Doing Business with
Russia

10 Years of Success in Eastern Europe & the CIS

   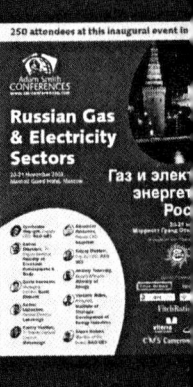

   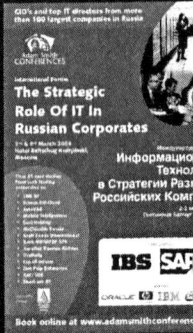

London
Adam Smith Conferences
9 Northburgh Street
London EC1V 0AH
United Kingdom
Tel. +44(0)20 7490 3774
Fax: +44(0)20 7505 0079

www.AdamSmithConferences.com

Mos
Adam Smith Confere
3 Uspensky per., buildin
Moscow 127
Russian Federa
Tel. +7 095 775 0
Fax. +7 095 775 0

SGS GOST Experts for Russia

ould you deal through a middle
an when the experts are within
ur reach? If you export to
ssia, you need to speak to real
OST experts

xpertise, Everyday, Everywhere!

ST R Certification (Gosstandart)
comply with Russian Standards for
duct Safety for a wide range of
ods.

sgortechnadzor (GGTN) Permits
industrial equipment used in oil
gas, petrochemical and mining
ustries.

epidemnadzor (SAN)
giene Certification)
products such as food,
metics, toys, clothing, textiles, fur-
re and some industrial/mechanical
ipment.

energonazor
osion proof certification.

stry of Internal Affairs
safety certification.

WWW.SGS.CO.UK

Call our GOST Helpline where our experts will be pleased to advise you on Russian certification for your products

Tel: +44 (0) 1276 697 890
Fax: +44 (0) 1276 697 888
Email: UKGost@sgs.com

S IS THE WORLD'S LEADING VERIFICATION, TESTING AND CERTIFICATION COMPANY

WHEN YOU NEED TO BE SURE   SGS

Russia – A well kept secret for the UK exporters
By Evelyne Flynn – SGS United Kingdom Ltd

Like most of the emerging markets, Russia is perceived by some exporters as a high risk market. The lack of confidence in political stability and the cultural difference, along with its bureaucratic system and the ever-changing legislation all contribute to such perception. But does trading with Russia have to be such a painstaking process? No, not if we know how to plan it first.

Time often works to our advantage when we plan our business activities in advance and this is especially the case when exporting to Russia. Many goods imported by Russia, particularly consumer goods, need to comply with Russian standards and legal requirements. The most common certificate needed for Russia is the GOST R Certificate of Conformity, which is governed by Gosstandart, the Russian State Committee for Standardisation, Metrology and Certification. GOST R Certificates are often required for customs clearance as well as for goods that are to be offered for sale or marketed within the country.

The purpose of the GOST R certificates is to protect the health and safety of Russian consumers. There are many other standards and safety requirements that could be applicable to your products which can also be quite confusing for both first time and routine exporters. It all depends on where, how and by whom your products are going to be used in Russia. It is also worth bearing in mind that international standards such as ISO and CE mark will not automatically be recognised by Russian officials.

The solution is to find a reputable Certification Body from whom you can gain advice on Russian standards and safety requirements before you engage in any business dealings. If you are a SME and find the Russian standards and regulations slightly complex, it may be a good idea to start by talking to a certification company that is near you speaks your language, understands your industry and shares your concerns.

Russia represents great opportunities for investors and exporters, however companies should pay attention to differences in legislation, in particular to certification. There are around 800 certification companies based in Russia and a few international companies that hold GOST accreditation outside of Russia who also offer their certification services. Our advice is to think and plan ahead, using the knowledge and expertise of your reliable certification partner.

GLOBAL MARKET BRIEFINGS

Doing Business with
Russia

A Guide to Investment Opportunities
and Business Practice

THIRD EDITION

Consultant editor:
Dr Marat Terterov

Published in association with:
The American Chamber of Commerce (Russia)

GMB

ELIHU BURRITT LIBRARY
CENTRAL CONNECTICUT STATE UNIVERSITY
NEW BRITAIN, CONNECTICUT 06050

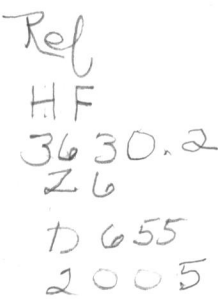

Publisher's note

Every possible effort has been made to ensure that the information contained in this book is accurate at the time of going to press, and the publishers and authors cannot accept responsibility for any errors or omissions, however caused. No responsibility for loss or damage occasioned to any person acting, or refraining from action, as a result of the material in this publication can be accepted by the editor, the publisher or any of the authors.

This fourth edition first published in Great Britain and the United States in 2005 by GMB Publishing Ltd.

Apart from any fair dealing for the purposes of research or private study, or criticism or review, as permitted under the Copyright, Designs and Patents Act 1988, this publication may only be reproduced, stored or transmitted, in any form or by any means, with the prior permission in writing of the publishers, or in the case of reprographic reproduction in accordance with the terms and licences issued by the CLA. Enquiries concerning reproduction outside these terms should be sent to the publishers at the undermentioned addresses:

120 Pentonville Road
London N1 9JN
United Kingdom
www.gmbpublishing.com

22883 Quicksilver Drive
Sterling VA 20166–2012
USA

© GMB Publishing Ltd and Contributors, 2005

ISBN 0 1–905050–01–1

British Library Cataloguing-in-Publication Data
A CIP record for this book is available from the British Library.

Printed in the USA by IBT/Biddles

Companies with Vision
Exhibit

Companies with Vision & Ambition

Exhibit in Russia

ITE is Russia's leading organiser of trade events in Russia and the CIS.

Whether you are building your business in Russia or looking at the market for the first time – You simply cannot beat the experience of exhibiting at the country's most important trade events for assessing the market, generating leads and making valuable business contacts.

Visit www.ite-exhibitions.com for more details about ITE's extensive calendar of trade events in Russia and the CIS, or call on +44(0)20 7596 5087

ITE Group PLC
105 Salusbury Road
London
NW6 6RG
UK

T: +44(0)20 7596 5000
E: enquiry@ite-exhibitions.com
W: www.ite-exhibitions.com

ITE LLC Moscow
42 Shchepkina Street
Building 2a
Moscow 129110
Russia

T: +7 095 935 7350
E: info@ite-expo.ru
W: www.ite-expo.ru

Contents

Foreword — xi
Andrew B Somers, President, American Chamber of Commerce in Russia

List of Contributors — xv
Map 1: Russia and its Neighbours — xxv
Map 2: Russia and its Regions — xxvi
Map 3: Moscow and its Boundaries — xxv

Introduction — xxix
Marat Terterov

PART ONE: BACKGROUND TO THE MARKET

1.1 Developments in the Political Environment — 3
William Flemming

1.2 An Overview of the Russian Economy: Money Matters — 11
Raiffeisen Bank

1.3 The Legal Regime and Regulatory Environment for International Business — 30
CMS Cameron McKenna

1.4 Latest Developments in the Foreign Investment Climate — 38
Andrew B Somers, President, American Chamber of Commerce in Russia

1.5 The Russian Investment Climate — 42
Branan

1.6 Russian Country Risk: Clouding Future Prospects for Russian Corporates — 55
Elena Anankina and Robert E Richards, Standard & Poor's

PART TWO: THE FINANCIAL SECTOR

2.1 The Russian Banking System: An Overview — 69
Eric Zuy, Allen & Overy

2.2 Retail Banking — 79
Deloitte & Touche

2.3 Twelve Years of the Russian Insolvency Regime — 82
Eric Zuy, Allen & Overy

2.4 The Issuance and Regulation of Securities — 91
Max Gutbrod, Partner, Baker & McKenzie – CIS, Limited

2.5 Currency Regulations — 95
Vladimir Dragunov, Partner, Baker & McKenzie – CIS, Limited

Contents

2.6	Corporate Governance Development in Russia *Branan*	99

PART THREE: MARKET POTENTIAL

3.1	Russian Oil and Gas *Bill Page and Mark Redhead, Deloitte*	109
3.2	The Business Climate in the Russian Oil and Gas Sector *Keith Rowden, Leader, Energy Industry Services and Igor Lotakov, CFA, Senior Manager, PricewaterhouseCoopers*	115
3.3	The Oil and Gas Industry: The Regulatory Environment and Legal Infrastructure *CMS Cameron McKenna*	123
3.4	Investing in a Reforming Electric Utilities Industry *Alexander Chmel, Partner and Vyacheslav Solomin, Senior Manager, PricewaterhouseCoopers*	128
3.5	Russian Energy Sector Policy *Sergey Maslichenko, OTAC Limited*	136
3.6	The Telecommunications Market *Vyacheslav Masenkov, Deputy General-Director and Alexander Chachava, Senior IT Analyst, RBC*	146
3.7	Telecommunications: The Regulatory Framework *CMS Cameron McKenna*	164
3.8	The Russian IT Market *Vyacheslav Masenkov, Deputy General-Director and Alexander Chachava, Senior IT Analyst, RBC*	168
3.9	The Automotive Industry *Alexander Raifeld and Andrei Kouzmin, Deloitte & Touche*	174
3.10	The Pharmaceuticals Market *Anton Timergaliev, Senior Market Analyst, RMBC*	180
3.11	Investing in Russian Pharmaceuticals: Crisis or Renaissance? *Denis Matafonov, Analyst, Antanta Capital*	190
3.12	The Development of Retail *Alexander Raifeld and Andrei Kouzmin, Deloitte & Touche*	198
3.13	The Brewing Industry *Deloitte & Touche*	205

PART FOUR: GETTING ESTABLISHED: THE TAXATION AND LEGAL ENVIRONMENT

4.1	Business Structures *CMS Cameron McKenna*	217
4.2	Establishing A Presence *CMS Cameron McKenna*	225
4.3	Russian Business Entities *Gennady Odarich, Lawyer, PricewaterhouseCoopers CIS Law Offices BV*	231

4.4	Business Taxation *Paul Quigley, Deloitte & Touche*	241
4.5	Russian Taxation *Natalia Milchakova, Tax Partner, PricewaterhouseCoopers, Moscow*	250
4.6	Auditing and Accounting *Andrei Elinson, Deloitte & Touche*	265
4.7	New Russian Customs Legislation *Alexander Dragunov, Director, Customs Practice, PricewaterhouseCoopers*	275

PART FIVE: BUSINESS DEVELOPMENT: OPERATING AN ENTERPRISE

5.1	The Property Regime in Russia *CMS Cameron McKenna*	283
5.2	Land Relations in the Russian Federation *Andrey Goltsblat, Managing Partner, Pepeliaev, Goltsblat & Partners*	289
5.3	Intellectual Property and E-Commerce *CMS Cameron McKenna*	294
5.4	Arbitration and Dispute Resolution *CMS Cameron McKenna*	304
5.5	Employment Law and Work Permits for Expatriates *CMS Cameron McKenna*	311
5.6	An Investment Project in Russia: Applicable Laws *Andrey Goltsblat, Managing Partner, Pepeliaev, Goltsblat & Partners*	317
5.7	Entrepreneurial Start-ups *Jamison Firestone, Firestone Duncan*	326
5.8	Property Rights *Andrei Soukhomlinov, Partner, Baker & McKenzie – CIS, Limited*	333
5.9	Competition Law *Paul Melling, Partner and Sergei Voitishkin, Partner, Baker & McKenzie – CIS, Limited*	344

APPENDICES

Appendix 1: Learning from the Russian Experience: Regional Debt Defaults and Recovery 1998–2003 *Eugene Korovin and Elena Okorotchenko, Standard and Poor's Ratings Direct*	353
Appendix 2: Placing Investment Projects within the Context of National Significance *Vitaly Mozharowski, Partner and Maxim Popov, Senior Attorney, Pepeliaev, Goltsblat & Partners*	366
Appendix 3: Useful Business-Related Websites	371
Appendix 4: Contributor Contact Details	374
Index	379
Index of advertisers	391

Foreword

It is my pleasure, for the second consecutive year, to introduce this very useful and respected volume containing the viewpoints of international companies operating in Russia. A number of the contributions will refer to the positive macroeconomic indicators and the remarkable legislative reform progress that have begun to attract the serious attention of investors to Russia. In my Foreword, I would like to emphasize the significant support that private business has been receiving from the joint co-operation between the US and Russian governments on economic and trade policy. Most importantly, the US and Russian governments have developed a strong institutional relationship that facilitates the progress that we see today.

A number of initiatives provide the opportunity for Russian and foreign business to influence government economic policy with the overall goal of improving the Russian climate for investment and trade. The American Chamber of Commerce in Russia is an active participant in many of these efforts. One such initiative in the energy sector is the US-Russia Commercial Energy Dialogue (CED), a private sector process that operates under American and Russian co-chairs representing their respective business communities. Five working groups, led by American and Russian companies, address specific areas of bilateral energy co-operation, including investment, market access, transportation, small business and electricity. In the past year, these working groups produced specific recommendations presented at the second US-Russia Commercial Energy Summit in St. Petersburg in September 2003, which were condensed into a shortlist of priority tasks. The US side has already responded to one of these tasks by assuring the Russian government that the US market and regulatory regime could accept a significant increase in Russian oil imports. The construction of a pipeline from western Siberia to the northwest port of Murmansk will facilitate the delivery of oil from Russia to the United States. We are optimistic that the CED will continue to make inroads into both governments' policy-making process.

Another example is the Russian American Business Dialogue (RABD), which focuses on such issues as intellectual property rights protection; customs code implementation, and the improvement of the environment for small business. Private business has scored some successes in this area in terms of improved regulatory and legislative steps by the government, and the American Chamber of Commerce will continue to press on those issues.

A third sector that has benefited from this co-operation is healthcare. Along with the US Commerce Department and the RF Health Ministry, our Chamber leads the Russian-American Interagency Council on Harmonization in Healthcare. The Council held a series of workshops for Russian professionals from the Health Ministry that focused on Western practices in the area of medical devices and pharmaceuticals regulation, and harmonization of quality systems and standards. For 2004, a work plan has been developed that includes more workshops, exchange visits and publications.

I mention these public-private sector co-operative processes to emphasize that the reforms of the Russian government and the new relationship between the United States and Russia are being supported by an open dialogue between the private sector and both governments in terms of formulating policies that are conducive to business and to improving the investment climate.

I trust that you will find the expert contributions in this volume of significant importance, as they outline the dynamic Russian economy and provide insightful forecasts for its continued growth.

Andrew B Somers
President, American Chamber of Commerce in Russia

List of Contributors

Allen & Overy is a premier international law firm and was founded in 1930. With over 4,800 staff, including some 430 partners, working in 26 major centres worldwide, they are able to provide effective, co-ordinated and decisive legal advice across three continents. Their clients include some of the world's leading businesses, financial institutions, governments and private individuals. Their aim is to understand business objectives and to be considered a critical arm of any organization they become involved with.

Eric Zuy, Senior Associate, Allen & Overy Legal Services, Moscow, has advised major Western banks, financial consortiums and companies on different types of banking transactions, project finance, and different financial arrangements with respect to insolvency and securities regulations. Eric's experience also includes advising on various types of secured lending, trade and export finance, financial and commercial transactions. He has broad experience of restructurings and insolvency procedures relating to banks and corporates. Prior to joining Allen & Overy, Eric was heavily involved in legal arrangements of foreign investments in the Russian Federation, transactions involving exchange control regulations, finance, corporate and insolvency matters.

The **American Chamber of Commerce in Russia** celebrates its 10th anniversary in 2004. Representing more than 750 member companies, the Chamber has established itself as one of the largest and most influential foreign business organizations in the Russian Federation. With its Moscow headquarters, its St. Petersburg chapter, and representatives in Washington DC, the Chamber advocates members' interests to the Russian and US governments, and provides a forum for dialogue between the international business community and policy-makers. The Chamber is a lead organization of the Russian-American Business Dialogue, initiated by Presidents Bush and Putin as a vehicle for the private sector to make recommendations to both governments on how to reduce barriers to trade and investment. The Chamber also co-chairs the US-Russia Commercial Energy Dialogue, the US-Russia Information Technology Roundtable and other important forums to advance business in Russia.

Andrew B Somers has been President of the American Chamber of Commerce in Russia since December 2000. He is the American co-chair of the US-Russia Commercial Energy Dialogue and a leader of the Russian-American Business Dialogue. He was Executive Vice President and General Counsel of American Express TRS Company in New York and headed his own consulting firm specializing in real estate and financial transactions in the Russian regions. His wife, Marina, is a partner in Somers & Cavelier, a Moscow-based executive search firm.

Antanta Capital Group started active operations in the Russian equity market in 2003. Since then it has become one of the fast growing private investment companies in Russia.

Although the company is young, it has already demonstrated good business results: in December 2003, Antanta Capital was rated 7th by RTS with a trade volume of over $145 million. Antanta's area of expertise is second-tier stock, which will become one of the most profitable investment options on the Russian equity market. Antanta Capital provides private investors and corporate clients with a full range of brokerage and financial services in the domestic and international stock markets. Contacts:

Arthur Alekyan, Director: aalekyan@antcm.ru

Eugene Kogan, Executive Director: ekogan@antcm.ru

Andrey Babenko, Head of Sales and Trading: ababenko@antcm.ru

Vladimir Lounkov, Head of Research Department: vlounkov@antcm.ru

Baker & McKenzie is an international network of more than 3,200 locally qualified, internationally experienced lawyers practicing in 68 locations worldwide. Over the years, their goal has been to offer clients the best of both worlds – wide-ranging global experience with in-depth expertise, and practical know-how in the laws and legal systems of the local jurisdictions, in which they are located. The significant size and level of development of the firm's world-wide practice ensures that they are, at all times, able to provide required resources from their worldwide network to complement their local offices. Combining more than 30 years of experience in Russia and the CIS, with a network of full-service offices in Moscow, St. Petersburg, Kiev, Almaty and Baku, Baker & McKenzie has the resources it takes to help clients capitalize on the wealth of business opportunities in the region. Their key practice areas include arbitration/litigation, banking & finance/securities, corporate law/M&A, IT/Telecom, intellectual property, labour/employment, natural resources, pharmaceuticals industry, real estate/construction, tax, venture capital.

Vladimir Dragunov is a partner in Baker & McKenzie's Moscow Office. He earned his Bachelor of Law with High Honors (1997) from the International Law Department of the Moscow State Institute of International Relations (MGIMO). He has also received an LL.M. degree in Banking and Finance (with a merit) at the University of

London (UCL) and has worked for nearly two years in the Finance Department of the firm's London Office. Prior to joining Baker & McKenzie, he worked for a Russian law firm, specializing in various commercial, corporate and foreign investment issues. Since joining Baker & McKenzie in 1997, he has been practising as a banking and finance lawyer. His primary focus is on bank and corporate lending, secured transactions, pre-export and trade finance, structured finance and securitization, derivatives, custody and currency control regulations. He has also broad experience in mergers and acquisitions as well as in capital markets work. In addition to his native Russian, he is fluent in English and has basic German.

Max Gutbrod is a partner in Baker & McKenzie's Moscow Office. Dr Gutbrod is a member of the firm's International Corporate & Securities Practice, as well as of the CIS Banking & Finance and Natural Resources Practice Groups. He also heads Baker & McKenzie's CIS IT/Telecommunications Practice. He is a member of the Financial Committee of Baker & McKenzie. He is Deputy Chairman of the German Business Association in Russia and Chairman of its Financial Services Committee. He is also a board member of the Russian Franchising Association. Dr Gutbrod is a graduate of the University of Tubingen and the University of Munich. In 1992, he earned a Ph.D. from the University of Munich. Dr Gutbrod joined Baker & McKenzie's Berlin Office in 1993 and has been practising in Moscow since 1995. He regularly advises on corporate and commercial matters, joint ventures, banking, securities and finance matters and government regulations. He is a frequent speaker at conferences on banking and finance, currency control, oil & gas, WTO issues, and the securities market in Russia. Dr Gutbrod has written numerous articles regarding Russian, German and international business law, including WTO, privatization, securities transactions and banking. In addition to his native German, he is fluent in English, Russian and Portuguese.

Paul Melling is the Managing Partner of the Moscow office of Baker & McKenzie. He supervises the firm's Corporate/M&A Practice in Russia and heads the CIS Pharmaceuticals Industry Practice. Mr Melling is an English lawyer and the founding partner of Baker & McKenzie's Moscow office, having been resident in Moscow since January 1989. He is a graduate of Oxford University and joined Baker & McKenzie in London in 1980 as a member of its East-West Trade Department, specializing in trade and investment in the then Soviet Union. In 1982, he became one of the first Western lawyers to appear before the USSR Foreign Arbitration Commission in litigation governed by Soviet Law. Mr Melling has been the Honorary Legal Adviser to the British Ambassador in Moscow since 1990 and the Honorary Legal Advisor to the Association of International Pharmaceutical Manufacturers in Moscow since its establishment. He is also

Honorary Legal Advisor to the Russo-British Chamber of Commerce and a member of the Chamber's Executive Council. He is fluent in English and Russian.

Andrei Soukhomlinov is a partner in the Moscow office of Baker & McKenzie. He heads the firm's Real Estate & Construction Practice in Russia. He joined Baker & McKenzie's Moscow office in 1997. Mr. Soukhomlinov has advised on acquisitions and sales of real estate, commercial property leasing, land use and planning, as well as on the real estate aspects of corporate mergers and acquisitions and lending secured against real estate. He received his Law Degree with Honors from Moscow State Institute of International Relations (MGIMO) in 1987. Prior to joining Baker & McKenzie, Mr. Soukhomlinov worked for several years as a legal adviser in a Russian real estate development company and also advised on real estate and construction matters while working for a Russian law firm. He speaks fluent English in addition to his native Russian.

Sergei Voitishkin is a partner in Baker & McKenzie's Moscow office and heads Baker & McKenzie's Russian M&A Practice. Mr Voitishkin earned his law degree from the Law Department of the Moscow State University in 1997. He also holds a degree in linguistics from the Moscow Institute of Foreign Languages. He specializes in corporate and commercial law matters. He served as a lead attorney on a number of multi-million dollar M&A transactions in Russia, advising major multinational and Russian clients on mergers and acquisitions in various industries, including oil and gas, manufacturing, chemicals, domestic appliances, tobacco and food products. The European Legal 500 *Law Firms in Europe & the Middle East 2003* refers to Mr Voitishkin as a 'respected partner' recommended for M&A work in Russia. In addition to his native Russian, he speaks fluent English and Swedish.

Branan is a Russo-British management consulting and corporate finance firm based in Moscow and with a strong focus on Russia. Branan provides services to clients in a wide range of industries, including energy and utilities, telecoms/media/technology, and manufacturing. The firm's main services are: strategy and organization; marketing and sales; financial management and accounting; mergers, acquisitions, disposals and capital raising. Since its formation in 1999, Branan has successfully completed more than 100 projects in Russia, Ukraine, Kazakhstan and Uzbekistan. The firm now employs over 40 people in offices in Moscow and Kiev.

CMS Cameron McKenna is a leading international law firm and a market leader. The firm has been recognized in several prestigious awards including most recently British Consultant of the Year – British Consultants Bureau in 2000 – for work on a water treatment project in Sofia, and the same award in 1999 for work on an airport project in Africa. CMS Cameron McKenna has practices in Central and Eastern Europe with offices in Moscow, Warsaw, Budapest, Prague and Bucharest and affiliated offices in Belgrade and Bratislava. CMS is a transnational legal services organization with member firms in the UK, Germany, France, Austria, Belgium, the Netherlands and Switzerland, and with 44 offices in 19 different countries.

Deloitte Touche Tohmatsu is an organization of member firms devoted to excellence in providing professional services and advice. It is focused on client service through a global strategy executed locally in nearly 150 countries. With access to the deep intellectual capital of 120,000 people worldwide, its member firms, including their affiliates, deliver services in four professional areas: audit, tax, consulting, and corporate finance. Its member firms serve more than one-half of the world's largest companies, as well as large national enterprises, public institutions, locally important clients, and successful, fast-growing global companies. Deloitte has over 800 local and expatriate professionals working in its offices in CIS countries: in Moscow, St. Petersburg, Kiev, Minsk, Baku, Tbilisi, Almaty, Astana, Atyrau, Bishkek and Tashkent. In the CIS, Deloitte provides a full range of professional services to both multinational corporations and growth-oriented local firms, including audit, tax and legal, corporate finance, consulting and corporate governance services. Its mission is to help its clients and its people excel.

Andrei Elinson joined Deloitte in 1997. He is an Audit Manager in the Moscow office of Deloitte & Touche CIS and has been working with the CIS practice for more than five years. Andrei has spent six months working in Deloitte's Forensic Department in the UK. In 2002 Andrei became the Forensic Leader of the Russian firm. He is also a member of the quality control group of the firm and serves as Deputy to Professional Practice Development Partner of our CIS Practice, who is responsible for treatment of Russian Accounting Standards. Andrei has served a wide range of local and international clients demonstrating a thorough knowledge of Russian, international and US accounting and auditing standards. Before joining Deloitte, Andrei also served as an expert in the stock department of DIAM Bank, Moscow for one year, where he honed his skills in securities trading and stock market valuation of various manufacturing clients. Andrei is a Certified Public Accountant and an Associate Member of Association of Certified Fraud Examiners.

Andrei Kouzmin has extensive experience in developing strategies for clients in various industries. He is skilled in market segmentation and analysis, competitor analysis, strategic diagnostic, marketing and sales improvement, competitive positioning, distribution channel development and project feasibility studies. He has also assisted clients in improving their business operations, organization design and development. Andrei has specialized in supply chain management, business process improvement, and corporate restructuring issues. He has strong experience in financial modelling and cost management. Before joining Deloitte, Andrei was a consultant in the supply chain management practice at PWC Consulting, and was previously an associate in the US with Coopers & Lybrand's cost management group. He holds an MBA degree in International Strategy from Georgetown University, Washington, and a Diploma in English and German from Kaluga State Pedagogical University.

Bill Page is tax leader for the oil and gas industry in the CIS. Bill has been practising tax for 17 years and for nearly five years in the CIS. He is a graduate of Oxford University and prior to joining the accounting profession was a tax inspector with the UK Inland Revenue. Bill has extensive experience in development and implementation of tax strategy and tactics for multinational and local energy companies, negotiation of hydrocarbon contracts, management of due diligence and tax reviews of target companies for foreign investors, management of various financing and business-related issues including optimization of trading operations for oil and gas companies. Bill has also worked extensively with construction and oilfield service companies, providing advice on cross-border transactions, support in negotiating with the local tax authorities and supporting clients involved in litigation on tax issues.

Paul Quigley is a VAT manager in the Indirect Tax Group in Moscow. Originally from the UK, he has been working in Moscow since 2001 and has wide experience of VAT both in Russia and the European Union. Paul serves a wide variety of clients from different industry sectors. Paul has specialized in VAT for the last six years. He started his career working with the UK tax authorities as a VAT inspector in the City of London. Before joining Deloitte, he also worked for another Big Four firm and in industry.

Alexander Raifeld is a Consultant in the Consulting Department of Deloitte in Moscow. He joined the firm in 2002. During his work with the firm Alexander participated in strategy development for retail and financial sectors and managed teams of business analysts. He developed a growth strategy for Russia's largest wholesaler of household items to increase corporate long-term value. Working closely with senior management of the largest Russian children's toy retailer, he conducted an extensive operations optimization project. He also participated in number of projects for Deloitte's main FMCG clients. Alexander graduated from Tufts University, Medford, Massachusetts and holds degree in Economics and Eastern European Studies.

William Flemming has been based in Moscow for the past five years, providing analysis of the Russian political scene in a variety of capacities. Prior to moving to Moscow, he was a graduate student of Oxford University doing research on Russian politics. He is currently opinion page editor of *The Moscow Times*.

Firestone Duncan is a midsize Moscow-based provider of high-quality legal, tax, accounting, and audit services and it maintains an affiliated office in Khabarovsk (the Russian Far East). The partners are American and Russian and the firm has been in operation since 1993.

Its areas of practice include most areas of Russian law that are likely to be of interest to corporate clients and entrepreneurs. The firm also maintains strong litigation teams. Several of Firestone Duncan's professionals have been trained to give expert testimony in the UK courts regarding matters of Russian law and have participated in international arbitration cases in various European forums. Firestone Duncan is able to undertake multi-jurisdictional projects and its abilities are enhanced by its membership in TagLaw, a worldwide network of prominent high-quality law firms. The professional members of Firestone Duncan speak Russian and English and are governed by western norms of professional responsibility, confidentiality and ethical conduct.

Jamison Firestone is also a Member of the Board and Co-Chairman of Enterprise Development Committee, AmCham.

OTAC Ltd, which was incorporated as a UK registered company in mid-1999, brings together a variety of overlapping and complementary consultancy experience and skills in a close-knit group that can also draw on a wide network of associates. OTAC was founded by Peter Oppenheimer, who is one of the most respected advisers and commentators on Russia's transition, combining the academic standards of Oxford University with wide-ranging experience of public bodies and business corporations.

OTAC personnel provide high-level support to governments, international institutions and private sector clients on strategic issues and the management of change. They offer wide-ranging experience on the key aspects of economic and social change:

- economic, social and institutional reform and national and regional strategies;
- development of broad-based growth and regeneration strategies;
- energy Sector Reform, including overall strategy and detailed reviews of specific industries and issues;
- strategic sectoral reviews ranging across manufacturing and service sectors and covering industries from automobiles to tourism;

- public sector finance and civil service reform, including poverty-focused strategies;
- government and institutional communications, public diplomacy and information.

Sergey Maslichenko is involved in OTAC Ltd. as a senior consultant. Over the last year he has been team leader of several FCO projects in Russia and Kazakhstan specializing in energy strategies. He has wide international experience of working in the field of energy policies, including consultancy work for the Ukrainian government. He got a PhD from Kiev National Economic University and carried out post-doctoral research at Oxford University in 2002/2003 as an FCO Chevening Scholar.

The lawyers of **Pepeliaev, Goltsblat & Partners** provide assistance in regulating rights to land plots and other real estate assets, and in solving other legal and tax problems. They specialize in:

- land and real estate due diligence, including examination of title documents for land and property;
- privatization of land and real estate;
- legal support for land and real estate transactions (purchase and sale, lease, mortgage, etc);
- drawing up contracts and negotiating contractual terms with counteragents;
- arranging an independent appraisal of land and real estate;
- acquisition of rights to land plots intended for commercial use;
- acquisition of rights to existing manufacturing facilities for setting up production;
- real estate mortgages as security for obligations under commercial contracts.

PricewaterhouseCoopers (www.pwc.com) is the world's largest professional services organization. Drawing on the knowledge and skills of more than 120,000 people in 139 countries, Pricewaterhouse Coopers builds relationships by providing industry-focused assurance, tax and advisory services based on quality and integrity. The objectives of its service offerings are to build trust and enhance value.

PricewaterhouseCoopers applies its industry knowledge and professional expertise to identify, report, protect, realize and create value for its clients and their stakeholders. PricewaterhouseCoopers serves many of the leading businesses in every sector on which it focuses. Those businesses value its rigorous, practical approach, characterized by a detailed understanding of individual client issues and by deep industry knowledge and experience.

In Russia PricewaterhouseCoopers has representative offices in Moscow, St. Petersburg, Togliatti and Yuzhno-Sakhalinsk. PricewaterhouseCoopers' offices are also situated in other CIS countries: Azerbaijan, Kazakhstan, Estonia, Latvia, Lithuania, Moldova, and Ukraine.

Raiffeisen Bank Austria (Moscow) is a leader in Russia's financial services market, providing a broad range of commercial, retail, foreign exchange, investment banking and brokerage services to both resident and non-resident corporate and private clients. RBA (Moscow) has been operating in Russia since 1996. A wholly-owned subsidiary of the Raiffeisen Banking Group, it was the first Russian bank with 100 per cent Austrian capital to have been granted a General Licence by the Central Bank of the Russian Federation.

RosBusinessConsulting (RBC) is Russia's leading media and IT company. It was created in 1993, and is currently the number one business information provider in Russia, as well as one of the major developers of software solutions for large and medium-sized businesses. The company has the widest business audience in the Russian media. RosBusinessConsulting was among the first Russian information agencies to create its own web portal (www.rbc.ru), which is now among the top three most popular resources on the Russian Internet. The website contains a wide variety of information and analytical materials on different segments of the market, which is available both in free and restricted access. RBC applies its extensive experience gained in the process of development and promotion of its own projects for the creation of IT solutions for its clients. RBC's highly-qualified specialists are able to develop and install various software, which is indispensable for the successful operation of large companies and state organizations. Direct targeting of web resources, along with high user hit rates, allows RBC to control more than half of the Russian Internet's advertising market.

Presently, there are over 1,000 specialists working for RBC, of whom more than 400 are highly-qualified IT engineers, web developers, programmers, designers, analysts and consultants. RBC is a source of independent, reliable and current information, which helps its subscribers (over 5,000) achieve success in a wide range of activities. RBC supplies state organizations, major Russian and foreign companies and the leading mass media with the widest range of information and news products. These consist of real-time news, financial data from Russian and world exchanges, RBC marketplaces, numerical, textual and graphical databases plus specialized financial tools for analyzing the market, analytical commentaries, corporate and branch research. Some 600 corporate reviews and over 100 industry surveys on all manufacturing industries have been published by RBC's analytical departments over the last five years. The largest databases and news agencies of the world distribute RBC's information: Bloomberg L.P., Bridge, LEXIS-NEXIS and Factiva (Dow Jones & Reuters). Dozens of clients who have used the services of RBC's analytical departments include the Russian Atomic Energy Ministry, Rosbank, Sumitomo Corp., NEC, Hitachi, Caterpillar, PRS-Presottorino Shatura, Radio Liberty, Dell, Sun Microsystems, and Russian regional administrations.

RMBC Company ('Remedium' group of companies) was founded in 1999. It is a leading market research and business consulting company on the Russian pharmaceutical market. In November 1999, RMBC won a tender organized by the Association of International Pharmaceutical Manufacturers (AIPM) on Retail Audit of drugs in Russia. At present the company has two subsidiaries, in Nizhniy Novgorod and in St.Petersburg, and 25 regional representatives in the regions. RMBC's primary goal is providing clients with the most up-to-date and full information on the Russian pharmaceutical market. Since 2003 it started operation in the CIS countries (Ukraine, Belorussia, and Kazakhstan in 2003) In 2002 RMBC became the first company on the Russian pharmaceutical market, whose methodology of statistical reports was approved by international audit company Deloitte & Touche.

The major activities of RMBC are various market researches, including portfolio analysis, positioning and promotion strategy development, identification of a new market niche etc; preparation of standard statistic reports covering pharmacy sales, hospital purchases and pharmaceuticals prescription; rent-a-rep service; monthly market bulletin published in co-operation with AIPM; analytical support of 'Remedium' publishing house periodicals – *Remedium*, *Rossiyskie Apteki* as well as the website: www.remedium.ru.

The major players, over 45 leading pharmaceutical companies of the Russian pharmaceutical market, are among RMBC clients: among them are Russian as well as foreign manufacturers Pfizer, MDS, Glaxo SmithKline, Boehringer Ingelheim, AstraZeneca, Organon, Nycomed, Lek, KRKA, Hoffmann La Roche, Schering, Schering Plough, Solvay Pharma, Boots, Servier, Schwarz Pharma etc.

Standard & Poor's was created in 1941 when a merger of Standard Statistics and Poor's Publishing Company took place. It is possible to trace its roots to 1860 when Henry Varnum Poor published his *History of Railroads and Canals of the United States*. Mr Poor was a leader in establishing the financial information industry on the principle of 'the investor's right to know'. Today, more than 140 years later, Standard & Poor's is the pre-eminent global provider of independent highly valued investment data, valuation, analysis and opinions and is still delivering on that original mission.

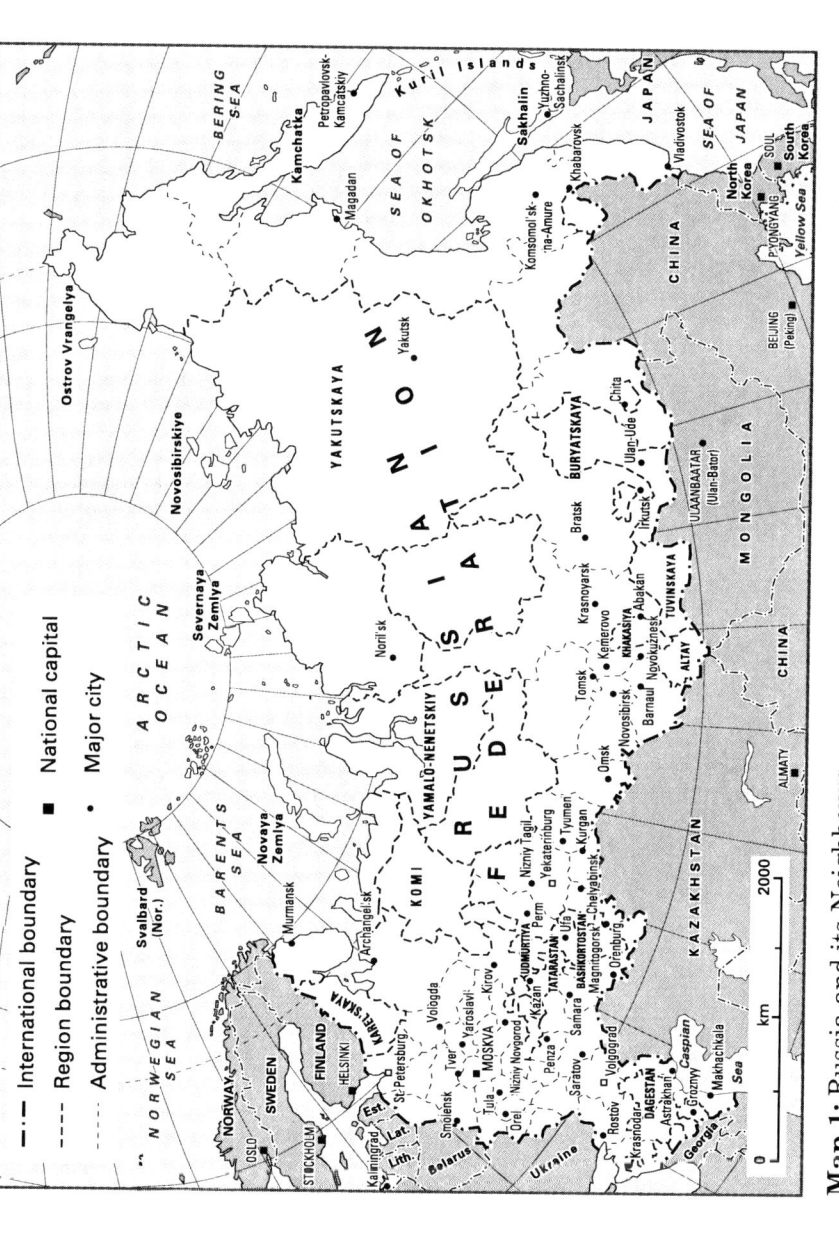

Map 1: Russia and its Neighbours

Map 2: Russia and its Regions

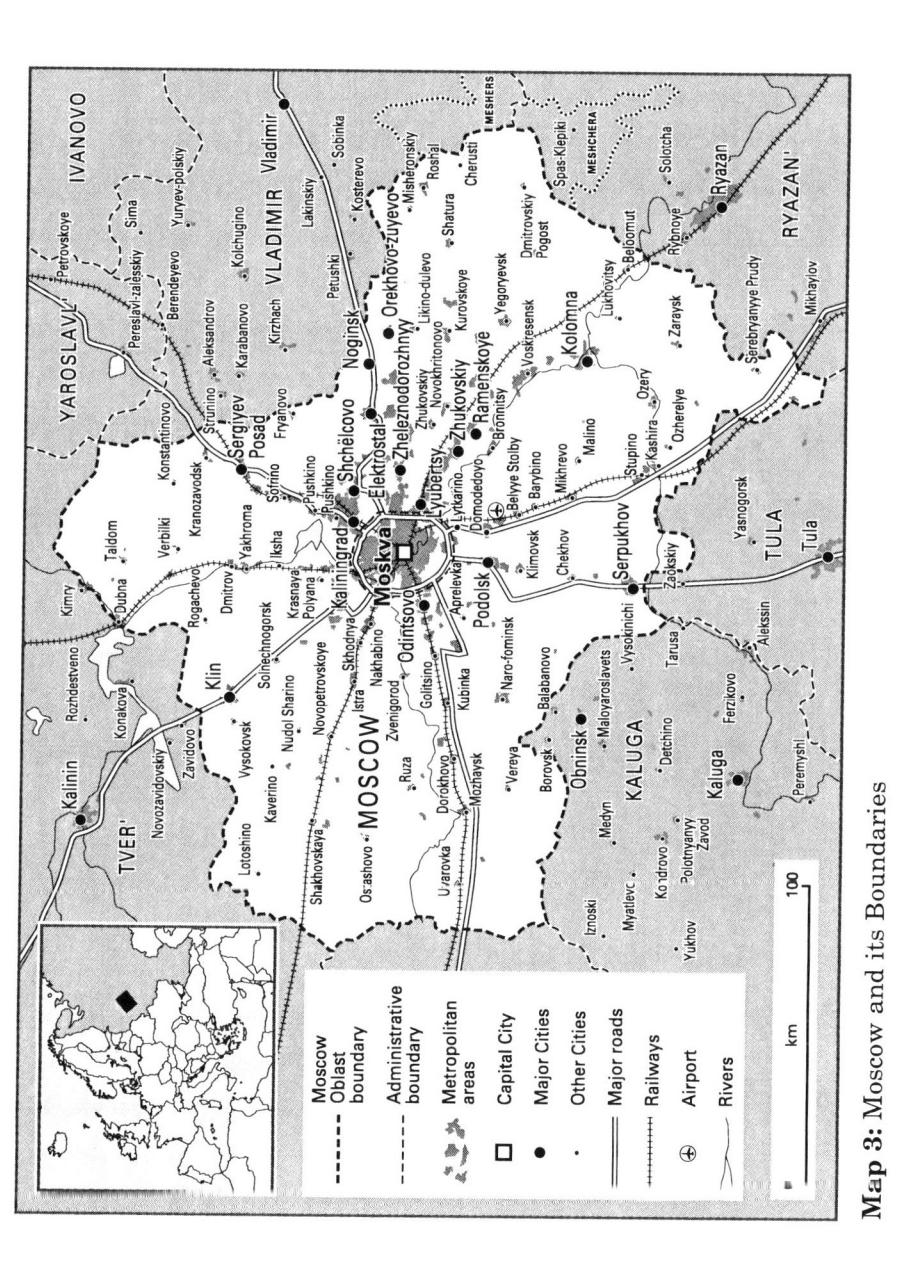

Map 3: Moscow and its Boundaries

Introduction

Dr Marat Terterov

This is now the third edition of *Doing Business with Russia* that I am introducing as editor, and it coincides with the very recent re-election as Russian president of Vladimir Putin, who convincingly won the vote for his second presidential term in March 2004. With Putin seemingly at the height of his political power – having been elected as the Russian Federation's second president in March 2000 and appearing set to remain president until at least March 2008 – and with the Kremlin seemingly having asserted such a strong level of influence over Russian political and economic life during Putin's first term, what are the most pressing questions confronting international business as it contemplates market opportunities in Russia during Putin's second term? There are two lines of discussion through which I would like to take the reader when contemplating this question, in addition to the general issues of doing business with Russia. The first of these is political, while the second pertains to the question of business culture.

The political

As international companies either already working with, or seeking to work with, Russia witness the commencement of Putin's second four-year term in office, several notable political (or policy-making) trends emerging from the first term are likely to consolidate and continue setting the framework for operations in the country. During the 1990s, under the presidency of Putin's predecessor, Boris Yeltsin, Russia's image as a destination for international business was marred by perceptions of economic stagnation and political instability. As the reader of previous editions of this book may recall, the established foreign view of Russian economic and business highlights during the Yeltsin decade was in fact one of 'low-lights', where production fell drastically in many vital sectors of the economy, where foreign and domestic investment was outstripped by capital outflow, and where social turbulence precipitated by economic shock therapy (reforms) and financial crises seemed pervasive. Economic and political uncertainty in Russia during the 1990s was further complicated by the State's inability – or unwillingness – to turn back the tide of organized criminal organizations engulfing the business sector, as well as the ongoing war in the break-away republic of Chechnya, which the government claimed was associated with terrorist acts against the population in several of Russia's cities, including Moscow.

If stagnation and instability were the main themes driving the foreign investor's perception of Russia during the Yeltsinite 1990s, recovery and stabilization appear to be the hallmarks of Putin's first term. Although Russia analysts will recall that Putin was initially appointed Prime Minister in August 1999 by Boris Yeltsin to bring the costly violence associated with the ongoing war in Chechnya under control, from the perspective of the foreign investor, Putin's first term as president will be remembered as a time when the Russian economy came under the management of a seemingly more diligent team of technocrats, who were able to realize consistently high rates of growth between 2000 and 2004. The Russian economy has been growing since the August 1998 financial crisis, reaching an annual high of 8.3 per cent in 2000. Average annual growth during the remainder of Putin's first term was in the region of 5 per cent, and, amidst the post-September 11 downturn in the US, these figures have been well received by many foreign critics. One of Putin's stated objectives for his second term has been to double Russia's GDP within 10 years. Such policy objectives and figures are certainly attractive for international business, as Russia's consistent years of economic growth, comparatively inexpensive cost of labour and high levels of human capital, together with improved levels of stability, are becoming noticed internationally.

A further defining trait of Russian politics under Putin's first term has been his government's continued acceleration of the economic reforms instigated during the Yeltsin years. Under Yeltsin, expulsion of prime ministers and changes of key government personnel was commonplace. During Putin's first four years in office, however, the Russian government has committed itself to encouraging the private sector, reducing bureaucratic controls on commercial activities, encouraging foreign investment, and further integrating Russia into the global economy by engaging in continued dialogue over Russia's entry into the World Trade Organization (WTO). A number of laws enhancing the process of economic liberalization have been passed under Putin, including a reduction in the country's tax on incomes to a flat 13 per cent, an overhaul of Russia's land code to one better geared to facilitating private property transactions, simplification in the procedures for the registration of new companies and the introduction of a new labour code governing employer–worker relations. Such reforms, although in their early stage of influencing Russia's overall investment climate, are nevertheless strengthening the country's business environment and capturing the attention of foreign investors.

Russia's enhanced image among the international community is further reinforced by the emerging confidence of the Russian business community, which, during the Putin years, has been reinvesting much of its profit back into the domestic economy. Although without doubt much of the economic growth mentioned earlier has been contributed by Russia's high-profile oil and gas industry (and high world prices for oil), a number of domestic enterprises from a diversity of spheres of economic activity are also performing visibly well. For the first time since the disbandement of the Soviet Union, investment coming into Russia has overtaken capital flight out of the Russian Federation, and the big Russian corporations – in oil and gas, the energy sector, metallurgy, telecoms, and food processing – are now tending to buy up existing assets and enterprises to further expand their business within the country. Major Russian companies such as Lukoil, Yukos, Gazprom, AvtoVaz, Norilsk Nickel, the electricity giant UES, Severstal, Sibneft, Vimpelcom and Tatneft are among the key drivers of the country's improved economic performance during the Putin years.

Twelve Russian companies – including those mentioned above – were recently listed among the world's largest corporations in *Forbes* magazine's annual rankings of the world's 2000 largest. Leading Russian companies are demonstrating their commitment to enhancing their management strategies by increasingly employing graduates from some of the top foreign business schools and universities, using foreign consultants to restructure their enterprises, and seeking to improve their understanding of concepts such as corporate governance. Although foreign investment in Russia still remains at relatively low levels compared to some neighbouring emerging markets, the reduction of capital flight and the reinvestment of domestic capital back into Russia has provided a substantial boost for the economy and has created many new jobs, particularly in the manufacturing sector. Furthermore, while the top Russian corporates dominate the business headlines, many secondary tier companies (some of which the reader will encounter in this book) are also seeking to operate to international standards and looking to expand their relationship with foreign business.

The West's positive appraisals of Russia's domestic economy and business environment during Putin's first term reached a peak of sorts in mid-2002 when the government of the United States proclaimed Russia to have acquired the status of a market economy. The American government's decision was based on a ruling from the US Department of Commerce, which carried out an extensive review process in arriving at its decision, that proclaimed that the Russian economy had transformed from its socialist past and was substantially driven by market forces. Also in the summer of 2002, the reputable international credit ratings agency, Standard & Poor's, upgraded Russia's rating from B+ to BB- (a rating that Russia last held prior to the August 1998 financial crisis), assigning a stable investment outlook and justifying its claim on the basis of continuing economic reforms and improved budgetary discipline. Similarly, another major ratings agency, Moody's, accorded Russia with an investment grade rating in October 2003. Furthermore, the Russian government and a number of private industry lobby groups have been actively staging numerous international business conferences in Europe and North America promoting Russia as a destination for foreign investors. The positive reviews that Putin's economic team have received during his first term have also been accompanied by some practical results in terms of attracting international business to Russia and numerous (major) international companies have a commercial presence of one form or another in the country.

The Yukos case

It is evident, then, that during the period of Vladimir Putin's first term as president the Russian government made a clear effort to improve the business environment in the country and concentrated notable energies into likewise improving the country's economic performance. Although a noticeable degree of good fortune has been on the side of the government's economic managers in recent years (ie, it is widely regarded that the Russian economy has been growing on a wave of favourable prices for oil and other raw materials upon which the country's exports are dependent), Russia, as a business opportunity, is arguably viewed more favourably today than at any time since the Soviet Union faded into history. However, while the positive signals are apparent from a business perspective, many critics are likewise concerned that Russian liberalism had reached a crisis during Putins' first term, while the country's nascent forces of socio-political plurality gave way to the Kremlin's newly asserted State centralism. Liberalism has never been a concept deeply rooted in the Russian national character, and although liberal economic reformers and self-proclaimed democrats were prominent in Russia's initial years of economic transition, such individuals are widely associated with the country's present social and economic problems. During Putin's first term, while the Russian government sought, selectively, to continue with economic reforms, the State became a more aggressive regulator of the economy than it had been under Yeltsin and exercised its preponderance over market forces when it determined that the latter had not acted in the national interest. The most evident example of the State's over-exuberance in its efforts to regulate the market has been the government's partial nationalization of Russia's leading oil company, Yukos (in October 2003), and the arrest of its leading shareholder and Russia's richest private individual, Mikhail Khodorkovsky.

Much has been written about the Russian State's recent pogroms against both Yukos and Khodorkovsky in the international press and the reader will further be able to gauge the opinions of a number of well-qualified commentators with regards to the Yukos case inside this book. The Russian government has justified its action by claiming that leading Yukos shareholders – including Khodorkovsky – had been involved in illegal privatization transactions during the 1990s and have grossly evaded their tax commitments, which, given the net value of Yukos' assets, has indirectly contributed to the economic deprivation of millions of Russian citizens. However, there is a wide degree of consensus among analysts that the State's attack on Yukos resulted from Khodorkovsky's increased activities in national politics (his funding of liberal opposition political parties, his public criticisms of the Russian political establishment, his alliances with Western capital and governments) and the potential challenge this may have created for the Putin regime. In terms of the 'the crisis of Russian liberalism', what is important from the Yukos case is not that the Russian government under Putin is showing any intention of reversing the inexorable process of economic liberalization that has been taking place in the country for well over a decade. Rather, we are now seeing a Russian political establishment that is promoting economic reform and courting international capital at the same time as expanding administrative controls over both the market and political orientations advocating a liberal nature that have been emerging in Russia during recent years. While in the short term such policies are, at best, sending confusing signals to foreign investors contemplating the Russian market, in the long term they are clearly in contradiction to what the West would like to see take root in Russia, as the former is firmly grounded in an ideology of the non-interventionist, unbiased State acting as an impartial referee in an open marketplace functioning within a liberal political framework.

Business culture

The Yukos case is also instructive for the foreign investor from the perspective of the type of business culture prevailing in Russia. Although the Russian government has sought to improve the country's investment climate in recent years, and has, indeed, supervised an improvement in macroeconomic management and monetary stability, it has yet to create an institutional environment for business where the 'rules of the game' apply equally to all parties. The application of such a philosophy in business life is one of the central features of the mature market economies of Western countries and something that the West has long been trying to impress on governments in countries like Russia. The arrest of Mikhail Khodorkovsky and the State's sequestration of a substantial part of his shareholdings in Yukos is, unfortunately, demonstrating that politicians in Russia are able to clamp down on businessmen when the latter, for whatever reason, fall out of favour with the State. It must be remembered that the same justification that the government employed to arrest Khodorkovsky, prosecute him through the courts and drive the country's second largest oil company towards bankruptcy could have been applied to numerous other leading Russian businessmen who continue to operate freely in Russia today. Personalities, rather than institutions, have remained the dominant feature of Russian business culture from Yeltsin to Putin, whether the subject of analysis is focused on the country's president and richest man respectively, or a regional state official and a local businessman somewhere in the vast Russian hinterlands. This aspect of Russian business culture is summed up in the following comment, which the reader can examine in more detail in Chapter 1.6 of this book: 'Instead of institutional frameworks serving as the foundation for fair and efficient economic activity, the application of laws and regulation in Russia is driven by personal agendas and rivalries and self-preserving or "rent-seeking" bureaucracies'.

It is evident that relationships count for a great deal when seeking to conduct successful transactions at a commercial level in

Russia, something that a foreign business should keep strongly in mind when conducting its due diligence into the Russian market. From a commercial perspective, many of these relationships are transacted somewhere inside, or on the fringes, of government bureaucracy and usually involve some level of 'rent-seeking' behaviour, a widespread form of economic corruption more often referred to as bribery in the West. Although in the West's mature market economies State bureaucracy is built on a tradition of individuals providing government services to the private sector and receiving a middle class income from the State, in both the Soviet Union and Tsarist Russia such traditions for the most part failed to entrench themselves. Instead, an individual's incentive to enter into a bureaucratic career in Russia has, historically, been motivated by the potential of gaining access to State resources and acquiring social status that accompanies holding a public office. Access to the State's resources, complimented by the political power that has traditionally accompanied the position of public office, has, over time, facilitated the emergence of rent-seeking bureaucracies in many ex-socialist countries. A culture of bribery, where bureaucrats exchange the State's goods and services for informal 'rents', or bribes, from private citizens, has been pervasive in Russia for centuries, and has shown little sign of abating in more recent years. Although Vladimir Putin has firmly stated his government's intentions to fight bribery and economic corruption, and aimed to reduce the size of the country's bloated public sector during the first term of his presidency, there is little sign that any tangible success has been achieved in this sphere. This aspect of Russian business culture was summed up by a headline in the well-regarded English language Russian newspaper recently: 'Kickback culture is a way of life' (*The Moscow Times*, 28 January 2004).

Nor has Vladimir Putin's government been able to disassemble Russia's business oligarchy and ownership concentration of the country's major economic assets from the narrow set of hands that control it. Russia's oligarchs, or business tycoons, emerged as the dominant players in the country's economy during the mid-1990s, when a group of these individuals colluded to finance Boris Yeltsin's re-election campaign in 1996 in return for the State's complicity in their acquisition of Russia's 'crown jewel' public sector enterprises at highly undervalued prices. Despised by millions of ordinary Russians, who blame these individuals for their own present economic misfortune, Russia's oligarchs consolidated their prominence during the latter years of Yeltsin's presidency. When Putin became president in 2000, it was initially felt by many that he would bring the oligarchs to heel and perhaps create an economic climate where Russia's economic wealth could be, to some extent, deconcentrated and disbursed throughout the economy and society in a more equitable manner. This was especially the case early on during Putin's presidency, after he effectively drove two of the leading oligarchs of the Yeltsin era, Boris Berizovsky and Mikhail Gusinsky, out of the country into foreign exile. However, although it is possible to argue that Putin's campaign against the oligarchs reached a new peak after the government's crackdown on Yukos, Russia's president has, for the most part, failed to break the country's oligarch-dominated economy.

This conclusion is confirmed by a recent study published by the World Bank's Moscow office, which argues that ownership concentration of Russia's economic assets is just as evident today as it has been in the 1990s. The study found that just 23 individuals or groups control more than a third of Russia's industry, 16 per cent of employment and 17 per cent of banking assets, and confirms the power of a few homegrown corporate operators when seen in the context of the Russian economy as a whole. Such studies point towards a two-fold conclusion: that the Russian economy during the Putin years continues to be dominated by either monopolistic or oligopolistic business groups operating within an underdeveloped competitive framework and weak anti-trust culture; and that the government's attacks on certain leading business figures have not constituted an attempt to break the oligarch-dominated economy, but, rather, bear greater resemblance to politically-motivated witch-hunts against selected targets that have fallen out of favour with the political establishment. Clearly, such an economic setting, where commercial success is highly dependent on political patronage, and where there is not one set of rules that can be applied equally to all players, can be quite a difficult one for most foreign enterprises to navigate. It also goes a long way towards explaining why Russia, as a country of such vast economic potential, has been a relatively poor performer in its efforts to attract foreign direct investment (FDI).

Despite some of these polemics that will confront international companies seeking to do business in Russia's unorthodox business culture, Russia is destined to continue to attract foreign investors into its nascent market. Russia's overall improved economic and political performance under Putin, the pro-global economic policies of his government and major Russian corporations, together with the country's abundant supplies of many of the world's most vital natural resources, all make the present time a particularly attractive one for embarking upon business co-operation with this vast country. Furthermore, the businessman or woman can no longer speak of their arrival in Russia's major European capitals such as Moscow or St Petersburg as a lawless or exotic encounter with early post-Marxist society. Even the first-time visitor to the country is likely to be surprised at just how much of 'the West' has now happily settled in present-day Russia. All the standard symbols, goods and services found in the most dynamic market economies are likewise found in contemporary Russia. Goods and services of every kind imaginable are both traded between Russia and the outside world, and produced inside the country. Street trading is particularly active in Russia's large, multicultural cities, rekindling memories of Russia's early capitalism in the late 19th and early 20th centuries. Russia today is a vast market populated by millions of avaricious consumers who are proving extremely resolute in finding the necessary disposable income to enthusiastically sample whatever new goods and services the market can offer them.

Furthermore, despite Russia's relatively poor performance in attracting FDI, many large foreign businesses are already well established in the Russian market. Among them are some of the world's biggest multinationals including Sweden's furniture company IKEA, which has been in the country for over a decade, the American giant of the automobile industry, General Motors, which has recently invested heavily in the Russian car industry, as well as Swiss-based Nestle, France's Danone, and the UK's British Petroleum, which in March 2003 announced a $6.75 billion planned investment in a joint venture with the Russian oil company TNK. Although this is a market where a foreign entity is far more likely to establish itself as part of a multinational company rather than a small- to medium-size enterprise, it is inevitable that more foreign companies will be coming to Russia in future years. As global business expands further, such companies will be attracted to Russia on the basis of market opportunity as well as by the many 'success stories' of foreign businesses such as some of the companies mentioned above, which put their confidence in Russia years ago and are now seasoned veterans of conducting business in the country. Most of these enterprises entered Russia with a long-term plan for their investments and have been flexible enough in their business strategies, adapting to some of the requirements of the local business environment. They have managed to demonstrate that, despite the complex nature of the Russian investment climate, Russia is a country where foreign companies can do business and reap the rewards in this highly prospective and challenging, emerging market.

About the book

In this volume, our third attempt at compiling a comprehensive publication on Russian business since the August 1998 financial crisis, the reader will find over 40 separate chapters covering a wide diversity of business topics relevant to one of the world's most significant countries. Furthermore, in keeping with the publisher's tradition of upholding objectivity and a range of specialist opinions with regards to a particular country, these articles are contributed by a great diversity of authors, all specialists in their particular area of doing business with Russia.

In Part One of the book, we present the reader with a comprehensive economic, legislative and political background to the Russian market. Contributors in this section include Austria's Raiffeisen Bank and the international law firm CMS Cameron McKenna, who focus on the country's economic and federal legislation as it relates to business and investment practices. There are also contributions from the Moscow-based political commentator, William Flemming, the Russian company Branan, and the President of the American Chamber of Commerce in Russia, Andrew B Somers, who discuss the Russian political system during the Putin presidency and present in-depth chapters addressing the Russian investment climate. We also present a chapter by the international ratings agency, Standard and Poor's, on Russian country risk.

In Part Two we focus on the Russian financial sector and include chapters by the law firm Allen & Overy on banking and insolvency, while Deloitte & Touche present a chapter on the status of retail banking in Russia. Branan also provides a detailed commentary on the latest trends in Russian corporate governance, and the international law firm Baker & McKenzie discusses currency regulations and the securities market.

Although most goods and services are today readily available in most large Russian centres of population, the country's consumer market is still very underdeveloped by international standards. Ample opportunity still exists for international companies to supply the Russian market. In Part Three, therefore, authors from PricewaterhouseCoopers, Deloitte & Touche, CMS Cameron McKenna and several local specialists review some of the more high-profile sectors of the Russian economy, including extraction industries such as oil and gas, reforming industries such as the electricity sector, and other traditionally important sectors such as automobile production and pharmaceuticals. We also look at some of the newer, dynamic sectors, including telecoms and the IT sector, retail and brewing.

In Parts Four and Five our lawyers, accountants and tax specialists provide an overview of Russia's tax regime and accounting practices, as well as intellectual property, the new land code, the recent overhaul in the labour code, the real estate market, the new customs code and other relevant topics.

The book is also complimented by an appendices section that we hope the reader will find useful, with its business briefs, some additional statistical information about the Russian market, and its collection of internet pages providing further practical information relevant to this once enigmatic country.

Dr Marat Terterov
July 2004

Part One

Background to the Market

1.1
Developments in the Political Environment

William Flemming

Introduction

Governing the Russian Federation – a country that spans 11 time zones, with approximately 145 million inhabitants and covering almost one-seventh of the world's land mass – presents a formidable challenge for any Russian president. This resource-rich country stretches from the Pacific Ocean to the Baltic Sea and from the Arctic Circle to the Black Sea and China. The Russian Federation came into being in 1992 as the Soviet Union's legal successor state, and since then has not enjoyed the smoothest of transitions from a totalitarian political system and centrally-planned economy to democracy and the free market.

In March 2004, Vladimir Putin won re-election with an overwhelming first-round majority of 71 per cent of the vote – a victory that cements his personal dominance of the Russian political system. As Putin enters his second presidential term, the course of the country's development will be dictated by him and his protégés to a much greater extent than was the case at the beginning of his first term, when he was still a relative political novice with an unconsolidated power base. Some four years after effectively being installed in the presidency by Boris Yeltsin and his inner circle, it could be said that Putin is finally his own man.

However, Putin also goes into his second term facing mounting criticism – both at home and abroad – over his administration's authoritarian tendencies and the absence of institutional checks on his power. The political system that Putin presides over has acquired the moniker of 'managed democracy' and the March 2004 presidential election, which was criticized for the lack of real competition or substance, is seen by many as symptomatic of this system's progressive entrenchment.

This chapter looks at the political landscape and the country's main political institutions, and then proceeds to a brief assessment of Putin's first term in office and the prospects for his second term.

The president and the presidential administration

Russia's first post-Soviet Constitution – adopted in 1993 – laid the foundations for what is sometimes referred to as a 'super-presidential' system, in which considerable formal powers are vested in the office of the president, in addition to which the president has an impressive set of informal levers for exerting influence over the body politic.

According to the Constitution, the president is elected to a four-year term and may sit for a maximum of two consecutive terms. The president sets the domestic and foreign policy agenda, is Russia's top representative on the international stage, and is commander-in-chief of the country's armed forces. He nominates the prime minister (as well as having extensive control over other government appointments), who must then be approved by the lower chamber of the parliament (the State Duma). He also has certain decree powers and can veto legislation passed by the parliament, which then requires a two-thirds majority in both lower and upper chambers to be overturned. Furthermore, the president has the power – indeed is obliged – to dissolve the Duma if his nominee for prime minister is rejected three times consecutively. And if the Duma passes two motions of no-confidence in the government within a period of three months, the president must either dismiss the prime minister and his government or dissolve the Duma.

The president has a staff of approximately 2,000 functionaries, called the presidential administration. *Inter alia*, it provides Putin with an indispensable tool for political control, and increasingly all decisions of any importance are made by the president and his staff. Head of the presidential administration is Dmitry Medvedev: a member of Putin's inner circle, he replaced the long-serving Alexander Voloshin, a pivotal Yeltsin-era holdover, in November 2003.

At the time of writing, the presidential administration is undergoing reform as part of a wider effort to slim down and revamp the executive branch, although initial indications are that reform of the presidential staff will be largely cosmetic and that most key figures will stay in place. Medvedev's only two deputies in the reformed administration, Vladislav Surkov and Igor Sechin, are members of the two main 'clans' in Putin's entourage (thereby preserving balance inside the Kremlin). Surkov, with ties to the Yeltsin clan, is rightly considered to be one of the Kremlin's most talented political managers and is responsible for ensuring that the parliament, media and regional governors are all kept in line and 'on message'. Sechin, one of the president's most trusted henchmen, has been by Putin's side since the early 1990s and is considered a core member of the so-called St. Petersburg *silovik* group in the Kremlin.

On the economic side of the adminstration, Andrei Illarionov, the president's outspoken economic adviser, has been reappointed. In Putin's first term, Illarionov was a sparring partner for the government over economic policy and for Unified Energy Systems' CEO Anatoly Chubais (over plans for restructuring the electricity monopoly, in particular). He is also credited as author of the ambitious goal of doubling GDP in a decade – a key objective established by Putin in his 2003 state of the nation address and reiterated in 2004. Arkady Dvorkovich, an able young economist and former deputy minister of economic development, has been made head of expert department (a new entity formed by merging the economic and expert departments of the presidential administration), which will be responsible for providing independent analysis of the government's economic policy and evaluating draft economic legislation.

Under Yeltsin and also under Putin, one of the key informal levers of influence at the president's disposal was – and is – the so-called 'household department' (*upravlenie delami prezidenta*). The department controls an empire of hotels, dachas, apartments, chauffeur-driven cars, top-notch medical facilities, etc and is responsible for taking care of the needs of government officials, Duma deputies, officials from the General Prosecutor's Office, Supreme Court judges, and so on. It provides the president with a rich source of patronage and largesse, which can be (and has been) used extremely effectively for political ends. Even the most ardent political opponents have tended to be susceptible to material incentives offered by the Kremlin, and this is perhaps no surprise given that official salaries – even of top government officials, judges and Duma deputies – up until now have been extremely meagre. This is now changing with the announcement of significant wage increases as part of the programme of government and civil service reform. It should also be added that, as Putin has tightened his grip on the political system, this lever has lost the importance that it once had for resolving political disputes in the Yeltsin era.

Government

Although the Russian Constitution has a number of features in common with the French Constitution of the Fifth Republic (both of which provide for a form of dual executive), the main difference – in practice at least – has been the preponderance of the Russian president over the parliament in forming the cabinet. Throughout the post-Soviet period, with the exception of the short-lived cabinet of Yevgeny Primakov, the government has depended on the president for support rather than resting independently on a parliamentary majority. As a result, the government has always been the junior partner in the executive, possessing limited political weight and lacking a proper political base of its own. During the Yeltsin era, this was reinforced by the president's efforts to consolidate his own position through frequent prime ministerial sackings, cabinet reshuffles and playing cabinet members off against one another.

Mikhail Kasyanov was prime minister for practically the duration of Putin's first term. Owing his appointment more to the Yeltsin clan than to Putin, he retained some measure of independence, publicly disagreeing with the president on a number of key issues. While he proved to be a competent manager, presiding over an impressive period of economic growth, he dragged his feet on key reforms, including administrative and civil service reform. Indeed, this served as the official pretext for Kasyanov's dismissal just three weeks before the end of Putin's first term and his replacement by Mikhail Fradkov, a former minister of trade and director of the federal tax police, who was ambassador to the EU at the time of his appointment.

The choice of Fradkov, which came as a complete surprise to most people, was probably determined primarily by four factors. First, he is seen as someone who will loyally implement the president's wishes. Second, he is an experienced bureaucrat. Third, he is a convenient compromise figure: not only is he acceptable to the key groups in Putin's entourage (without being a full member of any of them), but he is also a known quantity in the West and has enough of an economics background not to spook the markets. Fourth, he is seen as having no political ambitions of his own. The general feeling is that Fradkov will last for no more than a couple of years, after which Putin will probably replace him with his anointed heir, someone from the president's inner circle.

Most of the key ministers responsible for the economy have retained their seats in the Fradkov government, including Finance Minster Alexei Kudrin and Economic Trade and Development Minister German Gref. Moreover, the powers of both have been enhanced in the reshuffle and restructuring of the government, with the Tax Ministry being subsumed by the Finance Ministry and the Customs Committee and Property Agency being incorporated into Gref's Ministry.

Two new faces in the Fradkov government, set to play an important role, are Alexander Zhukov, the deputy prime minister in the new government, and Dmitry Kozak, cabinet chief of staff. Zhukov, who served as a Duma deputy for over a decade and as chairman of the Duma's Budget Committee from 1998 until his government appointment, is a respected liberal economist. Kozak, one of the more industrious reformers in the presidential administration and a close Putin associate, is probably the most powerful head of the government apparatus in post-Soviet Russian history. In addition to his core duties, he heads the government commission on administrative reform and is responsible for the implementation of sweeping reforms of the government and civil service (an area that Putin has repeatedly named as a top priority for his second term). He is also the Kremlin's enforcer in the Cabinet, responsible for ensuring that there is no deviation from the presidential line (in official bureaucratese, he is responsible for 'ensuring the unity of the system of executive power'). The powers conferred upon the prime minister's nominal subordinates – Kozak, in particular – have led some observers to question the extent to which Fradkov will really be in charge of the government.

The programme for overhauling Russia's bloated bureaucracy and reforming the government is still being thrashed out at the time of writing. However, the effectiveness of the executive branch and its capacity to implement policy will depend to a considerable extent on the success or failure of this crucial reform.

Parliament

Russia has a bicameral parliament, the lower chamber being called the State Duma and the upper chamber, the Federation Council. The Duma is made up of 450 deputies (MPs), half of whom are directly elected in first-past-the-post contests and half of whom are elected through party lists. Duma elections occur once every four years, providing the president does not dissolve the lower house before it serves out its full term (under one of the scenarios outlined above in the section on the president).

For most of Yeltsin's period in office, the Duma was dominated by the Communist Party and its satellites, while pro-presidential forces were weak in number. As a result, the executive and legislative branches were frequently at loggerheads and relations at best were characterized by grudging co-operation. Yeltsin never invited the parliamentary opposition to form a government, although he did from time to time appease the communists by removing ministers whom the opposition considered particularly odious and sometimes even co-opted individual members of left-wing parties into government. In the Yeltsin years, the government managed to push a certain amount of important legislation through parliament, normally through a mixture of cajoling and 'carrot and stick' methods. However, frequently the price was the emasculation of legislation or its capture by powerful interest groups.

The parliamentary elections in December 1999 fundamentally altered the balance of forces within the Duma, with pro-Kremlin parties strengthening their position considerably and the left opposition losing its prior dominance over the legislative process. The Kremlin's majority was further consolidated in the December 2003 parliamentary elections, in which the pro-presidential United Russia party won a resounding victory and emerged with more than 300 seats under their control – giving it a large enough majority to initiate constitutional amendments. United Russia's leader, Boris Gryzlov, became speaker of the parliament following the elections; he is viewed very much as a loyal executor of the Kremlin line, rather than an independent player.

The only other parties to get into the new Duma were the Communist Party, Rodina (Motherland) and Vladimir Zhirinovksy's LDPR – the latter two parties both purvey a mixture of nationalism and populism, and both are creatures of the Kremlin to a greater or lesser extent. Thus the only real opposition comes from the communists (with just over 50 deputies) but even their opposition is somewhat half-hearted. The liberal Union of Right Forces and Yabloko parties crashed and burned in the elections, failing to even clear the five per cent threshold necessary for representation in the parliament.

While the pro-Kremlin parliamentary bloc looks increasingly monolithic, appearances may well be deceptive. Many United Russia deputies have multiple allegiances, enjoying close ties – or being beholden – to the regional or business elite (numerous representatives of regional governors or major companies were included on United Russia's party list in return for financial and/or administrative support). Thus, while it is very unlikely that there will be open defiance of the Kremlin or the government, there certainly will be plenty of lobbying and horse-trading going on behind the scenes. Another issue is whether the party can outlive Putin's presidency, given that it has no real programme beyond supporting Putin.

The Federation Council, until Putin's accession to the presidency, was composed *ex officio* of the governors of each of Russia's 89 regions and the speakers of regional legislatures (ie 178 members in total). This provided the regional elite with additional clout at the federal level, as well as the ability to block federal legislation that did not serve their interests. The upper chamber has the power to veto legislation and send it back to the lower chamber, with a 2/3 majority then being required to override the veto, which under Yeltsin was very difficult to achieve.

One of the first major reforms undertaken by Putin following his inauguration in May 2000 was to weaken the governors by, *inter alia*, depriving them of their seats in the Federation Council (thus depriving them of their immunity from prosecution as well). This reform did not require amendment of the constitution, as the constitution itself is rather vague, stating only that: 'The Federation Council consists of two representatives from each of the regions of the Russian Federation; one each from the legislative and executive branches of the government.' Thus, governors and heads of regional legislatures have been replaced by full-time delegates elected by them.

The Federation Council has effectively been transformed from a hotbed of opposition to the federal government in the late Yeltsin years to a subservient body under Putin that does little more than rubber-stamp legislation. The speaker of the Federation Council is the accident-prone Sergei Mironov, whose chief qualifications for the job seem to be his blind loyalty to the president and his St. Petersburg provenance.

The Putin presidency

Looking back at Vladimir Putin's first term in office, his main achievement – for better or for worse – has clearly been the consolidation of his own position and the subjugation of rival centres of power and influence to the Kremlin, whether it be the regional governors, the oligarchs, the media, parliament or even the government. There can be little doubt that Putin now controls the 'commanding heights' of the polity. Putin has concentrated a great deal of power in the Kremlin and in his own hands, and there are very few, if any, institutional checks or balances; the political landscape has been purged of virtually all opposition. While this is unhealthy and gives considerable cause for concern, it should also be said that given the chaos and the weak state (captured by powerful business interests) that he inherited from his predecessor, Putin had little choice but to re-centralize power to some extent in order to strengthen the State's capacity to implement policy and reforms.

The big question, going into his second term, is whether Putin will use the power he amassed in his first term to push ahead with crucial reforms and seek to institutionalize his power, or whether he will merely continue to concentrate more power in his hands and avoid establishing transparent 'rules of the game'. As Standard & Poor's ratings agency stated in a recent report: 'At the moment, it is unclear whether Russia is poised for progress or will regress into an environment where businesses operate under the threat of political intrigues, personal power plays and ineffective or parasitic bureaucrats.'

There are worrying indications, from the past four years, that Putin much prefers backroom deals and strong-arm tactics to rules or laws applied openly and across the board. The ongoing Yukos saga provides a perfect example of this. The charges of fraud, embezzlement and tax evasion against Mikhail Khodorkovsky and one of his business associates could clearly be made against any number of other 'oligarchs' and businessmen. Russia's richest man was singled out most probably because he got ideas above his station (particularly in the realm of politics) and because by striking at one of the biggest and most powerful businessmen in the country, Putin could send a clear message to all the rest. However, rather than dealing with the excessive power and political influence of big business (a very serious problem) by tackling corruption, strengthening the anti-monopoly agency, introducing campaign finance legislation etc, and then enforcing one set of rules across the board, the president has demonstrated a preference for striking arbitrarily with the assistance of the General Prosecutor's Office. While he has 'whacked' several individual oligarchs over the past four years, Putin has shown no great desire to dismantle the system or to create a more transparent system governing relations between business and the State.

As Putin embarks upon his second term, however, there is some good news. The Fradkov government has announced a potentially far-reaching programme of reforms to revamp the government and streamline the bureaucracy. The predatory activities of government agencies and corrupt bureaucrats are a major source of risk impinging on the business environment and blocking the creation of a nationwide 'level playing field' for business. Progressive legislation is often blocked at the implementation phase or subverted to suit the rent-seeking ends of individual bureaucrats. Putin has repeatedly highlighted this problem over the past few years, reiterating that administrative reform is a top priority for his second term, and now he seems to be moving forward. However, without major progress on this front, the whole reform effort will likely be stalled indefinitely.

1.2

An Overview of the Russian Economy: Money Matters

Raiffeisen Bank

Over the last four years international oil prices have fluctuated in the range of $23–27 per barrel, boosting Russia's annual exports to $105–135 billion, or more than a third of gross domestic product. In turn, swelling export proceeds have significantly fortified reserves, setting the stage for exchange rate stabilization, and have fed into the money supply, making a play with the interest rates. The major impact of these trends on the real sector was giving a push to a consumption and investment boom, and counteracting tendencies toward autarchy in technology and R&D. Back in the monetary sphere, the impact of Russia's export boom has been most dynamic and visible in two major patterns that have persisted into 2004.

First, for about the last year, the rouble has been strengthening in nominal terms against the dollar, supported by both strong fundamentals at home and the weakening of the greenback around the globe. Second, interest rates have shifted down significantly. This is true not only regarding international assets, in the wake of monetary loosening by the US FED and the general ascent of emerging bond markets, but also domestically, due to increasing liquidity, surging demand for nominal assets, the lack of derivatives, and declining currency risks.

Growth in the real sector has more or less become conventional wisdom, and the main question now is not 'will there be growth?' but 'how much?'. At the same time, the monetary sphere in Russia is becoming the most intriguing one. Broadly speaking, investors and market players have been pondering over all three fundamental monetary issues: the exchange rate, inflation and the interest rate.

On this note, we will assess each issue individually and lay out our vision of future trends and their impact on the economy.

Exchange rate

'However beautiful the strategy, one should occasionally look at the results'

Winston Churchill

We really don't need to play up the importance of this particular issue, as the figures speak for themselves (see Figure 1.2.1). The rouble-dollar rate lies at the crux of any analysis of exchange rate trends for Russia. Among foreign currencies, the greenback still has pride of place in Russia. Looking at the current account, over 50 per cent of goods are exported in dollars or dollar-pegged currencies, and the similar share of imports is recorded in dollar terms. Domestically, 33 per cent of households and 56 per cent of corporate deposits are set in foreign currency, which is still mainly dollars. Turning toward the debt market, 80 per cent of sovereign bonds, 75 per cent of corporate bonds and the vast majority of domestic loans are issued in dollars as well. Based on both domestic and international trends, we are likely to see another 15–18 per cent of real rouble appreciation against the dollar for 2004, on the back of last year's figure of 17 per cent. (At the same time, against the euro, the rouble depreciated by 0.6 per cent in real terms, on a y-o-y basis).

With the rouble's rapid nominal ascent against the dollar becoming one of the key features of economic development in Russia, the future direction of the exchange rate has become a pressing question. The broad answer is that the oil prices will be the primary driver of the exchange rate, while in the short run (over the next twelve months),

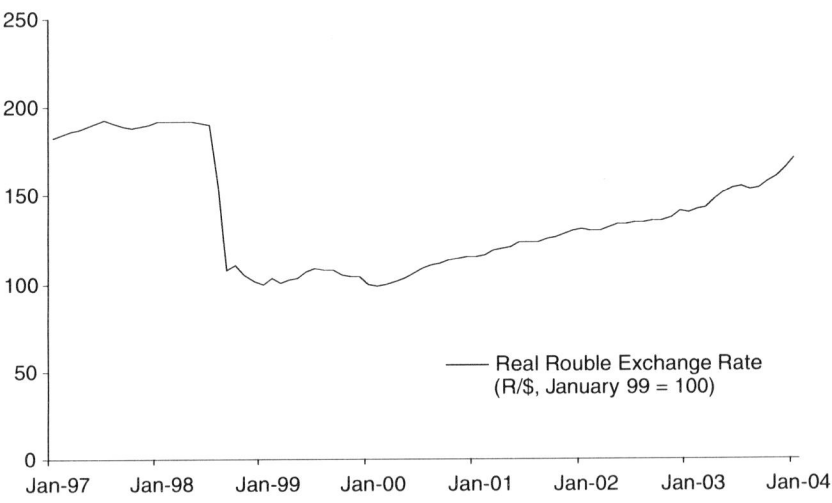

Source: Reuters, Raiffeisenbank estimates

Figure 1.2.1 Real rouble exchange rate (R/$)

the factor of major importance will be the policy mix chosen by the Central Bank of Russia (CBR).

Our forecast for the average oil price in 2004 is $27/bbl (see Figure 1.2.2). Accordingly, if current trends persist, we should see nominal rouble appreciation against the dollar continue. However, the actual figure will solely depend on CBR policy. Based on the current trends we could see the exchange rate at the level of R27.0/$1 or even lower by the end of the year.

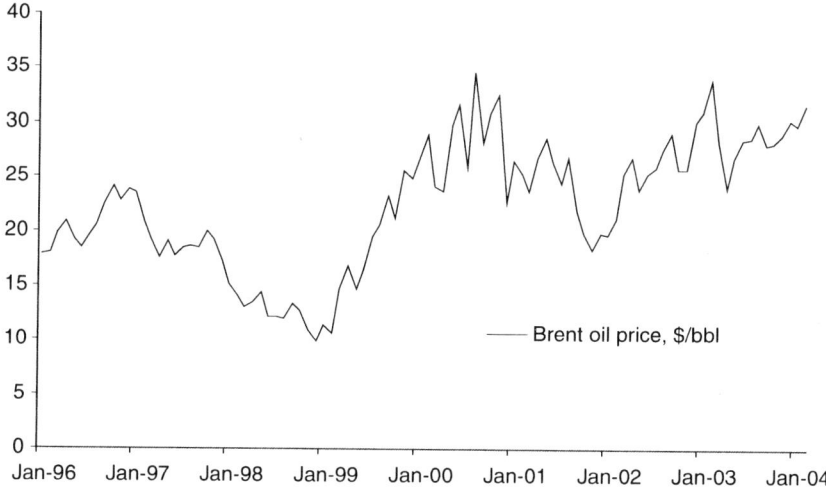

Source: Reuters
Figure 1.2.2 Brent oil price

Beyond the current year, there is a strong possibility that the oil price trend will reverse itself, which would result in a lagged reversal of the nominal exchange rate, perhaps as early as next year. Consequently, the risk of currency weakening – though greatly diminished at present – still exists for Russia's assets and should be taken into account for any investments beyond a one-year horizon.

What can the CBR do in the shorter-term perspective, while oils remain high? Broadly speaking, the play will again depend on what authorities view as most preferable – appreciation of the domestic currency through its exchange rate nominal values, or through accelerating inflation. The authorities are likely to base their targeted values for each of these parameters on what would be less distorting for domestic economic growth.

On the margin, the choices are the following:

1. 'Fix' the exchange rate implicitly at a certain level, allowing only minor fluctuations, while accumulating as many dollars on sales as

possible to insure against a worsening of external conditions and reversal of the real appreciation trend.

2. Instead of establishing a target for the exchange rate, an alternative would be making the liquidity constraint 'binding' by targeting measured increases in the money supply (and so reserves) within a certain time period (eg a month).

The consequences of the first option would be a rapid undervaluing of the rouble, with respective support of exporters and the relative cheapening of domestic inputs. Moreover, the CBR would accumulate sufficient reserves for a counter-cyclical play if and when global sentiment on commodities markets worsens, and/or the US FED abandons its loose monetary policy. This policy would ensure visible stability on the FX market while building a sufficient base to maintain it in the future. Interest rates would be poised to slide without extra regulations, suppressed by mounting liquidity in the financial sector.

This policy could be supportive for foreign investment inflows, in the sense that direct investors target cheap production factors on growing markets and portfolio investors seek out arbitrage opportunities on domestic asset price volatility. At the same time, it would also benefit exporters, domestic producers and households with dollar-denominated savings.

The main cost of this option is, as previously mentioned, an accelerating liquidity increase and growing problems with binding the excess money and keeping inflation framed. Achieving these goals would require regulation of interest rates, including issuing of own bonds, open market operations, and creating and developing a derivatives market. These measures should be implemented decisively and without delay under this policy choice. Otherwise, inflation would quickly spiral out of control, notwithstanding robust economic growth, the population's increasing propensity to save in banks (see the banking section below) and the mopping up of fiscal surpluses. In turn, this would eat into the rouble savings of households and revenues of domestically-oriented producers, and eventually might become distorting for the economy as a whole, even leading to a bubble on the domestic equity market (as investors switch over from bonds offering increasingly negative real yields). In the worst case, price growth significantly exceeding 10 per cent would undermine the benefits of maintaining a cheap and stable rouble.

An additional sterilization measure could be 'aggressive' capital account liberalization, allowing domestic investors to freely invest in foreign assets. However, this measure is highly unlikely, since it entails a spike in volatility on domestic debt and equity markets due to the constant in- and outflows of 'hot' money – something Russian monetary authorities undoubtedly aim to prevent.

The second option, if implemented, would require much less effort from the CBR to combat inflation, although it would fuel quicker appreciation of the rouble, cutting into the dollar-denominated income and savings of exporters and households. Moreover, it would generate higher volatility on the FX market, both in the short and long term, and likely push up domestic interest rates in the medium term – translating into an increasing cost of capital for domestic companies. Besides, both domestic and foreign portfolio investors would find exchange rate arbitrage increasingly attractive, and eventually find better options for playing on interest rate arbitrage on Russian and international money markets (more on this is detailed below), both of which would increase domestic asset market volatility.

Our educated guess is that in 2004 the CBR will use a kind of '50/50' policy mix: in the first half of the year the bank's policies will lean more heavily toward the first option, while in the second half more priority will be given to the second. In both cases, we expect step-wise gradual appreciation of the domestic currency to continue, but in the first case the 'steps' will be 'wider' – more broadly stretched out across time – and in the second case, 'steeper'. For example, the rate of R28.5/$1 has been maintained for more than a month since the end of January 2004, suggesting that the bank is currently giving larger weight to the first policy option.

The positive side of this 'strategy mix' is that it would be a measured trade-off between the benefits and costs of each individual policy and, respectively, require improvements in financial market regulation. In particular, this would mean developing absorption tools, since managing inflationary trends certainly won't be a piece of cake.

Inflation

'The lack of money is the root of all evil.' Adapting this popular saying to Russia's current monetary situation, one could also add: *'...and windfall money is much hassle as well.'*

Over the last three months the CBR's reserves have swelled by more than $20 billion, accelerating the growth of the monetary base and, respectively, M2. So far, while money supply has been expanding steadily at 44–46 per cent y-o-y, official data point to inflation gradually declining from 13 per cent to 11 per cent y-o-y over the same period (see Figure 1.2.3). Apart from the typical lag between growth in monetary values and inflation, a possible explanation for this apparent contradiction is the corresponding rise in demand for money, nominal dollar depreciation against the rouble, and absorption efforts by fiscal authorities.

Background to the Market

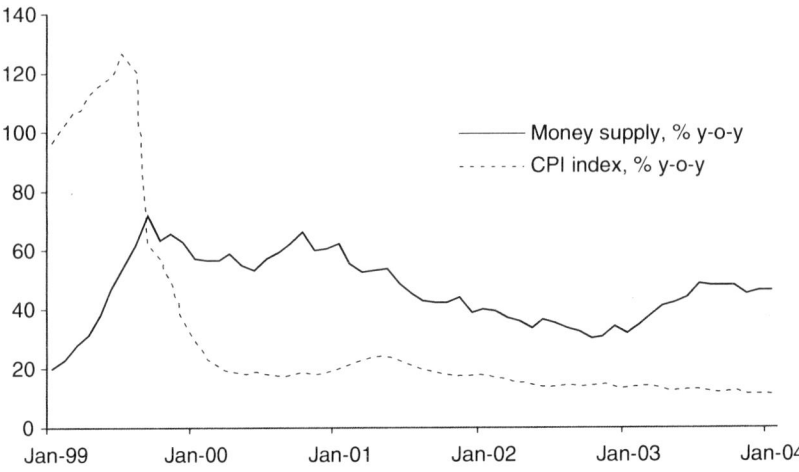

Source: Goskomstat, Raiffeisenbank estimates
Figure 1.2.3 Money supply vs CPI, y-o-y change

Barring any absorption measures, over the last quarter of 2003 the monetary base should have expanded by approximately R330 billion (eg the 'actual' GIR increase adjusted for rouble appreciation). At the same time, the CBR reported that the increase was in fact only R170 billion, suggesting that the authorities managed to absorb roughly half of the rise in liquidity.

These data tell only half the story, however. According to the CBR, cash on MinFin's accounts with the CBR increased by R45 billion, half the budget surplus value for the period (R106 billion in total), while MinFin's net issuance of bonds amounted to R36 billion over the period. The only feasible explanation for the remainder of the absorption is accumulation of financial reserves (and then either used for external debt service, or simply stored), which at end 2003 amounted to R258 billion, R108 billion of which have been earmarked for the Stabilization Fund, according to MinFin.

Apart from sterilization measures, slower price growth could also be a function of the nominal dollar depreciation against the rouble over the period (3.5 per cent over the second half of 2003 and another 2.8 per cent within the first two months of the current year). The link between domestic price dynamics and the exchange rate is a widespread phenomenon, at least in the non-food sector, which to a certain extent could explain the lower rate of overall price index growth. Abolishment of the 5 per cent sales tax could have also played a role.

Finally the acceleration of real sector development (7.3 per cent GDP growth in 2003 according to preliminary data) serves as a strong anchor on price growth.

However, even when all the above factors are taken into account, 15–20 per cent of money supply growth still remains unaccounted for, suggesting a higher 'fair estimation' of the level of inflation. Together with falling or flat interest rates, this implies that either the market will see accelerating inflation due to the lagged impact of monetary growth in the nearest months, or that perhaps there was a slip-up in official estimations.

Persistent inflation over 10 per cent would mean continued strong real appreciation of the rouble, the exact level of which will depend on the CBR's policy mix. What would this mean for the economy?

General implications of an appreciating exchange rate for the economy

Exports and imports

Persistent rouble strengthening would threaten first of all the 45 per cent of export revenue generated outside of the mineral sector. As for imports, the data for the period 2000–03 can be used as a proxy for estimating the impact of appreciation on its levels. An increase of imports by 14–23 per cent annually within the period corresponded to real rouble appreciation of 8–17 per cent against the dollar. This could be taken as a proxy for the domestic import elasticity of the exchange rate, though combined with the impact of income growth as well.

Growth and profits

Exporter's profits would certainly suffer from declining rouble-denominated revenues coupled with increasing domestic costs for factors of production, including labour, intermediary products, energy, etc. For non-exporters, losses would be felt indirectly, via the import substitution effect. A prime example is light industry, where the rate of growth remains in the range of negative 2–3 per cent for the second year in a row.

Capital inflows

Exchange rate and interest rate arbitrage
With nominal rates falling, portfolio investors would increasingly seek out arbitrage opportunities. On such a trend, borrowing money on international rates and then buying NDF for $/R, or a rouble debt instrument for a short term, would guarantee a positive return in dollars. Respectively, portfolio investments are likely to flow into the domestic market, though certain ambiguities in the new laws on currency control still pose a barrier to entry.

18   Background to the Market

...and not only that
Apart from the exchange rate patterns, assessing capital inflow entails several more issues that should be examined individually.

Growth of the economy
While in real terms 7 per cent growth is by itself an impressive feat, and a comparable rate is expected in 2004, in dollar terms Russia's GDP posts around 26 per cent y-o-y growth. Any way you look at it, these are certainly attractive figures for investors, reflecting a strongly growing market with comparably cheap labour and capital, and a suitable level of stability. Current examples of joint ventures in the real sector abound, especially in manufacturing (automotive, furniture production, construction materials, food industries, household appliances), not to mention large levels of foreign investment already poured into the oil sector and planned for telecoms.

In particular, rising relative costs would be compensated for, one way or another, by emerging opportunities and trends associated with economic expansion (growth in market size, demand, availability of resources, etc) For example, increasing labour costs might be offset by growth in labour productivity. Moderate, controlled appreciation will not, *ceteris paribus*, detract from foreign investment attractiveness, though certainly a 'freefall' of the dollar would cause concerns of a sudden correction and detract from overall economy stability.

Persistent stability, improved image of domestic borrowers
Currently, FDI – or rather the lack thereof – is less influenced by the exchange rate than it is by other factors: political risks, insufficient legislative base, poor contract enforcement and property rights

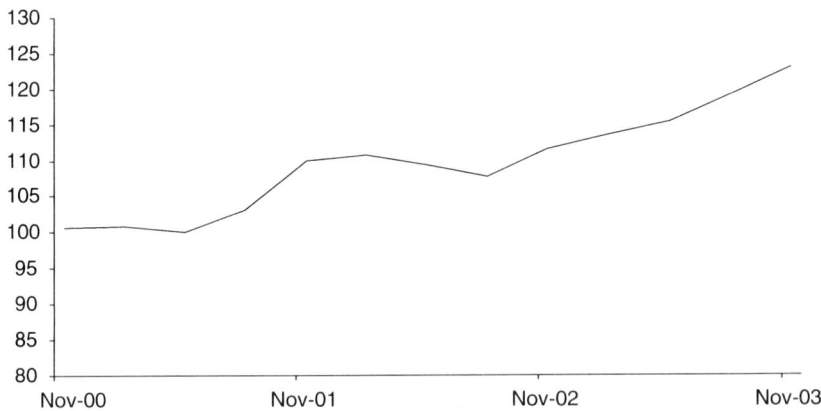

Source: Goskomstat, Raiffeisen research

Figure 1.2.4 Real average labour productivity index, Dec '00 = 100

An Overview of the Russian Economy: Money Matters

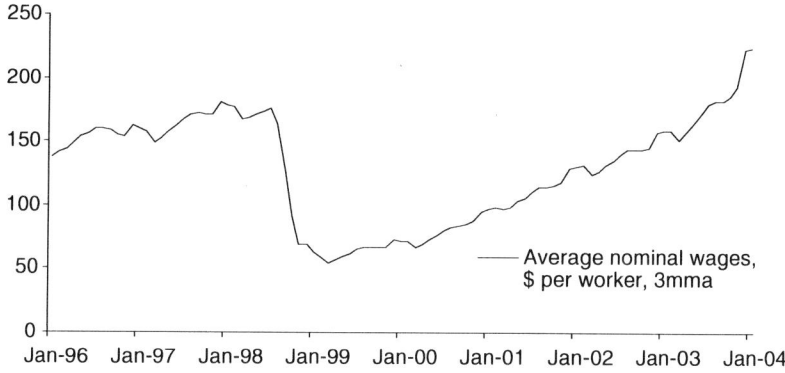

Source: Goskomstat
Figure 1.2.5 Average nominal wages

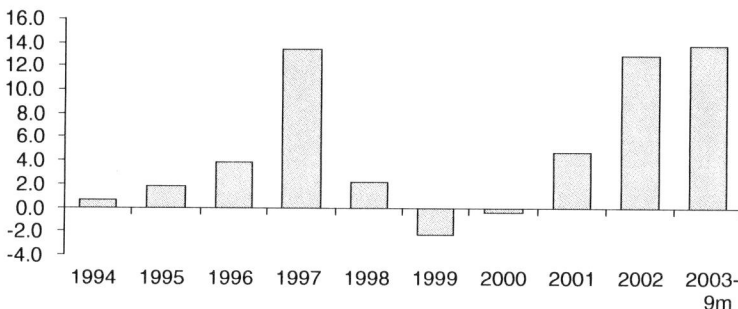

Source: CBR
Figure 1.2.6 Foreign loans and portfolio investment inflow to Russia's private sector ($bln)

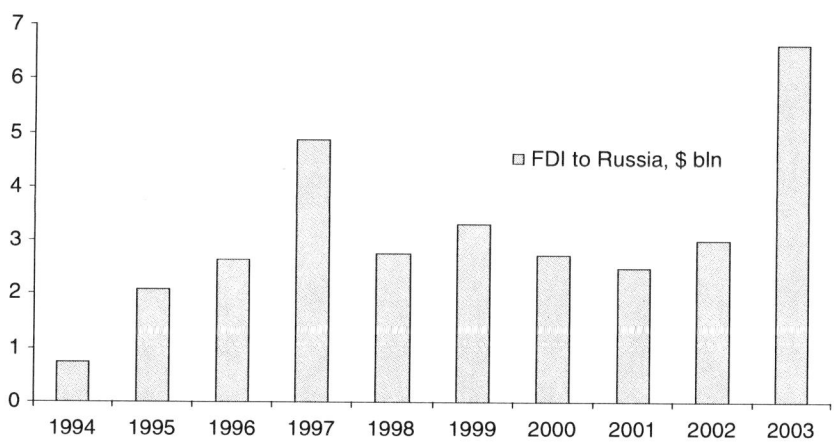

Source: CBR
Figure 1.2.7 Foreign direct investment to Russia ($bln)

protection, corruption, etc. Within this 'bouquet', appreciation of the domestic currency, which potentially raises costs, takes a backseat to broader political and legal considerations.

Turning to portfolio investments, on the debt side Russian corporate borrowing on international markets is burgeoning. The total value of issued corporate and bank Eurobonds has reached $13.8 billion, while total portfolio investment and loans to domestic borrowers should reach the level of $25 billion for 2003.

Interest rates: flat at best; external rates: all eyes on the US

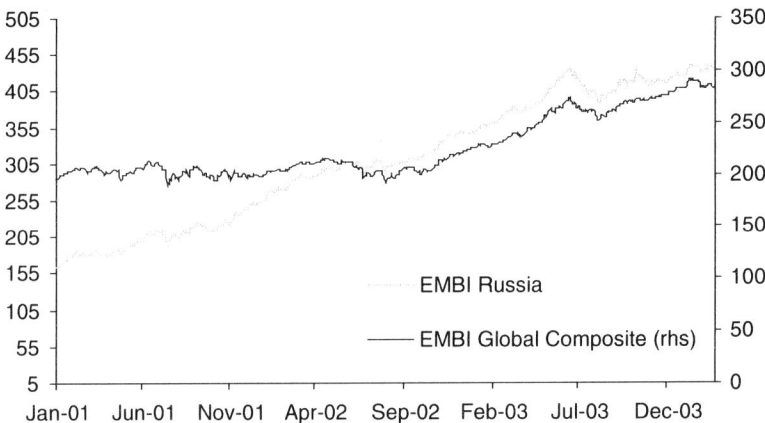

Source: Bloomberg

Figure 1.2.8 EMBI indices performance

Following the 'victory march' of emerging market bond prices over the last four years, the risk of a trend reversal appears tangible. While the markets are generally anticipating a rate rise by the US FED, as soon as the ever low 1 per cent US interest rates are actually moved up, the US Treasury market will immediately follow suit, pulling up global emerging market yields as well.

So at best we expect Russia's yield dynamics to remain flat, at the current level of 6.9 per cent (Russia'30) until the end of the year, though we assign high probability to a U-shaped trend, with year-end rates edging up into the 7+ range for Russia'30. Respectively, we do not foresee any high returns on sovereign Eurobonds, though Russia's spread contraction to UST should ensure a small positive return on sovereigns, especially after a possible S&P upgrade of Russia's debt to investment grade. For example, if yields remain unchanged from current levels by year-end, the gain on price for Russia'30 will be just 2 per cent.

That said, a switch to corporate dollar-denominated debt looks reasonable, preferably to semi-state companies. Our top pick is Gazprom bonds, which offer the highest liquidity and attractive yields. Among others, MTS also stands out, and it could be a good speculative buy on rumours of the acquisition deal with Vodafone. Corporate Eurobonds in general should enjoy spread contraction to sovereigns, which should compensate for the likely twist in global market trends.

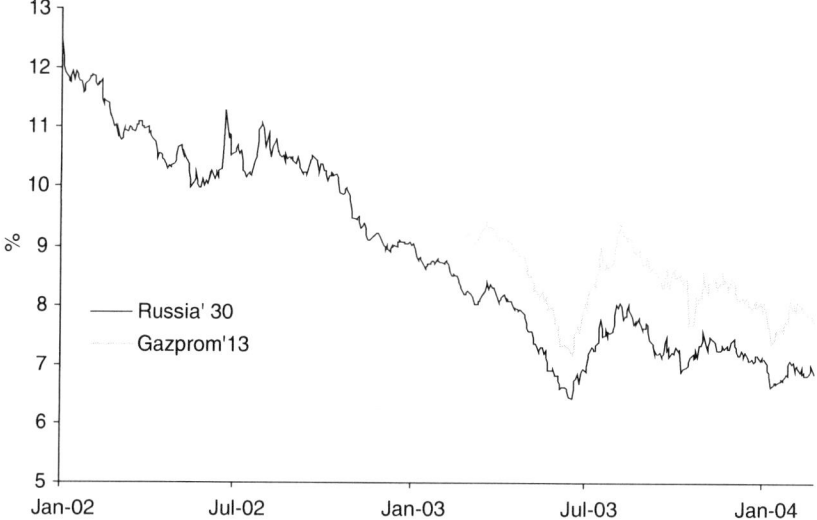

Source: Bloomberg
Figure 1.2.9 Russia'30 and Gazprom'13 yields

Domestically there are two crucial points:

1. movement of the exchange rate;
2. movement of international yields.

Rouble vs. dollar dynamics on Russian FX markets again will be the crucial factor driving domestic rate trends. Given our assumptions, we would expect interest rates to gradually drift down for the first half of 2004, and then stabilize or perhaps even edge upward in the second half.

The first half of the year will most likely continue to witness oils at their highs, and respectively strong external accounts, fuelling appreciation of the rouble against the dollar and pumping money onto financial markets. Assuming that international interest rates will not start to rise earlier than in autumn 2004, we expect domestic bond yields to slowly move down from their current levels.

A reversal of this trend would largely depend on global rate dynamics, as domestic rates are usually set with certain positive

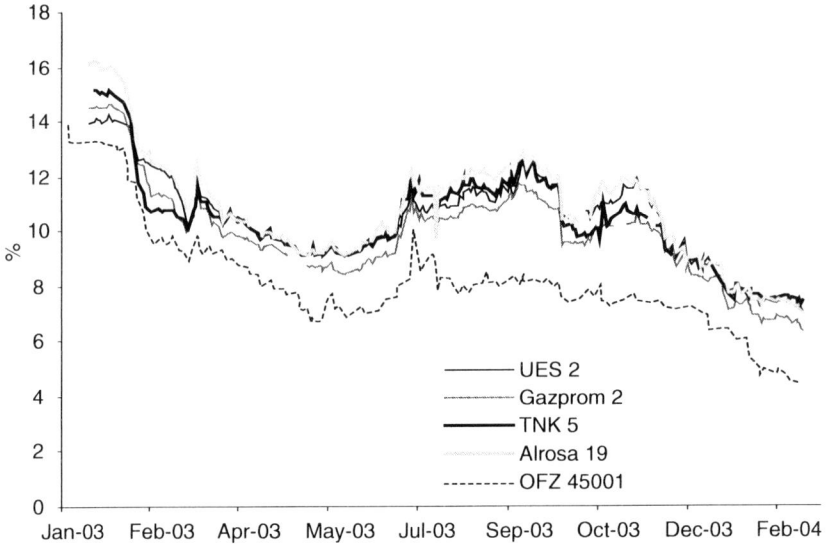

Source: MICEX, Raiffeisen research

Figure 1.2.10 Corporate vs sovereign bond yields

spreads to the Eurobond yields, a habit that seems to persist in spite of the already lengthy period of rouble appreciation.

At the same time, supply of bonds should increase. MinFin's borrowing plans are quite extensive, and are concentrated in the second half of the year. In particular, MinFin aims to issue several long and sizeable 'benchmark' OFZ issues for 3, 5 and 10 years, which will serve as benchmarks for the rest of the market. Each issue will be R30–35 billion.

In 2004 the authorities hope to make the market larger, more diversified and volatile, and much more competitive – ie to put an end to the practice whereby the State Pension Fund and Sberbank basically dictate new placements.

MinFin is targeting net borrowing of approximately $5 billion in 2004, including CBR plans on selling OFZs from its own portfolio this year. This should help absorb the swell of funds pouring into domestic markets. In order to improve market liquidity, MinFin will limit the share of newly issued papers in a single investor's portfolio to 35 per cent.

The authorities also promised two principally new instruments. The first is state savings bonds issued for the purpose of investing pension contributions. However, this will materialize no earlier than the second half of the year, as relevant legislation needs to be adjusted. In particular, amendments would include a list of investors authorized to purchase the bonds, such as pension and investment funds. Secondly, OFZ futures should create a derivatives market for government rouble bonds. Finally, the CBR will introduce new regulations for REPO that would allow not only GKO/OFZs to be used for collateral, but Eurobonds and MinFins as well.

Thus, the second half of 2004 should bring greater volatility, especially if a possible slide in oil prices puts a dent in Russia's external account performance, and also given uncertainty surrounding domestic exchange rate and international interest rate movements. There is a risk that the government rouble bond yield curve will shift outwards and steepen.

Turning to investment implications, the best strategy for rouble nominal assets continues to be staying at the short end of the curve for sovereign bonds, though switching to sub-sovereign and corporate debt would be an even better move. Given Russia's strong economic prospects, both these classes promise to perform well throughout the year, and offer good options for portfolio diversification on a risk-return basis.

One of the major risks related to the domestic securities market (apart from the already 'customary' political and oil-related risks) remains excessive short-term liquidity inflows, which have no place to go but into securities. At best this generates increased volatility, at worst – a bubble.

Fortunately for the economy, the principle of 'investment into real assets' is one that has been increasingly exercised by domestic banks. Development of credit is one of the bright spots for Russia's economy. Not only is international borrowing increasingly available and popular among domestic companies, but domestic banks are making significant headway in developing of all sorts of lending.

The Russian banking sector: an outlook

'An optimist sees an opportunity in every calamity; a pessimist sees a calamity in every opportunity.'

Winston Churchill

Despite information asymmetries and the customary emerging-market risks, Russian banks are increasingly showing themselves as optimists.

Four years of steady economic growth have substantially altered the landscape of Russia's banking environment. Compared to the crisis-ridden 1990s, a number of recent developments have set Russian banking on a principally new trajectory, including political and monetary stabilization, liberalization and structural reform, and tangible improvements in Russia's international status.

First and foremost, banks are becoming increasingly 'credit-oriented'. Sound public finance in 2000–2003 has resulted in the

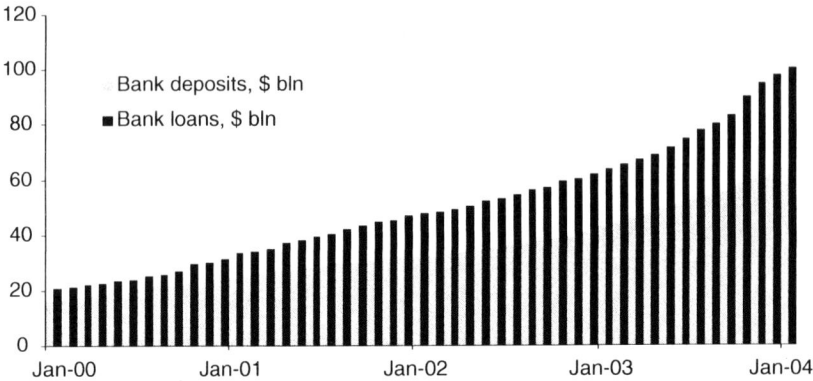

Source: CBR, Raiffeisenbank research
Figure 1.2.11 Bank deposits and loans

shrinking of the governmental securities market, as lending has become much more attractive than gambling on domestic markets. Attracted funds (primarily deposits) are increasingly used for financing conventional banking transactions, rather than plugging the gaps in the state budget, as was often the case prior to the crisis.

Table 1.2.1 Russian banks: credits, assets, investments

	1996	1997	1998	1999	2000	2001	2002	2003
Total assets, % GDP	23.2	33.9	38.8	34.9	33.4	34.9	37.8	40.8
Total credit to private sector, %GDP	7.3	8.6	12.8	11.5	12.3	15.4	16.9	19.6
Total credit to private sector, % assets	31.6	25.3	33.1	32.9	36.7	44.0	44.6	48.2
Investments into securities, % GDP		8.2	10.5	7.2	6.7	6.2	7.1	8.5
Investments into securities, % assets		24.1	27.0	20.5	20.0	17.8	18.8	20.8

Source: CBR, RET, Raiffeisenbank research

Broadly speaking, Russia's new business environment has provoked two key changes in bank strategies. Rapid development of the production sector has led to improvements in the financial status of many corporate borrowers, especially export-oriented companies, which have traditionally been the preferred category of clients for commercial lending. Declining credit risks associated with these companies and their improved reputation as borrowers, coupled with dramatically lowered international interest rates, have made their borrowing on international markets not only possible, but also affordable – especially taking into account nominal rouble appreciation since spring of 2003. This trend is most vividly demonstrated by the surge in the level of external borrowing, as well as the active tapping of the Eurobond market by major Russian companies and banks.

At the same time, the largest domestically operating banks are experiencing a shift in their client base. While in the previous two years exporters dominated the list of borrowers, banks are now giving increasing attention to relatively smaller companies oriented towards the domestic market.

The second innovation in banks' strategies is entrance into new market niches that previously were given scant attention, namely retail banking and services to SMEs. Both areas offer extremely high growth potential, though of course both also pose new challenges for banks, in terms of adjustments in technology, regional expansion and assessment of related risks.

Income growth and further development of the monetary sector have led to more optimistic expectations regarding stability. Besides, in an environment of developing financial markets, people have gradually acquired the habit of 'making money work' for them, at least to guard against inflation. This has fuelled strong growth rates for retail deposits in commercial banks, which have overtaken commercial deposits in relative value since last year. This, in turn, benefits banks in two major ways. First, mounting retail deposits help banks to solve the immediate problem of securing financing, albeit at a higher cost (interest rates on retail deposits tend to be higher). Second, they help banks to solve their liquidity problems. The Achilles Heel of the domestic banking system has been the substantial mismatch between the duration of assets and liabilities, an issue often mentioned in connection with the ubiquitous 'undercapitalization problem'.

Table 1.2.2 Retail deposits (1997–2003)

	1997	1998	1999	2000	2001	2002	2003
Retail deposits, % of banks' assets	19.0	19.1	18.7	18.9	21.5	24.8	27.5
Retail deposits, % of GDP	6.4	7.4	6.5	6.3	7.5	9.4	11.2

Development of the retail business is one of the ways to fill in the gap. Four years of financial stability and rouble appreciation have encouraged households to deposit money for longer terms. While two or three years ago deposits for one year and longer would have been considered a novelty in Russia, they currently make up over a third of

Background to the Market

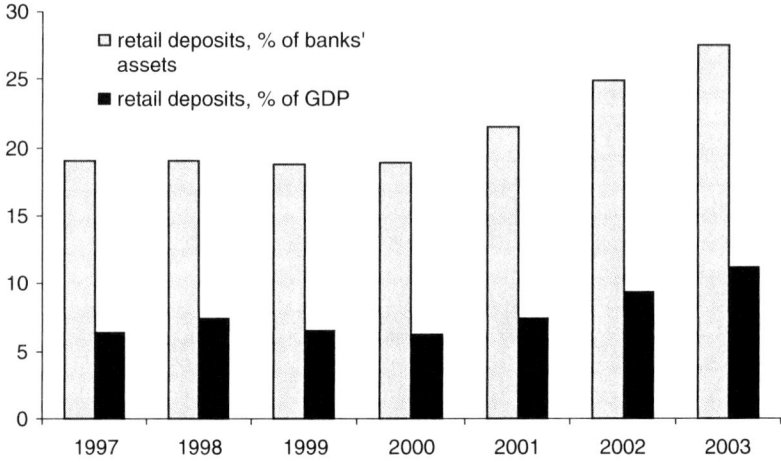

Source: CBR, Raiffeisenbank research
Figure 1.2.12 Retail deposit dynamics

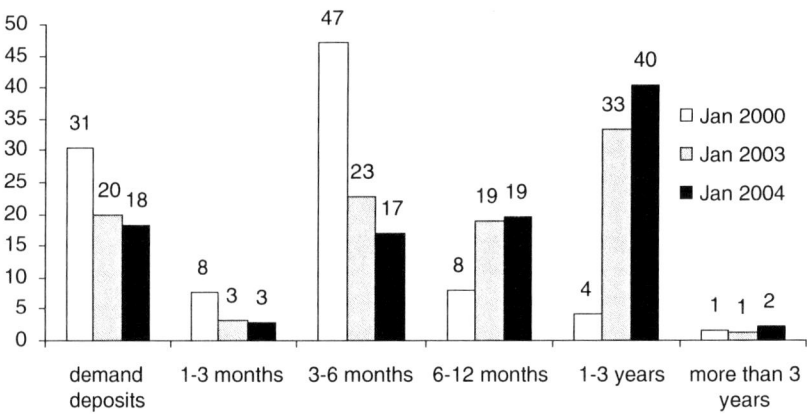

Source: CBR, Raiffeisenbank research
Figure 1.2.13 Retail deposits structure, % of total

total retail deposits. However, the 'devil in the detail' remains the perfectly legal option of early deposit withdrawal, which, in case of a bank run, could lead to a serious liquidity crunch.

Against the background of solid fundamental performance, households have raised their expectations for future income, providing a strong impetus for purchases of consumer durables and spurring demand for real estate. Retail lending began primarily with relatively small and short loans, mostly for household appliances. The next stage of development was car loans, and short-term, relatively small

An Overview of the Russian Economy: Money Matters

consumer loans (up to 3 years and $10,000 in value). However, the key breakthrough came with the launch of mortgage loan programmes by major retail banks. At the moment mortgage loans are one of the most profitable – and less risky – categories of lending. These loans offer fairly short terms (up to 10 years) in comparison with international norms as well as the highest dollar rates (10–15 per cent). Risk assessment is quite efficient, as banks require a range of supporting documentation and borrowers generally represent the wealthiest and most stable income cohort, who are most apt to play fairly with lenders.

Retail banking growth is not only based on fundamentals. General financial market sentiment is such that apart from an as of yet small corporate bond market segment, fixed income instruments can hardly offer banks acceptable returns (negative real rates remain one of the major impulses for banks to diversify their operations beyond financial market operations).

Despite robust development over the past years, Russia still demonstrates lacklustre performance in terms of financial intermediation, and particularly retail banking, according to both international standards and in comparison with other transition economies. The ratio of loans to GDP is roughly two to three times lower than in the other CEE countries, while figures for retail banking are almost negligible in relative terms.

However, the prospects for the Russian banking system are bright – basically it's just a matter of time. It has been less than four years since conventional banking services started to mature, and financial markets have been actively developing for an even shorter period. While the banking system can boast considerable achievements in

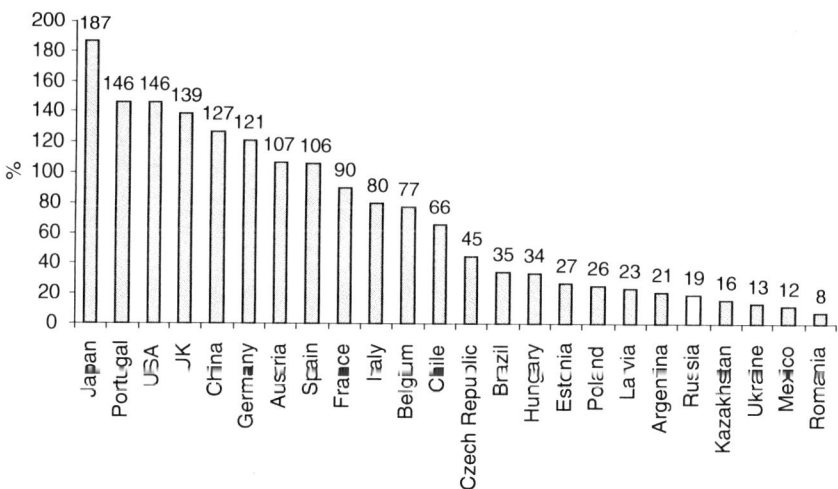

Source: World Bank, Central Banks' websites, Raiffeisenbank research

Figure 1.2.14 Loans to private sector (%GDP)

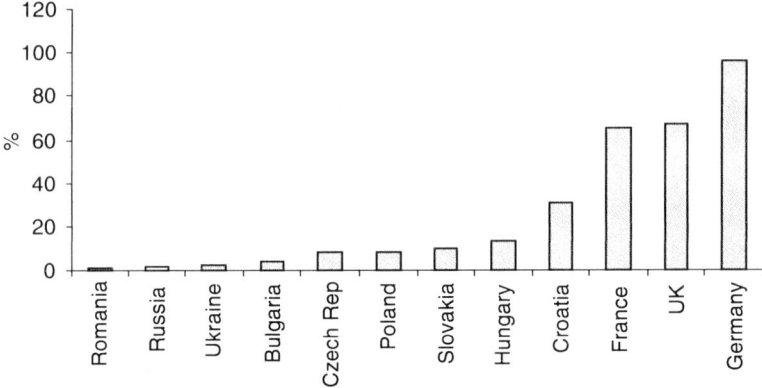

Source: CBR, Raiffeisenbank research
Figure 1.2.15 Retail loans (%GDP)

recent years, the memories of past failures to meet obligations still put a brake on further expansion. Indeed, the evidence points to a considerable capital flight problem, which, though improving, still plagues the domestic economy.

Continued economic and political stability is the main prerequisite for robust growth in banking services overall and the retail sector in particular. Authorities have taken the proper approach so far; gradual, step-by-step structural reform is exactly what the system needs in order to safeguard against possible market shocks. One of the most essential factors on the structural side is the further development of pension reform. Other major areas of progress include the laws on private deposit insurance and foreign currency control liberalization, which came into effect this year and should fuel growth and diversification in retail banking.

Table 1.2.3 Economic indicators

	1997	1998	1999	2000	2001	2002	2003	2004f	2005f
GDP, % yoy	1.4	-5.3	6.4	10.0	5.2	4.1	7.3	6.0	5.0
GDP $ bn	475.1	312.8	183.0	251.0	310.3	349.5	436.1	568.6	690.1
Industrial production, % yoy	2.0	-5.2	8.1	9.0	4.9	3.8	7.0	7.5	6.5
Capital investment, % yoy	-5.0	-6.7	4.5	17.7	8.7	3.5	12.0	10.0	10.0
CPI inflation %, eop	11.0	84.5	36.6	20.1	18.6	15.1	12.0	12.0	9.0
PPI inflation %, eop	7.4	23.0	71.0	31.6	10.6	17.5	12.9	13.0	12.0
Money supply growth, M2, yoy %	29.8	19.8	57.2	62.4	40.1	32.3	44.4	34.3	22.2
Domestic benchmark interest rate (OFZ >3y), %, eop				24.8	16.5	13.8	8.3	9.0	8.0
Eurobond yield 'Russia'30', %, eop				17.4	12.6	9.1	7.1	6.5	6.0
Federal budget revenues, % GDP	11.3	10.1	13.4	15.8	17.7	20.1	19.3	18.5	17.5
Federal budget expenditures, % GDP	18.0	15.1	14.6	13.4	15.3	18.7	17.7	18.0	17.0
Federal budget balance, % GDP	-6.7	-5.0	-1.2	2.4	2.4	1.4	0.7	0.5	0.5
Federal budget primary balance, % GDP	-2.4	-1.0	2.4	4.8	5.0	3.4	3.3	2.3	2.1
Exports, goods, $ bn	89.0	74.8	75.7	105.6	103.2	107.6	134.4	143.6	139.0
Exports, goods, % GDP	18.7	23.9	41.3	42.1	33.3	30.8	30.8	24.2	19.9
Export growth, % yoy	-1.7	-16.0	1.2	39.5	-2.2	4.3	24.9	6.9	-3.2
Export of crude oil, $ bn	13.8		14.2	25.3	24.6	29.1	39.7	47.4	44.5
Oil price, URALS, ave	18.3	11.0	17.2	26.6	22.9	23.7	27.0	26.5	23.0
Imports, goods, $ bn	71.6	57.4	39.5	44.8	53.8	61.0	74.8	87.8	96.6
Import growth, % yoy	7.1	-39.9	56.4	54.7	-14.1	3.7	13.9	18.0	10.0
Trade balance	17.4	17.3	36.1	60.8	49.4	46.6	59.6	55.8	42.4
Current account balance, $ bn	3.6	2.4	25.0	46.3	34.5	29.5	39.1	38.6	24.3
Current account balance, % GDP	0.8	0.8	13.8	18.5	11.1	8.4	7.9	6.5	3.5
Gross FX reserves, $ bn	17.8	12.2	12.5	28.0	36.7	48.5	70.6	101.8	112.6
FX rate R/$1, eop	6.0	21.2	27.0	28.5	30.1	31.8	29.8	27.0	28.0
FX rate R/$1, year average	5.8	9.8	24.8	28.1	29.1	31.3	30.8	28.5	27.5

1.3

The Legal Regime and Regulatory Environment for International Business

CMS Cameron McKenna

Russia is in the midst of economic and legislative reforms. Since 1990 the Russian government has put into place the statutory framework to bring the country up to modern standards and harmonize legislation. Although Russia does not yet have a stable and established legislative system, this issue remains one of the key priorities of the Russian government.

The legal structure developed during the 1990s at a rapid pace, with significant reforms being attempted in almost every sphere of law. The process of consolidating and rationalizing the legal framework of Russia's market economy remains ongoing with major changes anticipated in a number of key areas.

Constitutional structure

Constitution

The Constitution of the Russian Federation was adopted by the National Referendum on 12 December 1993. The Constitution defines the sovereign power of the Russian Federation, describes its federal structure, governing system and the principle human rights enjoyed by citizens of Russia. The Russian Federation is governed by a political system modelled after many in the West. The governing system is composed of three branches: the executive, the legislature and the judiciary.

Federal structure: local and federal government

The Russian Federation consists of 89 'subjects', including regions, ethnically-based autonomous republics, territories and the federal cities of Moscow and St Petersburg. The Constitution granted these 'subjects' certain autonomy over internal economic and political affairs.

The Constitution sets out a general list of powers reserved to the Federal authorities. Other powers are expressed as jointly exercised by the Federal and local authorities. The regional authorities are then allocated all other powers not specifically reserved by the Federal Government or exercised jointly. These powers include the power to manage municipal property, establish regional budgets, collect regional taxes, and maintain law and order. Bilateral power-sharing treaties between the central government and the 'subjects' of the Russian Federation have become an important means of defining and clarifying the boundaries of their respective power and authority. The Constitution gives regional bodies the authority to pass laws provided those laws do not contradict the Constitution and existing federal laws. Many 'subjects', however, have adopted their own constitutions, which in several cases allocate powers to the regional government that are inconsistent with the provisions of the Federal Constitution.

Executive branch and its structure

Under the Constitution, the executive branch is headed by the president, who is elected for a four-year term. The Constitution does not provide for a vice president. The president has the right to choose the prime minister, with the approval of the State Duma (the lower house of the Russian parliament). The president, upon the recommendation of the prime minister, appoints ministers, who are responsible for the introduction of primary and secondary legislation in their respective fields.

Russia's president determines the basic direction of Russia's domestic and foreign policy and represents the Russian State within the country and in foreign affairs. The president is commander-in-chief of the Russian armed forces; he approves defence doctrine, appoints and removes the commanders of the armed forces and confers higher military ranks and awards.

The president has broad authority to issue decrees and directives that have the force of law, although the Constitution states that they must not contradict other federal laws or the Constitution. In certain circumstances, the president has the right to dissolve the Duma.

Parliament and the basics of the legislative process

The legislative branch of the Russian Federation is the Federal Assembly (*federalnoye sobraniye*), which consists of the Federation

Council (*sovet federatsii*) (178 seats, filled by the representatives of executive and legislative branches of power of each of the 89 federal administrative units) and the State Duma (*gosudarstvennaya duma*) (450 seats, half elected by proportional representation from party lists, and half from single-member constituencies; members are elected by direct popular vote to serve four-year terms). The two chambers of the Federal Assembly possess different powers and responsibilities, although the State Duma is the most significant.

The Federal Assembly is a permanently functioning body, in that it is in continuous session except for a regular break between the spring and autumn sessions. Deputies of the State Duma work full-time on their legislative duties; they are not allowed to serve simultaneously in local government or to hold Federal Government positions.

Each legislative chamber elects a chairman who controls the procedure of the chamber. The chambers also form committees and commissions to deal with particular types of issue. They prepare and evaluate draft laws, report on draft laws to their chambers, conduct hearings, and oversee implementation of the laws.

Draft laws may originate in either legislative chamber, or they may be submitted by the president, the government, local legislatures, the Supreme Court, the Constitutional Court, or the High Arbitration Court. Draft laws are first considered in the State Duma and must pass three readings before being passed to the Federation Council. After adoption by a majority of the State Duma members, a draft law is considered by the Federation Council. If a bill is rejected by the Federation Council, a Conciliation Commission may be established, comprising representatives of the Duma and Federation Council, to review and amend the draft before it is presented again to the Federation Council. The establishment of a Conciliation Commission is the prescribed procedure to work out differences in bills that have been considered by both chambers.

When a draft law is adopted by the Federation Council, it must be signed into law by the president. The president has a veto, which if exercised can be overridden by a resolution passed by two-thirds of the members of the Duma and Federation Council.

Judicial system

The judicial system in the Russian Federation is split into three branches: the courts of general jurisdiction with the Supreme Court at the top, the 'arbitrazhniy' or commercial court system with the High Arbitrazhniy Court as the supreme body, and the Constitutional Court. The judicial system is also divided into a federal system and a system of local courts of the various 'subjects' of the Russian Federation.

The Constitutional Court decides whether federal and local legislation and regulations comply with the Constitution. The Constitutional Court also resolves jurisdictional disputes between federal or local authorities, and it may interpret and clarify the Constitution.

Criminal, civil and administrative cases involving individuals not engaged in business activity are dealt with by the courts of general jurisdiction. The initial stage in the system is the magistrate. Magistrates serve each city district and rural district. The whole system consists of the magistrates, district courts of general jurisdiction, Supreme Courts of the constituent subjects of the Russian Federation, and the Supreme Court of the Russian Federation. Decisions of the lower courts of general jurisdiction can be appealed through intermediate district courts and the Supreme Courts of the 'subject' of the Russian Federation up to the Federal Supreme Court.

As established by the New Arbitration Procedure Code, which came into force on 1 September 2002, economic disputes involving legal entities, individuals engaged in business activity and disputes between legal entities and their participants (shareholders) are dealt with by the 'arbitrazhniy' or commercial arbitration courts. These are sometimes referred to, rather misleadingly, as 'arbitration courts'. The arbitrazhniy court system consists of arbitrazhniy courts of the subjects of the Russian Federation, federal arbitrazhniy courts and the High Arbitrazhniy Court of the Russian Federation. The High Arbitrazhniy Court is the highest court for the resolution of economic disputes.

The Ministry of Justice administers Russia's judicial system. The Ministry's responsibilities include administrating the court system, supervising court activity and organization, as well as performing a number of other supervisory, administrative and systematic functions.

Law enforcement functions are performed by the Procurator General's Office (*procuratura*), which has local offices in cities and provinces, by the Ministry of Internal Affairs and by the Federal Security Service. The Procurator's office supervises the law enforcement agencies and investigates crimes and prosecutes offenders. The Ministry of Internal Affairs controls all the various police agencies and supervises prisons and the fire service. The Federal Security Service (formerly the KGB) is responsible for counterintelligence work and investigates organized crime and terrorism.

Basics of the civil law system

Legal system and legislative subordination

The Constitutional Laws, Federal Laws and Laws of the Russian Federation form the foundation of the legal system. Presidential

Decrees, Orders of the Government and decisions of various ministries support and describe the provisions of the primary laws and, as a matter of constitutional theory, should not contradict them.

The Russian legal system is a civil law system in the Continental European tradition. Various Codes govern all major spheres of business activity. The principal Codes are:

- Civil Code of the Russian Federation (*grazhdanskiy kodeks*);
- Tax Code of the Russian Federation (*nalogovyi kodeks*);
- Custom Code of the Russian Federation (*tamozhennyi kodeks*);
- Labour Code of the Russian Federation (*trudovoi kodeks*).

Civil and corporate legislation

Civil legislation of the Russian Federation is based on the Civil Code (Parts I, II and III) (the fourth Part should be adopted soon) of the Russian Federation of 1994. Pending adoption of Part IV of the Civil Code, some parts of the Civil Code of the Russian Soviet Federal Republic of 1964 and Civil Code of the USSR of 1991 remain in force.

Within the decade Russia has developed comprehensive corporate legislation covering all major issues of corporate activity. The general principles of corporate legislation are discussed in Chapter 4.1 'Business Structures'.

Tax legislation

Russia is currently in the midst of significant tax reform. In August 2000 Part II of the Tax Code was signed into law and became effective in January 2001. Many tax regulations are in transition. The main taxes are:

- *Profit Tax*. Profit tax is levied on the enterprise's gross profit. The general tax rate is 24 per cent of gross profit with some exceptions.
- *Value Added Tax (VAT)*. VAT is calculated on the sales value of goods (services, works) at a general rate of 18 per cent with certain exceptions. Imported goods are also subject to VAT.
- *Excise Tax*. Excise tax is levied on the sale or importation of certain goods (alcohol, tobacco, jewellery, cars, oil, gas, and other). The tax rate varies for each product.
- *Land and Property Taxes*. Land and property taxes are levied by the local authorities at a rate depending on the location of the property.
- *Personal Income Tax*. Personal income tax is calculated at a flat rate of 13 per cent.

Property, currency, custom and international legislation

The Constitution gives Russian citizens general rights to own, inherit, lease, mortgage and sell property; however, there are many gaps and ambiguities in the legislation that implements these rights. A new Land Code came into force on 29 October 2001 regulating the use and ownership of municipal and industrial land. Agricultural land is specifically excluded from the jurisdiction of the Land Code and is regulated by a separate federal law on agricultural land, which came into force on 27 January 2003. The law on agricultural land provides that agricultural land cannot be owned by foreign legal entities or individuals or Russian legal entities if more than 50 per cent of their charter capital is owned by foreigners.

Russia has extensive and complex currency control legislation. The Russian currency, the rouble, is the only legal tender in Russia. There are two types of currency operation according to the Law of the Russian Federation On Currency Controls of 9 October 1992:

1. Current operations: includes import/export contracts with deferral of payment for less than 90 days, loans not exceeding 180 days, and some other transactions.

2. Capital operations: includes direct and portfolio investments, import/export contracts with deferral of the payment for more than 90 days, loans exceeding 180 days and some other transactions.

Capital operations generally require permission from the Central Bank of the Russian Federation (CBR). Non-residents of the Russian Federation may have both foreign currency and rouble accounts to service their operations in Russia.

On 15 December 2003 the President of the Russian Federation signed the new version of the Federal Law On Currency Regulation and Currency Control, which replaced the existing version of the law. Most of the provisions of this law should come into effect six months after its official publication, (ie in June 2004).

This law contains an exhaustive closed list of capital currency operations, the performance of which may be regulated by the Russian Government or the Central Bank. Contrary to the previous situation the law changes the main principle of Russian currency control from 'everything which is not allowed is prohibited' to an opposite position of 'everything which is not prohibited is allowed'. Instead of specific permissions for certain types of 'capital operations' the Law establishes a liberalized approach to such operations (such as mandatory reservation requirements, 'special' accounts to conduct 'capital operations' etc).

The mandatory conversion requirement in relation to foreign currency export proceeds will remain the same (a maximum level of 30 per cent with the right of the Central Bank to establish a lower percentage).

Many of the currency control restrictions established by the Law are due to be abolished as of 1 January 2007.

The main legislative act governing the customs legislation of Russia is the Customs Code of the Russian Federation of 18 June 1993, which was in force until 1 January 2004. It will be replaced by a new Customs Code, which was signed into law in 2003. Russian import tariff rates vary from 0 to 100 per cent, depending on the imported item. The tariff rate for cars depends on the year of production of the imported car and varies from 1.4 to 3.2 EUR per cubic centimetre of engine volume. The import tariff rates for tobacco vary from 5 to 30 per cent. In addition to import tariffs, VAT and selective excise tax are also applied to imports. Import licences are also needed for certain types of goods (alcohol etc).

The Constitution states that general principles of international law and international treaties are part of the legal system of the Russian Federation. If Russia is a party to an international treaty that contains provisions contradictory to the provisions of the Russian legislation, the provisions of the international treaty prevail.

Foreign investment legislation

While the encouragement of foreign investment is a stated Russian government priority, there have been difficulties in creating a stable, attractive investment climate. Foreign investors' concerns about the legal system, corruption and taxation are key factors affecting foreign investment, rather than any explicit express restrictions imposed by the government.

Foreign investment law

The main legislative act governing the sphere of foreign investments is the Law of the Russian Federation On Foreign Investment in the Russian Federation of 9 July 1999 (Foreign Investment Law). The Foreign Investment Law provides the statutory basis for the treatment of foreign investment. The Law states that foreign investors and investments shall be treated no less favourably than domestic investments, with some exceptions. Such exceptions may be introduced to protect the Russian constitutional system, the morality, health and rights of third persons or in order to ensure state security and defence.

Russian legislation may also introduce special rights promoting foreign investments. The Law permits foreign investment in most sectors of, and in all forms available in, the Russian economy: portfolios of government securities, stocks and bonds, and direct investment in new businesses, in the acquisition of existing Russian-owned enterprises, in joint ventures, etc. Foreign investors are protected against nationalization or expropriation unless this is provided by the federal law of the Russian Federation. In such cases, foreign investors are entitled to receive compensation for the investment and other losses.

Restrictions on foreign investment

Currently, there are relatively few explicit restrictions on foreign direct investment. Foreign ownership in the natural gas monopoly, Gazprom, is limited to 14 per cent. Legislation limits foreign investment in the electric power company, Unified Energy Systems (UES), to 25 per cent.

The Russian Law On Insurance of 27 November 1992 established a ceiling of 15 per cent on the total amount of foreign investment in the insurance industry of the Russian Federation as a percentage of the total insurance capital in Russia. Insurance companies in which foreigners own more than 49 per cent of the Charter Capital may not engage in certain types of insurance business, including life assurance business.

The CBR has the right to use reciprocity as a criteria to specify the types of business that foreign banks may be licensed to operate in Russia, and is permitted to impose a ceiling on the total amount of foreign bank capital as a percentage of the total bank capital in Russia. At present, foreign banks' share of the total capital bank is well below the 12 per cent ceiling set by the CBR.

International treaties

Russia is party to a number of international treaties, which are aimed at the protection of foreign investments:

- *Bilateral investment treaties*: these treaties generally guarantee non-discriminatory treatment for foreign investments and investors in Russia, provide for compensation to be paid for expropriation or nationalization, and allow disputes to be referred to international arbitration. Russia holds such agreements with the United Kingdom, Germany, Italy, Spain, the Netherlands, Finland, France, Switzerland and others. The treaty entered into with the United States is waiting to be ratified.

- *Treaties for the avoidance of double taxation*: these treaties generally provide relief from double taxation, guarantee non-discriminatory tax treatment and provide for co-operation between the tax authorities of the respective signatory countries. Russia has such agreements with Austria, the United Kingdom, Greece, Denmark, Ireland, Spain, Italy, Canada, Cyprus, the Netherlands, the United States, Germany, France, Switzerland and many other countries.

1.4

Latest Developments in the Foreign Investment Climate

Andrew B Somers, President, American Chamber of Commerce in Russia

There are several key factors with respect to judging the investment climate in Russia, and the net effect in looking at these factors is positive.

The first factor is macroeconomic indicators. Russia has demonstrated a remarkable macroeconomic performance in the last few years in terms of its GDP growth, continued budget surplus, creation of a reserve fund in the event of a drop in world oil prices, accumulation of foreign exchange reserves by the Central Bank, and very sound fiscal policies. The fact that tax collection has increased significantly since Russia introduced a 13 per cent flat income tax is of extreme importance. All of these indicators remain very positive in the outlook for 2004.

The second very telling factor is the rapidly growing number of high-level American executives coming to Russia with either business plans for investment or serious intent to look at the options. This is essentially a final step before pulling the trigger on significant investments. These visits strongly indicate that the psychological hurdle that previously prevented American business leaders from looking at Russia as an investment destination has been removed. In many instances, these companies are pursuing a two-stage plan – first to manufacture for the Russian domestic market, and later to upgrade the technology and export abroad to a different niche of customers. This tells us that Russia is now on the map, along with China, India and Brazil; and among this list of countries, many CEOs have rated Russia as first.

The third factor in judging the investment climate is the government's commitment to continued reform. We think that the streamlining of the government that took place in the spring of 2004, reduction of the number of ministers by almost half and the number of deputy prime ministers from six to one, as well as the merging of functions which logically belong together, all point to the president's commitment in his second term to drive the reform effort deeper and broader than before. One such positive example is the alignment of the State Customs Committee under the Economic Development and Trade Ministry. This is especially interesting because customs collects 42 per cent of all budget revenues, and thus could have easily reported to the Finance Ministry. But the State Customs Committee leadership has stressed the importance of stimulating business as the agency's main priority, and this aspect of the mission should be enhanced by the structural connection to the Economic Development and Trade Ministry, whose basic mission is to increase GDP and facilitate business and investment.

The fourth important positive factor is progress in the WTO accession process. In the spring of 2004, Russia completed the essentials of its negotiations with the European Union, and concluded an agreement in principle with this very important trading partner. Negotiations with the United States continue apace, and the gaps between the two sides are slowly but surely closing. Although areas like access of foreign companies to Russia's financial and insurance sectors and tariffs for airplanes remain important obstacles to reaching an agreement, the most critical issue is protection of intellectual property rights. Recently, Russia has demonstrated some progress in this area as well, and we are betting that the last obstacles to WTO accession will be eliminated by the end of 2005, paving the way to a rules-based system and Russia's greater openness to international trade and investment.

The fifth positive factor is continuous support from the US and Russian governments for the bilateral processes that have been initiated by Presidents Bush and Putin to seek and act upon the recommendations of the private sector. The Russian American Business Dialogue (RABD) is such a public-private sector effort, and AmCham and the Russian Union of Industrialists and Entrepreneurs (RSPP) are its lead organizations. At the top of its agenda are recommendations to the two governments for improvements in the area of intellectual property rights protection, establishment of a business group to monitor the implementation of the new Customs Code that went into effect on 1 January 2004, and improvement of the environment for small business. Specifically on the latter point, we are asking the Russian government to increase the revenue level defining small business and thus expand the number of companies eligible for tax breaks and relieved administrative burdens as provided by the recently adopted legislation on small business. Another example of such public-private sector efforts contributing to the improvement of the investment climate in Russia is the US-Russia Commercial Energy Dialogue (CED). Within the framework of CED, Russian and American energy companies make recommendations to the two governments to improve the environment, and this initiative is beginning to show some successes.

Obviously, problems still exist. There are still cases when foreign businesses find themselves under pressure from their Russian partners trying to take over the ownership of a joint venture once it has proved to be profitable. In some of those instances, local administrations seem to have a relationship with the private interests that are trying to squeeze out the foreign business. Naturally, we are concerned about such situations and when they come to our attention, we intervene to get a hearing with the appropriate authorities or with the Russian private companies involved. We are very often successful in resolving matters, and this is encouraging. We do not lobby on behalf of individual companies, but when there is an issue affecting the investment climate, we consider it part of our mission to intervene at the request of our members. One very notable example of the Chamber taking an active role is the situation with Sakhalin-3, when the Russian government annulled the result of the 1993 tender that awarded the rights to develop the oil fields to two American oil majors. We view this issue as confined neither to these two companies, nor to the energy sector only – the issue at stake is property rights, and we have urged the Russian government to reach a solution that would not be threatening this very basic principle.

In this context, the effort by the Russian business community to initiate an alternative dispute resolution process is very promising. The RSPP has created a Business Ethics Commission to resolve disputes between businesses outside the legal system because this system is still very rudimentary in terms of property and investment rights. Essentially, it is a two-step process. When a company registers a complaint with the Commission, the Commission contacts the other company involved and suggests informal and private mediation to help the two sides find a compromise solution. If that doesn't work, then the complaining party has an option to ask for arbitration. The Commission has a list of about 70 qualified arbitrators, and each party selects an arbitrator from this list. Then, both arbitrators select the third – neutral – member of the arbitration panel. Following an informal arbitration hearing by this panel, both parties are committed to following the findings. The ruling does not have the force of law but it has the force of moral imperative. The process is very new but it seems to be working: in less than one year the Commission has had a few cases and decisions have been taken. AmCham has signed a protocol with the RSPP to support this effort to resolve business disputes in a civil manner. We view this as an effort from the Russian private sector to improve the environment.

On balance, we believe the investment climate in Russia continues to improve. The market continues to expand, and certainly American companies continue to have very successful results. 2002 and 2003 were banner years for the American companies in terms of revenues, profit margins and growth in market share. All prospects are very positive for 2004 and we think Russia is a very good investment bet for most sectors of the economy.

1.5

The Russian Investment Climate

Branan

Introduction and summary

The Russian investment climate has undergone spectacular transformation during the past decade and continues to offer new and attractive opportunities. Following the debt crisis in 1998 Russia's economic and political stability improved considerably and a combination of key structural reforms, solid foreign policy and high natural resource prices have propelled Russia to a new level of global competitiveness. Moreover, with the emergence of a viable local services sector together with strengthening consumer confidence, the country is slowly moving away from a natural resource dependent economy to a more diversified competitive market.

Several key risks remain however, which impact on the overall attractiveness of the Russian market. On the reform agenda Russia is yet to create a credible banking system, liberalize natural gas prices, and complete the restructuring of its electricity sector. Politically the country has found itself in the midst of several corporate quarrels, which continue to fuel negative investor sentiment and affect the Russian equity and debt markets. Although not as prevalent as in the early 1990s, local crime remains a concern in light of several recent assassinations. Law enforcement continues to be under a shadow of bureaucracy and corruption. Russia has come a long way since the dissolution of the Soviet Bloc in the late 1980s and has a long road ahead as it gradually converges with the economic competitiveness of its business partners around the world.

Economy

The Russian economy has been successful at maintaining its resilience, which in large part, is attributed to strong GDP growth, high natural resource prices, and diversification of its domestic demand components. Despite recent speculation around the banking sector and ongoing legal battles between the government and Russian oil major Yukos, the country's macroeconomic picture remains robust. The country's GDP expanded 7.4 per cent year-on-year in the first half of 2004. The government has also upgraded its year-end economic growth target to 6.9 per cent on the back of healthy export figures and positive outlook on the external markets. Construction, Transport and Retail Trade growth rates rose 14.2 per cent, 7.4 per cent, and 11.1 per cent, respectively. Russia's economics minister, German Gref, has set the GDP target for 2005 at 6.3 per cent. High oil prices continue to support domestic income growth via net exports, in addition to increasing consumption and investment. Russia's 1998 financial downturn brought about the low point of foreign investor confidence in Russia. Nevertheless, foreign investments in Russia are slowly on the rebound. Foreign investments include loans, trade credits, foreign direct investments (FDIs) and foreign portfolio investments (FPIs). Foreign direct investment has expanded impressively in the past three years going from $4 billion in 2002 to $7 billion in 2003 and is expected to reach $8 billion in 2004. Compared with other emerging markets in terms of FDI/GDP and FDI per capita, Russia ranks near the bottom, which doesn't seem to reflect its rapid economic recovery. Although Russia's FDI still remains quite modest compared to other countries, the recent positive trend reflects Russia's appeal to global businesses as a viable and lucrative place to invest.

Diversification away from the natural resource sector has recently been the major theme for the Russian economy and is a key to further economic growth. Total demand has been shifting toward the consumer and services sector where strong capital investment in Russia has boosted productivity and enhanced competitiveness. Going forward, however, the non-resource industrial sectors are not likely to grow as quickly as the output in the consumer and services categories, including telecoms, media, finance, transportation, etc. Nor are non-resource industries likely to expand faster than the extractive industries (fuel and metals) should commodity prices continue to rise or remain at high levels. Turning again to the gross domestic product components, the trend of stronger consumer-services growth is evident. In 2003, services comprised close to 62 per cent of the Russian GDP, and growth in the market-based service output exceeded growth in the goods sectors, similar to 2002 (the first time in Russia's history) (see Figure 1.5.1). The pricing power of services providers will remain strong, driven by domestic consumer demand.

44   Background to the Market

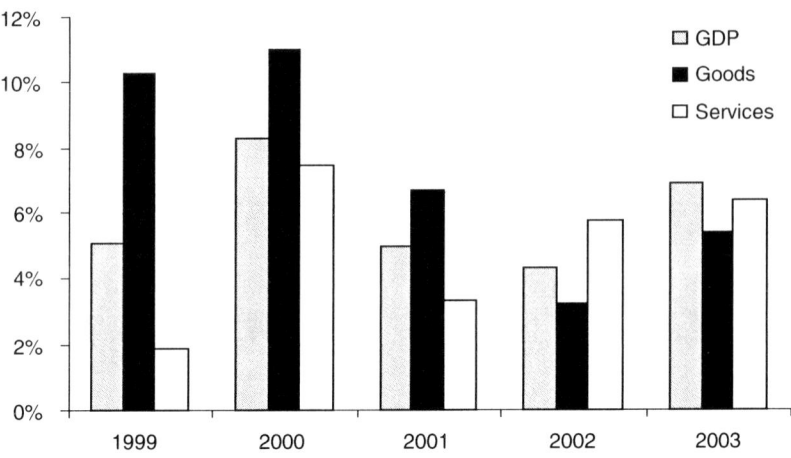

Source: Goskomstat
Figure 1.5.1 GDP growth rates

Other economic indicators re-emphasize the emergence of the consumer-services trend:

- Aggregate corporate profits have been substantially higher climbing 49.4 per cent in the January–May period of 2004. Although one of the reasons is a lower tax rate, which created better incentives to report income, the decompositions of the growth rate shows that consumer-driven sector profits contributed the most to the final figure. During the second quarter of 2004 communications, retail trade, and transportation led the growth, with 75 per cent, 34 per cent and 43 per cent, respectively.

- Services Purchasing Managers' Index (SPM) – a single-figure dissemination index compiled by the Moscow Narodny Bank – continues to stay above 50 (note: 50 is the threshold between growth and contraction). July 2004 marked another month of strong expansion as the SPM posted a 57.9 figure. Local services providers confirm higher future business confidence in the sector in response to growing demand and disposable income.

- Another indication of higher services demand is the relatively higher price inflation recorded in the consumer-services sector. Price growth for services was 16.8 per cent year-on-year in July 2004, higher than the overall inflation figure of 10.4 per cent for the same period (see Table 1.5.1).

Although the trend toward a more diversified economy is real and noticeable, the heavy reliance on the extractive sector will continue to

Table 1.5.1 CPI inflation y-o-y (July 04)

	July 04 (%)	June 04 (%)	July 03 (%)
Total	10.4	10.1	13.9
Foods	9.5	8.8	11.0
Non-foods	8.1	7.9	9.4
Services	16.8	17.4	31.0

Source: IntelliNews

hold back many investors. Fitch ratings agency, which reiterated its BB+ mark in August 2004, said it's unlikely Russia will obtain a second investment-grade rating by the end of 2004 citing two main reasons: 1) ongoing speculation around the Yukos case, which raised questions about the assessment of property rights in Russia, and 2) market dependence on the oil and gas sectors. Moody's Investors Service upgraded Russia's status to the high-grade category in October 2004 and remains the only rating agency to assign Russia an investment grade. Yury Lopatinsky, head of First Mercantile Capital Partners in Moscow, expressed similar concerns: 'High oil prices have had an inflationary effect on consumer product prices and real-estate, as political uncertainty has hampered longer term domestic investment necessary for economic diversification.'

Higher corporate profits, emergence of a strong services sector, and soaring oil prices have all contributed to the expansion of Russia's disposable income base. Real income grew 9.8 per cent year-on-year in the 1H04 and real wages climbed 14.1 per cent in the same period. Consumption will continue to be supported by strong trends in domestic income and, moreover, compounded by the rising ratio of disposable income to personal income. With a 13 per cent income tax rate, the lowest in Europe, and relatively low food and housing costs, Russia's emerging middle class has high ratio of disposable income to personal income, especially in major cities like Moscow and St. Petersburg. For the full year 2003, real disposable income grew faster than GDP. On average, Moscow and St. Petersburg consumers have close to 25 times more purchasing power than the rest of the country, which suggests that much of the future consumer demand growth will also come from the regional convergence.

The strong growth in Russia's financial reserves has largely ensured that any short- to medium-term balance-of-payments weakness would be manageable. The country accumulated over $89 billion in gold and foreign currency reserves through August 2004, compared to less than $6 billion that the government held in early 1998. These reserves are enough to service debt payments for several years even if oil prices decline significantly. Russia's foreign debt fell from 64 per cent of GDP in 2000 to just 28 per cent of GDP in 2003. Moreover, the government set up a stabilization fund in early 2004 with the purpose of hedging against possible future budget deficits. Revenues from oil and gas exports during periods of high energy prices will go into this fund and will cover the budget deficit during times of low energy prices. In the period between January and July 2004 Russia posted a budget surplus of $9.8 billion with 59 per cent of revenues coming from taxes and 34 per cent from customs. The stabilization fund grew to around $9.2 billion.

Both the European Bank of Reconstruction and Development (EBRD) and the International Finance Corporation (IFC) have made strong investment pledges to Russia and are optimistic on the investment climate overall. Some of EBRD's key objectives in Russia include: the development and practical implementation of the Corporate Governance Code; attraction of major international strategic investors; and the restructuring of the natural monopolies. With over 10 years of work experience in Russia, the EBRD has provided project financing for banks, industries, Russian companies and foreign strategic investors, both new ventures and investments in existing companies. For 2004, EBRD forecasts more than $1.5 billion in investments for Russia, with focus on the communications, transportation and energy sectors. The IFC has also made newly-pledged investments in Russia during its FY2003 in excess of $616 million, a 65 per cent increase over the previous year. Reflecting on its commitment to Russia, the IFC has grown geographically, investing across Russia in a variety of sectors, including infrastructure, media, general manufacturing and services, and financial services. IFC is also a leading investor in the IT sector and extended nearly $20 million to Russian IT companies in 2003. For 2004, IFC made a similar investment commitment of around $0.5 billion.

Capital flight continues to hamper the Russian economy despite falling in recent years and even showing a net inflow in 2003. Russia's finance ministry estimated that the net capital outflow from the country may reach $8.5 billion by the end of 2004. The main reason for this sudden shift toward capital outflow can be explained by the overall negative sentiment throughout the emerging markets marked by the recent downturn in China plus the speculation around the ongoing Yukos affair. However, despite the Yukos affair, investors remain interested in participating in joint work with other Russian oil companies, such as Lukoil. According to German Gref, Russia will experience net capital outflows through 2005. The accuracy of the capital flight in Russia though is questionable given the existence of the 'grey market', which could substantially increase or decrease the actual capital flows.

Structural reforms

Banking sector

One of the most anticipated structural reforms on the agenda today is the banking reform. Russia is currently dominated by two or three government-backed banks (Sberbank has a virtual monopoly attracting close to 63 per cent of total retail deposits), which can accommodate depositors and hundreds of smaller banks that have a history of liquidity problems, inefficiency and murky transactions. Guta Bank fell victim to a liquidity crunch and was forced to shut down most of its branches in the summer of 2004. Even the large business consortium Alfa Group saw thousands of worried depositors make a run on its Alfa Bank accounts on the back of financial sector jitters. The government did stabilize the situation by purchasing a controlling stake in Guta Bank through Vneshtorgbank and calming the public by injecting extra liquidity into the market. Although the situation did not develop into a widespread banking crisis, it did underscore the need to move forward urgently with the financial sector reform.

With deposit insurance and foreign exchange liberalization laws passed, Russia's central bank is implementing the laws with various decrees and measures. In the banking sector, it prepares to revoke licences of banks that do not meet the credit standards required for the deposit insurance system. However, it has recently eased the criteria of qualification for the deposit insurance structure by dropping eight of the 16 entrance criteria and softening others. Sberbank, which always enjoyed a government backing for its deposits, was scheduled to lose the guarantees on new deposits in October 2004 and will completely be void of them by 2007. This would open up Russia's banking sector for competition and growth. Later on, credit bureaux will be created by the Association of Russian Banks, which is pursuant of the Credit Bureau Bill passed in the legislature. The association aims to create the first national credit bureau by the end of 2004.

The Russian banking sector will encounter more turbulence going forward as smaller illiquid banks get filtered out of the system and the broader financial sector reform unravels. The bigger and more stable banks will only win from the transition period attracting a larger volume of depositors and revamping their organizational structures. According to Tim McCarthy, Chief Investment Officer at Troika Dialog Asset Management, with over $500 million invested in Russian portfolio securities, 'The Russian banking system will undergo significant reform during the next two years. Already, the effect of a lower tax rate has legitimized many businesses, stimulating growth of bank deposits. The recent laws passed on land reform, mortgages and securitization will greatly expand the role of banks in the Russian economy. Real estate is already privately owned and Russian corporations and individuals are relatively under-leveraged. The consumer debt to GDP and mortgage debt to GDP ratios are both less then 1 per cent in Russia, while these ratios are 19 per cent and 55 per cent respectively in the US. So, one can see that broad money supply expansion from the private sector is likely to fuel economic growth in the foreseeable future.'

Energy

The restructuring of the energy industry has become a major theme in assessing the overall development in Russian economic competitiveness. While both the natural gas and the utilities sectors remain under state control (Unified Energy Systems [UES]; Gazprom), the electricity reform has made considerable progress in moving toward a liberalized network.

The restructuring of Russia's main electricity group, UES, has won huge support in the West but proved to be a complex and sensitive issue at home. UES is an energy holding company with stakes in 251 subsidiaries, which own stakes in the national transmission grid, separate generation companies, and vertically integrated generation/transmission/distribution companies. The restructuring of the group includes unbundling, pro rata spin-offs, and privatization of its subsidiaries, which would lead to an efficient, transparent and more competitive electricity sector. The direction and the pace of the restructuring can be defined and forecast based on two different views of the parties who would benefit from the reform:

- Oligarch driven – The influence and reach of the wealthy minority in Russia would remain the dominant force in shaping the restructuring. Since most oligarchs are owners of local industrial groups whose business operations are tied to exports, they are interested in securing a steady supply of cheap energy to operate their factories. Therefore, their unique business interests run contrary to the objectives of the UES restructuring.

- Revenue driven – Since the ultimate effect of the reform should drive up energy prices, the managers whose compensation would be tied to the company's overall revenue stream would find it in their interest to support the reform. However, most of the managers own very little stock in the company and a stock option plan, which has been considered in the past, has not been implemented yet.

One of the main positive aspects of the restructuring is that unlike other state-owned energy companies where management opposes privatization and reform (China's State Power Company, Korea's Kepco, and Brazil's Eletrobras), UES's management is actually pioneering and sponsoring the restructuring.

Other reforms

Several other important issues remain on the reform agenda including the following:

- Liberalization of the natural gas sector. Russian domestic gas prices remain at deep discounts compared to the West, and lack of privatization in the state-owned Gazprom limits investments to modernize its network. Currently the state owns 37 per cent in the gas giant and plans to increase its stake to 51 per cent, thereby hampering any hope for privatization in the near future. The accession into the WTO also depends on the pace of the natural gas sector reform.

- Pension system reform. The government has passed a law that would ultimately transform the Russian pension scheme from a defined benefit to a defined contribution. The new structure is comprised of three layers: 1) notional defined contribution (NDC) pay-as-you-go pension plan, 2) mandatory funded second support trust, and 3) a benefit that will secure the distributional objectives of the pension system. The aim of the new structure is to reduce the complexity of the pension payment system through a simple benefit formula and transparent eligibility requirements. However recently, despite the new provision, the government appeared reluctant to give up control over the population's pension savings and transfer them to the private sector.

Politics

On the political front Russia has made strong steps forward to becoming a more integrated member of the global community and improved its image and integrity abroad. With the arrival of Vladimir Putin to the presidential post the administration made it clear that it intends to lead a more diplomatic and yielding foreign policy for Russia in the world and that it intends to do everything in its power to attract foreign direct investment and secure a viable trade system with the West and the East. After securing an easy victory for his second term, Putin increased his rhetoric on investment, economic development and social responsibility.

President Putin made an effort to narrow the gap between Russia and the West in terms of:

- Trade – Putin has signed a decree to form a free trade channel in the Commonwealth of Independent States (CIS), thereby facilitating a more efficient and profitable trade network between Belarus, Ukraine, Kazakhstan and Russia. The move is an important one, since many of the former Soviet republics have also actively sought business partnerships with Europe. Germany still remains one of the leading trade partners in terms of total volume, accounting for more than 10 per cent of Russia's foreign trade and close to 20 per cent of total capital invested. In 2003, the turnover between Russia and Germany totaled $18 billion.

- Convergence with Europe – Putin has made an effort to host several milestone European conferences where the Russian president solidified business contracts for Russian companies and discussed bilateral cooperation in the area of trade and security.

- Global security – Russia is playing an active role in the global fight against terrorism. With its main partner, the United States, Russia engages in the exchange of pertinent information to limit the escalation of world terrorism and illegal arms distribution.

- Overall image – Russia has found a new face abroad, with foreigners' perception shifting toward a more positive outlook on the country and the investment opportunities it can offer. President Putin is viewed as proactive leader with a pro-reform agenda.

Becoming a full pledged member of the World Trade Organization (WTO) has also been a key aim of the current Russian administration. Although the president was able secure much needed support from the European Union, no definite date has been set for the accession. According to the Ministry of Economic Development and Trade, Russia is losing close to $2.5 billion each year by not having access to the trade privileges granted to WTO members. The ministry hopes to win the backing of the world community to join by 2006.

On the domestic front, the political situation has become more choppy in the past two years as the government moves to limit the power of so-called oligarchs who managed to accumulate substantial wealth during the privatization era. Yukos has been in the news for quite some time, as the tax ministry claimed that Russia's largest oil company failed to pay billions of dollars in taxes and engaged in questionable activities when expanding its empire. While the speculation around the judicial proceedings will continue to add a degree of uncertainty for the Russian financial markets, most of the negative news have already been priced in and should not impinge on broad economic growth prospects.

The Yukos case does set a precedent though and the possibility does exist that the current administration may engage in further legal attacks on oligarchs, yet it should not trigger a wider-scale property rights reassessment or re-nationalization of state assets.

Law

As Russia transforms itself into a solid market-based economy and continues on the structural reform track it will need to further develop a law-based economy and strengthen the institutions involved. Most of the recent economic and political successes have been, on many occasions, shadowed by assassinations and blatant corruption in the law enforcing agencies. If the goal of the Putin administration is to present Russia as a secure and profitable place to do business, the government will need to seriously address the issues stated above. Summer 2004 was marked by the killing of the chief Russian *Forbes* editor, an American-born Paul Khlebnikov, whose work included an infamous article on Russia's 100 richest people. Other similar unsolved assassinations have been a common occurrence in the last decade, which considerably raises Russia's business risk for foreigners as well as for the locals. The legal code in itself is contradictory, cumbersome and unpredictable. Lack of sufficient compensation of judicial and law enforcement officials opens up the door for various inefficiencies in the work process and corruption.

The corporate sector is directly impacted by corruption as well, since the existence of the grey market diverts the flow of capital from the necessary investment channels. Small- to medium-size businesses lose out the most due to corruption, since they don't have enough reach and influence to protect themselves from fraudulent harassment. Small businesses are estimated to lose close to $2 billion dollars from corruption.

The Russian government has recently introduced several key measures to address the issues stated above:

- Compensation increases have been implemented for state officials in an effort to provide a level of income sufficient enough to disincentivize taking bribes. Although the move is in the right direction, the salary levels for government employees remain way below the corporate sector and it doesn't prevent those officials who engaged in corruption in the past from doing it again.
- The anticorruption committee was formed, which is responsible for passing appropriate legislation to improve the honesty and transparency of the Russian regulating and controlling bodies. A law has already been passed that prevents authorities from halting any enterprise's operations without a court order.

Corporate governance

The viability of doing business in Russia is in big part dependant on the presence of a well-defined process to protect shareholder and investor rights. Corporate governance emerged as the major theme in the post-debt crisis of 1998 and will continue to play a major role in the development of the Russian economy. Corporate governance, transparency and disclosure improved considerably in the last few years especially at Russian bellwether and blue-chip companies.

Russia's history of poor corporate governance dates back to the Mass Privatization Programme (MPP) initiated in 1992. While the MPP was meant to distribute ownership equally, the Russian government made strategic exceptions for industries like defence, natural resources, utilities, and telecommunications. The industries mentioned were privatized partially, remaining under the control of the state. A large portion of the shares not held by the government was made non-public and allocated to company managers and employees. Following the privatization, which partitioned huge stakes of state property to a few industry insiders at deep discounts, the business climate has become predisposed to transfer pricing, asset stripping and various abuses of minority shareholders. Most of the time the shareholder structure was unknown and the controlling group exercised great power to benefit only themselves. Recently the situation turned for the better, as more and more companies began to follow the internationally accepted accounting standards for their disclosure, increased transparency, and put in mechanisms to prevent transfer pricing. The Institute of Corporate Law and Corporate Governance (ICLG) was created in 2000, which aimed to improve corporate governance practices in Russia. The agency now performs regular reviews of Russia's biggest companies and assigns a rating that tracks their corporate governance development (see Table 1.5.2).

Conclusion

While several key risks remain, the Russian investment climate has become more competitive, more accessible to foreign businesses, and more diversified. Strong recent economic growth is sustainable, in the near-to-medium term, given high natural resource prices and an emerging consumer-services sector. FDI should continue to grow as more foreign companies enter the Russian market and invest into local businesses. Based on economic ministry forecasts, capital outflow will remain an issue at least in the medium term, in large part caused by jitters over the Yukos case and instability in the local financial sector. However, the true net capital flow figure may vary considerably due to the existence of a grey market.

Structural reforms will underpin further economic growth and convince the global community that Russia is committed to building a secure market-oriented environment. The banking reform is underway as illiquid and less transparent banks get filtered out and more secure

Table 1.5.2 Corporate governance rankings

Rank	Company	4Q03 (% of maximum)	Change (%) (since 4Q02)	4Q02 (% of maximum)	Change (%) (since 2Q00)	2000 (% of maximum)
1	VimpelCom	86.6	3.0	84.1	2.4	82.1
2	Norilsk Nickel	72.4	10.4	65.6	48.4	44.2
3	North-West Telecom	72.2	11.1	65.0	4.7	62.1
4	RAO UES	70.3	7.8	65.2	13.6	57.4
5	Lenenergo	67.0	3.2	64.9	-5.1	68.4
6	Rostelecom	64.9	7.5	60.4	-1.8	61.5
7	MGTS	62.9	15.2	54.6	3.4	52.8
8	Gazprom	62.3	5.2	59.2	13.2	52.3
9	Aeroflot	61.7	4.8	58.9	9.5	53.8
10	Volga Telecom	60.8	36.0	44.7		na
11	Lukoil	60.0	10.3	54.4	9.5	49.7
12	Kusbassenergo	59.2	-0.7	59.6	0.8	59.1
13	Sibneft	58.9	-5.8	62.5	25.3	49.9
14	Samaraenergo	57.9	3.2	56.1		na
15	Yukos	56.3	-9.6	62.3	37.2	45.4
16	Tatneft	54.4	17.7	46.2	-17.2	55.8
17	Tyumen Oil Company	52.7	-2.8	54.2		na
18	Irkutskenergo	52.2	-5.3	55.1	-19.4	68.4
19	Slavneft-Megionneftegaz	51.6	-2.3	52.8		na
20	Surgutneftegas	51.3	-2.1	52.4	19.6	43.8
21	Severstal	49.3	-2.8	50.7	-0.4	50.9
22	Bashkirenergo	48.9	-9.8	54.2		na
23	GAZ	46.2	1.8	45.4	1.8	44.6
24	Rosneft	44.3	33.4	33.2		na
25	Avtovaz	43.5	-3.1	44.9		na

Source: ICLG

financial institutions are granted licences from the Central Bank. The deposit insurance law was a landmark decree passed to pave the way for the financial sector reform. The energy sector has also attracted plenty of attention with the restructuring of the world's largest utility group, Unified Energy Systems. It is yet unclear how fast and where the reform will go given the existence of opposing interests influencing the process.

The Putin administration has no doubt created a more stable political environment than the one witnessed during the Boris Yeltsin years, and advocated a pro-reform and pro-investment agenda. Corporate governance will continue to play a key role in the overall assessment of Russian companies, specifically their transparency and managerial fairness.

The attractiveness of the Russian market will remain contingent on its ability to continue bold structural reforms, advocate higher standards of corporate governance and diversify its economic output.

1.6

Russian Country Risk: Clouding Future Prospects for Russian Corporates

Elena Anankina and Robert E Richards, Standard & Poor's

Despite the improving sovereign ratings of The Russian Federation, country risks still weigh on the credit quality of Russian corporate entities. Risks inherent from operating in The Russian Federation (foreign currency BB+/Stable/B; local currency BBB-/Stable/A-3) have long been factored into the credit ratings on Russian corporates. Despite improving sovereign credit quality, however, corporate entities in the region remain subject to the uncertain implementation of legislation and regulations, a centralized political regime where decisions are driven by individuals rather than institutions with well-established purposes, a concentrated economic structure with a lack of diversification, and a weak domestic banking system. These factors are tempered, however, by current incentives for transparency supported by strong international demand for emerging market debt.

Russia's weak institutional structure remains the key constraint on corporate credit quality in the country because it translates into an unpredictable regulatory, legal, and corporate governance environment and leads to the lack of a solid base for improving the country's economic structure. At the moment, it is unclear whether Russia is poised for progress or will regress into an environment where businesses operate under the threat of political intrigues, personal power plays, and ineffective or parasitic bureaucrats.

Standard & Poor's methodology for assessing corporate credit quality considers country risk a particularly important element of credit risk in emerging markets. This methodology distinguishes between the risk of sovereign default or direct interference – such as currency controls – which are captured by a country's sovereign credit rating, and other indirect risks endemic to a company operating in a particular country (see 'Local Currency Rating Criteria Update'). Endemic country risks are important considerations when rating Russia-based corporations, as important reforms and diversification of the economy lag behind the rapid fiscal improvement achieved by the Russian Federation itself.

On 27 January 2004, Standard & Poor's Ratings Services raised its long-term foreign currency sovereign credit rating on the Russian Federation to 'BB+' from 'BB', and its local currency sovereign credit ratings to 'BBB-/A-3' from 'BB+/B'. The upgrade was driven by the improved fiscal and liquidity position of the Russian government. This reduces the probability of the government's default and a reoccurrence of the turmoil and stress that such events cause for the corporate sector.

Russia's regulatory, legal, and corporate governance environments remain weak, however, as recently highlighted by the effective reversal of the acquisition of OAO Siberian Oil Co. (Sibneft; B+/Watch Dev/–) by another oil company, OAO NK Yukos (BB-/Watch Neg/–). On balance, such risks remain undiminished in light of recent evidence that Russian companies and their investors can be subjected to government pressure through selective implementation of regulations and legislation that is either politically motivated or triggered by competing business groups. This, in turn, threatens to negatively affect the investment climate, corporate governance environment, property rights protection, and incentives to transparency.

So far, there has been no significant increase in capital outflows from Russia as a result of uncertainty about principles and practices upon which the Russian government will be based after the March 2004 presidential election. These political and institutional risks are being counterbalanced in the short term by strong international demand for emerging market debt and Russia's robust macroeconomic and fiscal performance on the back of high oil prices. For individual firms, access to international funding should be an incentive to improve transparency, disclosure, and governance practices toward international standards. Whether Russian companies will continue to enjoy good access to the international financial markets and a healthy operating environment over the longer term, however, depends on the pace and effectiveness of economic, institutional, and legal reforms after the presidential election.

Credit strengthening of Russian corporates slows

Standard & Poor's currently rates 31 Russian companies on its global scale. The long-term ratings on these companies range from 'CCC+' to 'BB∣'.

Russian Country Risk: Clouding Future Prospects for Russian Corporates

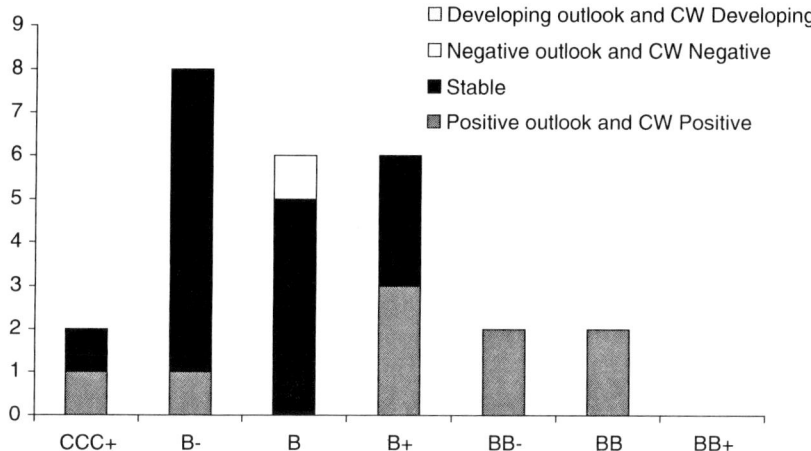

Figure 1.6.1 Outlook distribution of Russian corporate ratings on 13 May 2003

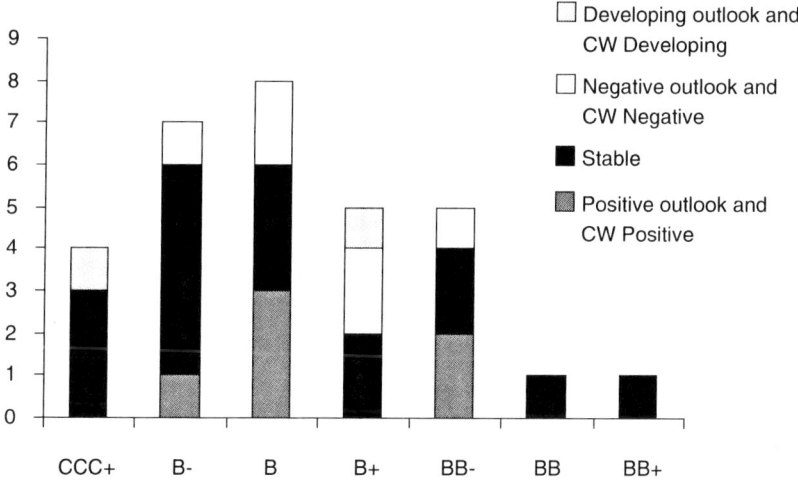

Figure 1.6.2 Outlook distribution of Russian corporate ratings on 4 March 2004

Since the 1998 financial crisis, the credit quality of Russian companies has improved steadily and significantly. During 2003 and January to February of 2004, there were 14 upgrades and one downgrade, although the majority of long-term ratings remain in the 'B' category.

The structure of outlooks and CreditWatch placements has became less positive, however, indicating that the remarkably strong positive trend of the past few years is slowing down. One year ago, all the corporate outlooks, with one single exception, were either stable or positive. Now there are four negative outlooks and four ratings on CreditWatch (two with negative implications and two with developing implications) (see Figures 1.6.1 and 1.6.2).

Even when accounting for the upgrades of corporate issuers, the gap between Russia's credit quality and that of the rated corporate sector has increased. Following the sovereign upgrade in January 2004, the only change in corporate ratings was an upgrade of the long-term foreign currency rating on OAO AK Transneft – the government-owned monopoly oil pipeline operator – to 'BB+', which reflected the improved transfer and convertibility risks that were accounted for in the raising of the sovereign foreign currency rating.

Bureaucracy continues to constrain credit quality

Instead of institutional frameworks serving as the foundation for fair and efficient economic activity, as well as raising the general standard of living for the population, the application of laws and regulation in Russia is driven by personal agendas and rivalries and self-preserving or 'rent-seeking' bureaucracies that burden businesses and impede the development of a more vibrant, diverse, and competitive economy. In recent months there have been worrying signs that conditions are getting worse, notwithstanding the passage of a number of pieces of reform legislation. Effective implementation of new laws and regulations and reduction of the bureaucratic burden on business through successful administrative reform is probably the most important challenge for the next administration.

Many of the reforms legislated or documented in 2001–2003 could serve as the basis for progress. From the corporate standpoint, the most significant new pieces of legislation include:

- tax reform;
- fiscal reform;
- the new bankruptcy law effective since 2003;
- electricity sector reform;
- changes to corporate law;
- currency control liberalization;
- deregulation of small businesses; and
- a more transparent tariff-setting framework for the electricity sector.

Questions remain as to the actual implementation and application of many of these and whether the government culture shifts toward serving the public, including private enterprises, as opposed to maximizing the power of the State and often its employees and their beneficiaries. In Russia's still-developing business and regulatory culture, personal or political motives, therefore, can prevail over economic rationale and result in biased decisions or decisions that are unpredictable from a purely business standpoint.

Managing high social costs and overcoming resistance to change by entrenched industrial and public sector interests are associated challenges. Russia's administrative burdens delay economic modernization and diversification and increase corruption risks. In the past, administrative burdens afflicted small and mid-size enterprises (SMEs) most seriously and were a deterrent to foreign direct investment, but now they seem an increasing threat to large Russian corporate entities as well.

Along with regulators and other bureaucracies, Russian courts remain unpredictable, which does not support fair and efficient economic activity. The weakness of the judicial system results in inconsistent and sometimes selective application of the law. It is not unusual to see different courts coming to contrary decisions on the same issue or overruling each other on unclear grounds. The courts lack independence and often appear to be influenced by federal or regional politicians or by powerful business groups. Corruption in Russian courts, therefore, remains a significant risk. Similarly, regulatory decisions are often non-transparent, unpredictable, and politicized.

Corporate governance remains an issue

Russia's corporate governance system is evolving and not yet firmly rooted. Its very short and dynamic history started with the murky privatizations of the mid-1990s and continued through the bitterly fought struggles to establish large industrial groups in the late 1990s. The idea that transparency and predictable corporate behaviour will support higher market capitalizations only began to surface with a few progressive corporate groups after the 1998 financial crisis, generally when the key industrial groups had achieved strong control over their key assets and ownership rights had been more or less settled. The mindset of most decision-makers, both in public and the private business environment, was formed in the Soviet era. As a result, private property, entrepreneurship, and value-creation are relatively new concepts, while government involvement in the economy and prevalence of personal relationships over prescribed rules is perceived as traditional. Many decision-makers still think in terms of control rather than value creation. This results in poor protection of ownership rights. The weaknesses of the country's legal and regulatory systems can still be exploited by the vested interests in the public and private sectors; for example, to gain control of certain assets or cash flows.

The Yukos affair and similar cases have discouraged transparency to some extent because it is perceived as making companies and shareholders vulnerable to outside threats. This reaction also hurts the legitimate interests of portfolio investors and lenders, however, by making it more difficult for them to assess risk and value and spot conflicts of interest. It will be unfortunate if a fear of regulatory actions or heavier government involvement in corporate affairs – be it politically motivated or at the instigation of rival business groups with political influence – induces more companies to regress back to the sort of aggressive corporate practices that prevailed in the late 1990s.

The legal, regulatory, and corporate governance uncertainties can be illustrated most clearly by the Yukos affair, as well as the recent questioning of the Moscow telecommunications licence of Vimpel-Communications (JSC) (Vimpelcom; B+/Stable/–) and other lower-profile cases. Yukos and its subsidiaries and shareholders are the subject of numerous tax and legal investigations, including ones into tax optimization practices that are widely used in Russia. Because of legal and tax charges against the company's beneficial shareholders, the court froze a 44 per cent stake in the company that the major shareholders owned indirectly, via offshore legal entities. Meanwhile, the former core shareholders of Sibneft – in which Yukos had acquired a 92 per cent stake just before Mikhail Khodorkovsky (the former chief executive and major shareholder of Yukos) was arrested – refused to transfer governance and management control to Yukos and started to reverse the transaction. Subsequent canceling by the court of Yukos' share issue used to purchase a 57 per cent block of Sibneft shares, and the resulting conceivable loss of that block (unless the share cancellation is successfully appealed), was a further manifestation of court actions that can impede corporate governance and finance in Russia.

The risk to companies under high-profile investigations can be compounded by lower-level officials, some of whom – in apparent attempts to demonstrate their loyalty and zeal – have initiated narrower investigations of their own into taxes, oil production licences, or assets. Although there have not yet been any high-profile defaults as a result of official actions, these actions compound the normal financial and business risks that companies face in markets where legal regulatory and governance systems are more developed and predictable.

The practical implementation of regulatory and judicial reforms will be key for Russia's corporate sector environment. In particular this should include:

- Administrative reform – which streamlines the compliance process and reduces the unnecessary interference of government in business including greater accountability, reengineering of work processes,

Russian Country Risk: Clouding Future Prospects for Russian Corporates

and staff optimization within the bureaucracy. Real reform, not just a redistribution of the government functions in token compliance with legislation, is essential to boost the efficiency, flexibility, and competitiveness of Russian companies.

- Judicial reform that must increase the fairness, efficiency, and predictability of the environment that businesses and creditors face. Judges also need to be more aware of the needs of the business community. On many occasions, individual judges' lack of knowledge and conservatism have posed a greater obstacle to development of business than the legislation.

- Interplay between corporate governance and regulation that encourages a better governance, credit quality, market, and regulatory culture.

Centralized and personality-driven political system adds risk

For large businesses, particularly in the resource sector, the growing concentration of power in the presidential administration creates new uncertainties. Without effective checks or balances from the legislative or judicial branches, and with a civil service in need of drastic reform, this concentration of power threatens to increase the already personalized relationships between business and government that, coupled with a resurgence of nationalist sentiment and questioning of existing contractual and property rights, heralds a period of uncertainty for the Russian corporate sector.

The December 2003 parliamentary elections were a victory for the pro-president centrist party United Russia. They also demonstrated the popularity of a nationalistic economic policy aimed at strengthening the government's role in the resource sector and increasing the sector's tax burden. If centrist parties play to the popularity of a nationalistic agenda, it could negatively affect the tax regime and undermine some recent efforts to liberalize the business environment. A nationalistic tilt might also hamper foreign direct investment, expose selected companies or businessmen to political pressure, and affect corporate governance and transparency incentives and practices.

The Yukos case is unique because of the company shareholders' unusually heavy involvement in politics, but without clear-cut protection under the law and principles of government other companies or institutions have to rightly factor in the risk that they too could attract the particular attention of the authorities. For example, Vimpelcom was subject to a licence investigation that was both begun and ended with suddenness and little explanation. In the pre-eminent oil and gas sector, the government recently invalidated the licence for Exxon Mobil Corp. (AAA/Stable/A-1+)-led Sakhalin-3 oil exploration project. Although massive nationalization looks very unlikely at this stage – because private property is already deeply entrenched and the key industries have been essentially privatized – the security of title, property rights, and contracts is a risk factor that must be weighed in by both direct and portfolio investors in Russia.

The trend toward political and fiscal centralization should help ease the threat of pressure or action by regional authorities against businesses in the future. In regions where governments have been heavily involved in the economy, however (such as Bashkortostan, Tatarstan, and Yakutia), the centralization process might imply uncertainties in shareholding or corporate governance, sometimes in the form of tax or regulatory pressures. For example, right before the elections in late 2003, in the Republic of Bashkortostan (B+/Stable–) the region's key oil firms, Bashneft and Bashneftekhim, were privatized in a questionable way by the setting up of a cross-shareholding structure that was effectively controlled by the management, which is close to the family of the former head of the region. The companies were subject to tax investigation, while the share issue of the region's key bank, Ural-Siberian Bank (OJSC) (B-/Stable/C), was contested in the court, triggering an outlook change from positive to stable. Both cases appear to have been settled after the president of Bashkortostan achieved a compromise with regional authorities and was re-elected to his office.

Standard & Poor's believes that creditors of government-owned companies are unlikely to benefit from the recent rise of nationalistic sentiment and the trend toward centralization. These organizations continue to face regulatory risks, which have been incorporated in the ratings on the entities. It is important to bear in mind that government interests are typically focused on the companies' current operations and long-term strategic projects rather than on avoiding a corporate default, because a default does not necessarily imply bankruptcy or liquidation. Recent fiscal legislation makes it almost impossible for the government to arrange for a timely direct financial support in the event of a liquidity crisis. Russian state-owned companies, therefore, receive little, and normally no, benefit in the ratings as a result of their ownership. Although these companies' business profiles might benefit from a degree of state support or even occasional politically motivated lending by the state-owned Savings Bank of the Russian Federation (Sberbank), their stand-alone credit quality can be affected by nontransparent populist-driven regulations, pressure for politically motivated investments, and generally less sophisticated management and corporate governance risks as well. For example, the rating on OAO Gazprom (BB-/Stable/–), Russia's gas monopoly in which the government holds majority control, is constrained by its low regulated domestic prices. In effect, the company shoulders the social burden for the government. RAO UES of Russia (B/Positive/–), the country's majority government-owned electricity monopoly, has a rating that reflects restructuring, regulatory, and other uncertainties.

Despite many uncertainties about the nature and extent of the influence of the government sector on corporate ratings, political unrest looks very unlikely. President Putin's wide popular support, coupled with Russia's strong presidential system and the Duma's composition after the December 2003 election, ensures wide legislative support if the new presidential administration wants to continue current reforms. Of importance is how committed to, and effective, the new administration will be in achieving desperately important administrative reforms that will both facilitate the broader range of policy implementation and lift the burden of government from business.

Economic concentration adds further constraints to growth

Russia's economy remains very concentrated in terms of its dependence on oil and gas and a few other natural resources as well as the concentration of private firm ownership in a relatively small number of financial industrial groups (which are controlled by Russia's 'oligarchs'). These structural characteristics mean that a downturn in the oil sector is a risk even for firms with little direct or obvious exposure to it. This vulnerability is not likely to be reduced in the near to medium term.

The dependence on oil and gas can be seen in the fact that those sectors accounted for 58 per cent of exports and an estimated 23 per cent of GDP in 2003, while metals accounted for a further 17 per cent of 2003 exports. The dominance of large financial industrial groups in Russia increases the risk that problems at one or more major members of a financial industrial group could ripple through the group affecting members and their main counterparties. The diverse economic cushion of modern SMEs remains underdeveloped and faces impediments to growth from the administrative burden of government bureaucracy and the underdeveloped banking system.

Incentives for transparency provide hope

The general level of transparency and disclosure in Russia is improving, albeit from a very low base and with large variances from one company to another. As capital markets become a more important source of financing, this improvement is expected to continue. The government is planning a gradual implementation of IFRS- or US

GAAP-based reporting starting with banks and listed companies and continuing somewhat later more broadly. Even if the process takes more time, the positive trend is obvious. For most rated companies, the key issue is the timeliness, rather than the level, of disclosure. Timeliness is hampered by the limited supply of accountants with a good understanding of IFRS or US GAAP accounts and the typically two-stage approach of basing these accounts on Russian statutory accounts with necessary adjustments and clarifications.

Transparency and corporate governance has markedly improved in recent years, but still remains an important issue. Complex corporate structures emerged during privatization, to avoid burdensome regulations or to optimize taxes. This applies to many newcomers to capital markets – such as OAO Caustic (CCC+/Stable/–) and OAO Plastcard (CCC+/Stable/–) – but also to some large corporate players. Typically, such companies have significant related party transactions and it is difficult to determine whether they trade at an 'arms-length' basis and to create an appropriate financial and accounting picture to analyze.

Shareholding structures are often obscure. National disclosure standards only require disclosing large names listed in the shareholder register and do not extend to the beneficial shareholding level. In many cases, therefore, the actual interests behind a particular company cannot be known with confidence. Shareholder disclosure is hampered by the fear of corporate raiders, property rights protection, large tax bills, or government pressure. The progress in this area is slow, although there are some examples of improving standards of disclosure such as Mobile TeleSystems OJSC (B+/Stable/–), Wimm-Bill-Dann Foods OJSC (B+/Negative/–), LUKoil (BB/Stable/–), and OAO Severstal (B+/Negative/–) as well as some smaller companies.

Concentrated shareholding structures affect predictability and transparency by making companies overly reliant on several key decision-makers and prone to large unexpected transactions such as dividends and M&A. Even if such transactions are disclosed, the company's destiny is very much in the hands of a particular individual with little accountability to minority shareholders or creditors.

In the future, the incentives to be transparent will largely depend on the balance between the access to capital markets, particularly the ADR market where shareholding disclosure is required, and the risks of pressure from the government or aggressive takeover attempts. After looking at the Yukos affair, some companies might be more cautious in their disclosure but because the story has not affected their access to the capital markets so far, the incentives to be more transparent in order to raise capital should prevail.

Increased appetite for emerging market debt offsets weak banking system

Russia continues to have a weak and undercapitalized banking system, which increases liquidity risk for Russian corporations. Many banks are captive or treasury operations of large industrial groups and a lack of economic diversification affects the banks' ability to grow and diversify their customer base. The level of intermediation is lower than in peer countries: the amount of credit issued by domestic banks to the private sector is low at only 21 per cent of GDP. Most Russian banks are rated well below Russian corporations (see Figure 1.6.3).

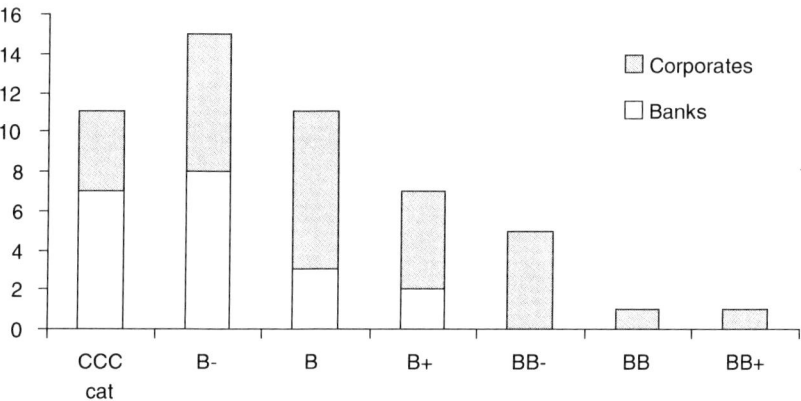

Figure 1.6.3 Russian corporate and bank ratings distribution on 4 March 2004

Although progress is being made, Russia's credit culture remains immature. Bank and bond markets are vulnerable to shocks and surprises due to investment and lending decisions being based on relationships, reputations, or other considerations rather than solid information and analysis. As a result, some companies can opportunistically borrow to fund aggressive investments in M&A, or borrow while keeping large cash balances and thereby expose themselves to weak financial institutions or currency risk.

Russian companies do now, however, have much better access to capital, both domestically and internationally, and this is a significant positive factor for credit quality. Since 2002–2003, large companies have had easy access to the international bond and bank loan markets, supported by strong international demand for emerging market debt and Russia's solid economic growth. As a result, foreign corporate debt grew fast in 2003. Notwithstanding the Yukos affair, the international demand for Russian debt has not decreased, as illustrated by several successful eurobond placements in late 2003 to early 2004. Even if international investor interest is volatile in the mid term, Russian issuers are not likely to be totally cut off from financing, as they were shortly after the 1998 crisis. Russia's ability to service all its debt in the short term remains relatively strong and the risk of a sovereign default is minimized by the country's very strong external liquidity position and the government's short-term fiscal flexibility.

Meanwhile, domestic bank credit and capital markets have been growing fast, albeit from a low level, so that Russia now has the largest bond markets in Eastern Europe. Oil revenues have created a liquidity cushion on the domestic financial market and provided funding opportunities for midsize companies. These factors improve corporate liquidity in the short term, but Russia's corporate sector would still benefit greatly from a strengthening of the domestic banking system.

Country risks still dominate outlook

The diverse range of outlooks and a significant number of CreditWatch placements suggests that Russian corporate ratings are likely to be volatile in the year ahead following their strong, steady, upward movements in recent years. In the short term, the ratings will be significantly driven by industry and company-specific factors rather than by sovereign rating dynamics.

Transparency and predictability of companies' financial policies in areas like M&A, debt, and liquidity will become as important as operating and financial indicators. Although general country risk is already factored in Russian corporate ratings, if a company becomes exposed to an unusual amount of regulatory or legal pressure – such as with Yukos – a CreditWatch placement or downgrade is possible. Overall, these factors are company-level reflections of two country-level issues: corporate governance and government interference.

The mid- to long-term outlook for Russian corporate ratings will be significantly determined by indirect sovereign factors, particularly by the country's progress – or regress in a worse-case scenario – in terms of establishing robust and independent legal and regulatory institutions, developing healthy corporate governance practices, making the relationships between the government and the corporate sector more predictable, and reducing the bureaucratic burden on business. These indirect factors will be no less important for corporate ratings in Russia than the sovereign's fiscal and macroeconomic performance.

Part Two
The Financial Sector

2.1

The Russian Banking System: An Overview

Eric Zuy, Allen & Overy

Regulatory system: The Central Bank

The Russian banking system is headed by the Central Bank of Russia (the CBR) – the institution that prints money, maintains Russia's currency reserves, implements currency control legislation and licences, regulates and supervises Russian banks and other credit organizations (eg those of clearing houses). It also owns a controlling interest in Sberbank, the national savings bank, and, until recently, Vneshtorgbank (VTB), the country's foreign trade bank (together Russian's largest banks), keeps budgetary accounts and accounts of state agencies and authorities, runs the national settlement system and conducts banking transactions. All of this is done at the same time by the same entity.

These extensive powers have been, and still are, the subject of a lengthy and rigorous political struggle, which has resulted in the CBR gradually, over the course of the last few years, losing some of its powers and privileges. For example, since 1997 the CBR has been obliged to transfer 50 per cent and, as of 2004, 80 per cent, of its profits to the federal budget (but still retains the remaining 20 per cent) while previously it kept all its profits, including seniorage. Around 1996–1997 the CBR lost out to its long-standing rival – the Federal Financial Markets Service (the FFMS) – and as a result the activities of Russian credit organizations in the securities markets (eg broker-dealer operations) are now licensed by the FSMC rather than by the CBR. In 2001, the CBR lost the fight to control money-laundering activities under the new anti-money-laundering law – these are now controlled by a separate, newly-created agency, with the CBR playing a more limited role. However, the worst year in the CBR's history was the year 2002, when the new Law on the Central Bank of Russia, adopted at the initiative of the Russian President, Mr Putin, expanded the authority of the National Banking Council, the public body designed to supervise the CBR, and significantly increased the influence of the Government, the legislature and Russian regions, over CBR policy. In addition, in 2002, the Government 'persuaded' the CBR to sell its shares in VTB at their nominal value and to receive in exchange rouble denominated bonds bearing just six per cent interest and having a maturity of nine years.

Nevertheless, despite these developments, the CBR is still a powerful agency keeping tight day-to-day control over virtually every Russian credit organization. In order to carry out its functions the CBR employs roughly 83,000 people and maintains 78 local branches throughout Russia.

History

The modern Russian banking system originally emerged through the introduction of the 1990 Law on Banks and Banking Activities. In just a few years, more than 2,000 banks came onto a scene previously occupied only by the CBR, Sberbank, Vnesheconombank (VEB), Promstroybank and a few other ex-Soviet state banks. This high number of banks, however, neither represented the same quality nor corresponded to the level of economic development in Russia at that time. Most of the banks profited either by servicing accounts of state authorities (with the most lucrative ones being, perhaps, the customs and tax authorities) or by trading on the speculative GKO (ie state short-term bonds) market.

The August 1998 Crisis

Not surprisingly, the collapse of the Russian GKO market during the so-called August 1998 Crisis (the 'Crisis') was a heavy blow to the fledgling Russian banking system. The results were shocking: many banks went bankrupt (with the most famous examples being SBS-AGRO, Rossiiskiy Credit and Inkombank) and hundreds of thousands of people lost their savings. The adoption of the Budgetary Code in 1998 and the subsequent transfer of most of the budgetary accounts to the Federal Treasury left many surviving banks without stable sources of income. According to the CBR, during the period from 1997 to the end of 2001 the number of operating banks dropped from 2,029 to 1,319. Despite the CBR's plans to tighten control over the existing banks and, thus, to force banks 'without a future' to close, the total number of banks has slowly grown during the last two years and, on 9 July 2004, reached 1,579.

Current status of the Russian banking system

Obviously, it is easier for the larger banks to survive. However, the current level of merger and acquisition activity is rather low. Immediate post-Crisis restructuring activities were limited to asset stripping and changes of name, as bank owners busied themselves hiding assets from their creditors. Many of the reported mergers represent intergroup restructuring (eg the merger of Alfa Bank with Alfa Capital, and the merger of Bank Austria with International Moscow Bank due to the merger of their parent companies/banks in Germany and Austria), rather than mergers in the true sense. While various acquisitions of small regional banks by their larger counterparts have been reported, the only memorable examples of any real M&A activity are the successful acquisition by Nikoil of Avtobank and UralSib, acquisition of the 1st OVK group of banks by Interros Group (which includes Rosbank), and the most recent acquisition of the failed (during the summer 2004 banking 'crisis') GUTA-Bank by VTB and acquisition of Russian Standard by BNP Paribas.

The current league table of the largest Russian banks is headed by ex-Soviet giants such as Sberbank, VTB and VEB. However, the league includes newer names as well, eg Alfa Bank, Gazprombank (controlled by the Russian gas monopoly Gazprom), International Industrial Bank, Rosbank, Bank of Moscow, MDM, Nikoil (controlled by Lukoil, one of the largest Russian oil producers), UralSib (undergoing acquisition by Nikoil) and Sobinbank.

There is no prohibition against foreigners establishing Russian banks or buying shares/participation shares in existing Russian banks. However, the acquisition of more than 5 per cent of the shares/participation shares in a Russian bank needs to be declared and the acquisition of more than 20 per cent of the shares/participation shares requires prior consent from the CBR. The Government plans to change both these figures to 10 per cent. Federal law can dictate the overall limit on foreign investment in the Russian banking system. To date, however, no such law has been adopted. As of 1 April 2004 there were 128 (compared to 126 in January 2002) banks with foreign capital, including 33 (23 in January 2002) that are wholly foreign-owned, and 8 banks with a majority foreign participation. This demonstrates a significant rise in foreign investment in the Russian banking sector over the last two years. The top 100 banks include several subsidiaries of foreign banks, eg ABN AMRO, Citibank, CSFB and ING.

Obviously, size alone does not necessarily correspond to the level of commercial activity/profitability. For example, the commercial activities of VEB are rather limited and it mainly performs agency functions in relation to Russian external debt.

The strongest Russian banks are typically members of the larger financial–industrial groups and often perform mostly treasury functions. The most probable explanation for this is that there are simply not enough trustworthy banks in the country to service the large Russian corporates and, as a result, they have had to establish/acquire their own banks. In 2002, the Ministry of Anti-monopoly Policy declared its plans to prohibit shareholders/owners of banks from maintaining their own bank accounts in the banks they control, as this reduces the competition as it means there are simply not enough valuable clients left in the banking services market for other banks. Not surprisingly, these plans have been widely criticized and, as a result, they have not been implemented.

The main problem of the Russian banking system is, of course, its under-capitalization. As of 1 April 2004, Russian banks as a whole had only 814.19 billion roubles (compared to 453.9 billion roubles on 1 January 2002) of their own capital (approximately $27.99 billion at the exchange rate of $1 to 29.09 roubles) and their total assets were approximately 5.6 trillion roubles (approximately $192.5 billion at the exchange rate of $1 to 29.09 roubles), compared to 3.2 trillion roubles on 1 January 2002. Thus, the capitalization of the Russian banking sector has almost doubled over the last two years, but is still at the very modest level.

National currency and currency control legislation

The Russian rouble, the national currency of the Russian Federation, is not yet freely convertible. The new Law 'On Currency Regulation and Control' No. 173-FZ dated 10 December 2003 (the Currency Law) envisages that the Russian rouble will become freely convertible from 1 January 2007. Due to the instability of the Russian economy and high inflation levels, the rouble often loses out to the dollar and other hard currencies in terms of people's preference. Banks, corporates and individuals often prefer to keep their reserves and savings and to receive their income in dollars or other hard currencies, rather than in roubles. It is worth mentioning that even the Russian budget is prepared on the basis of the estimated rouble to dollar exchange rate. Capital flight is estimated to be in the region of $20–40 billion per year.

In order to support the rouble, Russia maintains rigid currency control legislation. As a general rule, all settlements between Russian residents may be conducted only in roubles. Exporters must repatriate their hard currency proceeds back to Russia and convert 25 per cent of their export proceeds into roubles on the Russian currency market within seven days of receipt of hard currency. At some stage after the Crisis, the portion of the export proceeds subject to mandatory conversion into roubles was further increased to 75 per cent; however, it was later reduced initially to 50 per cent and then back to the original 25 per cent level. The Currency Law envisages that mandatory conversion, as well as certain other restrictions (such as special accounts, prior registration of the transaction and reserve requirements) will be cancelled altogether by 1 January 2007. As a general rule, Russian exporters should receive export proceeds within 180 days of the export of goods or services (this is one of the positive changes introduced by the new law on currency regulation and control). The acquisition of hard currency is no longer restricted.

While the Currency Law clearly introduced a more favourable legal regime for exporters and importers, it remains to be seen how this will affect foreign and Russian investors, manufacturers and other businesses.

Russian banks with a CBR licence permitting them to conduct operations in hard currencies, the so-called Russian Authorized Banks, act as 'agents of currency control', ie they control every single payment by residents and non-residents. The Currency Law has weakened the position of Russian Banks by allowing Russian residents (legal entities – from 19 June 2005) to open foreign bank accounts in OECD or FATF countries. It is expected that this will significantly increase competition between Russian and foreign banks.

Bank lending

As described above, Russian currency control legislation creates various barriers to the use of hard currencies. Russian law, however, allows the parties to a contract to express monetary obligations in hard currency (or any other equivalent) so long as the obligation is actually performed in roubles. Not surprisingly, the bulk of bank loans in Russia are either made in hard currency or are linked to a particular hard currency, which results in borrowers bearing the risk of exchange rate fluctuations.

Due to high inflation rates (which are usually higher than those reported in official statistics), few banks offer long-term loans. Loan terms rarely exceed three years and interest rates are prohibitively high.

The Russian tax system is undergoing significant change and the situation is slowly improving. Nevertheless, the effective taxation level is unreasonably high when compared with that in the West. Russian accounting standards are designed mainly for taxation purposes rather than for the purposes of making investment decisions. They differ from international and US accounting standards and do not always reflect the true state of companies' financial affairs. As a result, 'creative tax planning and accounting' is widely used in Russia; the

Yukos case is just one example of such practices. Coupled with the fact that there are no credit reporting bureaux in Russia, this often leaves banks in a difficult position when considering whether to grant a loan, as they have to assess credit risks on the basis of limited and often unreliable information. Therefore, banks generally grant loans only to their long-standing customers, though exceptions may be made for large companies with proven track records, especially in export-oriented industries. It is expected that the credit bureaux will be created soon, as the relevant draft laws have already been submitted to the State Duma.

Since foreign banks have access to international capital markets they are often able to offer lower interest rates and longer-term loans to Russian borrowers of an appropriate calibre than their Russian rivals can. As a result, foreign banks, together with their subsidiaries, occupy a significant share of the corporate lending market for large Russian borrowers (transactions are often, for various reasons, negotiated in Russia, but are documented as taking place abroad).

Investment banking

The Russian securities market is at a fairly early stage in its development and is slowly recovering after the Crisis. Legally, Russian banks are not divided into investment banks and commercial banks. Generally, all major banks are big players in the Russian securities market, whether directly or through their investment companies. It is worth mentioning that while Russian banks occupy most of the positions in the relevant league tables, first place is often taken by CSFB.

Retail banking

As many people suffered and lost out during the Crisis, the level of trust enjoyed by Russian banks is generally relatively low. In order to overcome this situation, Russia finally introduced, at the very end of 2003, a system for guaranteeing private deposits/mandatory insurance of private deposits. The CBR majority-owned banks (eg Sberbank) will continue to enjoy special status until 1 January 2007: their contributions to the relevant insurance fund cannot be used to make payments to the depositors of other banks and the Russian Federation will be secondarily liable for their debts to private depositors.

The Government and the CBR claimed that the new deposit insurance system would make any new banking crisis and related panic impossible, as depositors would be confident that their savings would be protected. The summer 2004 banking crisis emerged from nowhere and proved that both the Government and the CBR are often wrong.

GUTA Bank failed completely and was purchased by VTB for a nominal consideration of 1,000,000 roubles. Alfa Bank lost half of its private depositors and managed to survive only through the support of its shareholders (who have injected into it £700 million cash) and the, unprecedented for the Russian market, introduction of a 10 per cent commission for early withdrawal by private clients of their deposits – a measure considered illegal by the legal community.

The CBR rushed to lobby for legislation that would provide compensation to the depositors of those banks that did not join the mandatory deposit insurance scheme. This was not exactly consistent with the idea that only selected banks would be allowed to join the mandatory deposit insurance scheme and only depositors of such banks would be provided with some sort of state/CBR guarantee/support. Perhaps this is explained by the fact that, at the outset of the summer 2004 banking crisis, there was not a single bank that had managed to complete the lengthy procedure for joining the mandatory deposit insurance scheme.

The retail banking market is heavily dominated by Sberbank, which attracts most private deposits; its market share has increased since the Crisis and the collapse of its nearest competitors such as SBS-AGRO and Inkombank. For example, in 2001, Sberbank attracted 72.1 per cent of all private deposits (82.5 per cent of all private rouble deposits and 51.3 per cent of all private hard currency deposits), had the largest credit portfolio and received the largest profits in the whole banking sector. This achievement reflects the high public confidence enjoyed by Sberbank, which enables it to pay a relatively low interest rate on deposits. However, the increased competition in the market for retail banking services has led to Sberbank losing its position to competitors. For example, in 2002, its share of the private deposits fell to 64.2 per cent.

After the Crisis, the CBR urged foreign banks to start retail operations. Some foreign banks have complied with the request and several of their subsidiaries (eg Raiffeisen Bank and International Moscow Bank) have achieved notable success in attracting the funds of high-income individuals. However, their operations are limited to just a few branches in Moscow and some other major Russian cities and cannot be compared with the tens of thousands of branches maintained by Sberbank. It is worth mentioning that foreign banks pay an even lower interest on deposits than Sberbank.

At present, foreign banks do not target low-income clients and structure their tariff policy accordingly. ABN AMRO, for example, does not offer private banking for individuals unless they are employees of its corporate clients. However, in 2003, Russian banks became increasingly attracted to the retail banking market and many of them rushed to offer their services to individual customers. As a result, the competition in this market increased.

Mortgage financing

Mortgage financing is at an early stage in its development, but is developing at a rapid pace. Interest rates begin at over 10 per cent per annum for hard currency or hard currency linked loans.

Apart from the problems described above in relation to banking transactions generally, there is one further obstacle to the development of mortgage financing. According to Russian law, in order to be valid, a real estate mortgage has to be notarized. The notary fee is set by law at the ridiculously high level of 1.5 per cent of the 'value of the contract', ie the mortgaged property. This requirement creates an unjustified expense for borrowers and seems unnecessary in view of the introduction, in 1998, of state registration of rights to, and transactions in, real estate. The Government has finally prepared and submitted to the State Duma a set of 19 draft laws designed to improve the legal environment for mortgage financing and residential development, which will get rid of mandatory notarization of mortgages and will introduce a significant number of other improvements to the relevant legislation.

Plans for reform

On 30 December 2001 the Government and the CBR released their joint Strategy for the Development of the Banking Sector of the Russian Federation (the Strategy). The Strategy lists plans for future reform of the banking system. Among rather general statements of the goals, the Strategy includes several specific steps worth mentioning (some of which have already been implemented):

- The Government will dispose of its minority interest (25 per cent or less) in all banks, will consider on a case-by-case basis whether it should dispose of its interest in other banks where its participation exceeds 25 per cent and will not create further new state banks – this process has already started but is far from complete.

- The commercial business of VEB will be transferred to VTB, with VEB continuing to perform agency functions in relation to Russia's foreign debt. The press reported that this process has now been completed.

The Russian Banking System: An Overview 77

- The Government, jointly with the CBR, will tighten control over Sberbank; the CBR will continue to be the majority shareholder in Sberbank.

- All Russian entities (and not just banks) were to switch to international accounting standards by 1 January 2004. In fact, as of July 2004, this has been implemented in relation to banks only. It remains to be seen when this will be implemented in relation to non-banking institutions.

- Creation of aA system for guaranteeing/mandatory insurance of private deposits will be created – this has been implemented.

- Credit bureaux will be created. The relevant draft law was included in the 'mortgage package' recently submitted to the State Duma.

- There will continue to be no legal restriction on banks combining investment with commercial business.

- There will be no limit on the overall foreign investment in the Russian banking system.

- The CBR will consider allowing foreign banks to operate in Russia through their branches. It appears that this process is taking CBR considerably more time than might reasonably have been expected.

- The CBR will dispose of its interest in 'Soviet Foreign Banks' (ie its foreign subsidiaries). The press has reported that this plan has encountered strong resistance from the regulatory authorities in the countries where these banks are located.

- Improvement in the protection of pledgees; a system for registering pledges of movable assets. At this stage there is no evidence of any progress on this matter.

The press reports that the Government is currently considering the Strategy of Development of the Russian Banking System in 2004 and up to 2008. However, this document has not yet been officially published.

Experience shows that not all plans are implemented as intended, especially where the plans are those of the Russian Government and the CBR. However, despite the failure to implement all plans within the original time-frame, the steps already taken by the Russian President and the State Duma in the sphere of currency control legislation and the ongoing efforts in relation to the development of mortgage financing send a clear message that they are eager to avoid old mistakes and to make things happen, albeit at a relatively slow pace.

Table 2.1.1 Major Russian banks (as at 28 July 2004)

No.	Name
1	VNESHECONOMBANK
2	SBERBANK OF RUSSIA
3	VNESHTORGBANK
4	ALFA-BANK
5	GAZPROMBANK
6	INDUSTRY AND CONSTRUCTION BANK
7	CITIBANK
8	MDM BANK
9	BANK OF MOSCOW
10	ROSBANK
11	URALSIB
12	INTERNATIONAL INDUSTRIAL BANK
13	INTERNATIONAL MOSCOW BANK
14	RAIFFEISEN BANK AUSTRIA
15	SBS AGRO
16	PETROCOMMERZ
17	INCOMBANK
18	NOMOS BANK
19	VOZROZHDENIYE
20	PROMSVYAZBANK
21	AUTOBANK-NIKOIL
22	SOBINBANK
23	GUTA BANK
24	MENATEP SAINT PETERSBURG
25	NIKOIL
26	ABN AMRO BANK A.O.
27	BANK ZENIT
28	GLOBEX
29	TRANSCREDITBANK
30	IMPEXBANK

Please note that GUTA-Bank was acquired by VNESHTORGBANK.

2.2

Retail Banking

Deloitte & Touche

Russia's renaissance since the August 1998 crisis has been staggering. While the US economy has grown by 2–3 per cent a year and Europe's economic growth has practically flat-lined, Russia's real GDP has grown by over 20 per cent and its industrial production by 30 per cent. In different circumstances the currency's subsequent depreciation would have been viewed as undermining the economy, but for Russia it has done no harm, boosting local production, export and investments and making industry much more competitive overall. Oil prices have brought Russia significant revenues and in the banking sector, deposits and loans have doubled. Anyone who invested in Russian equities can now retire.

However, despite making significant strides, reform in the economy and, more particularly, reform in the banking sector, is far from complete and manifold problems persist.

The Russian banking sector remains highly concentrated and, at the same time, fragmented, with all banks apart from Sberbank, Russia's largest retail bank, holding only tiny market shares. Unfortunately the consolidation that would make the system more efficient and better capitalized upon, is not materializing. This can be largely attributed to the fact that Russian merger laws stipulate that in order to consolidate banks, the permission of each and every individual depositor is needed before a deal can go ahead.

The recent appearance of major US and European players on the Russian banking scene (Citibank, Credit Lyonnais, Deutsche Bank, etc) promised a profound change in the way retail banking business was being run. Awaiting quick improvements, changes in the Law on Registration of Banks and Foreign Participations were made, eliminating the 12 per cent foreign ownership limit. However, this initiative has failed to result in a flood of foreign capital. Generally, foreign banks still view the market as risky, ruling out other potential paths to reform. Even the recent upgrade of Russian sovereign debt to investment grade by Moody's did not contribute much to the overall sense of stability. The outflow of capital from Russia due to the relatively high level of political and national risk is still weighing down on the Russian banking system. Another major obstacle for attracting foreign investment is the 'specifics' of doing business in Russia, including the rigorous administrative and bureaucratic requirements.

The introduction of deposit insurance, a much-needed step towards increasing the overall trust in the banking system, is being constantly delayed due to political disagreements. The same situation affects improved supervision, greater transparency, etc. One of the major problems, however, is the lack of reliable and accurate credit information on Russian companies and individuals, since there are no parallels to credit bureaux and rating agencies. The lack of trustworthy information sources creates situations whereby banks cannot evaluate the credit standing of a potential borrower. International banks and companies seeking to extend credit to Russian companies are also unable to evaluate the credibility of a potential borrower. Such situations are aggravated by the fact that banks are unwilling to share whatever information they may have accumulated on their own. It is generally expected that this lack of publicly available information will exist for the foreseeable future.

One of the consequences of this trend is that the banks are reluctant to extend credit, due to the lack of the information necessary for risk assessment. This constitutes a significant problem for individuals as well as small- and medium-size enterprises (SMEs), who either cannot qualify for or attract credit on reasonable terms. This in turn leads to a situation where both individuals and SMEs have to rely on personal ties, connections and informal channels, thus narrowing the circle of potential partners, buyers and suppliers and hindering the overall development of the retail banking business.

In spite of the above-mentioned issues, bank deposits have been growing. At the same time, Sberbank's market share has dropped from 75 per cent in 2000 to 68 per cent today, and brokerage Troika Dialog foresees it falling to 63 per cent by 2005. The most aggressive local player in the retail market is Alfa Group, with its Alfa Bank Express project, though rivals such as Rosbank and MDM Bank are also expanding. However, foreign banks have better chances of attracting clients, partly due to their non-involvement in the devastating 1998 crisis and partly due to their offering of services new to Russians, such as online banking and security alerts to prevent unauthorized transactions. Additionally, foreign banks are bringing Western standards of customer service that are new to Russian customers.

As far as lending is concerned, Russian Standard Bank, the first local bank to specialize in consumer loans, has extended over $410 million in loans since it was set up in 1999. At the same time Raiffeisen Bank has $90 million in retail loans. Rising incomes and consumer demand have led to a surge in car loans and mortgages. These loans are a high-profit business. The margin on a retail loan in Russia is typically around double that on an equivalent loan in Western Europe. Average interest rates on rouble deposits are little more than 5 per cent, while rates on retail loans average at around 15 per cent. The big challenge for many newcomers, however, is distribution. Citibank, for instance, currently with only two branches, is relying on telephone and Internet banking, a network of automated-teller machines at British Petroleum gas stations around the capital, and alliances with local retailers. Societe Generale is also well behind its schedule of opening branches, due to a lack of appropriate real estate, a problem which other players have so far managed to avoid.

What is clear is that as Russia's economy stabilizes and the memories of the 1998 crisis fade, middle-class Russians are increasingly turning to banks to keep their money. At present, it is estimated that only 33 per cent of savings are kept in the banking sector, so there is a huge opportunity to attract new customers to the industry.

It is obvious that the country still has a long way to go and any let-up in the reform process could be devastating. Potential as well as existing players in the Russian banking market, both domestic and foreign, should carefully weigh up all the downsides of the initiative to avoid being blinded by the potential revenues.

2.3

Twelve Years of the Russian Insolvency Regime

Eric Zuy, Allen & Overy

History

Initial legislation

Back in the old days of the Soviet Union, there was no insolvency legislation because almost everything was owned and controlled by the State. Later, when the market reforms got under way there arose the need for a mechanism to deal with the insolvency of market participants. The legal vacuum could not exist for too long and on 14 June 1992 the President issued Decree No. 623 on Measures for the Support and Rehabilitation of Insolvent State Enterprises (Debtors) and the Application to them of Special Pro-cedures (the Decree).

The Decree was fundamentally flawed. Firstly, as follows from its title, it applied only to state enterprises (which included enterprises in which the State had a shareholding of at least 50 per cent) and did not apply to private companies or individuals. Critics of the Decree could not see much point in the State initiating special insolvency procedures in relation to wholly-owned state enterprises rather than simply liquidating them – a process which was already within the powers of the State in its capacity as owner of the enterprise.

Secondly, the Decree envisaged out-of-court insolvency proceedings to be administered by the relevant State Property Committee – in the case of wholly-owned state enterprises – or a commission of the owners of the enterprise – in the case of partially state-owned enterprises (both referred to hereafter as the Owners). Obviously, the Owners of insolvent enterprises did not prove to be the right people to protect the interests of the creditors of those enterprises.

Thirdly, the Decree envisaged that the Owners would review the insolvency petition and determine whether the debtor was insolvent by applying the so-called 'inability to repay/inadequate assets' insolvency test, (ie a debtor was deemed to be insolvent only if its total debts exceeded twice the value of its assets). In practice this was a difficult test to meet as most state enterprises had numerous non-productive, and often absolutely illiquid assets, on their balance sheet.

Once a debtor was acknowledged to be insolvent, its Owners were to prepare a rehabilitation plan specifying the time frame for which the insolvent enterprise was to be under so-called independent management (6–18 months) of an independent manager (which could also be a foreign entity) selected through an auction process (and which had to have provided security in the amount of not less than 10 per cent of the balance sheet value of the debtor's assets). While the powers of the independent manager were quite wide, it could not make more than 30 per cent of the workforce redundant, which often left little room for manoeuvre.

In light of the above, the Decree was never considered successful in achieving its ends.

The first insolvency law

On 19 November 1992 the legislature took a lead from the President and adopted the first Russian law on bankruptcy (the First Law). The First Law was a step forward in comparison with the Decree.

Firstly, it applied to all commercial legal entities and entrepreneurs irrespective of their form of ownership. Secondly, the insolvency proceedings were to be administered by the Arbitration Court (ie the Russian State commercial court) rather than by the Owners.

The First Law reduced the insolvency threshold by half (ie the debtor was considered insolvent if its total debts were equal to or exceeded the value of its assets). An insolvency petition could be filed by a creditor only if the debtor failed to pay debts equal to or exceeding 500 minimal monthly wages within three months of the same becoming due. In addition, the First Law required the creditor to send to the debtor a last-minute warning to the effect that the creditor would file an insolvency petition if the debtor failed to pay its debt within seven days of the date of the warning.

The major flaw of the First Law, from the perspective of the debtor, was that it did not relieve the debtor from interest, fines and penalties accruing during insolvency proceedings in relation to the debtor's breach of its obligations. Thus, while the moratorium imposed during insolvency proceedings would prevent the creditors from collecting their debts, it would not stop interest/penalties/fines from accruing. As a result, even where debtors were able to qualify for external management or rehabilitation proceedings (and thus, initially avoid liquidation), most of them still ended up in liquidation immediately after the termination of the initial proceedings since, once the moratorium ended, debtors would find themselves unable to meet their liabilities in respect of the interest, fines and penalties that had accrued during the insolvency proceedings.

With time it became apparent that the First Law did not serve its purpose of restructuring inefficient businesses as it did not give debtors sufficient opportunity to recover. The number of bankruptcy cases was relatively small (eg in 1993, the courts completed 74 cases and in 1994, 231 cases) and did not match the level of non-payments/defaults in the economy.

The tough monetary policy of the Government and the Central Bank led to a lack of cashflow in the economy: the so-called 'crisis of non-payments'. Cash settlements were rare and businesses preferred to settle debts between themselves and even with the State via barter, set-off, promissory notes and other arrangements not requiring cash payments. These arrangements were often associated with creative tax planning. The President tried to remedy the situation and on 18 June 1996 adopted the famous Decree No. 1212, which prohibited, among other things, debtors with outstanding tax obligations from having more than one bank account. Many Russian businessmen, however, preferred not to use any bank accounts at all rather than see their money being interfered with by the tax authorities. It became apparent that where the State was not able to change a business's practices, it would need to create a mechanism to change the management and the ownership of troubled entities by modernizing insolvency legislation.

The second bankruptcy law

On 8 January 1998, Federal Law No. 6-FZ the 'Law on Insolvency (Bankruptcy)' (the 'Second Law') was adopted. The Second Law was intended to make insolvency proceedings easily accessible to creditors in the hope that this would help the restructuring of troubled companies, would replace the old management with a more efficient one and would cope with the so-called 'crisis of non-payments'. The reality turned out to be very different.

The Second Law eliminated the 'inability to repay/inadequate assets' insolvency test for indebted legal entities, but left the test intact for debtors who were individual entrepreneurs. An insolvency petition could be filed by a creditor if a debtor failed to pay debts equal to or exceeding 500 minimal monthly wages (approximately $3,000 at the time) within three months of the same becoming due, irrespective of the cause of the non-payment. The Arbitration Court had to review the insolvency petition (basically, on formal grounds) within three days of its date of filing. Insolvency proceedings were due to commence automatically following the acceptance of the insolvency petition by the Arbitration Court. The Second Law did not require the Arbitration Court to invite the debtor to the hearings. Later the Constitutional

Court acknowledged such practice to be unconstitutional, but that was long after the initiation of the most famous insolvency proceedings – Imperial Bank and Inkombank.

Once the Arbitration Court accepted the insolvency petition, it was obliged to appoint a temporary manager who would identify the state of the debtor's financial affairs, take measures to preserve its assets, identify its creditors and convene the first creditors' meeting. The creditors' meeting would then decide whether to petition the court to liquidate the debtor (if the debtor was hopelessly in debt) or to put it into so-called external management (if the debtor had a chance of recovering). The creditors could also enter into an amicable settlement with the debtor.

The arbitration managers (temporary managers, external managers and liquidators) were meant to be independent licensed professionals who would protect the creditors and play a key role during insolvency proceedings. This was quite a challenging role for a newly-created profession. The Second Law provided for a transitional period during which no licences were required and the functions of the arbitration managers could be performed by so-called 'anti-crisis managers'. In practice, this meant that virtually any 'man off the street' could become an arbitration manager by completing a one-month course and passing a simple test. Clearly, this was not always enough to prepare a manager to cope with the insolvent entities, many of which were giant companies or some of the largest Russian banks, run by huge management teams.

The draftsmen of the Second Law did not take into account the possibility that arbitration managers and the Arbitration Court could be serving the interests of people other than the creditors. The Second Law created a solid basis for abuse: it lacked any system of checks and balances, it did not differentiate between independent creditors and affiliates of the debtor, it excluded the shareholders/participants of the debtor and its management from the insolvency proceedings, it limited the role of the creditors and created a fairly poor mechanism for supervising the activities of arbitration managers. It was not surprising then that the Second Law became a popular mechanism for ruining and taking over the business of a competitor, cheating creditors and the State. The Second Law well deserved its reputation as the Russian Federation law that did more than any other to promote the development of corruption.

Following the adoption of the Second Law, the number of insolvency cases snowballed year by year. While initially one could argue that the increasing number of insolvency cases was due to the August 1998 financial crisis caused by the collapse of the Russian GKO market, later it turned out that the growth in the number of insolvencies continued for years after the crisis (see Table 2.3.1).

Table 2.3.1 Insolvency statistics

	1992	1993	1994	1995	1996	1997	1998	1999	2000	2001	2002
Number of petitions filed	*	*	*	*	*	*	*	19,041	47,762	55,934	106,647
Number of cases completed	–	74	231	716	1,226	2,269	2,628	5,959	10,485	18,993	44,424
'Backlog'	*	*	*	*	*	*	*	13,082	50,359	87,300	102,820

*No data available

While the Second Law envisaged that it was the specific duty of the temporary manager to identify the debtor's creditors and while the creditors had the right to file their claims (eg if for some reason their claims were not properly identified by the temporary manager), the Second Law was interpreted and applied in such a way that creditors wishing to participate in insolvency proceedings and to be entitled to repayment, had to file their claims (together with the relevant supporting documents) with the debtor in order to 'establish' their claims, irrespective of whether the debtor and the temporary manager knew or should have known about the relevant creditor and the amount owed to it (except for claims confirmed by the court decision). The debtor had seven days to object to the claim. The failure to object meant that the claim was 'established' and should be included in the register of claims. In practice, temporary managers often raised objections or refused to enter the relevant claim in the register even where the debtor did not object to or even acknowledge the claim.

Cases of disputed claims had to be resolved by the Arbitration Court. The Second Law neither required the debtor to have sufficient grounds for objections, nor provided for any sanction for frivolous objections being made to creditors' claims either by the debtor or by the temporary manager. As a result, the courts were inundated with disputed claims. The hearings of such claims would typically take just a few minutes and, what was still more frustrating, the relevant court resolutions on the establishment or dismissal of the claims were not subject to appeal. One could only imagine a creditor's reaction and the impact this had on an investor's confidence where the validity of multi-million dollar claims depended on the outcome of a brief hearing, which was often little more than a formality. Later, the Constitutional Court acknowledged such practice to be unconstitutional, but for many creditors/insolvency cases it was already too late.

Insolvencies of credit organizations

Dissatisfied that its role had been downgraded to the position of a mere creditor, the Central Bank lobbied for the adoption of Law No. 40-FZ the 'Law on the Insolvency (Bankruptcy) of Credit Organizations' of 25 February 1999 (the Banks Insolvency Law), which put the Central Bank back in a position to control insolvency proceedings of banks and other credit organizations (eg the Central Bank became entitled to impose additional qualification requirements on arbitration managers of credit organizations and to issue special certificates to them).

In line with the First Law, the Banks Insolvency Law provides that insolvency proceedings can be initiated against a bank only after revocation of its banking licence by the Central Bank. Taking into account the fact that after revocation of its banking licence the former bank cannot conduct banking business and, thus, cannot recover, the outcome of the the Banks Insolvency Law is that the system of external management does not apply to banks, ie if a bank becomes insolvent it should be liquidated. For some reason the Banks Insolvency Law also prohibits bankrupt banks from entering into amicable settlements with their creditors.

On 8 July 1999, Federal Law of Russia No. 144-FZ, 'The Law on Restructuring of Credit Organizations', was adopted. This law envisages various insolvency prevention measures that can be taken in relation to a bank and also deals with the rehabilitation of banks by the state Agency for Restructuring of Credit Organizations (ARCO). The procedures envisaged by this law effectively serve the same purpose as external management and financial rehabilitation (see below) procedures serve in relation to corporate debtors. If none of these measures work, the Central Bank would revoke the debtor's banking licence and would effectively put it into liquidation in accordance with the procedure envisaged by the Banks Insolvency Law. The press reports that ARCO will soon be liquidated as it 'has already performed its purposes', therefore the relevant legislation will be amended accordingly.

Natural monopolies

Astonished by the scale of criminal activities arising from the Second Law, the legislature rushed to protect Russian corporate monopolies and on 24 June 1999 adopted Law No. 122-FZ, the 'Law on Specifics of the Insolvency (Bankruptcy) of the Subjects of Natural Monopolies in the Fuel and Energy Complex' (the Natural Monopolies Law), which increased the minimum level of indebtedness required in order to file an insolvency petition by a thousand times, reverted back to the 'inability to repay/inadequate assets' insolvency test and introduced special qualification requirements for arbitration managers. It is not surprising that this law has rarely, if ever, been tested in practice.

Current status

On 26 October 2002, the President of the Russian Federation signed the new 'Law on Insolvency (Bankruptcy)' (the Insolvency Law). The Insolvency Law came into force (with some exceptions) on 28 November 2002.

The Insolvency Law replaced the Second Law as well as the Natural Monopolies Law. However, it still envisages that the insolvency of banks will be subject to a separate legal regime. Thus, both the Banks Insolvency Law and the 'Law on Restructuring of Credit Organizations' continue to apply. The press has reported that the Banks Insolvency Law will be significantly amended soon, presumably in connection with the introduction of a system for insuring private deposits in banks.

The scope of the Insolvency Law has been extended. It now applies (with some exceptions) not only to commercial legal entities but to non-commercial legal entities as well (such as state corporations, public organizations, non-commercial partners, and autonomous non-commercial organizations and condominiums (partnerships of owners of apartments)). It also now applies to natural monopolies (including nuclear power stations, which were previously exempt from insolvency proceedings).

The Insolvency Law was drafted with the primary purpose of preventing the numerous abuses that occurred on the basis of the Second Law. To this end the Insolvency Law:

- makes it more difficult to initiate insolvency proceedings, ie an insolvency petition can be filed against a debtor only if its indebtedness is confirmed by a court judgement that has come into force (in case of civil law claims) or by a decision of the relevant tax or customs authority on the levy of enforcement over the debtor's assets (in case of tax claims); and such indebtedness is not satisfied within 30 days after the submission of the writ of execution to the bailiff (in the case of civil law claims) or after the relevant decision of the relevant tax or custom authority on the levy of enforcement over the debtor's assets (in case of tax claims);

- gives the debtor, its shareholders/participants/owners and the state authorities a greater say in insolvency proceedings, eg both the debtor and its shareholders/participants/owners can now officially participate (though with no voting rights) in insolvency proceedings, and the state authorities (eg tax/customs/municipalities) have equal status with other creditors and can vote at each creditors' meeting and not just at the first meeting, as was the case under the Second Law;

- increases state and public control over arbitration managers, eg the qualification requirements for arbitration managers have been tightened, the creditors can introduce certain further qualification requirements for the arbitration managers, and the procedure for the appointment of arbitration managers has been complicated and now resembles to a degree the jury selection process;

- introduces various measures to avoid abuse of process, eg all claims are established by the court only. The arbitration manager or the creditors can elect to transfer the function of keeping the register of creditors' claims to an independent registrar, and the arbitration manager no longer has the authority to manage the debtor during the supervision stage even where the head of the debtor's executive has been removed by the court – a tactic often used in the past to gain complete control over the debtor.

Along with 'closing the loopholes' in the Second Law, the Insolvency Law introduces various further changes with a view to improving the efficiency and outcome of insolvency proceedings. For example, the Insolvency Law:

- introduces (in addition to supervision, external management and liquidation) a new stage of insolvency proceedings, namely, financial rehabilitation, whereby either the debtor's shareholders/participants/owners or the state authorities or third parties may guarantee and procure the performance of all the debtor's obligations in full;
- specifically authorizes the debtor to issue additional shares (by closed subscription) in order to repay its debts;
- has reduced the number of classes of ranked claims from five to three. More importantly, is that it has improved the position of secured creditors, ie claims secured by a mortgage/pledge are satisfied in priority to all other claims except for claims of first (claims for harm caused to health or life) and second (salaries, severance and copyright payments) priority arising prior to the creation of the pledge. This is in contrast to the position under the Second Law whereby the claims of secured creditors were satisfied after all claims of first and second priority, irrespective of when they had arisen. In addition, the Insolvency Law clarified that secured creditors' claims be satisfied in priority to unsecured claims out of the value realized upon the sale of the pledged/mortgaged assets rather than from the pooled property of all secured creditors and potentially all property of the debtor.

On paper, the Insolvency Law constitutes a significant improvement in the Russian legal environment. There is no doubt that it will stop many of the abuses conducted on the basis of the Second Law. However, it remains to be seen whether it will be widely used in practice as a civilized way of dealing with insolvencies, or whether it will go the way of the Natural Monopolies Law, which was not used due to the complexity of initiating insolvency proceedings. The absence of any significant reported bankruptcy cases (except for the potential bankruptcy of Yukos) initiated under the Insolvency Law during the past two years supports the second premise.

2.4

The Issuance and Regulation of Securities

Max Gutbrod, Partner, Baker & McKenzie – CIS, Limited

Introduction

Generally, the securities markets and securities transactions are regulated by the Russian Federal Law on the Securities Market (the Securities Law), enacted 22 April 1996. The offering of corporate securities is regulated by the Law on Joint Stock Companies (the JSC Law), enacted on 26 December 1995, and to some extent by the Law on Limited Liability Companies (the LLC Law), enacted 8 February 1998, and by the Law on Banks and Banking, enacted 2 December 1990 (regarding credit institutions).

During the last few years, there has been a fair amount of discussion on changes to the applicable legislation and on the structure of the securities markets in general. To date, this has resulted only in a new Federal Law on Mortgage-Backed Securities (the MBS Law), which came into effect on 18 November 2003, introducing two new types of securities, namely mortgage-backed bonds and mortgage participation certificates.

Only open JSCs can issue publicly-traded shares. Russian securities are also subject to a number of regulations issued by the FSFM (previously, the FCSM), the Russian Civil Code, and the regulations issued by other regulatory agencies.

The stock exchange

In Russia, there are several well-established stock exchanges, both in Moscow and throughout the Federation. Stock exchanges are governed by regulations of the FSFM (previously, the FCSM), and other governmental bodies. However, only a small percentage of transactions occur on the stock exchanges. Most sales of securities in the Russian Federation are executed over the counter (OTC) between licensed brokers and investors. Procedures for obtaining a licence to carry out broker/dealer activities and requirements for potential brokers/dealers are set forth in regulations adopted by the FCSM.

There has been a fair amount of discussion on the role of stock exchanges over the last few years, which has resulted in an expectation that requirements for listing are likely to be tightened soon.

Corporate securities

Russian JSCs may issue shares, options on shares, corporate bonds, and other securities authorized by the Russian Civil Code and the FSFM. Open JSCs may raise capital either by issuing shares to the public or by private placement. Shares of closed JSCs may not be offered to the general public.

Securities in general

Unless a particular instrument is specifically recognized by law as being a security, it will not be considered to be a security. Article 143 of the Russian Civil Code provides a list of recognized securities. These securities include bonds, shares, negotiable promissory notes, cheques, deposit and saving certificates, bills of lading, and securities issued in the process of privatization. In addition, option certificates have been included within the Russian legal definition of 'securities'.

The Securities Law outlines the procedure for the registration of securities issuances and clarifies when a prospectus is required. A prospectus is required when either:

1. securities are to be distributed to an unlimited number of holders; or

2. the number of holders is known and exceeds 500; or

3. securities are intended to be listed or otherwise publicly traded.

The Securities Law generally requires quarterly reporting of financial and other information and the publication of information describing material events that will affect the finances or the business activities of the issuer within five days after the occurrence of such events. Issuers must provide such information if they have ever registered a prospectus or if they are issuers of 'publicly offered securities'.

Regulation of the securities market

The Federal Service for the Financial Markets (FSFM)

Pursuant to Presidential Decree No. 314, dated 11 March 2004, the FSFM has replaced the Federal Commission for the Securities Market (the FCSM) as the primary regulator of the Russian securities market. The FSFM functions, which it carries out either directly or through its pre-authorized agencies, include the licensing and supervision of professional securities-market participants, the authorization of self-regulatory organizations, the registration of securities issuances and prospectuses and the approval of standards therefor, and the classification and definition of different types of securities.

The FSFM has the authority to take certain actions against professional securities-market participants who violate the securities regulations. These measures include the suspension and revocation of licences, enforcement actions, and petitions for criminal prosecution. In addition, the FSFM has the power to fine legal entities or individual entrepreneurs for various securities law violations. Any action pursued against issuers, such as the invalidation of an issuance, must be effected through the courts. Consequently, the ultimate jurisdiction over breaches of the securities laws remains with the courts.

Self-regulating organizations (SROs)

The requirement of obligatory membership in an SRO for professional participants in the securities market was repealed by the Presidential Decree of 16 October 2000. Pursuant to a FCSM press release dated 23 October 2000, professional participants may now apply directly to the FSFM to receive a licence. According to the Licensing Regulation, the FSFM must make a decision on issuing a licence to an applicant within 30 days of a direct submission of the documents to the FSFM or within 15 days if an applicant presents a recommendation from an SRO along with the documents. Since the requirement that an SRO recommendation be received prior to the licensing still exists in a number of the FSFM regulations previously adopted by the FCSM, some representatives of SROs consider an SRO membership an ongoing requirement for receipt and possession of a licence.

Regulatory measures

The FSFM shares its regulatory authority over the securities market with the Central Bank, the Ministry of Finance, and the Federal Anti-Monopoly Service (the FAS). For example, the FAS regulates trading in options and futures, while the FSFM regulates derivatives with underlying assets.

The Securities Law also imposes disclosure requirements on holders of securities and on professional securities-market participants. A holder of an issuer's securities (other than bonds non-convertible into shares) is required to disclose its holding when such a holder possesses 20 per cent or more of the issuer's securities. Moreover, as long as a shareholder's ownership continues to be above this 20 per cent threshold, such a shareholder is required to disclose any further acquisitions of 5 per cent or more.

The Securities Law requires that notification be provided to the FSFM of transactions whereby foreign parties acquire shares in Russian companies, foreign ownership of which is restricted by law (eg the gas and electricity monopolies and insurance entities). In addition, the FSFM must approve securities issued by Russian issuers for placement and organized trading outside of the Russian Federation.

Legislation enforced prior to the passing of the Securities Law prohibited the use of 'insider' information. The Securities Law provides a somewhat more sophisticated and potentially broader definition of 'insider trading'. The legislation refers to the utilization and passing of 'inside' information for use where the information was gained by virtue of office, job position or contract.

Bonds

The issuance of corporate bonds is regulated by the Russian Civil Code, the JSC Law, and the LLC Law. The public issuance and trading of bonds is governed by the Securities Law.

The above Laws introduced the concept of secured and unsecured bonds. Secured bonds must be fully secured with a third-party guarantee or suretyship, or with a pledge (or a mortgage) of the issuer's and/or third party's securities or immovable property. Only companies, including credit institutions, that have existed for a minimum of three years may issue unsecured bonds. The above Laws provide that the par value of all unsecured bonds issued by a company must not exceed the charter capital of the company and that no bonds may be issued until the charter capital is fully contributed.

In April 2002, a new FCSM resolution providing, *inter alia*, for standards applicable to the issuance of bonds convertible into shares was adopted. These new Standards of Issuance set forth more detailed procedures for the issuance of bonds convertible into shares and further developed some relevant provisions of the JSC Law.

2.5

Currency regulations

Vladimir Dragunov, Partner, Baker & McKenzie – CIS, Limited

Introduction

Article 140 of the Russian Civil Code declares that the rouble is the national currency of the Russian Federation. Although agreements may refer to the rouble value equivalent of foreign currency, all transactions conducted inside the Russian Federation, as a general rule, must be settled in roubles. Article 317 (3) of the Civil Code, however, permits the use of foreign currency in cases provided for by law.

The main piece of federal legislation regulating currency transactions is the Law on Currency Regulation and Currency Control (the Currency Law) of 9 October 1992. The Currency Law governs 'foreign currency transactions', such as the transfer of ownership or other rights to foreign currency. The Currency Law also regulates the powers of currency control agencies and the rights and duties of individuals and legal entities to possess, use and dispose of 'currency valuables', and imposes liability for the violation of currency legislation. Currency valuables include foreign currencies, securities in foreign currencies, precious metals, and precious stones.

On 17 June 2004, the Currency Law will be replaced with the new Federal Law No. 173-FZ, On Currency Regulation and Currency Control (the New Currency Law), dated 10 December 2003. It is expected that in the meantime certain implementing regulations will be adopted by the Russian Government (the Government) and the Central Bank of Russia (the CBR). The New Currency Law is an important step in the process of removing most of the currency control restrictions, which is expected to occur in 2007.

Foreign investors must monitor currency regulations very carefully since these rules change frequently in the Russian Federation. In light of the high penalties for failing to observe the Currency Law, foreign investors should seek the most up-to-date legal advice to ensure that they are in compliance with all Russian currency requirements.

Resident vs non-resident status

The Currency Law gives the CBR authority to regulate the possession and use of foreign currency by individuals and legal entities on the territory of the Russian Federation. The Currency Law divides individuals and legal persons into two groups: residents and non-residents. Residents include Russian citizens and other individuals whose permanent place of residence is the Russian Federation, legal entities created in accordance with Russian legislation, representative offices (branches) of Russian legal entities outside of Russia, and enterprises/organizations that are not legal entities but are located inside the Russian Federation. Non-residents are defined as individuals whose permanent place of residence is located outside of Russia, legal entities incorporated outside Russia, and representative offices (branches) of foreign legal entities in Russia. The distinction between residents and non-residents is retained in the New Currency Law with minor changes.

Bank accounts

A non-resident company may open the following types of accounts in the Russian Federation:

- rouble 'convertible' account ('K' account);
- a rouble 'non-convertible' account ('N' account);
- a foreign currency account; and
- a special purpose rouble account for state-issued securities and certain 'blue chip' corporate securities issued by Russian companies ('S' account).

A non-resident company can open any of the above accounts regardless of whether it is accredited to do business in Russia or not. Certain restraints are imposed on 'N' accounts and 'S' accounts. Funds from 'N' accounts, for example, may be used for the purchase of foreign currency not earlier than 365 days after presenting a purchase order to an authorized bank. Cash withdrawals from both 'K' and 'N' accounts may be effected only for the purposes authorized by the CBR, while cash withdrawals from S accounts are prohibited.

The New Currency Law does not expressly provide for such limitations. However, it remains to be seen whether the limitations existing under the current currency regime will continue after 17 June 2004.

Movement of capital

The Currency Law divides foreign currency transactions into two categories: capital movement currency transactions and current currency transactions. Capital movement currency transactions include:

- direct investments;
- portfolio investments, ie the acquisition of securities;
- money transfers to pay for the title to buildings, real estate, land, and other property;
- grant or receipt of a payment deferment of more than 90 days for the import and export of goods; and
- extension or receipt of financial credit (loans) for more than 180 days.

Capital movement currency transactions must be carried out pursuant to a CBR authorization for which only resident legal entities can apply, unless otherwise exempted by the CBR. Examples of such exemptions, which are conditional upon satisfying certain requirements, include, among others:

- foreign currency transfers by resident individuals to and from Russia in amounts not exceeding US$75,000 during the course of a calendar year in order to acquire foreign currency denominated securities or to exercise rights in such securities;
- loans from non-resident entities; and
- transfers of currency by non-residents to resident entities under Russian real estate sale or lease contracts.

Current currency transactions do not require a CBR authorization. Such transactions include:

- foreign currency transfers to and from the Russian Federation making immediate settlements of payments for import and export of goods;
- settlements connected with credits granted for not more than 90 days for import-export transactions;
- extension or receipt of financial credits (loans) (not to exceed 180 days);
- transfers to and from the Russian Federation of interest payments, dividends, investments, credits, and other transactions linked to the movement of capital; and
- transfers of a non-commercial nature, including the transfer of wages and salaries, pensions, alimony, business trips expenses, inheritances, and other similar transactions.

The New Currency Law abolishes the distinction between current transactions and capital movement transactions. The New Currency Law will also substantially limit the authority of the CBR to restrict currency operations in Russia. Firstly, it provides for an exhaustive list of currency operations subject to administrative regulation and establishes a 'free hands' regime with respect to other currency operations between residents and non-residents. Further, it limits the list of regulators to the CBR and the Government of the Russian Federation and clearly states that these bodies may not introduce new requirements to the currency regime established by the New Currency Law, except as provided by the New Currency Law itself. Finally, the New Currency Law explicitly prohibits imposing of any requirements to obtain individual permits for a particular type of currency transaction.

Instead of individual permits and requirements, the New Currency Law introduces new types of limitations, namely 'special account' and 'mandatory reserves'. A special account should be used for conducting certain types of foreign currency transactions. The regime for such accounts is yet to be defined. The requirement to keep a mandatory reserve would be imposed on residents and non-residents according to a number of currency operations specified in the law. Residents or non-residents thus may be required to block a certain amount of money in roubles (up to 100 per cent of the value of the relevant currency operation as may be determined by the CBR or the Government) in a separate non-interest-bearing account with a Russian authorized bank for a certain period of time (eg 2, 12, and 24 months). The authorized bank will further reserve an equivalent sum at the CBR. In most cases, such reserves shall be established not later than the day of the currency operation subject to a mandatory reserve. However, in certain cases (eg purchase by non-residents of securities issued in Russia, by residents of securities issued abroad, or by residents of participation interest in foreign companies), residents and non-residents may be required to establish such reserves in advance.

Liability for violation

Persons violating Russian currency regulations may be subject to civil, administrative, and criminal liability. Administrative penalties for the violation of Russia's currency regulations are currently provided for in Articles 15.25–15.26 of the Russian Federation Code of Administrative Offences, which entered into force on 1 July 2002. These penalties are mainly fines that may be imposed upon different types of offenders: individuals, officers of enterprises, and legal entities. The amounts of fines vary from a tenth to the entire amount of profit gained as a result of the illegal currency transaction. In addition, violators, particularly authorized banks, can be fined for failure to submit the proper documents to the authorities and can also lose their licences to conduct foreign currency transactions.

2.6

Corporate Governance Development in Russia

Branan

Improvement of corporate governance is one of the prerequisites to further successful development of the Russian economy.

It is difficult to give a precise and exhaustive definition of corporate governance. The essence of the term is relationship between a company's management bodies, shareholders and other interested parties; it also encompasses the principles the company enforces to manage and control decision-making processes and operations in general.

The model of the corporate governance currently shaping in Russia is in many ways different from the traditional concepts that evolved in other countries, namely Anglo-American, German (or European) and Japanese (or Asian) models.

The main mechanisms of functioning of the Anglo-American model (also referred to as Shareholder Wealth Maximization Model, or SWM) are a board of directors elected by shareholders on a one-share-one-vote principle, management chosen by the directors and working towards maximization of the company's share value, which is based upon the present value of expected future dividends. In this model, suppliers of equity capital, ie shareholders, bear the entire risk of the enterprise and are residual claimants of the income.

The German or European model (also referred to as Corporate Wealth Maximization Model, CWM) is based on the social interaction principle: apart from shareholders, there are other groups that have a stake in the operations of the enterprise, eg key suppliers of the company, its personnel, as well as suppliers of debt capital (banks), public organizations, the State, etc. The objective of management decision-making in this case is to increase wealth and power of the company as an entity. In this model, it is usually difficult for outsiders to take the control away from the management, and voting power in the governance of the corporation is usually not one-share-one-vote.

Two-layer management is practised with supervisory and management boards in place where all the stakeholders are represented, cross-ownership is a frequent phenomenon, and banks often hold substantial stakes in the companies.

The Japanese or Asian model is characterized by the great State involvement into the companies' activities, and the shaping of large vertically and horizontally integrated groups (pyramid structures) comprised of financial institutions, State and businesses, usually under control by one family (*keiretzu* in Japan and *chaebols* in South Korea). In this situation, distortions in corporate governance structure have been inevitable, the main being immature mechanisms of interaction between controlling and minority shareholders, conflicts of interest and lack of transparency, which resulted in inefficiencies in companies' management partly contributing to the Asian crisis at the end of 1990s.

Corporate governance in the countries in transition, however, does not fit precisely into any of the above models. Some experts refer to the corporate governance model currently shaping in the transition economies as the entrepreneurial model. Its main principle is that it has all the recognized necessary elements of corporate governance, but none of them work in reality, as State regulation and economic policy are unpredictable and strongly depend on the political interests of the officials and oligarchs. The main characteristic of this model is the absence of division of competencies and responsibilities between the owners and the management, as well as a high degree of political and economic uncertainty.

The current situation in Russia, in our opinion, cannot be described using a single model. At the beginning of 2004, corporate governance appeared to have gone beyond the entrepreneurial model and to be approaching the European one, with social responsibility being one of the priorities for the most advanced corporations. However, the way the situation with the largest Russian oil company Yukos has later developed suggests that the State is still able to exercise far greater influence on private companies than their management bodies and shareholders, which has thrown the Russian corporate governance system back to the entrepreneurial model. Besides, share value remains one of the main indicators of corporate governance effectiveness, as in the Anglo-American model. However, the State remaining the largest Russia's shareholder, and large vertically and horizontally integrated financial and industrial groups still being in place, the situation suggests adherence to the Asian model. Therefore, conclusions about the character of corporate governance in the Russian Federation should be made only on the basis of an overall analysis of the business development of the country as a whole.

Later an historic overview and explanation of the peculiar nature of corporate governance development in Russia will be given. In the meantime, let us outline the main driving forces behind the recent positive change in companies' attitudes to corporate governance.

Firstly, the Russian companies realized the need to attract outside capital, including foreign investment, which called for greater transparency in operations and improved corporate governance mechanisms. According to McKinsey, when evaluating companies in transition economies, large investors normally focus more on the quality of corporate governance rather than financial and economic performance. Moreover, having foreign businessmen among shareholders of the company and especially on the board makes it easier for Russian companies to enter highly-competitive international markets and successfully operate there, as demonstrated in the findings of the recent research by the Higher School of Economics and the Institute of Comparative Studies.

Secondly, the effort of existing minority shareholders, especially those represented by non-resident investors, aimed at better protection of their rights, played its positive role in development of corporate governance in Russia.

Thirdly, the companies realized that improved corporate governance standards and enhanced business transparency can be used as a new *PR tool*, especially if the company succeeds to reserve the 'first-comer' status here, which will help the company to achieve competitive edge and shape a positive image in the opinion of the general public.

The peculiarities of corporate governance in Russia can be largely attributed to the specifics of privatization strategies applied in Russia in the 1990s.

Privatization in the first half of the 1990s was supposed to transfer state-owned enterprises into companies with a broad ownership base, as well as to ensure economic development via competition between efficient owners and skilled managers.

Back at the end of the 1980s, under Gorbachev, employees and managers were granted a right to lease and subsequently buy from the State the assets of the enterprises they were working at. Later, with the overall collapse of the administered planning system and disruption of vertical economic links, the new Mass Privatization Programme (MPP) was initiated, where individuals would be given undifferentiated vouchers to be used as a bid for shares in newly privatized enterprises. In the course of MPP, over 30,000 joint-stock companies were created. Within the programme, enterprises from several selected 'strategic' industries, utilities being one of them, were made non-public with the State holding a controlling stake in them and with the rest of the stock allocated to the insiders and management. Thus, large well-performing companies in 'strategic' sectors became controlled by the State and the insiders; majority stock at non-strategic SMEs with stable performance was acquired by the management and employees; and finally shares of non-resource companies with poor operating performance became available to the general public in exchange for the vouchers at privatization auctions.

The main drawback of the privatization idea as a whole was that the Russian businesses had to travel all the way from state-owned enterprises via individual firms and partnerships to the corporations, the highest business organization form, within an extremely short period of time, whereas it took dozens of years in other economies. Ill-preparedness of the companies for corporate relations caused a mismatch between the form and the content and resulted in numerous conflicts of interest, creating situations running counter to the initial goals of privatization. Some of the results of MPP were the concentration of ownership and control in the hands of the insiders and the so-called 'oligarchs' nurtured by government policies, as well as undervaluation of enterprise assets at privatization auctions stemming from the absence of assessment and valuation practice and experience. Institutional investors, who in other emerging economies would traditionally act as 'depositary vehicles', exercise oversight in the privatization process and act to protect minority shareholders' rights, were underdeveloped in the period of privatization and in most cases pursued profiteering goals. Lack of legal infrastructure, blind reliance on the Western practices often non-applicable to the Russian reality, and the 'shock therapy' nature of MPP exacerbated the situation.

After the MPP, until 1995, the Russian government largely retained control over the majority of the strategic enterprises. However, due to unfavourable political conditions and budget deficit, it consented to the 'loan-for-shares' programme offered to Yeltsin's government by some oligarchs. The programme implied offering low-interest loans to the government by a consortium of the Russian banks, and conducting cash auctions between commercial banks (mostly led by the oligarchs) for the State shares in the strategic enterprises, which would be later transferred to the winners as collaterals. Until the government were able to repay the loans, the strategic enterprises would remain under control of the auction winners; if the State failed to repay the loans, its share would be transferred to the creditors, which eventually became the case. Apart from transferring control to the financial industrial groups, the government continued subsidizing them as if they remained government enterprises. This peculiar partnership between the government and large businesses gave way to various kinds of abusive self-dealing and wealth expropriation from minority shareholders. The main types of the shareholder rights violation were share-dilution, asset-stripping, related party transactions, transfer pricing, hostile bankruptcy and delayed dividend payment.

The gaps in legislation, excessively stringent tax policy and political uncertainty created no incentives for the managers of the companies to introduce and apply corporate governance principles. In the situation of an undeveloped and illiquid secondary market, the managers were not interested in share price increases; they were not inclined to pay dividends, for they perceived the payments as depriving them of a part of profits; strategic goods prices being still controlled by the State, the managers tended to strip assets for sales abroad; they resorted to various measures to conceal actual income, which had disastrous effects for corporate accounts transparency. Besides, managers were not interested in attracting outside investors and voted for restricting, if not prohibiting, bankruptcy procedures, so preventing restructuring of loss-generating companies.

Paradoxically, the crisis of 1998 had a positive overall effect on the ownership structure of the financial industrial groups: to avoid bankruptcy, many of the holdings and the banks sold their stakes in underperforming or illiquid assets. As a result, the number of 'management' and 'employee' holdings decreased while the number of 'outsider' holdings, as well as non-financial firms, company holdings and largely unaffiliated banks, rose. An increase in foreign and individual investment was a sign of increased diversification of the ownership base, too. This increase in investment came largely as a result of the actions of the large business group owners, who had been initially busy with acquiring, retaining and restructuring assets, but now finished assets consolidation and became interested in raising funds from outside sources.

Another important development of the period was the emergence of institutions dealing with shareholders' rights protection, such as the Investor Protection Association, the Investor Protection Program of the National Association of the Professional Participants of the Securities Market, the Institute for Corporate Law and Governance, etc.

However, the management of most of the Russian companies still had an upper hand in the disputes, as compared to the minority shareholders. The situation with Yukos, which in 1998 became subject to 'greenmail' by notorious US investor Kenneth Dart, is a good illustration for the point. Having a minority stake in the company and being aware of the upcoming acquisition by Yukos of its several subsidiaries, Dart decided to block the management decision and negotiate with Yukos management to sell his shares in the companies at extremely high prices. However, the management took a decision to conduct an additional issue of shares of subsidiaries, thus diluting Dart's stake and depriving him of the blocking right. On the one hand, the situation could be regarded as shareholder rights violation; on the other hand, it could be viewed as clearly obstructing the introduction of corporate governance principles, namely the transition to single shares that Yukos was to undertake. The conflict lasted for almost two years and despite a controversial public attitude and the clearly negative effect on the company's image, the decision was never revoked.

Several new laws were adopted during 1997–2001, mainly focusing on information disclosure, shareholders rights' protection, specifics of the management bodies (Board of Directors, Revision Commission, and Management Board), and improvement of auditing and accounting standards. The New Tax Code with lower tax rates and mechanisms of prevention of minority shareholders' rights violations was adopted. A new bankruptcy law and the new Code of Arbitration Procedures, for instance, had clauses protecting the rights of majority shareholders, which, paradoxically, have also been an issue in Russia; with improved legislation it became more difficult to initiate and conduct hostile takeovers via bankruptcy and share seizure.

Greater government involvement was observed: functions of the Federal Commission on Securities Market (FSCM) were expanded; a Co-ordination Council for Corporate Governance was set up within it in 2000. Later, in 2003, the National Council for Corporate Governance (NSKU) was established at the initiative of the Russian Union of Industrialists and Entrepreneurs (RSPP), Chamber of Commerce and Industry (CCI), and the FSCM. The council includes leading businessmen and representatives of government and other agencies.

In 2001, the Federal Commission for Securities Markets started to work on Russia's first Corporate Governance Code, which was introduced in April 2002. The Code does not have a status of a law; it is rather a set of recommendations describing 'best practices' of corporate governance. In 2001–2002, several large Russian companies (Gazprom, RAO UES, Yukos, Sberbank, and Magnitogorsk Iron & Steel) developed proprietary corporate governance codes. According to 2003 research by International Finance Corporation, 20 per cent of the large Russian companies have a Corporate Governance Code or are in the process of approving one; 30 per cent began to draft the Code, and 35 per cent are planning to have one in the future.

Summarizing the main stages of corporate governance development in Russian companies, it can be said that the initial step was enabling the management to exercise control, have information on the cost and income structure and carry out uniform policy towards all the parts of the holdings. The second step was to carry out transition of all the companies of the group to a single share, a lengthy and cumbersome process involving radical changes in legal and property structure. After, and sometimes in parallel with, the process, delegation of powers from owners to professional managers started to take place, even though almost all the managers previously had had some relationship with the owners and could not be considered 'hired managers' in the strict sense of the term. With the delegation of powers, transition to modern standards of corporate governance started, with more transparency in reporting on companies' activities, Western standards are steadily being adopted and in-house corporate codes are being developed. Some companies, eg Yukos, have created extra incentives for top and middle management, such as a system of options similar to that used in the US. Many large companies, such as Lukoil and INTERROS, have incorporated the principle of accountability and social responsibility in their corporate strategies.

In a nutshell, the period of 1997–2003 saw some tangible improvements in the corporate governance practices of the Russian companies. The specific areas where the changes occurred were in the composition of the Board of Directors (greater shareholders' empowerment took place with an increased number of minority shareholders and independent directors on the Boards of Directors); dividend policy (dividends have increased, clear-cut schemes of their payment were developed); information disclosure (international and US accounting standards started to be adopted in many large companies, at the same time patterns of constant communication with shareholders and analysts were developed and maintained); investor advocacy groups (several cases of successful recourse under the law were observed).

However, the challenges still remain, among them weak law enforcement mechanisms with corruption and illegal means of disputes resolution still widely used, and lack of transparency and accountability, especially in the large government-owned enterprises. Some companies prefer to conceal the real results of their financial performance so as not to attract extra attention on the part of the state authorities, especially in the light of recent events concerning large industrialists. Therefore, minority shareholders non-affiliated with the management often do not receive 'real' information on the company's operations.

The taxation system in Russia still leaves much to be desired from the corporate viewpoint: eg dominant owners still consider dividends a waste of money in a way, due to the additional tax payments. Administrative barriers, too, remain a very effective method of afflicting companies, with no real market for land, estate and communal services established yet.

Despite the fact that many large Russian companies have made steps towards improved corporate governance practices or at least have claimed to do so, numerous cases of discrepancies between the norms of the corporate governance codes and companies' bylaws and their practical application still exist. For instance, distortions in the composition of management bodies are in place, with no truly independent directors present on most of the boards.

Ownership concentration is still very high, with the State remaining the largest shareholder, and there is still a lack of large institutional and strategic investors, especially foreign. The risks associated with the unpredictable political situation, especially in terms of the relationship between the State and large businesses, well illustrated by the Yukos case, create disincentives for large overseas investors, which impedes Russia's further integration into the world economy.

In general, Russian business has two possible routes to globalization. The first is simply utilizing Russia's natural advantages and exporting raw materials and agricultural produce; it certainly requires less time and effort on the companies' part. The second implies a step-by-step integration of the country into the global economy in every aspect, including corporate culture, and, despite being laborious and time-consuming, in the long term appears more productive and welfare-creating. Therefore, adherence to best practice in corporate governance by Russian companies can be viewed as one of the powerful instruments for Russian integration into the world economy.

Part Three
Market Potential

argus media

Argus FSU Energy is a market-leading weekly newsletter on the oil and gas industries in the former Soviet Union, and central and eastern Europe. It provides timely news of the latest regional developments as well as analysis of political and economic events.

Argus Nefte Transport is a monthly newsletter focusing on crude and product transportation from and within the former Soviet Union. It is an invaluable guide to understanding how FSU oil gets to market, providing vital intelligence and data about the ever-changing sector.

Every day the industry faces new challenges and issues. Every issue of Argus FSU Energy and Argus Nefte Transport steps back to analyse these changes, explain what they mean and why you should be paying attention to them. You can see for yourself how vital this information is to you and your business by applying for a free trial. Simply fill out the form below and fax back to us on +44 20 7359 6661

apply for a free trial now!

please complete these details to receive your free trial:

Name: ....
Position: ....
Company: ....
Address: ....
....

Tel: ....
Fax: ....
E-mail: ....

☐ Nefte Transport   ☐ FSU Energy

if you have any questions please contact us on
+44 20 7704 4770.
FAX THIS FORM TO +44 20 7359 6661
or e-mail us at marketing@argusmediagroup.com

code: DBR04

www.argusonline.com

3.1

Russian Oil and Gas

Bill Page and Mark Redhead, Deloitte

Russia continues to provide both domestic and foreign investors with tremendous opportunities in the oil and gas sector. The drive to replace reserves and to seek alternatives to Middle East crude, coupled with the burgeoning markets of China and South East Asia, continue to make Russia, with its vast reserves of oil and gas, a magnet for the oil and gas industry, as illustrated by BP's decision to form its joint venture with TNK, formally launched on 1 September 2003. The events of the past 12 months have, however, reminded us that with these opportunities comes risk. The Yukos affair has highlighted the political risks of doing business in Russia, whilst the continuing delay in developing new export routes poses a threat to planned production growth.

As of 1 January 2004, market indicators were highly encouraging: crude production rose 11 per cent in 2003, and the reserve replacement was around 85 per cent for oil, with new gas finds almost twice the level of production.[1] This was attributable to a general recovery from the endemic slump that gripped the sector in the 1990s (production growth of 38 per cent over the past five years), aided by consistently high crude prices, benefits from rouble devaluation, relative political stability and the application of new technology. On the other hand, production is still significantly less than during the late 1980s. Also, the temporary cessation of Iraqi supplies had opened up new markets in the Mediterranean. However, the gap between domestic prices and export ones evidenced a structurally oversupplied market with export supply bottlenecks and administrative barriers on export trade. Transneft, the state-owned pipeline operator, is to be commended for managing to accommodate around 2 million barrels per day (bpd) production growth between 1999 and 2002; however prices rose accordingly, with per-barrel transportation costs for major Russian oils averaging around $7 per barrel in 2003. Bottlenecking was also evidenced by the amount of crude being transported by train and river (around 4.5

---

[1] All figures from Renaissance Capital's *Russia Oil and Gas Yearbook*, 18 July 2003.

million bpd in 2003), although this costs around three times as much as pipeline freight. A table of the 2003 results of the biggest six companies in production terms is provided in Table 3.1.1.

Table 3.1.1 Oil production in 2002–2003, in thousands of barrels per day

Company	Jan-Dec 2002	Jan-Dec 2003	% Increase year-on-year
Yukos	1,398	1,615	15.5
LUKoil	1,510	1,578	4.5
Surgutneftegaz	984	1,081	9.8
TNK	750	859	14.6
Sibneft	527	628	19.2
Tatneft	492	493	0.2

Source: Aton Capital, company data

Figures remained encouraging on the face of things as of 1 July 2004: crude production rose 10.5 per cent year-on-year in the first half of 2004, with exports (via Transneft) up 22 per cent.

Although the situation may appear promising, with analysis suggesting 7.4 per cent growth in 2004 overall,[2] concerns have been expressed about several issues threatening the prosperity of the sector as a whole. Two of the reasons previously given for Russia's good performance: the devalued rouble and political stability, are now questionable. The picture is also darkened by uncertainties about the transport infrastructure and recent changes to the tax legislation. However, on the positive side, oil prices look set to remain strong with predicted benchmark Brent prices of around $25.50 per barrel predicted for 2004,[3] and some analysts predicting that prices could even touch $50 per barrel on the back of recent record highs. One indicator of the current strength of the sector is the westward movement of Russian oil majors to operation in North America. In January 2004 LUKoil purchased 795 gas stations from ConocoPhillips, doubling its market share in the US Northeast,[4] and in-country investment in fixed assets is also on the rise, up 13 per cent year-on-year in the first half of 2004.

However, high oil prices, combined with the dependency of the exchange value of the rouble on these prices, could be drawing the sector into something of a vicious circle. The problem is that many of

---

[2] Aton Capital's *Russian Oil and Gas Outlook 2004*, 20 January 2004.
[3] Aton Capital's *Russian Oil and Gas Outlook 2004*, 20 January 2004.
[4] See 'LUKoil Doubles Share of Stations in US', *Moscow Times*, 28 January 2004.

the oil majors' revenues are measured in dollars, with a high proportion of costs measured in roubles, therefore any rise in prices would cause a strengthening of the rouble and corresponding undermining of profitability. Conversely, a fall in prices would mean lower revenues, without the converse benefit from a falling rouble, as it is believed that the rouble would remain strong even at oil prices below $25 per barrel.[5] Some companies are more at risk from a strong rouble than others, with Yukos, Surgutneftegaz and Tatneft particularly vulnerable.[6]

The arrest of Yukos CEO Mikhail Khodorkovsky in October 2003, following the arrest earlier in the year of his associate Platon Lebedev and seizure of a 42.1 per cent stake in the company, set alarm bells ringing amongst investors, with the question being raised of whether property rights were under threat. Russia's equity risk premium rose by 54 basis points to 5.8 per cent in July 2003 alone.[7] When it became clear that the bailiffs were moving in on Yuganskneftegaz, one of Yukos's major subsidiaries, the stock exchange fell from 606 to 518 points in the space of eight days. On reflection it is clear that this was a matter uniquely concerning Khodorkovsky and his associates and his political aspirations; after all, had the Kremlin wished to attack other oil companies a pretext to do so could easily have been found. However, the broadly discussed intention of the Government to sell Yuganskneftegaz (Yukos's main production entity) poses a vital question as to whether the biggest Russian oil producing company may become bankrupt as a result of a tax offence. Recently Yukos was presented with a tax bills for the year 2000 to the amount of $3.4 billion, and this debt may grow as a result of further tax inspection.

Doubt also surrounds the pipeline system. Investment has been made in recent years (in 2000–2003, 23 new pumping stations and 1,030 km of new pipelines were put into operation), and the de-bottlenecking process is ongoing, with the elimination of problems in Novorossiysk for example. However, Transneft has simply been unable to keep up with sector growth, as is shown by the fact that in January 2004, with production hitting a post-Soviet high of 8.94 million bpd, exports actually fell five per cent. Inclement weather at the Black Sea ports was blamed, raising fears of a domestic glut.[8] This underlined the fact that transportation could act as a brake on future growth. Future expansion plans are outlined in Figure 3.1.1.

It is estimated that the pipeline/combined ratio (that between pipeline transport and rail/river freight) can only be changed through major

---

[5] Aton Capital's *Russian Oil and Gas Outlook 2004*, 20 January 2004.
[6] Ibid.
[7] Renaissance Capital, *Russian Oil and Gas: Gauging Risk*, 21 July 2003.
[8] See 'January Oil Output at Post-Soviet High', *Moscow Times*, 3 February 2004.

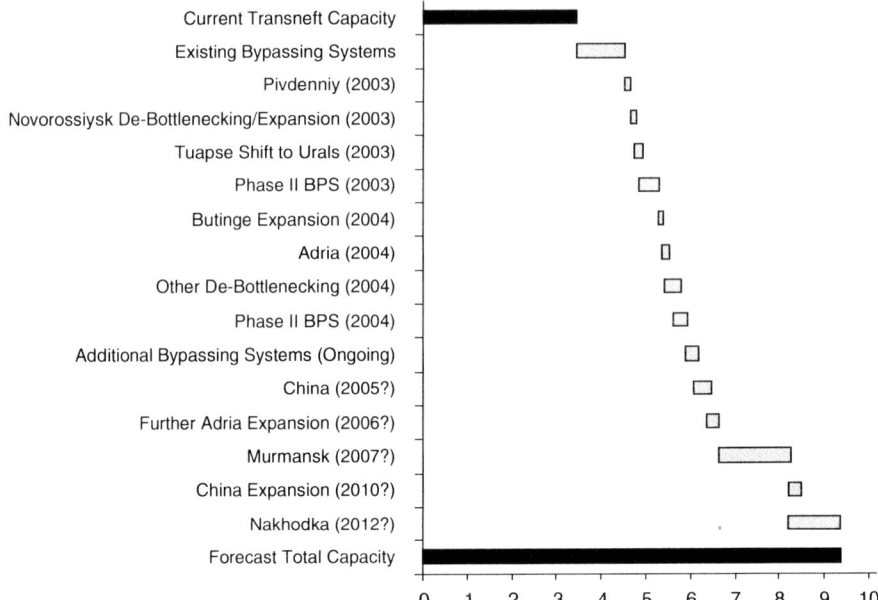

The 'Additional Bypassing Systems' caption overlooks Sakhalin projects, where we estimate crude production could approach 25 mtpa by the end of the decade. As offshore projects, these will not rely on core shared transportation infrastructure to reach export markets.

Source: Transneft, Ministry of Energy, Petroleum Argus FSU Energy, Nefte Compass, CERA, Renaissance Capital

Figure 3.1.1 Forecast expansion of non-CIS crude export capacity (million bpd)

projects such as the proposed pipeline from Western Siberia to Murmansk, from Siberia to Nakhodka (near Vladivostok) or to China (which of the two proposed Eastern routes will be constructed remains to be seen). As evidence of this, in January 2004 Yukos made a deal with Russian railways for transportation of 12,000 tons per day of crude to China, pending future potential pipeline construction which will do away with the need for rail freight.[9] To complicate matters, the railway system is also nearing capacity on some lines (eg along the Trans-Siberian). Transportation problems will hurt those companies with the highest rates of growth (ie Yukos, Sibneft, TNK-BP) the hardest, as infrastructure will be unable to keep up with their planned production increases.

Another question mark regarding the future concerns a forthcoming update of the tax legislation. The current regime dates from 2001, and is somewhat regressive in nature. It has not, however, successfully captured the economic rent generated by a period of prolonged high oil

---

[9] See 'RZD Rides China Oil Boom, *Moscow Times*, 26 January 2004

prices in the opinion of many observers. President Putin has repeatedly called for increases in taxation of the oil majors, and new legislation looks inevitable, barring an unexpected sudden fall in prices. The Energy Ministry has been pushing for a raise of $6 billion per year, which it claims would bring the Russian regime into line with that of Kazakhstan, Norway, Canada and other oil-producing countries.[10] Starting 1 January 2004 certain changes were made, including increase in mineral extraction tax rate, increase in excise taxes rates and the elimination of tax concessions, which allowed Yukos, Sibneft and others to save an estimated $1–1.5 billion per year. TNK/BP and LUKoil, no doubt with one eye on the Yukos affair, have agreed to co-operate, LUKoil even going so far as to cease voluntarily taking advantage of existing tax concessions.[11] During 2004 the Government continued to increase the tax burden on oil companies by raising export duties on oil and oil products (the rate of oil export duty increased from $41.6 to $69.9 per ton from 1 August 2004). Starting from January 2005, the rates for all specific oil taxes (mineral extraction tax, excise duties) will be further increased. Considering the continuing high price level it may be concluded that with the global oil prices staying at the level of $33–$37 per barrel, around 40–45 per cent of export revenues received by Russian oil companies will be collected through these specific taxes.

Over the past couple of years it has become clear that Production Sharing Agreements (PSAs), though permitted in law, will only be made available under a very narrow range of circumstances. The creation of a legal framework for PSAs was long sought by foreign oil companies who found the predictable fiscal conditions available under a PSA regime very attractive. Domestic oil companies were less happy with what they saw as unfair concessions to foreigners. The result of this is the restriction of availability of new PSAs to the most complex and difficult projects. ExxonMobil struggled for 10 years to obtain a PSA for the Sakhalin 3 block, only to be disappointed in early 2004, when the government decided not to issue a production licence without an auction.

Three pre-existing PSAs remain in operation, including the ExxonMobil-operated Sakhalin 1 and Shell-operated Sakhalin 2 projects. Taken together, these constitute the majority of foreign investment in Russia, and are two of the largest and most complex oil and gas projects in the world today. The proximity of Sakhalin to Far Eastern markets, particularly Japan, Korea and China, gives them a definite advantage over Siberia as an investment location. Importantly, the fields covered by these two projects include very large amounts of gas, and both consortia are investigating export options,

---

[10] See 'Ministry Wants $6bn Tax Hike', *Moscow Times*, 4 February 2004
[11] See 'Kremlin Mulling Ways to Raise Oil Tax Ratio', *Moscow Times*, 22 January 2004.

with Sakhalin 1 considering a pipeline to Japan, whilst Sakhalin 2 has commenced construction of an LNG plant on the island.

The future of the gas industry in Russia remains closely linked to the gas behemoth, Gazprom. This company controls approximately 94 per cent of Russia's gas production and 25 per cent of the world's gas reserves; it also controls the domestic gas distribution system and export pipelines. Although Gazprom has significant private shareholders, it remains closely linked to the State. Over recent years there has been considerable speculation that Gazprom will be broken up and the gas market liberalized. Recently the government has drawn back from this option. The management team at Gazprom is clearly committed to defending its position, and the political aspects of gas market liberalization (particularly the impact on domestic gas prices) are no doubt on the government's mind.

Russia remains an exciting opportunity for oil and gas investment. The key question is how much excitement investors are prepared to tolerate. It is clear that the government wishes to retain a significant level of control over the sector and this has created friction with investors. Tax concessions are under attack, ExxonMobil has apparently lost Sakhalin 3, Yukos is in the firing line and Gazprom's position is being reinforced, despite talk in the past about reform of the gas sector. Export routes are under pressure and discussion of private investment in expansion of the pipeline network seems to be stalled. On the positive side however, BP has made a major commitment to the sector, which could not have happened without government support. Oil prices remain buoyant and the long-term shift to gas as fuel for power stations underlines the prospects for Russia as home of the largest oil reserves outside the Middle East and the world's largest gas reserves.

3.2

The Business Climate in the Russian Oil and Gas Sector

Keith Rowden, Leader, Energy Industry Services and Igor Lotakov, CFA, Senior Manager, PricewaterhouseCoopers

It's official! Russia is an energy superpower.

During the Soviet era, Russia and the other republics were among the largest energy producers in the world. However, because the Soviet energy sector was off-limits to outsiders and due to Cold War animosities, the country's accomplishments in the energy sphere were not duly recognized on the world stage.

After the collapse of the Soviet Union, Russia's production of oil, and to a lesser extent of gas, fell so sharply that Russian energy exports, of oil at least, ceased to be a factor in world markets. While leading Western energy companies recognized Russia's tremendous reserves of natural resources, it was generally believed that a thicket of political, bureaucratic and infrastructure hurdles combined to make the development of Russia's oil and gas resources uneconomic. In fact, views of Russia's potential were so negative that during the early to mid-1990s almost all global growth in energy production and demand simply bypassed Russia – as if the country didn't even exist on the energy map.

But, as is almost always the case in the energy industry, the forecasters turned out to be wrong. The Russian energy industry has transformed itself into one of the most important sources of oil and gas in the world. Asia, Europe and North America are now all knocking on Russia's door seeking partnership and energy security through Russian oil and gas resources. Many Western companies are operating in Russia, or are seriously considering investing in Russia so as to get a jump on the competition.

What has driven Russia's energy renaissance and what is needed to keep it going?

While most Western energy majors (with a few notable exceptions) were ignoring Russia in the early to mid-1990s, a number of home-grown Russian entrepreneurs saw an opportunity and jumped to take advantage of it. The resulting privatization of much of Russia's oil industry, while controversial, effectively laid the foundations for most of Russia's future oil majors. Several of these companies quickly enlisted Western service firms to help them manoeuvre the technological learning curve, and, as a result, Russia's oil production began to grow at an impressive rate.

Led by companies such as Yukos, Sibneft and TNK (now TNK-BP), Russian oil production grew from 6.17 million barrels per day (bpd) in 1998 to 8.54 million bpd in 2003, representing an average annual growth rate of 6.7 per cent (and 10.9 per cent growth at the 2002 production level of 7.70 million bpd!).

At the same time, oil exports grew by an average annual rate of 10.5 per cent to reach 4.56 million bpd in 2003 from 2.51 million bpd in 1998, and jumped by 20.6 per cent with the 2002 export volume of 3.78 million bpd.

According to data from the RF Ministry of Energy, the first six months 2004 saw a 10.3 per cent year-on-year increase in crude production (223 million tons), which supports the generally anticipated production growth rate of 8 per cent to 9 per cent for 2004 as a whole.

Thus, as far as the world oil market is concerned, Russia with its current production of 8.96 million bpd has clearly become a key global player and a leading competitor for the OPEC countries (see Figure 3.2.1).

In contrast to Russia's petroleum sector, the gas industry has not undergone any large-scale privatization. State-controlled Gazprom enjoys a monopoly in gas transportation and exports and holds licences to the lion's share of Russia's gas reserves. Nonetheless, Gazprom and Russia play a central role in the current energy picture within Europe and promise to be key players in meeting the growing demand for natural gas in Asian countries, primarily China, where annual consumption is expected to reach 70 billion cubic meters (bcm) by the end of this decade and whose own production will then cover only about 80 per cent of increased consumption levels.

In terms of reserves and production, Gazprom is the largest hydrocarbons company in the world with 28.8 trillion cubic meters (tcm) of proven and probable reserves. Gazprom also supplies Europe with nearly 30 per cent of its natural gas needs.

Even as the more dynamic oil industry increased its production at such incredible rates, Gazprom has not been sitting idle. The gas giant increased non-FSU exports from 96.5 bcm in 1990 to 133 bcm in 2003, representing an average annual growth rate of 2.3 per cent.

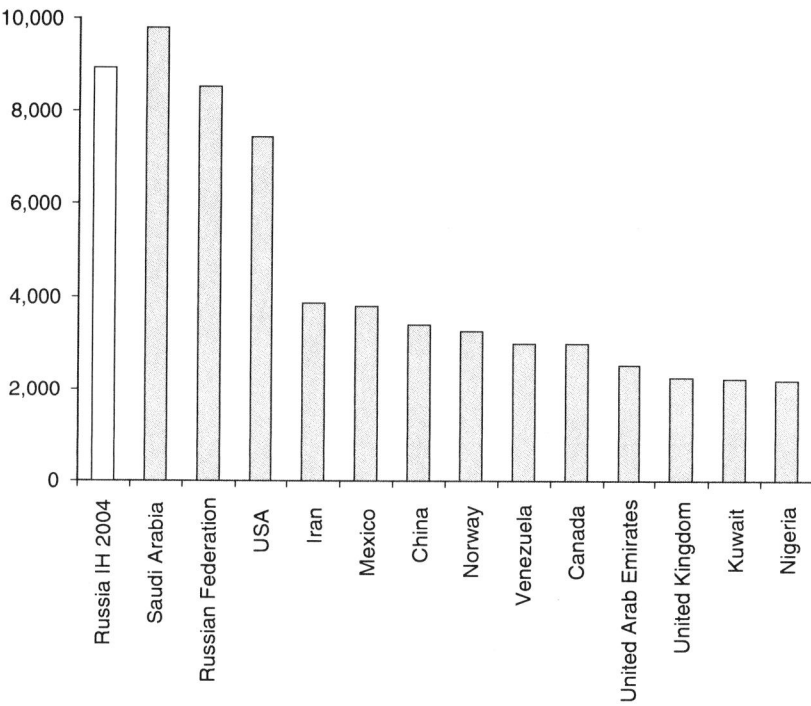

Source: BP Statistical Overview of World Energy, the RF State Statistics Service
Figure 3.2.1 Top global crude producers (2003), million bpd

Russian energy supply side: what to expect

However, the biggest question currently on the minds of investors and analysts is: can the impressive growth of Russia's oil industry be sustained?

There is a consensus among energy industry experts that, from the standpoint of adequate hydrocarbon reserves and technical capabilities, the answer is a resounding yes. But huge capital investment will be needed. The Russian government itself projects that the country's energy industry will require approximately $240 billion worth of investments by the year 2020. Meanwhile, estimates of overall investment in the global energy industry over this period reach as high as $16 trillion. Naturally, given such levels of capital investment, companies will go to those areas of the world where they believe they can earn the highest return on investment.

For Russian companies to compete for capital and for Western companies to invest at the levels needed to continue the remarkable growth of Russian hydrocarbon production, several factors must be considered to encourage continued domestic and foreign investment in the sector. Likewise, new investors in the Russian market would be well advised to have a complete understanding of the potential impact of these issues on their current business plans. Several of these key issues are outlined below.

Transport infrastructure

The impressive recent growth rates of crude production, which it is believed will level off at a long-term sustainable rate of 4 per cent after 2008, should help Russia to cross the pivotal 10 million bpd production threshold within two-to-three years and go well beyond that by the end of the decade.

One of the largest looming threats to continued production growth is represented by potential export restraints caused by capacity bottlenecks in the export infrastructure. The infrastructure of Russian crude exports is based primarily on oil pipeline monopoly Transneft's high-capacity crude pipeline system, which accounts for 79 per cent of current Russian crude exports. Transneft's system is the world's largest, spanning 11 time zones with 48,900 km of pipeline and two world-class ports – at Novorossiysk on the Black Sea and Primorsk on the Baltic Sea.

While Transneft boosted its export capacity from 3.28 million bpd in 2002 up to 3.48 million bpd in 2003 and expects to achieve another 4 per cent increase in 2004, the output of Russia's oil companies has grown at a faster rate, thus forcing the industry to rely on Russia's railroads as an alternative. The Russian railway system (RZD), which now accounts for 17 per cent of current oil export capacity, is also becoming prone to bottlenecks and, in any case, while economically viable at the current level of oil prices, does not offer a cost effective long-term alternative to pipeline transport.

The solution to today's clogged oil transport system would come in two parts and would allow Russia to maintain sustainable production of over 10 million bpd. The first part would entail building a pipeline to the northern ice-free port of Murmansk as well as increasing pipeline capacity to Baltic Sea export terminals, which would minimize reliance on problematic shipping routes that go through Turkey's crowded Bosporus Straits. The second component envisages the construction of a pipeline to China or, alternatively, to the port of Nakhodka on Russia's Far Eastern coast.

The Murmansk pipeline would be 2,500–3,600 km long and cost an estimated $3.4 billion to $4.5 billion to build. One of the major advantages of the Murmansk route is that it would allow for oil shipments to ports on the East Coast of the United States, a journey of only 9,300 km as compared to 20,600 km on average from the Persian Gulf.

While both of these proposed alternative routes have been vigorously championed by the private sector, for their part the Russian government and Transneft have insisted on maintaining state control over crude oil transportation and export quantities and, thus, want any and all future pipeline projects to be carried out and owned by Transneft. This includes determining when, and how, capacity will be increased.

However, there is more to the current infrastructure constraints than merely limiting export growth. The limited pipeline export capacity has resulted in a system of quota allocations for each oil producing company based on its share of total production. In turn, this creates an artificial stimulus to increase production in order to gain a larger share of export quotas and encourages companies to continue to own and operate marginal wells because they need the production to maintain quotas.

Simply put, the government must put politics aside and move quickly to adopt and implement solutions to the looming capacity crisis.

There are obviously many other factors that will affect growth prospects, including the sustainability of high oil prices to finance necessary construction, or the necessity for sufficient future growth in global oil demand that can accommodate Russian production growth and keep OPEC from attempting to prevent Russia from enjoying its fair share of the world energy market.

On the gas side of the equation, Gazprom controls access to transportation and, thus, opportunities for oil companies and emerging independent gas companies to tap into the Unified Gas Transmission System (UGS) are restricted. In addition to the gas monopoly's vast reserves, Russian oil companies also have gas reserves estimated at 19.2 tcm, the development of which is currently stalled in part because of low domestic gas prices and the aforementioned lack of access to the UGS. Russia's goal is to significantly increase its gas exports to Europe (and possibly to the United States). In order to achieve this objective, the domestic market will need such currently untapped gas reserves as well as significant investment by oil companies and emerging independent gas companies. In turn, these companies must be given access to the UGS as well as opportunities to construct their own pipelines.

Tax regime

A fair and predictable tax regime is a fundamental requirement for a healthy investment climate. Russia has made great strides in lowering the tax burden on business in general and the energy industry in particular. But, this situation is likely to change. It has been widely reported recently that the Russian government believes that energy companies do not pay their fair share of taxes relative to their net income.

A key element of the current tax regime is that the unified production tax is effectively a regressive tax, as it is based on export prices. Since domestic oil prices are typically lower than export prices and, in part due to the infrastructure issues noted above, do not always move in tandem with world prices, the tax burden is greater on domestic oil. This makes it difficult for non-integrated producers to make an adequate return and is stifling the development of 'independent' oil companies.

If the government decides to tinker with the tax regime in order to increase taxes on the industry, it should also move to eliminate the disproportionate burden of the unified production tax on non-integrated small producers so as to stimulate the development and growth of small oil companies.

Whatever shape the tax regime eventually takes, it should be fair and predictable so that investors can make long-term decisions and have confidence that tax disputes will be resolved in an impartial manner. Obviously, a sound legal system is an inherent component of a fair and predictable tax system. While it certainly appears that businesses will be paying more tax, they must be able to remain confident that tax disputes, or any legal dispute, can be resolved in a fair and transparent manner.

Licensing regime

As is the case in most countries, the Russian Federation retains ownership of all mineral resources. Oil and gas companies gain rights to exploit hydrocarbon reserves by being awarded licences by the State through a competitive tender process or by acquiring an interest in a company that already holds a licence.

Russia's current licensing regime has been in place since the fall of the Soviet Union and has remained fairly stable. However, licences can feature numerous administrative and detailed minor technical requirements that make ongoing compliance with licence terms difficult. The RF Ministry of Natural Resources, which is responsible for administering licences, has consistently demonstrated a willingness to work with licence-holders in amending licences so that companies can continue to hold a licence. But, this process is overly bureaucratic and costly and also exposes companies to the vagaries of politics or bureaucratic meddling.

Likewise, transferring a licence is a difficult process and can take from 18 months up to two years to accomplish, if at all. As a result, it is difficult for large companies to dispose of non-core properties and for new companies to enter the market or grow through acquisition.

Finally, although licence terms require preparation of and adherence to a development plan that covers the life of the given field, essentially all existing licences are for terms of no more than 25 years. Since most Russian oil and gas fields have reserve lives substantially greater than 25 years, energy companies face the risk, albeit small, that licences may not be renewed. As the end of a licence term approaches, this uncertainty could impact investment decisions or impair proper field exploitation.

Streamlining the licence regime by making tenders more transparent, reducing the bureaucracy involved in maintaining a licence, making licence transfers easier and extending all licences to the life of the given field would help to reduce costs for large companies and attract smaller entrepreneurial companies into the industry. In markets like the United States, Canada and the North Sea, historical experience has shown that smaller companies were able efficiently to grow production and reserves in areas where large companies could not. Thus, a growing number of small companies in the industry could spell significant production growth for Russia.

Environmental regulation

Currently, Russia has few environmental restrictions, thus making it easier to do business here than in many developed countries. But, Russia has never had comprehensive environmental laws or regulations with the result that oilfields, pipelines and other infrastructure facilities may require costly and substantial environmental clean-up efforts in the future. Existing Russian companies and companies considering investment in the energy sector face the risk that new regulations will come into play requiring large-scale clean-ups, thus saddling current licence-holders or property owners with massive environmental liabilities.

Russia must balance its environmental regulation needs with the abilities of the industry to fund clean-ups and ongoing regulation. Whatever the solution, energy businesses need a clear and fair regulatory framework in order to make proper investment and capital allocation decisions.

Corporate governance

A lack of effective regulation together with a willingness by owners to exploit weaknesses in corporate and securities laws represented a significant barrier to foreign investment in the past. However, improved laws, and increased awareness that good corporate governance can tangibly add value to businesses, have resulted in a marked improvement in corporate governance practices in Russia. However, more needs to be done to insure the free flow of capital necessary to maintain the pace of oil and gas resource development.

At a minimum, securities regulation should require that public companies report at least bi-annually on a group basis and that those companies have a truly independent board of directors. The planned requirement that these companies report under International Financial Reporting Standards (IFRS) should also be accelerated.

Besides the obvious benefits of such regulation, the mandatory adoption of IFRS would likely lead to accelerated development of management systems and reporting processes, resulting in more efficient management, lower costs and increased transparency for stakeholders. This would in turn lead to more investment in the energy sector.

Russia has come a long way and its accomplishments to date should not be diminished. ExxonMobil and its partners have committed an estimated $12 billion to the Sakhalin I project. Royal Dutch Shell and its partners also expect to invest close to $12 billion in Sakhalin II. BP has invested nearly $7 billion in the TNK-BP joint venture. Likewise, Russia's five largest oil majors have been investing around $6 billion in their up-stream operations every year, largely from their own cash flows, and are planning to increase this figure up to $8 billion by 2005. So, clearly these companies believe that the risk reward model is favourable.

But, in order to tap the vast resources yet to be developed and to improve Russia's status as an energy superpower, more capital will likely be needed. Direct investors into Russia and those investing in Russian companies would be wise to gain a full understanding of the issues discussed above and to work constructively with Russian regulators to improve conditions for businesses and all of their stakeholders.

3.3

The Oil and Gas Industry: The Regulatory Environment and Legal Infrastructure

CMS Cameron McKenna

Introduction

Russia's extensive oil and gas reserves have attracted energy companies from all over the world. This chapter describes the most important Russian oil and gas legislation and summarizes a number of its most important provisions.

Russia's oil and gas sector is overseen by the Ministry of Energy of the Russian Federation. Russia's oil sector is dominated by large joint-stock companies created by privatization. Russia initiated a two-step oil privatization process in 1993. The first phase, which involved organizing state-owned enterprises as joint-stock companies, ended in 1994 and resulted in the establishment of several vertically integrated oil companies. The second phase, which has been ongoing since 1995, involves the auctioning off of government shares in these companies.

Legislation

Russian oil and gas legislation is based on the Constitution of the Russian Federation and the following three laws constitute the basic legal framework for oil and gas exploration and production:

- Law On Underground Resources of 21 February 1992 (Sub-soil Law);

- Law On Production Sharing Agreements of 30 December 1995 (PSA Law);
- Law On Gas Supply in the Russian Federation of 31 March 1999.

Russian legislation provides two distinct regimes for oil and gas exploration and production. First, the Sub-soil Law establishes a general licensing and administrative law regime under which federal and local authorities issue, amend and terminate rights granted by licence. Second, the PSA Law establishes a quasi-contractual regime for production sharing agreements (PSAs) between the investor and federal and local government.

The Sub-Soil law

The general principles of the oil and gas legislation are set out in the Sub-soil Law, which establishes the administrative system for the exploration and production of mineral resources and defines the State as the owner of all mineral resources in the earth. The Sub-soil Law also defines the scope of authority of the federal and local governments in the mineral resources sphere. Every 'subject' of the Russian Federation may adopt its own legislation on the use of natural resources within the scope of authority granted to it by the federal legislation and by any agreement defining the scope of authority that may have been entered into by the Federal Government and the government of the 'subject'. There are 89 'subjects' of the Russian Federation including the republics, oblasts and federal cities.

The Sub-soil Law states as a general principle that a licence to use sub-soil resources may be issued to Russian or foreign legal entities. A licence to produce oil will be issued in most cases only after a tender and on the basis of a joint decision of the federal and local authorities. The Ministry of Natural Resources of the Russian Federation and its territorial agencies issue the licences to use sub-soil resources. The issuance of the licence may also be subject to approval by federal mining safety and environmental agencies.

A licence confirms the right of the licence-holder to use sub-soil resources according to the terms and conditions defined in the licence. The terms and conditions stipulated in the licence remain in effect for the period stipulated or for the whole term of validity of the licence. The terms and conditions may be changed only with the consent of the licensee and the authorities which granted the licence, or in certain other cases defined by law.

The basic criteria applied by the relevant authorities when deciding a tender are the scientific and technical level of the proposed programmes for geological study and use of sub-soil, the extent of mineral extraction proposed, the contribution to the social and economic development of the territory, and the effectiveness of the environmental protection measures proposed and national security interests of the Russian Federation. Usually however, the winner of an auction for a sub-soil licence is determined on the basis of the total amount offered to be paid for the right to use that sub-soil block.

All information on forthcoming tenders for sub-soil user rights is published in the Russian national media and local media for the different 'subjects' of the Russian Federation.

The PSA Law

The PSA Law establishes a special regime for production sharing agreements. Russia has had a law on PSAs in place since 1996 but, due to delays in adopting additional legislation, few projects have gone forward on production sharing terms. PSAs according to Russian legislation should be treated as civil law contracts subject to a special statutory regime and entered into between the Russian Federation and an investor or investors.

In general, a PSA is implemented as a result of an open tender conducted by the Russian Federation. The winner of the tender negotiates the terms and conditions of the PSA with the federal government and the relevant local government. The PSA defines the rights and obligations of the investor and the Russian government – for example, the PSA will set out a formula for calculating how the winner of the tender and the Russian government will share the hydrocarbons produced. Production is split into 'cost production' and 'profit production' (though such 'distribution' may be changed in accordance with a PSA). The 'cost production' belongs to the investor to pay off the costs of the project, while 'profit production' is divided between the investor and the Russian government.

The PSA Law does not eliminate the requirement to obtain a licence for the use of mineral resources under the Sub-soil Law, but the government is obliged to issue the licence within 30 days from the date the PSA is signed. The PSA Law prohibits the government from revoking the licence once the PSA is concluded. For a field to be developed on a PSA basis, it must first be approved by a Federal Law, often referred to as a 'List Law'.

Tax

The tax burden is one of the most significant issues for those oil and gas producers in Russia that operate under the Sub-soil Law regime.

Among the numerous taxes that producers are required to pay are excise tax, property tax, tax on production of mineral resources, transportation tax, unified social tax, profit tax, and value added tax. In addition, the Sub-soil Law requires producers to make regular payments for the use of sub-soil as well as one-off payments upon the occurrence of certain events stipulated by the licence, and payments for geological information on sub-soil. A fee is also charged for participation in a tender (auction) and for the issuance of licences.

Producers involved in projects developed on production sharing terms under the PSA Law are also required to pay the following taxes: excise tax, mineral production tax, tax for use of mineral resources, transportation tax, land and environmental taxes, unified social tax, profit tax, value added tax.

The PSA Law provides that parties to the PSA may elect international arbitration for dispute resolution. For the purpose of a PSA the Russian Federation may waive its sovereign immunity.

The PSA Law still contains some disincentives to foreign investment. Each PSA is required to have at least 70 per cent of equipment, materials and technical assets used in the PSA project (measured by cost) produced by Russian companies or by foreign companies carrying on business and registered for tax in Russia. At least 80 per cent of employees must be Russian citizens with foreign employees restricted to the first stages of the project or when no appropriately qualified Russians are available.

The Sakhalin I and Sakhalin II projects, each being developed by consortia that include Western companies, currently operate under PSAs. Those PSAs, however, were signed in 1995 before the PSA Law came into effect. The Sakhalin II project produced its first oil in July 1999.

Gas

Russia's gas sector is dominated by the joint-stock company Gazprom (RAO Gazprom), which is 38 per cent owned by the government of the Russian Federation. RAO Gazprom was established by the decision of the government of the Russian Federation of 17 February 1993. It has a dominant position in the gas production and distribution market owning almost all gas production, transportation and distribution facilities in the territory of the Russian Federation.

Transport issues

The company Transneft has a monopoly over crude oil transportation, while the company Transnefteprodukt transports petroleum products.

Tariffs are generally established by the State. Oil companies and joint ventures are constrained in their ability to export crude oil by two factors:

- there is only limited capacity in Russia's oil pipeline system for transporting oil to points outside Russia;
- the Russian government limits exports to ensure domestic supplies.

For a variety of reasons, the price of crude oil is significantly lower in Russia than abroad, which makes it unprofitable to sell oil domestically.

3.4

Investing in a Reforming Electric Utilities Industry

Alexander Chmel, Partner and Vyacheslav Solomin, Senior Manager, PricewaterhouseCoopers

This chapter provides a short overview of the Russian utilities industry and a more detailed analysis of current and anticipated future developments with regard to Unified Energy Systems of Russia (RAO UES Rossii), the all-Russia electric utilities holding company, a Company whose operations are spread over 12 time zones and which employs about 600,000 employees.

Background on the Russian electricity industry

The electricity sector is one of the last branches of the Russian economy that has yet to change significantly the administrative methods it inherited from the Soviet era. In addition, virtually all of the major present-day power stations and electricity grids were inherited from the Soviet period. It is clear that this historic system has limited flexibility and significant structural problems. Today everyone in Russia who consumes electricity and heat, effectively benefits from the investments made under the Soviet Union, but change is essential as this is no longer a tenable situation.

The current structure of the electricity sector includes:

- RAO UES Group, a 53 per cent state-controlled holding company, which controls and operates the power system in Russia. The company controls 73 vertically integrated regional energy utilities (known as 'Energos'); 23 stand-alone thermal power plants (TPPs); 8 hydro-generation plants (HGPs); and a huge network of high-voltage transmission grids. The RAO UES Group's generation facilities boast a total installed capacity of over 155 GW, which represents approximately three-quarters of the country's total installed capacity. The RAO UES Group also controls over 96 per cent (in length) of the electrical grids in the country;

- Rosenergoatom, a state-owned holding company controlling all 10 of Russia's nuclear power plants (NPPs), which have a combined installed capacity of approximately 22 GW;
- independent producers (Irkutskenergo, Tatenergo, Bashkirenergo, Novosibirskenergo), which have a combined installed capacity exceeding 27 GW;
- other producers, including generation facilities owned by enterprises in other industries (eg oil and gas producers).

As illustrated above, RAO UES Group is effectively a monopoly in the area of energy supply, which additionally operates and co-ordinates the power system in Russia. Consequently, the future strategy for the reform of RAO UES is a hugely important issue for the development of the national economy.

The main areas of the RAO UES Group's business activities are:

- electricity and heat production, transmission and distribution;
- management of the Unified Energy System of Russia (UES of Russia), organization of UES of Russia operations, provision of services for the Federal Wholesale Market of Electricity and Capacity (FOREM);
- operational dispatch management of the technological process of power generation and supply;
- technical monitoring of the condition of UES of Russia power plants and power grid facilities;
- construction and commissioning of power industry projects, as well as analysis and forecasting of changes in power supply and demand.

RAO UES Group controls, via its wholly-owned subsidiary, CDR-FOREM, the FOREM, where all the participants sell and buy centrally prescribed volumes of energy based on government-regulated tariffs.

Through another wholly-owned subsidiary (CDU-System Operator), the RAO UES Group exercises operational dispatch management of the technological process of power generation and supply by all FOREM participants.

RAO UES Group also owns, through its 100 per cent subsidiary Federal Grid Company (FGC), a system of high-voltage transmission grids, which extends to almost all parts of Russia and connects all regions of the country, with the exception of certain remote areas in Siberia and Russia's far east.

Energos, regional utility companies, with exception of a few, are subsidiaries of RAO UES Group. Energos are currently vertically-integrated companies that produce, distribute and sell electricity and heat to industrial and residential customers using cost-based tariffs approved by local governments. Energos can sell any excess energy they produce through FOREM to either other Energos or other participants or, similarly, replenish any deficit of energy by acquiring energy from TPPs, NPPs and HGPs. Although controlled by RAO UES, most Energos have significant minority shareholders.

Change imminent

It is commonly recognized that the current structure of the Russian electricity sector does not meet the needs of any of its principal participants:

- Energos complain that regional authorities and their energy commissions are setting artificially low tariffs for retail customers, for populist reasons, at the expense of industrial consumers (so called cross-subsidies) and that current tariffs are insufficient to allow Energos to maintain the system in a working state or deliver a return on equity.

- Regional authorities blame Energos for overstating costs in coming to their cost-plus tariffs (and resisting any reduction in their costs) and for discontinuing energy supply to slow-paying customers, especially ones that are financed by the government.

- Industrial and retail consumers complain that they have to pay high prices for energy, but a safe and stable supply is still not guaranteed.

Electricity pricing is clearly affected by political and human factors in Russia. As mentioned above, cross-subsidizing, where the industrial consumers have to, in effect, subsidize power tariffs for residential customers by overpaying for their own electricity, is still a widespread feature of the industry. Such practices, together with inefficient energy consumption by most industries, sometimes makes certain products uncompetitive. Under the existing structures, Energos often lack any motivation to reduce costs and consumers, particularly residential consumers, lack any motivation to conserve energy.

Macroeconomic factors are also involved. Amongst Russia's key short-term objectives is the development of a stable market economy and sustainable economic growth. Given the key role played by the electricity sector in any successful economy, the need to make effective progress in 'liberalizing' the sector in Russia is a major issue. The country inherited a huge invested infrastructure from the Soviet era, but that infrastructure is aging and demand shows strong signs of growth.

In order to solve or mitigate potential regional or national supply problems, the electricity sector needs significant capital investment. Volumes of this investment are such that they are unlikely to be financed by the State. Some private capital is available in Russia and there are also financial institutions and companies in the world that specialize in large investments in the electricity sector. However, for many national and international investors the Russian electricity sector continues to be perceived as being too risky for significant direct investments, not least because of uncertainly over future market structures and because individual Energos often do not meet the minimum investors' requirements of financial and operational transparency.

Reform: Objectives and principles

The problems highlighted above demonstrate the need for structural reforms in the Russian electricity sector. In response to these problems, the State has adopted legislation to conduct reforms in a series of steps. Most fundamentally it is envisaged that monopolistic (energy dispatching and transportation) and competitive (generation and selling) businesses will first be separated and then market conditions introduced to the competitive part of the electricity sector (see Figure 3.4.1).

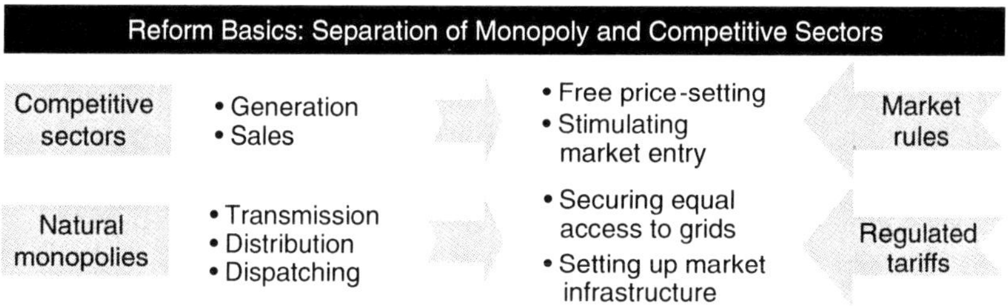

Reform Basics: Separation of Monopoly and Competitive Sectors			
Competitive sectors	• Generation • Sales	• Free price-setting • Stimulating market entry	Market rules
Natural monopolies	• Transmission • Distribution • Dispatching	• Securing equal access to grids • Setting up market infrastructure	Regulated tariffs

Figure 3.4.1 Reform basics

As was mentioned above, all major stakeholders in the electricity sector, including the government, acknowledge that some structural changes are needed in the sector if it is to meet the challenges created by its history and the current economic environment.

The major objectives and steps of the reform programme include:

- Optimizing the industry's structure by:
  - creating a transparent and competitive market place;
  - improving overall economic efficiency of the system;
  - ensuring financial viability of individual market participants;
  - securing affordable end consumer electricity prices.

- Creating an attractive investment profile by:
  - encouraging capital investment into areas where new build is required;
  - raising economic competition and quality through involvement of foreign strategic investors;
  - establishing a clear and effective regulatory framework;
  - enhancing shareholder value;
  - ensuring fair treatment of minority shareholders.
- Address social consequences of reform by:
  - ensuring smooth transition to a deregulated market with minimal price shocks;
  - ensuring reliability of the new system.

Reform will, or is already, affecting all the segments of the RAO UES Group and other elements of the Russian electricity sector. The key features are:

- *Energos* will be divided by line of business (generation, distribution grids, sales), as shown in Figure 3.4.2. After an initial process of unbundling, a second process of interregional integration along lines of business will take place. In effect, the newly separated regional generating and grid companies will merge to form larger, single activity companies.
- *Territorial* (interregional) *generation companies*, formed from the mergers of spun-off generation companies, will then become electricity market participants.
- *Ten wholesale generation companies* will be formed, based on thermal and hydro-generation plants.
- *Inter-system and high-voltage electric grids* will be merged into the Federal Grid Company which, as a natural monopoly, will then be acquired by the state.
- *Dispatching of energy* will be conducted by another state-owned entity, the System Operator.
- *Markets:* The RAO UES Group will still manage the regulated FOREM, while the Administrator of the Trade System (power exchange) will become the forum for all sales, pricing, negotiating and contracting of purchase and sale on the non-regulated sector of the power market; it is envisaged that this market will account for 5–15 per cent of the total volume of energy traded in Russia for the period to 2006.

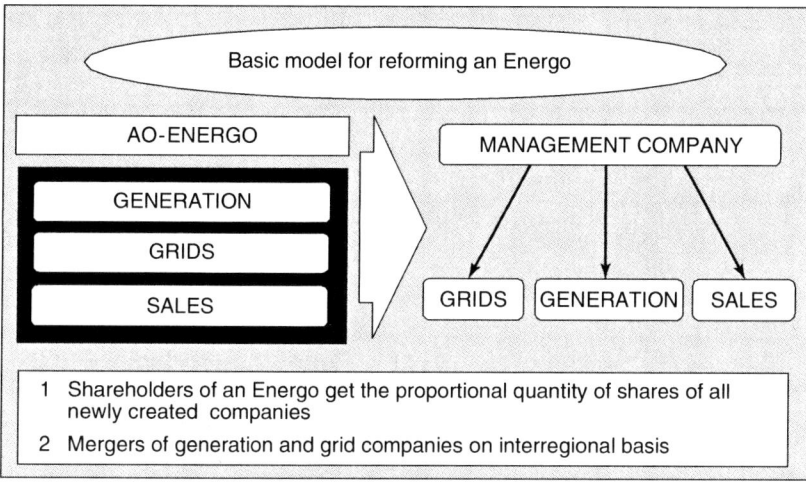

Figure 3.4.2 Regional Energos: Basic model of unbundling

The anticipated timeline of proposed reforms is illustrated in Figure 3.4.3.

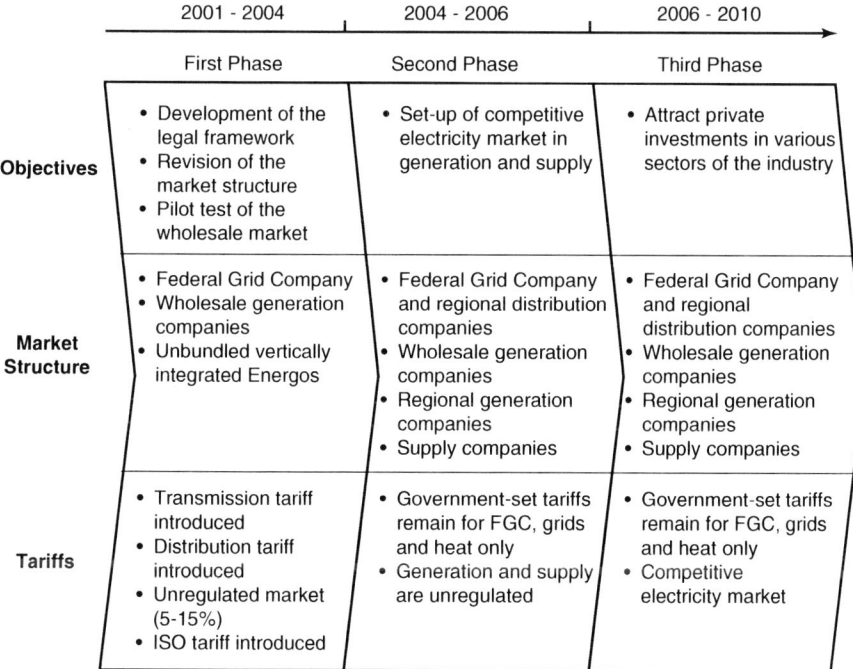

Figure 3.4.3 Anticipated timetable

Although it is clear that separation of competitive and monopoly (regulated) activities is vital for further development of market principles in the electric utilities industry in Russia, there has been considerable debate as to whether the scenario of spinning off various businesses with proportionate shareholding (as adopted by the Russian Government) is the most appropriate or equitable one in the current Russian environment.

Stakeholders

This question of the equity of reform is centered on the various shareholder groups currently invested in the electricity sector in Russia. It is important to remember that there are two levels of shareholders, who openly (or via nominal holding structures) own shares in:

- the parent company, RAO UES Rossii;
- underlying Energos/power plants.

The State, is the main stakeholder and shareholder (about 53 per cent of shares) in the Parent company RAO UES Rossii, and, hence, indirectly, in its subsidiaries.

Other shareholders in either the Parent company and/or the underlying Group entities have changed dramatically over the last 1–2 years. Those who in principle agreed with the government's base scenario of reform, were predominantly portfolio investors; in general these shareholders wished to retain an investment in the electricity sector. Recently such shareholders have tended to be bought out by a cohort of strategic investors who have had quite different interests. In particular, they appear to be less interested in 'fair', proportionate spin-offs. Instead, they appear to wish to obtain control (paying a fair price if needs be) over specific businesses in specific regions.

The first pilot reform project (Tulenergo) was completed in November 2003 and illustrated how an 'unhappy' strategic investor with a blocking stake could, in practice, stop the reform process. This example and the underlying range of 'motives' for shareholders mean that the forthcoming 2004 reforms will be most intriguing. More than 20 major Energos are expected to hold their extraordinary shareholders' meetings during April to October of 2004 to make decisions as to whether they accept the current reform scenario or not. In this context, and with regular changes in government personnel, the future shape and speed of reform remains uncertain.

Investment opportunities in a new industry

One of the justifications of reform being pushed from the top is the perceived need for new investments amounting to many billions of dollars in the industry. New investment opportunities mirror key features of the proposed reforms:

- Separation of competitive and regulated businesses (accompanied by establishment of a separate transmission tariff and real market price for electricity) should result in a higher level of transparency of the industry, which in turn should make it more attractive to investors.

- The new competitive electricity market (appropriately supported by market reforms in natural gas supply and municipal consumption) could make generation businesses attractive for IPP-type investments, which appear vital in light of current very low efficiency and high obsolescence of generation assets in use.

- As the restructuring process is going on, the number of independent entities operating in the industry will increase many times, creating a solid mass of entities ripe for corporate acquisitions, mergers etc. Significant corporate reform is expected to happen in the post-reform period under pressure from strategic investors, whose interests may not be met during the main reform process.

The combination of the above factors should ensure that the electricity sectors role in the stock market becomes more interesting for those who prefer to remain portfolio investors.

Conclusion

As the brief discussion above highlights, the electricity industry is facing major change over the coming few years. The proposals regarding the structure of reform, and indeed experience around the world of similar reform programmes, suggest that reform will bring both significant challenges and opportunities for all participants in the electricity sector in Russia. Given the scale of the industry and its key role in the Russian economy, the prospects look electrifying.

3.5

Russian Energy Sector Policy

Sergey Maslichenko, OTAC Limited

Introduction

Russian Energy Sector Policy envisaged in the Energy Strategy to 2020 (the Strategy) and adopted by the Government on 28 August 2003 has become a hot topic in professional discussions among Western and local economists. The scope of these debates range from the appraisal of the future level of energy savings required to meet optimistic GDP growth forecasts up to revealing the role of lobbies in gas, oil and coal production estimates with a view to obtaining additional financial preferences from the State. In short, a variety of interrelated political, economical, legal and social issues at the micro and macro levels are involved in the analysis of the energy strategy.

This chapter examines the dominant constraints in Russian energy strategy to 2020, and the process of elaborating a feasible energy policy in Russia. It focuses on the policy-oriented investigation of energy balance forecasts, based on the Ministry of Energy's decisions, on expert judgements, and mass media publications in regard to supply and demand for gas, oil, coal, and electricity. This includes an assessment of energy consumption based on estimation of GDP growth and level of energy efficiency that will be achieved to meet energy constraints, and an analysis of the feasibility of market reforms and investment in the sector.

GDP growth

The most important element that determines the general energy strategy and particularly the energy balance forecast is the estimation of the GDP growth rate. As all energy consumption in Russia will depend on the country's economic growth, accurate estimations of

1) growth rates of GDP; and 2) the structure of GDP have to be undertaken in order to plan the energy sector development.

According to the optimistic scenario of the Strategy, Russian GDP will increase from 2000 to 2020 by 3.3 times (2.3 under the moderate scenario). This means that the economy is projected to grow by an annual average of 5.2 per cent during 2000–2005 and 6.6 per cent during 2006–2020 under the optimistic scenario and by about 4.4 per cent per annum under the moderate scenario.

Russia has indeed experience several years of relatively strong GDP growth: 10 per cent in 2000, 5 per cent in 2001, 4.3 per cent in 2002 and 7.3 per cent in 2003, but the Russian economy has remained very dependent on hydrocarbon exports.

In this regard, many analysts suggest that Russia's recent strong economic performance was due to an equally impressive increase in the price of hydrocarbons. Employing the results of a World Bank study, the most plausible estimate implies that 3 per cent of the 7.2 per cent growth in the first half of 2003 was due to the direct and indirect effects of the oil price increase and 4.2 per cent to non-oil factors. In other words, had oil price stayed constant, the growth of Russia's economy in the first half of 2003 would have been only 4.2 per cent.

In addition, the study reveals some interesting facts: since the 1998 crisis, Russia's economy has only grown faster than 5 per cent when the oil price has increased at the same time. This means that, given the way in which Russia's economy is currently organized, growth rates of above 5 per cent will require either an additional increase in the oil price, which in the long term is unlikely, or growth of the economy's productivity, which means that more reforms and more structural changes are needed.

Apart from the estimate of GDP growth to 2020, the structure of industry output needs to be considered in order to forecast the energy demand and supply. A key question that defines future energy consumption is the extent to which economic growth will be independent from hydrocarbons. The only estimate that the Strategy provides is the forecast of the energy sector share of industry output to 2020. It is estimated at 18.7 per cent under the favourable scenario and 19.2 per cent under the optimistic scenario, which is significantly less than the 29.5 per cent of energy sector production in the total industry output in 2000.

Energy efficiency constraints

The Strategy provides some estimations of the size of energy savings to be achieved by 2020. Overall energy efficiency potential in Russia is estimated at 39–47 per cent of current energy consumption, or 360–430 million tce.[1] According to the Strategy, a third of this potential is in the energy sector itself, 35–37 per cent in industry and 25–27 per cent in public services.

From 2000 energy intensity is forecast to decrease by 26–27 per cent to 2010 and 45–55 per cent to 2020. Half of GDP growth will be achieved without energy consumption increases, due to the structural reforms in the economy, 20 per cent of GDP growth will be generated by technological energy efficiency measures and the rest – 30 per cent of GDP growth – will require an energy consumption increase.

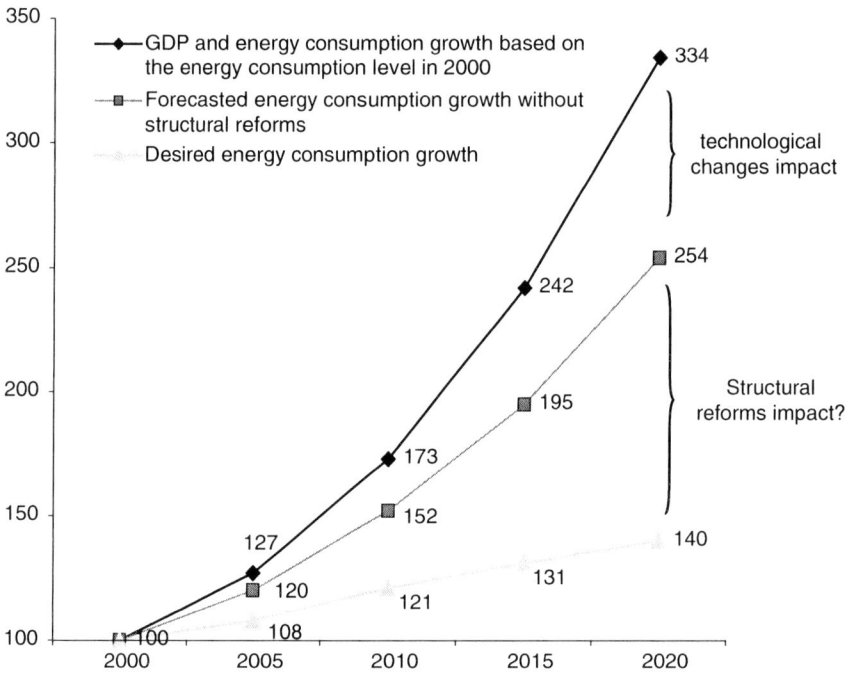

Source: Russian Energy Strategy to 2020

Figure 3.5.1 Forecast GDP and energy consumption growth (%)

Thus, while GDP is supposed to grow – 2.3–3.3 times between 2000 and 2020 – the energy consumption of the Russian economy is forecast to increase only 1.25–1.4 times. Moreover, over 50 per cent of the energy efficiency increase will depend on structural reforms, which are not clarified in the Strategy; neither is there any clear identification of what economic mechanisms (and their relative impact) should be

---

[1] Tce – tonne of coal equivalent – the unit of energy consumption measurement based on the ability of fuel to generate energy, which allows comparison with different types of fuels (gas, oil, coal, etc).

employed to reach the targeted efficiency. The only mechanism that the Strategy provides is the price increase of gas and electricity, with no explanation of its impact on energy efficiency.

In this respect, we think that the relatively high level of forecast energy efficiency that is supposed to be achieved by undertaking significant progress in structural reforms may underestimate energy consumption in Russia. This may cause additional pressure on the energy sector, which would require either additional production of energy or a decrease in energy exports.

Energy balance forecast

In general, the Russian Energy Strategy to 2020 has been written in such a way that energy consumption forecast (demand for energy) has been given much less attention than energy production (supply side) estimates. To some extent, this can be explained by the prevalence of a 'central plan' approach in elaborating the Strategy, which is still prevalent in various Russian ministries. Apart from that, some analysts (eg ISDEI) suggest that the relatively detailed forecast of energy supply, as opposed to energy demand, resulted from 'lobby' pressure on the Ministry of Energy. To this extent, some influential Russian financial-industrial groups (particularly oil companies) were not happy with the future course of structural reforms, which could potentially decrease their share of GDP and reduce their current privileges (tax exemptions, investments, etc). In other words, to retain status quo and perhaps obtain new privileges such business groups envisage expansion of the energy sector in Russia's economy with no accompanying analysis of how such an increase in production could be met by energy demand. This argument is also supported by the significant increase of investment requirements that are claimed by energy companies in order to support forecast growth of the Russian energy sector (see below).

Energy consumption

Given the lack of detailed estimates of future demand for energy in Russia, the Strategy provides only a 'rough' approximation based on the GDP growth forecast and desired level of energy efficiency that might be achieved. Assuming that today's demand for energy in Russia is about 915 million tce and energy consumption will increase by 1.25–1.4 times by 2020, the energy demand is forecast to be 1,145–1,270 million tce.

It is supposed that the gas consumption share of energy demand will drop from 50 per cent to 45–46 per cent by 2020. Oil and oil products will have a 20–22 per cent share, and coal 20–22 per cent. Apart from these aggregate figures, which seem to represent only desired intentions and are not supported by any economic justification, the Strategy doesn't provide any evidence on what sectors will consume energy resources. The general perception is that these figures were inserted in the Strategy without any preliminary forecast of the energy-consuming sectors' development.

Analysis of the dominant energy consumers in Russia based on Goskomstat 'Input-Output' tables ('Sistema tablits 'Zatraty-Vypusk' Rossii za 2000 god') revealed the following conclusions:

- a significant share of primary energy resources (gas, oil, coal) is consumed within the energy sector itself (82 per cent of oil is utilized by the refining industry and 14 per cent by the oil industry itself; 31.6 per cent of gas is consumed by the electricity sector and 11.1 per cent by the gas industry itself, 20.8 per cent of coal demand is used by the electricity sector and 12.2 per cent by the coal sector);

- as a large part of primary energy resources are consumed by the electricity sector, the forecasted development of the whole energy sector will depend heavily on the progress in the electricity sector and on demand for electricity from the electricity consuming industries;

- as electricity was consumed mostly by service sectors (transport, communal services, and social sectors), ferrous and non-ferrous metallurgy, machine building and the chemical industry, the energy consumption forecast will depend on the economic and technological reforms in these branches of industry in particular, which determine the level of their future growth as well as energy efficiency gains;

- the energy efficiency and consumption forecast for the Russian economy will depend, to a great extent, on the administrative and budget reforms that the Russian government has to undertake in the near future in order to increase the energy efficiency of public organizations and communal services companies.

According to the Strategy, higher coal consumption is assumed to substitute for some share of gas consumption. The main reason, according to the Strategy's authors, is to halt the 'gas pause' when cheap gas is inefficiently consumed by the Russian economy, and to employ the large potential of the coal industry instead. This is intended to be achieved by increasing the gas price, which will result in stabilization of the gas/coal price ratio at the level of 1:1 in 2006, 1.4:1 in 2010, and 1.6–2:1 in 2020 (in 2002 the ratio was 0.62:1 in tce).

As the increase in coke production is forecast at significantly lower rates (29 per cent – from 62 million tonnes in 2002 to 75–80 million tonnes in 2020) than production of steam coal (83 per cent – from 191 million tonnes in 2002 to 325–350 million tonnes in 2020), the main consumers who will have to substitute coal for gas are supposed to be the thermal power stations.

The authors of the Strategy believe that the projected increase in gas prices will induce the electricity sector to decrease demand for natural gas in favour of steam coal. Apart from the environmental consequences of such a policy, there is great concern about the feasibility of such a scenario for the electricity sector.

Most experts and executives of RAO UES (the company that owns the majority of thermal power stations in Russia) suggest that despite the desired increase in the gas/coal price ratio (which is itself questionable: RAO UES predicts that the ratio won't exceed 1.29 by 2020 as the coal price will be increasing faster), there are technological, economical and environmental factors constraining the electricity sector's switch from gas to coal:

1. A working group of RAO UES and the Russian Academy of Science created in 1999 investigated 82 thermal power stations and found out that only 28 stations have the potential to be converted to the consumption of coal. To do that, moreover, these stations will require an additional $3.5 billion investment for restoring the coal-consuming technology (including storage facilities for coal and coal waste) and providing ecological safeguards. At the same time, they can economize on gas consumption for about 10 bcm (equivalent to $400 million, at an assumed gas price of $40 per tcm). Even then, this scenario implies conservation of outdated, depreciated and inefficient technology.

2. Whereas 80 per cent of thermal power energy is produced in the European part of Russia, most coal production is located in Siberia. So there will be a 'transportation constraint' upon increased coal consumption in the electricity sector. A significant part of the coal price (49 per cent for Kuznetsk basin coal, and 73 per cent for Kansko-Achinskiy basin coal) is in transport expenditure. Another scenario that suggests the production of electricity in Siberia and its subsequent transportation by power lines to the European part of Russia is also constrained by the relatively small capacity of these lines, which require investment of about $2.8 billion. Apart from that, there is also the problem of the high level of energy waste when transporting electricity over such long distances.

3. A higher gas price could bring efficiency improvements in gas consumption rather than the expansion of coal consumption. There are several options for decreasing gas consumption by installing new gas and steam equipment. Investment in new gas-steam engines (with an efficiency saving of 50–60 per cent) is estimated at

$500 per 1 kW capacity, while technological changes for coal use will cost $600 per 1 kW and investment in new coal engines (with an efficiency saving of 45–46 per cent) is estimated at $1,000 per 1 kW (RAO UES website).

Energy supply

Coal production

According to the Strategy, the main incentive for a rise in coal production is the forecast of a gas/coal price ratio increase. It is estimated that coal supply will increase from 258 million tonnes in 2000 to 430 million tonnes in 2020 (optimistic scenario) or 370 million tonnes (moderate scenario) (see Figure 3.5.2). Given the fact that actual production of coal decreased to 253 million tonnes in 2002, this means that between 2003 and 2020 coal extraction will have to grow by an average 6.5–9.8 million tonnes per annum which, taking into account the recent trends in coal production and the presence of a number of constraints, seems unlikely to be achieved.

While Russia has huge deposits of coal (200 billion tonnes, 12 per cent of the world total), extraction of additional coal is constrained by unfavourable geographic, geological, and economic factors (Strategy, p.60).

The dominant constraint is the extensive physical depreciation (75–85 per cent on average) of the sector's fixed assets and the outdated level of

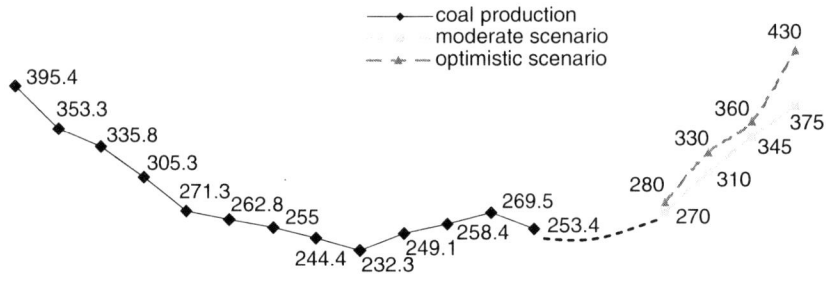

Source: Ministry of Energy statistics, Russian Energy Strategy to 2020

Figure 3.5.2 Coal production in 1990–2002 and its forecast to 2020 (million tonnes)

technology. Taking into account that the level of state support for the industry has declined dramatically and that its own cash flow is quite inadequate (in 2002 balance losses, before taxes, of the coal industry reached 1,439.3 million roubles (about $48 million), it is unlikely that sizeable progress in the renovation of the industry's capacity and in the provision of new efficient technology will occur in the near future.

As a result, with existing low rates of investment in the industry the production of coal is, at best, likely to grow perhaps to 280–290 million tonnes in 2020 (*Russian Coal* magazine) compared with the 370–430 million tonnes suggested by the Strategy.

According to the Head of the Coal Industry Department of the Russian Ministry of Energy, the coal industry needs investment of 15 billion roubles ($500 million) per annum just in order to maintain production of 270 million tonnes per annum – never mind increasing it (*Russian Coal* magazine). For comparison, in 2000 the overall investment in the coal industry was 8 billion roubles, the forecast for 2001 was 13.3 billion roubles.

Oil and oil products supply

According to the Strategy, oil production growth between 2000 and 2010 will be the largest of all the energy sectors – from 324 Mt in 2000 to 445 Mt in 2010 under the moderate scenario and to 490 Mt under the optimistic scenario. Moreover, it will exceed the overall growth rate of Russia's GDP up to 2007–2008, contradicting the Russian Government's intention to diminish the dependence of GDP growth upon exports and energy resources. All these facts raise doubts among many experts in Russia.

Given that internal consumption of oil has been stable for the last six years (about 175–180 million tonnes) and there will be no sizeable increase in consumption during 2000–2020 (according to the Strategy, p.66), it follows that the proposed substantial growth in oil extraction is to be exported.

At the same time, the recent trend in oil exploration and production do not suggest much future increase in oil production. Moreover, the volume of exploration drilling, which, to a great extent, should be the evidence for any future trend in oil production, declined during 2001–2002. According to Ministry of Energy, the volume of production drilling decreased by 16.8 per cent in 2002 compared with 2001 and the volume of exploration drilling dropped by 40.1 per cent.

Apart from that, the depreciation of existing oil wells reached 53 per cent (43 per cent in Western Siberia) ('Russian Strategy on Nuclear Energy Development'), which resulted in a decreasing rate of oil production. At the same time, the productive potential of new oil wells is significantly lower than old ones and the proportion of oil wells with difficult access is about 60 per cent of the industry total and continues to grow.

Gas production

The Strategy forecasts a significant increase in gas production by 2020, from 584 bcm in 2000 to 730 bcm (or 680 bcm under the moderate scenario). There are concerns among energy analysts as to the ability of gas producers to accomplish this task. Since the collapse of the Soviet Union in 1991, investment in the Russian gas industry, particularly in gas extraction, has fallen sharply. A decline has begun at Gazprom's three main fields, which accounted for 78 per cent of production in 2001. The rate at which they will decline in the future is unknown, as is the speed with which new capacity can be developed to replace the old fields. There are two main obstacles. First, because of their arctic location, there will probably be a lag of at least five years between the commencement of a project and the first significant extraction of gas. Second, at present Gazprom is in no condition financially to begin these projects.

Electricity production

The Strategy forecasts a gradual increase in electricity production from 878 billion kW in 2000 to 1,215 billion kW (under the moderate scenario) or to 1,365 billion kW (under the optimistic scenario) in 2020. This is to be achieved by raising thermal energy production (40 per cent), through increased use of coal (see discussion above). In addition, production of nuclear energy is to double.

Investment constraints

The Russian Energy Strategy to 2020 calls for massive investments in the energy sector over the 2003–2020 period (see Table 3.5.1).

Table 3.5.1 Energy sector investment requirements by industry to 2020 ($bn)

Industry	Strategy (2000)	Strategy (2002)	Current Strategy (2003)	% change 2003/2002
Oil	159–197	150	230–240	+53 to +60
Natural Gas	164–171	180	170–200	−5 to +11
Electricity	147–217	130–160	120–170	−8 to +6
Coal	18	20–29	20	0 to −31
Heating	n.a.	n.a.	70	–
Energy Efficiency	n.a.	n.a.	50–70	–
Total	**488–603**	**480–519**	**660–770**	**+38 to +48**

Source: Russian Energy Strategy to 2020 (various versions)

As Table 3.5.1 shows, there have been substantial changes in energy sector investment requirements envisaged in the last version of the Strategy, resulting in a significant increase of both total investment requirements and investments for the majority of energy industries. It is now projected that the Russian energy sector will require $33–38 billion investment per annum between 2001 and 2020, which is double what the Russian energy sector obtained in 2002 (about $16 billion) and half of aggregate investment in the Russian economy in 2002 (about $70 billion). The most dramatic increase in investment requirements is in the oil sector, which needs a third of the total investment in Russia's energy sector ($230–240 billion between 2000 and 2020 or $11–12 billion per annum).

Such optimistic forecasts of investment in Russia's energy sector raises doubts both on the general ability of the Russian economy to attract such investments and on the energy industries' finances. In general, the poor investment climate in Russia will continue to hinder foreign direct investment. The current investment environment is characterized by fiscal, legal and regulatory instability and by a significant lack of transparency.

Besides, given the Russian Government's experience with regulation of the national economy (ie employing direct mechanisms such as tax or custom duty privileges, decrease in rent payments, zero-interest bank credits, budget financing for some projects, etc), some Russian analysts (in particular, ISDEI) suggest that projected investments will have a negative impact on the whole economy by redirecting financial capital from non-energy sectors (with higher value added) to the primary industries.

3.6

The Telecommunications Market

Vyacheslav Masenkov, Deputy General-Director and Alexander Chachava, Senior IT Analyst, RBC

General description of the market

Unlike other industries, the Russian telecommunications market is quite mature, and it keeps on developing. The Russian communications industry has lived up to expectations. There has been a boom in both the cellular telecommunications segment and elsewhere throughout the industry, with major telecom projects now underway. Alternative telecom operators have secured the bigger share of the market, offering their customers advanced technologies. Very soon multimedia, telematics and other services will become something commonplace and will be available through multifunctional smartphones. The main problem, however, is too fast a technological growth that makes returns on recent investment hard to earn quickly. At the same time, while these innovations are intended for residents of large cities, rural areas would probably be happy to settle for a mere three TV channels, to say nothing of MMS.

What was left from the Soviet Union was a telecom network that was much better than in some countries with a similar level of national welfare. What hampers telecoms development in the country are such weak points of the central network as lack of long-distance communication lines, outdated switches (although this problem is now almost solved), and obsolete local networks, which are often in poor condition. Russia is distinct from Europe and most Asian countries, where the industry is dominated throughout by former monopolies, in that its telecom industry is decentralized. This could be said of the USA as well, but that country's network was split up after it had been integrated to cover the whole US territory. In Russia, this industry structuring approach leads to considerable differences in the level of services. For instance, leaders among alternative operators, such as Sovintel and Comstar, do offer state-of-the-art services, but only large corporate customers can afford them. The rest have no choice but turn to cheaper services that are often of poor quality.

The situation in the telecoms market has changed for the better recently owing to the policy pursued by the Communications Ministry and the Ministry for Economic Development and Trade, private companies, and also Russian and foreign investors. The biggest operators rely on latest technologies to upgrade their equipment, expand product lines, diversify services by adopting future-oriented technologies, and capture new markets.

Volume of the telecommunications market

The telecommunications market accounts for a major share (72 per cent) of the national IT industry sales that were assessed at $12.13 billion in 2002 (see Figure 3.6.1).

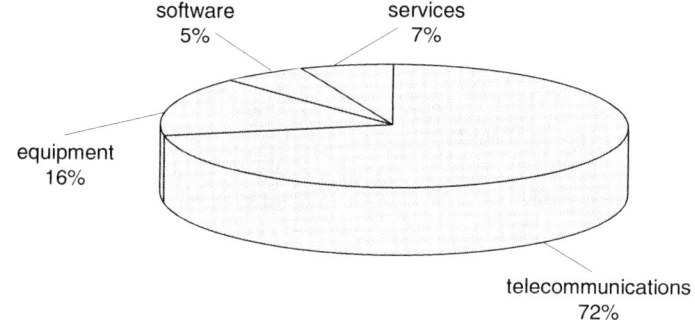

Source: www.ibusiness.ru

Figure 3.6.1 Market shares of information technologies (experts' assessment)

Telecommunications is the biggest and, in some segments, the communications industry's fastest growing market. It is quite a successful business, according to the Communications Ministry, with a turnover of $8.7 billion in 2002, up from $6.7 billion in 2001. The year 2003 is expected to see a 40 per cent gain. Russia controls about 0.7 per cent of the world telecommunications market. Experts forecast a further increase in the telecoms share of GDP from 2.5 per cent in 2002 (see Figure 3.6.2). The corresponding figure in Western Europe and North America stands at 4–6 per cent of GDP.

The industry's economic results in 2003 were impressive. In the first six months, the range of services grew by 50 per cent from a year before.

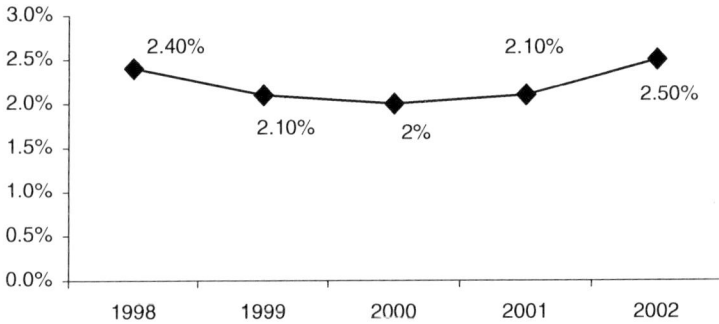

Source: Communications Ministry, RosBusinessConsulting

Figure 3.6.2 Communications industry's share of GDP (%)

Small wonder that foreign companies have an incentive to invest in the Russian telecom market. In particular, over the first nine months of 2003, foreign investments had climbed to $575.2 million, a 43.1 per cent gain on the same period in 2002, of which direct investments amounted to $73.4 million, portfolio investments totalled $18.8 million, and $483.1 million were other investments. Besides that, some $800 million of domestic capital was invested in the industry over the same period. Thus, more than $7 billion has been invested in the Russian telecommunications industry over the past four years. The trend is expected to continue in 2004, with emphasis placed on development of cellular telecommunications in regions and expansion of services offered.

Since different segments of the market often overlap, the market is hard to assess by merely summing them up. An objective assessment of the aggregate volume of the telecommunications market can be made based on an estimate of the communications industry as a whole. The telecoms equipment segment occupies some 81 per cent of the market, while the share of telecom services is 19 per cent.

The share of telecoms equipment in the total volume of the segment is quite small because investments are closely linked to technological innovations. To adopt new technologies, operators have to invest large sums in equipment that will pay off in several years. According to experts, there will be no more major investments in the cellular telecommunications segment; while the 3G technology is yet to come to Russia, the more so because it is not yet as profitable in Europe as expected. In 2002, Europe found itself in a situation where 3G technology was unnecessary. As a result of the regulators' miscalculation, market growth slowed down, players changed, and traditional operators such as Deutsche Telekom and FranceTelecom suffered losses, while new operators such as Vodafone emerged. Europe is not, however, going to remain static in this situation for long.

The Telecommunications Market   149

Table 3.6.1 Communications industry indicators (January–September 2003), in millions of roubles

Index	January–September 2003				Gain over same period in 2002, %			
			Operators				Operators	
	Total	New		Traditional	Total	New		Traditional
Total operating revenues, including	**281,654**	**150,993.5**		**130,660.5**	**148.9**	**155.0**		**142.4**
Mail service	19,383	796.7		18,586.3	137.9	175.7		136.6
Special communications	850.3			850.3	120.4			120.4
Long-distance communications	53,033.6	13,529.6		39,504	106.4	101.4		108.3
Urban telephone service	47,966	13,425.8		34,540.2	129.8	167.3		119.4
Rural telephone service	3,896.8	83.3		3,813.5	133.9	161.6		133.4
All types of payphones	2,069.1	155.5		1,913.6	*	*		*
Recording communications*	17,992.4	13,680.7		4,311.7	*	*		*
Radio communications, radio broadcasting, TV and satellite communications	9,060.1	7,041.7		2,018.4	138.3	147.8		113.0
Wire broadcasting	1,893.6	32.4		1,861.2	115.1	114.8		115.1
Mobile telecommunications	100,154.3	98,330.1		1,824.2	161.1	161.8		129.2
ISDN services	425.1	255.0		170.1	*	*		*
Intelligent network services	400.7	248.7		152	*	*		*
Connection and traffic transmission services	23,252	3,413.9		19,838				
Radio frequency centres	1,277.1			1,277.1	154.3			154.3

Source: Communications Ministry

* No comparisons can be made between the structure of services in 2002 and 2003

Key players in the telecommunications market

Russian telecom operators can tentatively be divided into three groups: traditional, institutional and new (alternative).

Traditional telecom operators

Traditional operators are companies that provided telephone and telegraph services before the 1990s, and continue to do so today. These include companies more or less controlled by OAO Svyazinvest, MGTS, Lensvyaz, the Komi Republic's Svyaz, and the largest interregional operator, Rostelecom.

The authorities' influence has a dual effect on investment prospects in such companies. On the one hand, they cannot avoid bearing social responsibilities in their areas, quite often holding enormous debts owed to them by government agencies and other public sector entities that cannot be left without telephone communications.

On the other hand, traditional operators have the most extensive networks and are monopoly operators in an overwhelming majority of regions, which guarantees them regular minimum incomes regardless of economic conditions or the political situation, given a steady demand for telecommunications services.

The telecom rate setting powers have recently been transferred from local authorities to the Antimonopoly Policy Ministry to minimize regional authorities' influence on local companies. The pricing policy has become more predictable and economically sound, and political considerations have become less overbearing.

Institutional telecom operators

Institutional telecom operators have traditionally provided services to enterprises of the transport industry, oil and gas industries etc, and were controlled by the respective ministries. The major institutional operators are Transtelecom (Ministry of Railways), Gazsvyaz, Gaztelecom, Gazcom, UES Telecom, Macomnet, and Metrocom.

Alternative (new) telecom operators

Development of the telecom industry has given rise to a great number of alternative operators. Initially, most of them were joint ventures with a big share of foreign capital. Subsequently, following mergers and takeovers, many companies became fully-fledged Russian-owned businesses. Today alternative operators control almost 100 per cent of the mobile communications market, a considerable share of the Internet access services market, and a big share of telephone communications services, particularly those they provide to corporate customers. In 2002, the aggregate sales of services provided by alternative operators in Moscow exceeded the revenues of traditional communications operators.

The main advantage of alternative operators is a high quality of communications, wide range of services, and no burden of social responsibilities. Most alternative operators use public telephone networks of traditional operators, and many of them build digital overlay networks providing voice mail and high-speed data transmission services.

Major alternative operators include Golden Telecom (OOO SCS Sovintel), ZAO MTU-Inform, ZAO Combellga, OOO Ekvant, ZAO Transtelecom Company, ZAO Comstar, ZAO Peterstar, ZAO MTU-Intel, OAO Central Telegraph, OAO RTComm.RU, ZAO Telmos, and OAO Komincom.

In December 2003, Golden Telecom bought from Norwegian Telenor 100 per cent of shares in OAO Komincom, the sole owner of ZAO Combellga, in exchange for its stock. The merger, which is expected to be completed within 12 to 16 months, will produce one of the largest alternative telecom operators in Russia. Alfa-Bank will have 30.02 per cent in the stock of the new company, Telenor will get 19.5 per cent, Rostelecom 11.2 per cent, European Bank for Reconstruction and Development 8.4 per cent, Barings 7.2 per cent, Capital International 6.1 per cent, and the remaining shares will continue to be traded openly. By taking over Komincom-Combellga, Golden Telecom aims for synergies, especially in the regions.

Leaders in the Russian telecommunications market

According to 2002 performance results, MTS topped the list of Russia's major telecom operators, ahead of long-distance communications operator OAO Rostelecom, with OAO VimpelCom edging up closer to the leaders.

In July 2003, the number of cellular phone users in the GSM, TDMA/DAMPS, NMT, IS-95 and IMT-MC-450 standard networks reached 27.01 million (according to J'son&Partners), and by the end of December 2003 the figure had jumped to 33.5 million. The overall cellular phone penetration rate in Russia is 18.6 per cent. In Moscow and the Moscow oblast that exceeds 56 per cent, St. Petersburg and the Leningrad oblast trail with 45 per cent.

Telecom operators in the stock market

Russian telecom operators have made considerable headway in the stock market for two years in succession. This fact can, to an extent, be attributed to the favourable situation in the stock market. Yet the operators' improving operating and financial performance is not to be overlooked.

152   Market Potential

Table 3.6.2 Major telecom operators in Russia

Company	Sales, $ million***		2002 on 2001
	2002	2001	% change
MTS***	1,361.8	893.2	52.5
VimpelCom***	768.5	422.6	81.9
MegaFon (consolidated)	409.0	215.0	90.2
Rostelecom	810.2	638.0	27.0
Uralsvyazinform*	471.7	337.3	39.9
Tsentrtelecom*	522.6	424.7	23.1
VolgaTelecom*	349.7	278.1	25.8
Sibirtelecom*	389.4	318.0	22.4
UTK*	335.8	271.2	23.8
MGTS	322.1	263.4	22.3
North-West Telecom*	321.8	266.3	20.8
Transtelecom**	40.4	6.9	485.5
Dalsvyaz*	170.0	139.9	21.5
Sovintel	145.0	116.9	24.0
Central Telegraph	40.2	24.9	61.3
Bashinformsvyaz	73.1	65.0	12.5
Svyaz (Komi)	35.5	30.1	17.9
Lensvyaz	335.0	28.2	18.7
Kazan GTS	12.5	8.2	51.8

* Aggregate turnover of amalgamated operators
** Telecoms services sales
*** Consistent with GAAP

Source: company reports, RBC

Table 3.6.3 Major cellular telecommunications operators in Russia

Operator	Subscribers in August 2003	Subscribers gain since January 2003, %
MTS	9,910,000	49
VimpelCom	7,950,000	54
MegaFon	4,645,350	57
SMARTS	860,000	59
Uralsvyazinform*	837,373	67
NSS	268,142	56
Tomsk Cellular Communications	169,926	68
Eniseitelecom	160,486	111
Ekaterinburg-2000	155,699	96
Sibchallenge	138,000	119

* Consolidated data

Source: IAA Sotovik

Table 3.6.4 Russian telecom operators in the stock market

Company	Market value, US$ millions		Trade volume from 01.07.02 to 30.06.03, $ millions	Pre-tax profit, $ millions	Net profit, $ millions	Dividends on stock (ordinary/preference) in 2002, Rb
	July 2003	July 2002				
MTS	5,880.31	2,475.49	n/a	427.30	277.10	1.7/-
VimpelCom (GAAP)	2,561.09	1,147.29	0.494	178.00	130.00	n/a
Rostelecom	1,266.11	728.33	2,480.739	168.43	98.62	0.543/1.27
Uralsyazinform	725.11	85.25	106.510	43.93	28.97	n/a
MGTS	570.78	482.97	2.273	40.67	35.89	0.68/7.055
Tsentrtelecom	460.30	101.61	11.381	52.30	34.55	0.096/0.206
VolgaTelecom	443.98	78.76	10.490	63.42	46.90	0.706/1.795
Sibirtelecom	341.12	61.56	11.866	29.19	15.09	0.007/0.012
North West Telecom	277.07	184.49	4.465	20.89	10.43	0.064/0.14
UTK	259.79	72.47	7.777	73.17	49.76	0.081/0.161
Dalsvyaz	84.11	16.76	3.799	12.36	5.89	0.31/0.58
Bashinformsvyaz	73.08	31.45	0.239	26.19	19.99	0.025/0.02
Svyaz (Republic of Komi)	20.28	16.74	0.058	4.45	3.68	0.1222/0.0407
Lensvyaz	17.90	17.90	0.065	3.31	2.50	3.938/11.814
Kazan GTS	7.32	9.15	0.003	3.36	2.59	0.005/0.1
Central Telegraph	5.48	9.44	0.009	1.40	0.74	0.042/0.042

Source: Companies' data and RBC data

The stock prices of traditional and alternative telecom operators have risen dramatically. Specifically, in the first half of 2003, growth rates varied between 70 per cent and 100 per cent. Among the factors contributing to the increase in the companies' capitalization value are improvements in their financial performance, greater transparency, growth in business activity in Russia, mergers of telecom companies, recent changes to Russian laws and rapid development of the world stock market for high-tech companies' shares.

The shares of traditional telecom operators have grown more expensive following reorganization of Svyazinvest JSC and mergers of numerous regional companies into seven interregional communications firms. Factors contributing to the increase in stock prices include:

- growth in the liquidity of the companies' stocks as new shareholders have become more active after their stocks were converted from shares in former communications companies and following an increase in the number of shareholders;

- aggressive activism of Western investment trusts. Following mergers, the new companies' investment risks have fallen dramatically, with little effect on the companies' capitalization until recently;

- availability of foreign capital. The rationale behind the mergers of communications companies was to boost their capitalization figures by entering international capital markets. Some of the operators have already announced their intention to implement Level Three ADR programmes.

In 2003, traditional operators did their best to slow down the decline of their market share. Svyazinvest group operators launched reorganization of business and investment planning patterns in an effort to enhance transparency of the business and facilitate development of strategic plans on the competitive market. Enhanced solvency was one of the most immediate favourable effects of regional operators' mergers. This development has enabled the operators to lower interest rates on investments and to increase the volume of investment funds.

The AKM-com index, which can be considered an indicator of the industry's stock position in the market, grew by 52.4 per cent from January to December 2003. In 2002, the operators' stocks, too, saw a certain growth, although the yearly growth was half as fast, giving a gain of 25 per cent. Telecom operators' shares were only less attractive than those of energy and metal producers.

The fastest growing shares in the period under review were the ordinaries of Uralsvyazinform (+100 per cent), which are slightly less attractive than those of Rostelecom in terms of liquidity. Today Uralsvyazinform is not only a fast growing company in the Perm region, but also an operator in Russia's oil-rich regions boasting the country's highest GRP and per capita incomes. Moreover, Uralsvyazinform is more than just a fixed telephony monopolist in the region, it is also Russia's fourth largest operator for the number of cellular telecommunications subscribers. In this area, Uralsvyazinform is more profitable than any other Svyazinvest company.

Table 3.6.5 OAO Svyazinvest operators' stock prices in January to December 2003

Operator	Ordinaries growth rate, %	Preferences growth rate, %
Uralsvyazinform	100.6	62.3
VolgaTelecom	88.7	–
Rostelecom	60.3	70.5
Dalsvyaz	40.0	53.0
Sibirtelecom	23.0	30.0
Tsentrtelecom	21.7	42.8
UTK	19.5	33.4
North-West Telecom	11.1	38.4

Source: RTS

VolgaTelecom was another fast growing operator (+88.7 per cent). It plans to consolidate and develop its cellular telecommunications assets, the announcement of which has had a favourable effect on the stock market.

Rostelecom shares grew by 60 per cent, which is a sign that it is attempting to fight off growing competition from alternative operators.

Telecom operators' shares will remain just as attractive in 2004. However, existing risks have a depressing effect on their popularity. Small wonder, buying Svyazinvest operators' shares is a risky business, but, as happened before, may turn out to be quite profitable.

One can safely assume today that the Russian Federal Property Fund's plan to sell the government stake in Svyazinvest (or any part of it) will not come off even though the plan has not been dropped yet. Nothing is known about many of the terms and conditions of this transaction, in particular, the date of the auction has not been set, potential buyers are unknown (bidders are generally believed to include Alfa-Group, Sistema JSFC and Telecominvest Holding Company), nor are the conditions of the sale. Market players are expecting more certainty about Svyazinvest privatization prospects in 2004. Moreover, investment projects will be accumulated along strategic lines, which will give the market a benchmark to assess the operators' market value.

Equally important for the financial performance of Svyazinvest's interregional companies in 2004 is a possible rise in tariffs on local communications, expected to increase by 18–20 per cent in the second half of 2004.

Market for communications facilities

According to the Russian Communications Ministry, the volume of the domestic telecommunications equipment market totalled about $3.3–3.4 billion in 2002 and it is expected to grow to $6.3 billion by 2010. The report prepared by the Russian Ministry of Communications also profiles the structure of the communications equipment market. It is hard enough, however, to get an idea of the kind of equipment the Communications Ministry implies in, for instance, the 'mobile communications' line of its report.

More specific data are given in surveys carried out by telecommunications equipment suppliers. For instance, according to Alcatel, equipment sales for purposes of developing the Russian communications infrastructure accounted for about 1.4 per cent of overall international sales in 2003. According to data provided by Gartner, these estimates give a market capacity of $1.6–1.8 billion for this equipment class. As the company says in its study, the overall equipment sales for operators and corporate networks will total $2.2 billion in 2003.

According to the Russian Goskomstat (State Statistics Agency), manufacture of communications equipment in Russia grew by 30.6 per cent in January to August 2003, up from the same period in 2002. The range of communications equipment, on which statistics is available, is quite interesting: while radio sets, TV sets, and telephones can typically be classified as 'communications equipment', VCRs can hardly be regarded as such. The fact that VCRs were included in this category must be due to their considerable growth rate of 82.9 per cent, which has had a positive effect on overall statistics.

Foreign manufacturers dominate in most communications equipment market segments, and despite official reassurances (from the Russian Ministry of Communications, etc) there are no viable prospects for a significant increase in the market niche held by domestic suppliers.

Experts believe, however, that telecommunications equipment from Russian manufacturers could be in demand in small market niches. For instance, domestic developers stand the best chance in the 'physical line' modem segment. This segment comprises such Russian companies as the Kroniks Design Office, Zelaks, the Nateks Centre for Science and Technology, NSG, Granch, etc. Their equipment was initially designed for Russian communications lines, taking into account their specificity as early as at the development stage. The line of their products spans almost all existing digital subscriber line technologies, except for the ADSL technology, which is almost 100 per cent foreign-made modems.

Rotek, one of Russia's flagship telecommunications equipment manufacturers, boasts high achievements in optical equipment. At the recent TRBE 2003 show, Rotek displayed a CWDM (Coarse Wavelength Division Multiplex) system designed, first and foremost, to transmit a great number of video and audio signals via a single fibre of an optical cable.

At the present time, new services considerably increase line load capacity and adversely affect performance of obsolete equipment. Almost all telecommunications operators today face the prospect of developing and upgrading (digitalizing) their telephone exchanges, modifying their layouts, and replacing obsolete equipment throughout vast regional networks. As of early 2003, only 26 per cent of the hardware used in the Russian telecommunications sector met international requirements. Almost three-quarters of existing communications networks are to be modernized in the next few years in order for Russian communications networks to operate efficiently.

The share of digital channels operating in the primary public communications network had grown to 83 per cent by early 2002. Relatively new and small-size telephone exchanges are the most digitalized option. The Khantymansiyskokrtelecom Company operates the most advanced network, at a digitalization level that had reached 88.6 per cent by early 2002. Meanwhile, MGTS has the smallest number of modern automatic telephone exchanges, at a digitalization level of 11.43 per cent.

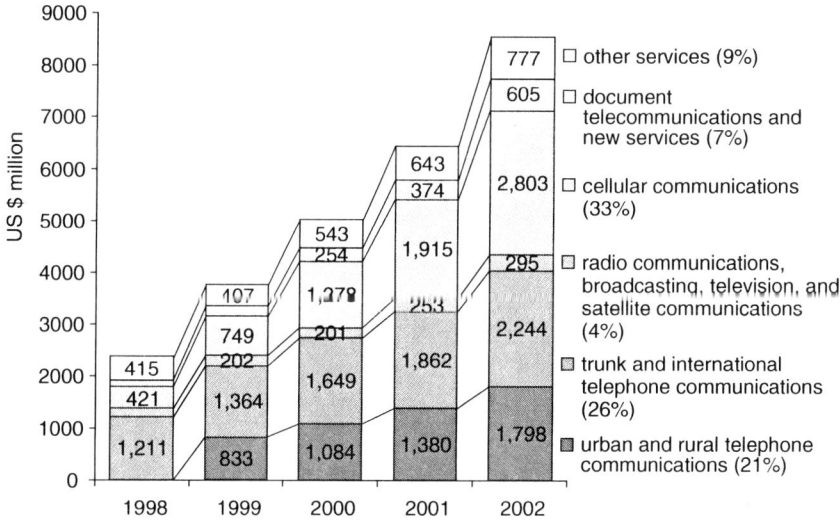

Source: Russian Ministry of Communication

Figure 3.6.3 Russian telecommunications market segments

Cellular telecommunications

According to Alcatel, the cellular telecommunications segment, which has always been the driving force of the telecommunications market, accounted for about two-thirds of the 2003 overall operator-class equipment sales. The cellular phone segment, in which the 2003 sales are expected, according to available studies, to top $1 billion in Russia, should be taken into consideration on its own merits.

The cellular phone boom currently underway in Russia gives the numerous cellular phone manufacturers and cellular telecommunications equipment suppliers a good opportunity to make high profits. Besides, next generation cellular networks, including IMT-MC-450 standard networks (CDMA-450 technology), are currently under development, with the US Lucent Technologies, the Canadian Nortel Networks, and the Chinese ZTE Corporation and Huawei Technologies being the key bidders for supply contracts.

In the equipment market, fast absorption of small-size cellular telecommunications companies has resulted in this market being now dominated by the Big Three operators accounting for 90 per cent of the overall sales of relevant equipment. At the same time, the companies taken over in the process are capable of expanding their operations by attracting more customers by offering the low prices of their parent companies, while the remaining small-scale independent operators are forced to slash investments, being unable to compete with the big players.

Fixed communications facilities

In the past four years, the Russian fixed communications equipment market has grown 3.6-fold. According to various estimates, the total

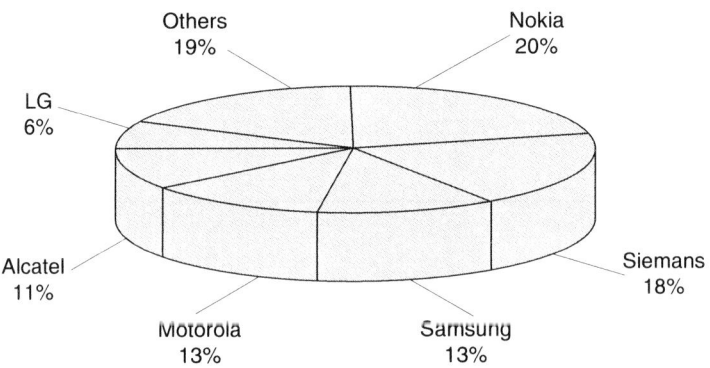

Source: RBC

Figure 3.6.4 Cellular phone sales structure in 2002 (legitimate sales) (%)

cost of new automatic telephone exchanges sold in Russia in 2002 equalled $150–$200 million. In terms of monetary value, though, the market has changed little: while sales rose, equipment prices dropped. The overall cost of maintaining, expanding and upgrading the hardware already installed equals $30–40 million.

Unlike the steadying mobile communications segment, the fixed communications equipment market is going through its most critical period in the recent decade: traditional operators have for the first time been largely replaced by cellular networks in the voice communications segment, in a process that has been facilitated by both reciprocal trends in price policies and an almost complete federal coverage by, and also easy connection to, GSM networks. Traditional operators have already been confronted by the prospect of choosing between the two business areas when planning investment expansion in the most developed regions, for instance, the Ural region. Should Svyazinvest be privatized, the new owner will also have to think twice about the need for a massive replacement of obsolescent equipment that is still fit for operation.

Despite the gains made by US and Chinese manufacturers in the Russian telecoms equipment market, Siemens and Alcatel are likely to remain leaders in the fixed communications market in the near future. Although no drastic leap is expected in demand for automatic telephone exchanges in local communications networks in Russia, a considerable increase in automatic telephone exchange capacity is clearly in evidence. In 2002, Svyazinvest took out its highest-ever loan, a centralized credit of four billion roubles from Sberbank (Savings Bank), to purchase equipment for regional operators, and the year 2003 will see the greatest number of digital telephone exchanges put into service.

The Internet

As of early 2003, Russia had about 3.5 million active Internet users, whose numbers registered an annual growth rate of 40–50 per cent. The overall number of Internet users, going online at least once in several months, equals about 10 million. The data transmission, telematics and Internet equipment market segment has the greatest potential for dynamic growth.

Satellite communications

The Russian satellite communications market is yet to be developed. The Kosmicheskaya Svyaz Federal Unitary Enterprise, which owns ten satellites, provides the bulk of all satellite communications services. At the moment, Kosmicheskaya Svyaz is primarily responsible for broadcasting federal television channels and providing presidential communications, and now the company plans to digitalize and compress television signals, which will enable it to free up some of its satellite channels and

Table 3.6.6 Communications equipment statistics

Communications equipment	As at 1 October 2003	2003 on 2002, %	Gain (loss) in nine months of 2003, %
Telephones (including office exchange telephones), total, including:	*37,502,353*	*104.73*	*3.5*
Urban and rural communications network telephones, total,	**36,452,867**	**104.64**	**3.6**
of which operated by traditional operators	32,377,962	104.72	3.2
Main urban and rural communications network telephones	35,244,972	104.94	3.7
Urban and rural communications networks apartment telephones	28,541,930	105.26	3.6
Urban and rural communications network telephones, linked to office telephone exchanges, total	**1,049,486**	**107.97**	**0.5**
of which operated by traditional operators	879,462	99.99	–2.2
All types of payphones, total	*188,622*	*95.35*	*–2.2*
of which by traditional operators	165,918	91.86	–2.7
of which phone card-operated	132,868	109.63	6.7
Trunk (international) payphones, total	**7,409**	**73.47**	**–33.7**
of which operated by traditional operators	7,126	73.37	–35.9
Urban and rural communications network payphones	**106,400**	**82.36**	**–6.1**
of which operated by traditional operators	97,590	81.54	–6.6
Urban and rural communications network general-purpose payphones	**74,813**	**127.76**	**11.6**
Main radio relay stations, total	*19,615,852*	*92.24*	*–5.7*
Mobile communications, total subscribers	**30,418,894**	**219.25**	**42.2**
of which serviced by traditional operators	637,888	**177.74**	33.4
Including cellular telecommunications subscribers	29,890,499	**221.19**	42.6
of which serviced by traditional operators	469,664	**199.77**	39.4
Telematics and data transmission services, total subscriber sets	*3,437,442*	**189.00**	*35.3*
Including Internet subscriber sets	3,173,438	194.18	37.1

Source: Russian Communications Ministry

use them for commercial purposes. Two other operators, namely Gazcom and Voentelecom, which provide services to Gazprom and the Russian Defence Ministry, respectively, are also exploring the feasibility of going commercial. Cellular mobile satellite communications are provided by Globalstar and Thuraya. Globalstar has a total of about 8,000 users, and Thuraya has just started providing such services.

Corporate Intranet equipment

Institutional communications operators have been established to provide intranet communications to large industrial holding companies, ministries, and government agencies. This market segment is specific in that its consumers comprise establishments of various ownership patterns: government agencies, corporate organizations represented by natural monopolies with a considerable share of government presence (such as the Gazprom Gas Company and the Unified Energy System), or their specialized subsidiaries, and private corporate operators.

The communications networks of various government agencies and corporate organizations in the fuel and energy and transportation industries, and also other government agencies, offer large niches for telecommunications manufacturers. Particularly fast growth rates have recently been registered by communications networks of the Russian Ministry of Railways.

Well-known foreign companies and domestic enterprises (claiming 25–30 per cent of overall supplies) are the main hardware suppliers for this market segment.

Switching equipment manufacture

The capacity of the market for switching equipment for institutional and corporate communications networks may be compared to that of the local public communications network (65–75 per cent).

Switching equipment manufacture is one of the areas, in which the domestic industry maintains a significant potential. The Russian

Table 3.6.7 Demand for switching equipment for establishing an interlinked communications network in Russia in 2001–2010

Communications network type	Millions of numbers	$ billion
Local urban communications	24–26	2.4–2.5
Local rural communications	3–4	0.3–0.4
Mobile communications	23–25	2.7–3.0
Total demand	50–55	5.4–5.9

Source: Russian Ministry of Communications

Ministry of Communications promotes the domestic industry, even though most production facilities are owned by foreign companies that have succeeded in obtaining the status of domestic manufacturers in Russia.

Russian companies and Russian-foreign joint ventures having the status of domestic manufacturers have developed and launched into production of a wide range of digital automatic telephone exchanges, which meet modern technological standards.

The total output of switching equipment produced by domestic manufacturers may reach 4.5–5 million phone lines a year. This figure considerably exceeds the annual rate of phone numbers introduced by public telephone networks. Most existing production capacities remain untapped. This fact has a direct impact on the profitability of products manufactured and manufacturers themselves.

In the first half of 2003 the local telephone network capacity grew by about 1.5 million ports. The domestic industry, primarily joint ventures, sold 60–70 per cent of all equipment in service. The remaining equipment required to install these port numbers was delivered by foreign companies such as Siemens, Alcatel, Ericsson, and so on. Demand for cellular, trunk and international, and most of the corporate communications equipment is almost fully satisfied from imports.

There are two ways to meet demand for switching equipment. The first is to purchase new hardware, and the second is to upgrade existing equipment, still with much service life left, so that it could efficiently meet modern requirements made on equipment by the Russian Interlinked Communications Network. Given relatively low costs (30–40 per cent of the cost of new equipment per port), modernization will allow the service life of most switching equipment to be extended, and in individual cases it will even allow for increasing the phone number capacity of communications networks operating on existing equipment.

At the present time, requirements made on switching equipment are being revised thoroughly. The traffic structure is shifting from voice information to data transmission. This suggests the need to make drastic changes to switching equipment, namely, effecting a changeover from channel switching to packet switching. This is a time-consuming process, however, and so channel switching will remain in demand for some time to come.

Government regulation of communications equipment manufacture

Communications equipment is manufactured under government supervision. Most future-oriented science-intensive developments have been carried out in compliance with the federal target programme 'Development of Telecommunications, Television, and Radio Broadcasting Equipment'. Baseline development was supported simultaneously with commercialization of the results of the federal target programme 'Electronics Development in Russia'.

The capacity of the domestic industry at the first and second stages (until 2006) will primarily depend on the impact of the launch of new equipment designed in compliance with the above programmes into production. At the third stage, the domestic industry is to introduce technologies and manufacture equipment developed under federal programmes adopted by the Russian Government, such as 'Basic National Technologies' and 'Electronics in Russia'.

These programmes set guidelines primarily for traditional equipment developers and manufacturers. A significantly larger number of companies are making attempts to stay on in the equipment market on their own, often at the risk of unjustified expansion of the range of identical equipment manufacture.

The Conception for Developing the Russian Telecommunications Equipment Market in 2002–2010 adopted by the Russian Ministry of Communications is aimed at protecting the domestic telecommunications equipment market, supporting Russian manufacturers in availing themselves of their competitive advantages, and raising the share of domestically-manufactured equipment in the domestic communications equipment market to 60–65 per cent. At the present time, it is imperative to create conditions for developing new types of equipment and new technologies, channelling investments into the industry, and establishing new, and upgrading existing, workstations. The Conception also deals with laws and statutes regulating the market for telecommunications equipment and communications services.

3.7

Telecommunications: The Regulatory Framework

CMS Cameron McKenna

Introduction

Rapid developments in technology and the growth of the Internet are among the drivers of fundamental change in the structure of the old telecommunications, broadcasting and media industries across the world. Russia is no exception. The Internet, mobile, telephony and digital broadcasting are likely to grow at exponential rates, although starting from a comparatively low base. Significant investment is still needed in the public service telephone network if penetration rates are to be lifted from the current national average level of 21 per cent to the target level of 60 per cent, which has been set by the Ministry of Communications and Information Science. The Ministry has calculated that some $60 billion of investment in telecommunications will be required over the next 10 years to achieve this.

Privatization

Until 1993 the Russian telecommunication network was fully controlled and owned by the state authorities of the Russian Federation. In 1992 the Russian government announced plans for privatizing the telecommunications sector and local network operators were privatized according to the following scheme: 51 per cent of common shares were kept by the State; 5 per cent were transferred to the companies' management; 10 per cent were transferred to the companies themselves; 25 per cent were transferred to the employees as preferred shares; and the remaining shares were sold by the local state property management funds to investors. Later the government formed a holding company, Svyazinvest, which owned all government shares in all regional telecommunications companies. Currently, each 'subject' of the Russian Federation has its own telecommunications company. These companies tend to suffer from regulated low tariffs but enjoy a monopoly position in their respective regional markets.

The government developed a two-stage scheme to privatize part of Svyazinvest. In July 1997, 25 per cent of the capital plus one share in Svyazinvest was sold for $1.875 billion. The second step of privatization (25 per cent minus two shares) was postponed owing to poor market conditions after the financial crisis in 1998. Subsequently, the second step of privatization was postponed again pending the termination of the reorganization of the company; this should significantly increase its capitalization.

Rostelecom is Russia's main international and long-distance telecommunications carrier. Svyazinvest currently owns 51 per cent of Rostelecom. Other strong players on the Russian telecommunications market are the state-owned natural monopolies, such as the Ministry of Railway Transportation, Gazprom and RAO Unified Energy Systems, which use their infrastructure networks for telecommunications business.

Legal regulation

The general principles of Russia's telecommunication legislation are set out in the Federal Law on Communications dated 17 July 2003, which came into force on 1 January 2004. It sets out a legal framework for the rapidly developing telecommunications industry and is intended to stimulate investment in the telecommunications sector, as well as to foster competition among local telephone operators in the sector, which is monopolized in some spheres.

Governing agencies

The principal ministries and committees that have jurisdiction over telecoms operators and equipment suppliers are set out below.

The agency responsible for regulating the telecommunications market is the Ministry of Communications and Information Science of the Russian Federation, which in turn is responsible for a number of state committees that have delegated authority in relation to specific areas. The Ministry is responsible for state policy and state management of the communications industries, including postal and courier services. The Ministry also manages a number of state enterprises operating in the telecommunication sphere and is responsible for issuing licences to telecoms operators. The Ministry supervises, on a day-to-day basis, telecoms operators and has the power to inspect equipment and generally monitor compliance with licence terms.

A number of other state agencies and institutions have authority over the telecommunications sector. The Federal Agency for Government Communication and Information certifies and licenses the use of encryption codes and equipment. Jointly with the Ministry of Anti-Monopoly Policy, the Ministry of Communications and Information Science develops and coordinates tariffs and tariff policy for the telecommunication services. The State Committee for Radio Frequencies assigns radio frequencies, monitors the use of frequencies, and defines technical standards in broadcasting. The State Commission on Electronic Communication coordinates the development and construction of telecommunications networks and systems and supervises their operations. The State Commission on Information Science is responsible for state policy in the sphere of information distribution and control, as well as for developing state standards for licensing. The Ministry of Health Protection regulates certain issues regarding the location of the telecommunications equipment.

Licensing

The Law determines the licensing requirements applicable to companies providing communication services and gives a detailed list of circumstances when a licence can be suspended or revoked. The list of telecommunication services that are included in the licences and relevant licensing requirements is yet to be established by the Russian Government. When established, this list will be reviewed by the Government annually.

A licence will be issued by the Ministry of Communications and Information Science for a period up to 25 years with a possibility of extension. The list of documents and fees necessary to obtain a licence is provided in the Law and includes:

- an application letter (standard form);
- the constitutional documents of the applicant;
- the certificate of state registration of the applicant;
- a description of the communication services with relevant technical data;
- a document confirming the payment of the application fee.

The Law provides for specific cases when a licence for performing communication services will be granted via a tender, such as:

- if the State Radio Frequencies Commission establishes that there are limited number of available frequencies in a particular territory; and

- if the Ministry of Communications establishes that the capacity of communication networks in the territory is limited, thus the number of telecommunication operators in this territory should be limited.

The new requirements are designed to stimulate competition among telephone operators.

Telecommunication equipment

The Law contains a requirement that most telecommunication equipment, either manufactured in Russia or imported, must be certified. A list of specific equipment subject to mandatory certification is yet to be established by the Russian Government. The certification is performed by accredited certification institutions. The Russian Government has not yet established the procedure for the accreditation of these institutions.

The Law also provides that some telecommunication equipment is not subject to mandatory certification, and voluntary certification conducted by a manufacturer itself will suffice (if confirmed by a declaration of compliance). This is a new provision for Russian legislation regulating telecommunication operations, which is expected to encourage the development of the telecommunications market in the Russian Federation.

3.8

The Russian IT Market

Vyacheslav Masenkov, Deputy General-Director and Alexander Chachava, Senior IT Analyst, RBC

The Russian IT market developed at a faster pace compared to the world IT market in the 1990s, gradually decreasing the gap between the levels of their development. Amid a recession in Western countries in 2000 to 2001, the Russian market was booming after the financial crisis of 1998 – it added 40 to 50 per cent annually. As a result, the Russian IT market emerged and reached a volume of $4.7 billion by 2002.

Table 3.8.1 The IT market volume in billion dollars and the shares of regions

	The market's volume in 2002	2001 %	2002 %	2003 %
The USA	305	30.3	30.9	30.6
Europe*	408	42.7	41.3	40.0
Japan	120	11.9	12.1	12.3
4 tigers**	24	2.4	2.5	2.6
Russia	4.7	0.41	0.47	0.52
The rest of the world	126.3	12.29	12.73	13.98
Total	**988**	**100.0**	**100.0**	**100.0**

*Europe without Russia and the CIS
**4 tigers – Hong Kong, South Korea, Singapore, Taiwan

Source: EITO 2003 data

According to estimations of the RBC's department of consulting, growth in the IT market, including the 'grey' market, amounted to about 17 per cent in 2003. Our achievements are especially impressive amidst the gloomy situation on the world IT market. According to information from the US consulting company IDC, the year 2002 was the worst year in the history of development for the world IT sector.

Table 3.8.2 The ratio of the IT market and the GDP of different countries

Country	The IT market in 2002, $ billion	The share of GDP, %
Russia	4.7	1.2
The USA	310	6.38
Germany	75	3.65
France	58	3.99
Italy	28	2.45
Spain	13	2.3
Poland	3.3	2.1
The Czech Republic	1.9	3.8
Estonia	0.19	3.7
The UK	71	5.17

Source: EITO

Robert Farish, the IDC regional director for Russia, Ukraine and Central Asia, said that Russia continued to be one of the few dynamically developing markets in the whole world in 2003. According to IDC estimations, the total volume of the Russian IT market was $4.92 billion in 2002, and by 2007 it is forecasted to reach $10.31 billion. The market's dynamics over the past few years have also been high. In 2002 the market added 18.4 per cent, while in 2003 its advance was 22.7 per cent to $6.04 billion, according to preliminary estimations. According to Robert Farish, the highest growth was performed by such segments of the market as services (system integration) with a 23.4 per cent gain and software (47.2 per cent). At the same time the market retained its 'technical orientation', since the share of expenses on services and software in the structure of total expenses on Information technologies was just 37.6 per cent in 2003.

Services and software will keep growing at a higher pace than the whole IT market. The share of services and software is expected to be up to 50 per cent of the IT market by 2007.

The market of custom programming amounted to about $300 million in 2003 (according to estimations of the RBC department of consulting). The market's advance against 2002 was 30 per cent. The forecast for 2007 is about $800 million, amid annual growth of about 25 to 30 per cent.

Table 3.8.3 Services, software and custom programming

	2001, $ bln	2002, $ bln	2003E, $ bln	Growth in %
Services in the sphere of system integration	0.7	0.84	1.01	20
Standard software	0.34	0.43	0.58	36
Custom programming	0.17	0.23	0.3	30

Source: estimations of the RBC's consulting department

On the whole, Russia looks excellent against a gloomy background. However, one should realize that growth on the domestic IT market is also due to the fact that it has room for development. Specialists say that even with the current pace of growth, Russia will need more than 100 years to reach the volume of the IT market of the USA registered in 2002.

The largest investor that provided the lion's share of the demand for IT was the State: expenditure of state agencies on electronic communication development amounted to almost $3 billion in the period from 2001 to 2003. This expenditure is expected to be about $5 billion in the period from 2004 to 2007. The government will spend this money on providing state agencies with access to the Internet, computers, office appliances and necessary software. In particular, the expected IT budget of the Russian Tax Ministry is about $600 million for the next four years, including $150 million that was attracted as a credit from the World Bank in 2002. Another $150 million were allocated by the World Bank at the end of 2003.

Tens of millions of dollars per year are invested in IT by the Russian State Customs Committee and the Federal Treasury. Total computerization has started in the Pension Fund. About $2–3 million were spent on IT by branches of the Pension Fund in large regions and $10 million in Moscow in 2002. The recent census also contributed to the revenues of developers. The Russian State Statistics Committee spent about $25 million on IT within the framework of the census.

However, the most global project in the IT field is undoubtedly the Electronic Russia programme (which as was suggested would give a totally new incentive to the development of the IT market). Despite the fact that the government allocates much less resources for global 'informatization' than was initially planned, the growth dynamics still inspires optimism. For example, in 2003 expenditures of the federal budget for Electronic Russia more than doubled and reached R1.43 billion ($44.5 million) compared to R600 million ($20 million) in 2002.

To sum up, it is worth mentioning another significant event that happened almost without the influence and will of the government. This concerns Internet trade. In 2002, the volume of retail via the

Internet doubled in Russia. According to the Brunswick UBS Warburg investment company, the assumed turnover of all Russian Internet stores reached $240–260 million in 2002 against some $100 million in 2001. Brunswick UBS Warburg forecasted another more considerable jump in 2003. According to expert estimates, this year Internet vendors will have sold goods worth $650 million.

Table 3.8.4 The structure of Russia's IT market

	2001, $ bln	2002, $ bln	2003E, $ bln	Growth in %
PC	1.55	1.7	1.86	10
Spare parts and peripherals	1.15	1.34	1.56	17
System integration services	0.7	0.84	1.01	20
Software development	0.34	0.43	0.54	26
Custom programming	0.17	0.23	0.3	30
Electronic commerce	0.2	0.27	0.36	35
Total	**4.11**	**4.81**	**5.63**	**17**

Source: estimate of RBC's department of consulting

Despite the industry's obvious success, the very structure of the Russian IT market is rather primitive, as yet, compared to that of Western European countries. While the IT market in Western Europe is several times larger than the telecommunications market, in Russia it is almost half the size. While in Western Europe the share of equipment is some 30 to 50 per cent, depending on the country, in Russia this figure is 63 per cent. Apparently, our country is completing the first stage of 'informatization' that envisages basic equipping of workplaces with computers, their integration into networks and connection to the Internet, and the purchasing of PCs by home users.

The next stage we are to go through is the transition to a higher technological level where not hardware but software solutions, services and electronic commerce are visible to the naked eye. It is worth pointing out that as compared to 2001, Russia has made several steps towards this. For instance, the share of computers, spare parts and peripherals declined in total sales volume (grey imports taken into account) from 66 per cent ($2.7 billion) to 63 per cent of all resources spent on the IT market ($2.96 billion), while revenues from software development went up from 12 per cent ($500 million) to 13 per cent ($630 million).

While in the West the software market gained only 0.8 per cent, it is accelerating in Russia. As for the market growth rate, the majority of analysts agree on a rather high figure of 25 per cent (this is the data cited by IDC).

Table 3.8.5 The largest participants on the IT market

No.	Name	The field of activities	City	2002 Turnover, thsds of roubles	2001 Turnover, thsds of roubles	Growth, %	No of employees	Production per capita
1	LC Group (1)	Distribution of computer equipment	Moscow	10,972,500	7,295,000	50	900	12,192
2	Rover / Bely Veter	A group of companies (6)	Moscow	8,621,250	6,653,040	29.58	1,200	7,184
3	IBS	A group of companies (2)	Moscow	8,151,000	6,682,220	21.98	2,000	4,076
4	R-Style	A group of companies (3)	Moscow	6,865,650	5,789,312	19	647	10,612
5	Lanit (8)	Integration	Moscow	5,788,724	4,202,950	37.73	1,500	3,859
6	Verysell	A group of companies (4)	Moscow	5,172,750	3,209,800	61	300	17,243
7	TechnoServ A/S	Integration	Moscow	5,135,130	4,397,426	16.78	485	10,588
8	Rosco	Distribution of computer equipment	Moscow	4,702,500	4,960,600	-5.20	120	39,188
9	OCS	Distribution of computer equipment	Moscow	4,608,450	2,801,280	64.51	300	15,362
10	Aquarius	A group of companies (5)	Moscow	4,284,749	2,371,946	80.64	318	13,474

Source: CNews, RBC's department of consulting

Meanwhile, among the top ten of the Russian IT market in the first national rating compiled by CNews.ru and RBC's department of consulting, there are no companies that are involved in software development only or project integration only, and these are the enterprises in today's Russia that are the most highly technological in the industry.

As for forecasts, in the opinion of the Telecommunications Ministry and IDC, the market's growth rate will be preserved in general but IT services will gradually replace the volume of hardware supplies. According to the forecast of RBC's department of consulting, in 2003 growth will continue and reach 12 to 18 per cent. At the same time, the software, electronic commerce and IT consulting market will demonstrate the most dynamic growth.

3.9

The Automotive Industry

Alexander Raifeld and Andrei Kouzmin, Deloitte & Touche

Introduction

According to industry experts, the number of motor vehicles in Russia has increased by approximately 50 per cent over the last five years, reaching 22 million passenger cars, 540,000 buses and 3.5 million heavy trucks in 2003. This translates into car ownership of 148 cars per 1,000 people, significantly lower than in emerging markets with comparable per capita GDP levels. In the period 1998–2003, domestic passenger vehicle output grew in line with GDP, but sales rose much faster due to second-hand imports. Car prices in Russia are still relatively low, and most consumers are highly price sensitive.

The Russian automotive market is also characterized by a significant proportion of obsolete vehicles. Statistics show that 50 per cent of all cars in Russia are 10–15 years old. These figures suggest that a significant latent replacement demand exists, which is likely to materialize as disposable incomes grow. Industry analysts believe that the main beneficiaries of this trend in the medium term will be domestic producers, as they are able to offer low prices for their products. Analysts predict car ownership to continue rising at a rate of 4–5 per cent per annum until 2005, due to the growth of disposable incomes, the increased availability of bank auto loans, and protectionist government policy.

In July 2002, the Russian Government approved 'The Concept for Automotive Industry Development', an eight-year programme designed to upgrade the Russian car sector. The Government's objective is to encourage foreign car-makers to set up domestic production facilities during the transitional period, and give domestic producers time to focus on improving the quality and design of their automobiles. Meanwhile, tariffs on new car imports will go up and stay at an increased level for five years. Only in 2010 will tariffs be reduced again, in compliance with the requirements of the WTO.

While relatively slow in breaking from its centrally-planned past, the vast majority of Russian automotive manufacturers have now been privatized. These companies have begun to benefit from an expanding middle class, better internal management and protectionist policies. They are also becoming the main acquisition targets of domestic Financial Industrial Groups (FIGs) and metal production companies. We see these trends continuing and accelerating as the Russian economy continues its expansion.

Soviet manufacturing had virtually 100 per cent vertical integration due to central planning, and the Russian automotive sector continues that trend. Major original equipment manufacturers (OEMs) often achieve over 80 per cent internal content, which is significantly higher than their Western European and North American counterparts. Domestic OEMs currently refrain from importing major components, as it would make their final production costs unaffordable for most consumers.

Western car manufacturers are interested in producing cars in Russia due to a large, unsatisfied demand, the availability of an inexpensive labour force, a vast resource base and the geographical location of the country. However it is unlikely that the world auto giants would purchase any domestically manufactured cars, due to the notorious reputation for poor quality and outdated production standards. Russian automobile producers have so far not been able to take advantage of existing protecting import tariffs, or to bring the quality level of their products up to Western standards. We believe that world auto leaders would prefer to move to Russia by constructing their own assembly plants and gradually expanding the number and the complexity of tasks performed in their production facilities. This is currently being done by Ford Motor Company, Kia and BMW; these automobile manufacturers have already opened plants in Russia. We expect a few other companies to move to Russia in the short- to medium-term future.

The domestic automotive sector is dominated by three large OEMs: Volgski Automobile Plant (AvtoVAZ), Gorky Automobile Plant (GAZ) and Ural Automobile Plant (UAZ). KaMAZ dominates the heavy truck sector while Pavlov Autobus Plant (PAZ) is the leading manufacturer of buses. Recent production statistics reported by the State Statistics Committee show that in the most lucrative sector, personal automobiles, AvtoVAZ heavily dominates the market. As Russia's largest car producer, it accounted for 75 per cent of domestic cars, leaving its two main competitors, GAZ and UAZ, far behind. Its new joint venture with General Motors, which started production of the Chevrolet-Niva in September 2002, will further solidify AvtoVAZ's position among traditional domestic producers.

The Russian 'big three'

AvtoVAZ

The personal car market is dominated by the Volgski Automobile Plant (AvtoVAZ) with its popular and virtually omnipresent Lada brand name. The history of AvtoVAZ dates back some 30 years to when it was developed with Fiat. The plant was built as a high volume manufacturer of passenger cars, and is constantly expanding its production capacity. Lada cars are deeply inferior both in terms of quality and design. The company does not use existing tariff barriers as an opportunity to work on improving its automobiles and bringing them up to world standards. As a result, Lada continues to lose its position on the local market and suffers from a poor reputation. We believe that AvtoVAZ's market share will continue to diminish, especially once import tariffs are lifted in compliance with WTO requirements. According to AvtoVAZ's CEO and news agencies, in 2003 the company manufactured a total of over 800,000 vehicles and generated a net profit of 5 billion roubles, which is a dramatic increase from 700 million roubles in 2002.

In February 2004, AvtoVaz signed a 3-year 240 million dollar loan from Deutsche Bank. Although the company has not yet announced its plans, we believe the funding will go to upgrading, improving and updating the company's current product line. Although we view this loan as a very positive step not only for AvtoVAZ but also for the automotive industry as a whole, we do not believe that it will radically change AvtoVAZ's situation. Major Lada problems are likely to remain, discouraging consumers from purchasing VAZ vehicles.

GAZ

GAZ is Russia's second-largest automotive producer, producing large passenger cars, light and medium trucks, and minibuses. Despite new management, the company continues to suffer from poor sales of its flagship business-class automobile Volga, characterized by poor quality and an out-of-date Soviet era design.

GAZ however is very successful (more than 55 per cent of domestic output) in the light commercial vehicle (LCV) sector, which it dominates with the Gazelle. The automobile has a load capacity of 1.35 tonnes and 9 cubic metres of cargo space. Lack of competition and low costs have made it a bestseller with Russian enterprises and entrepreneurs. Overall the company was able to increase its production by 4.3 per cent to 213,000 automobiles in 2003.

UAZ

While UAZ is by far the smallest of the Big Three, it is the most Western-oriented company. Despite the company's strong production growth of approximately 16 per cent in 2003 its market position remains vulnerable, as most of its products have not benefited from investments in design enhancements. UAZ produced almost 33,000 vehicles in 2003. Mainly a producer of LCVs and minivans, the 3,160 and 3,162 sport utility vehicles may provide the impetus it needs to become a stronger competitor. Severstal, a metallurgical giant, owns a controlling stake in UAZ. New strategic investors, experienced management, imported Swiss and German equipment, and a relatively good corporate structure make UAZ a potentially successful company on the domestic market.

Recent trends

There are two significant trends currently affecting the auto manufacturing industry in Russia; the shift from 'screw-driver assembly' to full local production of foreign industry giants, and the continuing loss of market shares by major Russian car manufacturers. The first trend creates a strong positive impact not just on the automotive sector but on the whole economy as well. Foreign automobile manufacturers bring in the knowledge, technology, skills and investment necessary to produce high quality cars in Russia. World automobile giants will be the major driving force of the automotive sector expansion as more and more foreign companies decide to open their production facilities in Russia.

On the other hand the market share in the passenger car segment of 'traditional' domestic car manufactures will continue to shrink. Both AvtoVAZ and GAZ were unable to offer a product of quality and design comparable to those of Western companies. Their most important advantage – low price – will diminish in importance as national welfare continues to increase. Russian manufactures will need to make major investments in R&D in order to create competitive passenger vehicles. These investments, however, seem unlikely at present.

Major FDI projects

General Motors' joint venture with AvtoVAZ is the largest project of this kind. GM, AvtoVAZ and the European Bank of Reconstruction and Development (ERRD) signed a general agreement setting up a joint venture in June 2001. Under the deal, AvtoVAZ provides the facilities, equipment and expertise while GM mainly contributes cash and some equipment. GM and AvtoVAZ each receive a 41.5 per cent stake worth $99.1 million each, while EBRD owns the remaining 17 per cent of stock, worth $40 million. The bank provides an additional $90 million in loans. The joint venture started production of the Chevrolet-Niva

AWD vehicle in September 2002 and is planning to increase its present output capacity. However, GM withdrew its plans to start Opel Astra production at this plant in 2005.

The Ford Motor Company opened a $150 million assembly plant in Vsevolozhsk near St. Petersburg in July 2002 and started the production of Ford Focus cars. The company reduced the original price it charged in Russia for its European-produced Ford Focus by almost 21 per cent, creating a strong competitive advantage by offering its consumers an attractive price-quality combination. As a result, demand for the Ford Focus model produced in Russia (which retails for $11,400 and is available on credit) exceeds supply to such a degree that consumers have to wait up to 3–4 months before getting their cars, having made a down payment or paid full price for them. Currently the number of unfulfilled orders for the Ford Focus produced in Vsevolzhsk stands at 9,000.

Avtotor currently owns assembly factories for BMW and Kia automobiles in Russia. The company is constantly expanding the range and complexity of tasks it performs. The company invested approximately $100 million in BMW production facilities and is currently able to reach an output of 15,000 cars annually. Avtotor can serve as a good example for the future of the Russian automotive industry, where foreign luxury and economy brands being produced in Russia will play a major role.

Consolidation

Consolidation has begun in the industry driven by cash-rich investors, hungry to invest the profits from their primary businesses or create profitable alliances. Siberian Aluminum (SibAl) has been the most active, acquiring a controlling stake in PAZ and a blocking stake (over 25 per cent) in GAZ. It reportedly owns controlling stakes in Likinsky Autobus Plant (LiAZ) and several component suppliers to the industry, focusing mainly on high-value components such as engines. Severstal, another metals giant, has acquired a controlling stake in UAZ. In almost all instances the new owners took immediate action to restructure the acquired companies by reducing debts, improving procurement and distribution, and eliminating barter schemes. We view such consolidation as a positive step for automobile manufacturers, as they can benefit from additional financial resources and experienced management.

Conclusion

According to industry specialists and our estimates, a demand for low-price (under $6,000) automobiles will remain, which will be fully met by domestic producers. However, as disposable incomes of consumers grow, people's preferences will shift towards better quality and better designed foreign car manufacturers. Another significant recent trend in the automotive market is the fast development of auto loans. According to recent data, by September of 2003 Russian banks gave out car loans for a total of 2 billion dollars. This number is projected to grow at a high speed given the fact that most Russian banks currently develop their loan programmes and that consumers are more willing to borrow money from a bank. While the development of auto loans is likely to boost sales in all segments of the car market, we expect the major impact to take place in a segment of foreign inexpensive mid-sized cars with a price tag of $15,000–$20,000. Domestic car makers would not be able to benefit fully from this market trend as their products are not competitive against foreign auto giants. Thus, we are sceptical about how domestic auto producers would be able to withstand tough competition from international giants.

Our somewhat pessimistic approach towards traditional domestic car manufacturers has recently been echoed by Arkady Dvorkovich, Deputy Head of the Ministry of Economic Development, who did not mention the automotive industry as a growth industry. Moreover, he called it 'the most risky industry'. This falls in line with our opinion, as we see the greatest potential for growth in the automotive sector coming from Russia-based production of foreign manufacturers. This is especially true as Renault, Toyota and other giants are seriously considering launching their factories in Russia.

3.10

The Pharmaceuticals Market

Anton Timergaliev, Senior Market Analyst, RMBC

Market size

The Russian pharmaceutical market has now passed the serious breakdown period following the financial crisis of 1998 and, since 2000, has experienced steady growth. As the income of the population increases, this growth shows no signs of weakening (see Figure 3.10.1). While the 16 per cent growth of 2002 was mainly due to the 10 per cent VAT imposed since January 2002, and actual growth of the market in pre-VAT prices was about 6 per cent, the growth rate of 2003 accounted for 17 per cent[1] in actual prices or over 9 per cent in fixed prices. The

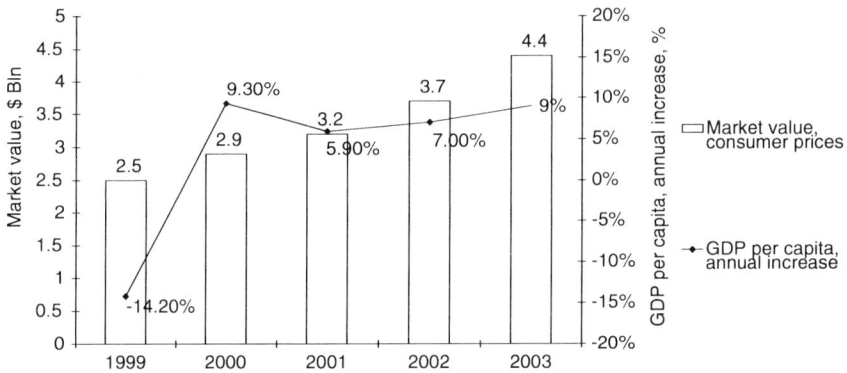

Source: Goskomstat, RMBC

Figure 3.10.1 The Russian pharmaceutical market values ($ billion)

---

[1] Market growth in actual US$ prices accounted for 19 per cent, but this figure was affected by the dynamics of the exchange rate R/$ in 2003. The nominal average exchange rate rise was about 2 per cent, thus the market value growth (ie in rouble prices) accounts for about 17 per cent.

average annual consumption of drugs increased from $17 per capita in 1999 to $26 in 2002, and $30 in 2003. These figures are the result of the significant upturn of the Russian economy and ensuing growth of the income of the population. But, since the income growth resulted from favourable external conditions, some slowdown in market growth is expected for the next few years. According to our forecasts, during the next three years the Russian pharmaceuticals market will be increasing at annual rate of 7–8 per cent (in fixed prices), and in 2006 its value will total $5.5 billion in final consumer prices. This estimate is based on the assumption that the Russian political system will remain stable and that no major changes take place in the Russian legislature.

Market structure

In 2003, sales of pharmaceuticals to pharmacies accounted for about 80 per cent of the total sales in the market, over 15 per cent were for hospital purchases, and federal state procurements accounted for about 5 per cent. The retail sector is dominated by Rx (prescribed) drugs, which account for about 62 per cent of the retail sales (see Figure 3.10.2). Sales to pharmacies have a tendency to increase in the autumn/winter season, a cough and cold period, and have a stable minimum in the summer months (see Figure 3.10.3).

Sales of the Russian pharmaceutical market are concentrated in Russia's major economical and populated regions. In 2003, the cumulative share of the top 10 regions by retail sales value accounted for about 41 per cent of the market, with over half of this figure being accounted for by Moscow and St Petersburg. The population of these two cities together accounts for about 10 per cent of the country's total,

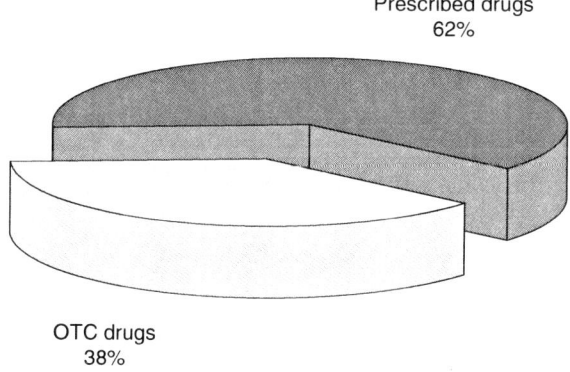

Source: RMBC

Figure 3.10.2 Structure of the retail sector of the pharmaceutical market in 2003, consumer prices

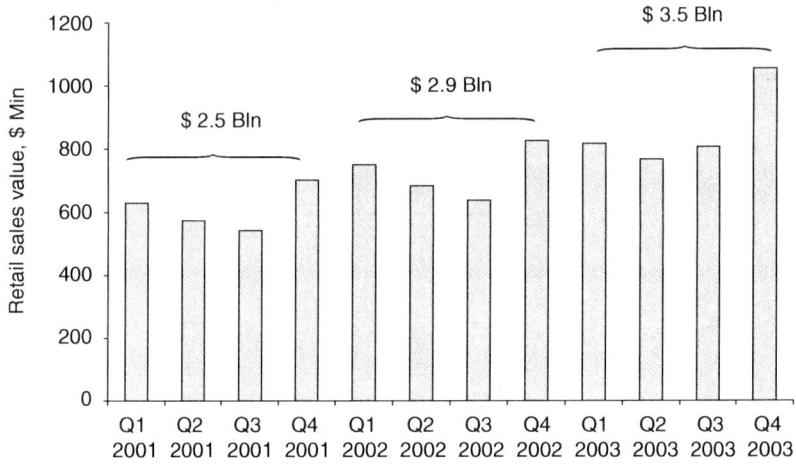

Source: RMBC

Figure 3.10.3 Pharmacy sales of drugs, quarterly dynamics

while in the retail sales of drugs in 2003 Moscow and St Petersburg accounted for 17 and 4.2 per cent of the total, respectively (see Figure 3.10.4). This cumulative share in 2000 accounted for 19.9 per cent of the retail sales, and has been slightly increasing since then at annual rate of 0.5 per cent points, which illustrates the trend of the population's income becoming centralized.

Pharmaceutical supply

The pharmaceutical market in Russia is dominated by imports. In unit terms the cumulative share of domestically-manufactured drugs for

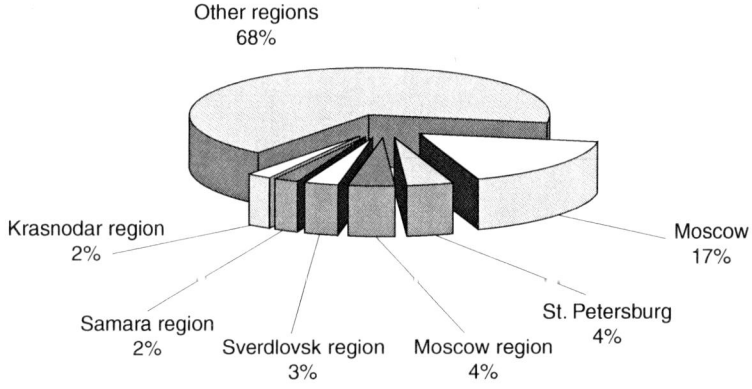

Source: RMBC

Figure 3.10.4 Pharmacy sales of pharmaceuticals by regions in 2003, retail prices

the retail and hospital sectors accounted for over 75 per cent in 2003, but in monetary terms its value was below 30 per cent of the market. This means that the average per-package price for imported drugs is much higher then the average price for domestic drugs. During the last three years the cumulative share of imported drugs in retail sales was almost the same and accounted for 72–73 per cent in value terms. In 2002 it decreased slightly due to the price increase after VAT introduction, but in 2003 the growth of the domestic drugs' total sales value was slower than for the imported ones, and thus the share of the domestic drugs accounted for 27 per cent, the same as in 2001 (see Figure 3.10.5).

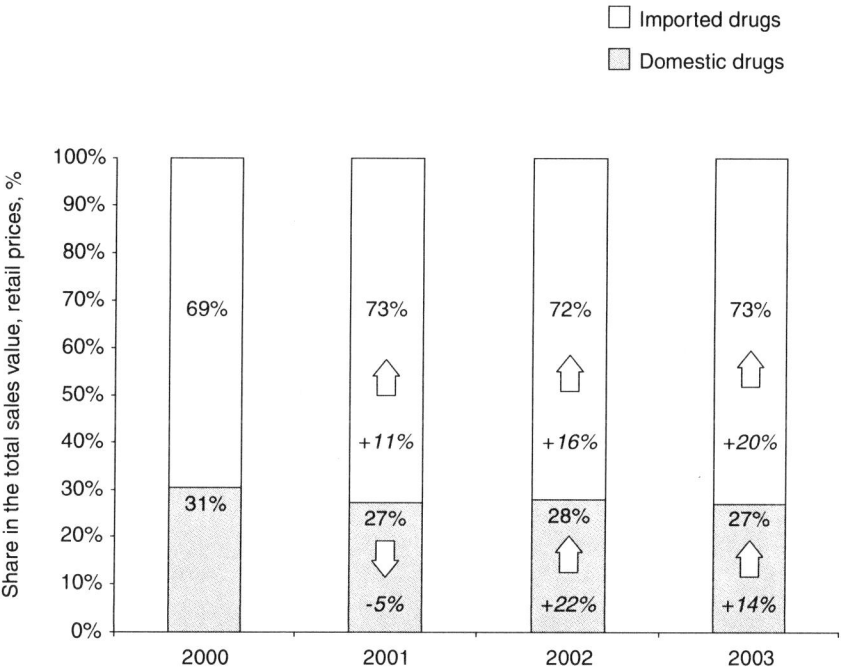

Source: RMBC

Figure 3.10.5 Retails sales of foreign and domestically-manufactured drugs, shares in the total retail sales and annual increase

Annual imports of pharmaceuticals in Russia have been increasing rapidly since 2000 and totalled $2.12 billion in 2003 (see Figure 3.10.6). The announcement of VAT introduction strongly stimulated imports at the end of 2001. This led to an enormous increase of imports that year, followed by a subsequent recession due to the over-stock effect. This explains the recession of the imports values in 2002 and rapid growth in 2003.

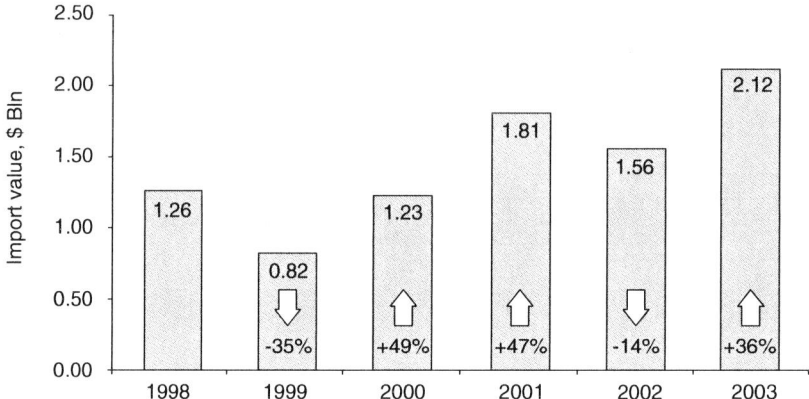

Source: State Customs Committee

Figure 3.10.6 Imports of pharmaceuticals in Russia

The main importers of drugs into Russia are Western countries, and in 2003 the cumulative share of Western Europe, USA, Canada and Japan accounted for 66 per cent of total pharmacy sales and hospital purchases of imported drugs, by value. This is 1 per cent rise over the 2002 figure. The share of Eastern Europe manufacturers accounted for 24 per cent of imported drug sales. Indian manufacturers have about 7 per cent of the market.

The list of the top 10 manufacturers by retail sales and hospital purchases in 2003 includes only foreign companies. The only domestic manufacturer present in 2002 (which includes five pharmaceutical factories that previously belonged to ICN Pharmaceuticals Inc. and were sold in 2003 to a domestic investment company, Profit House) left the top 10 in 2003 (see Figure 3.10.7). The list of the leading producers is relatively stable: apart from the ex-ICN factories, the only company that has left the top 10 in 2003 is Servier Pharmaceuticals. The two new entrants to the list are Nycomed and Lek D.D., which rose from 11th and 14th positions respectively. Apart from these, two other companies had significant sales increases in 2002–2003 – sales of Pfizer International Inc. grew by 30 per cent, and sales of Berlin-Chemie/Menariny Pharma G.m.b.H. grew by 43 per cent.

Domestic manufacture of drugs in Russia in 2003 just reached the pre-1998 crisis level. After a 38 per cent increase recorded in 2000, growth almost stopped during 2001–2002, and only in 2003 did it nearly reach the total market growth figure (see Figure 3.10.8). The list of the leading manufacturers by value in 2003 has not changed since 2002 (see Figure 3.10.9). The shares of most of the leaders slightly increased (the exceptions are Bryntsalov-A, Biosintez, Biohimik); thus, the total share of the top 10 companies accounted for 52 per cent of the total domestic production value, compared to 51 per cent in 2002.

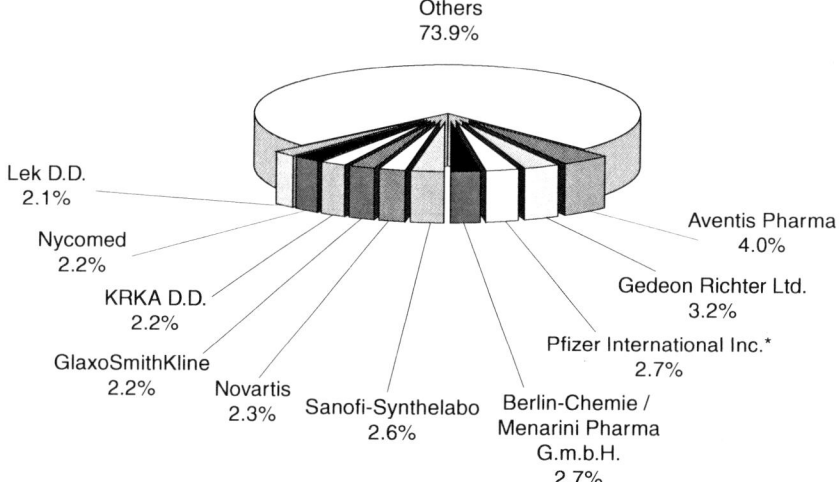

* including Pharmacia N.V./S.A.
Source: RMBC

Figure 3.10.7 Top 10 drug manufacturers by retail sales and hospital purchases value in 2003, wholesale prices

It should be mentioned that by 2005 all pharmaceutical manufacturers in Russia must pass certification under the GMP international standards. Today most of Russia's current pharmaceuticals production facilities employ obsolete equipment and experts estimate that the transition to the GMP standards for the entire Russian pharmaceuticals industry will need some $2 billion worth of new investment. As a result, most of the drugs manufactured in Russia are of a quality

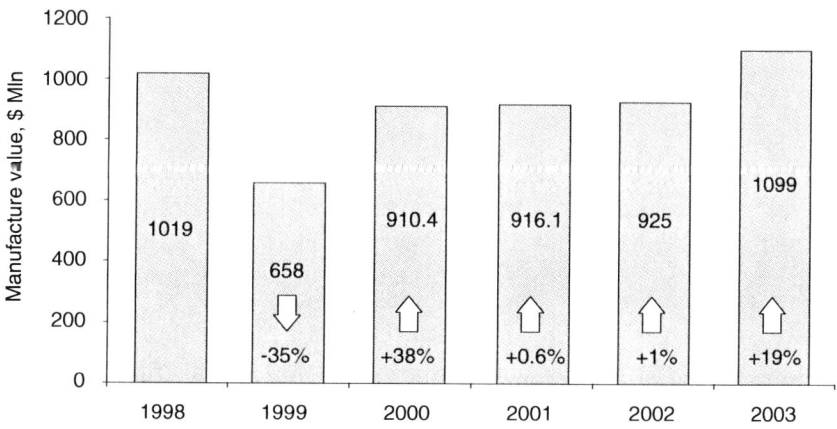

Source: Goskomstat (RMBC analysis)

Figure 3.10.8 Domestic production of pharmaceuticals in Russia

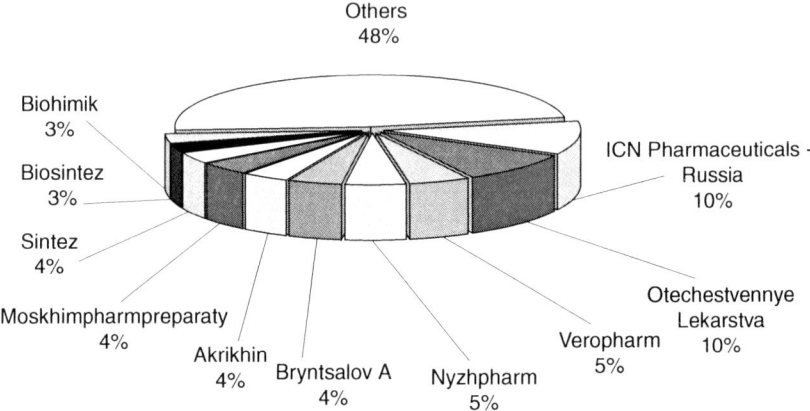

Source: Goskomstat (RMBC analysis)

Figure 3.10.9 Top 10 manufacturers of pharmaceuticals in Russia by production values in 2003

suitable for domestic use only, or for exports to other post-Soviet republics and developing countries. At present only a few companies, about 1 per cent out of a total of 800 pharmaceutical manufacturers, will be able to meet GMP by 2005, and because of this there is the possibility that the GPM transition terms could be changed. On the other hand, these companies are mostly the market leaders and several of them form the active lobby (ARMP),[2] which supports the introduction of the GMP standards in 2005. Thus, the future of the domestic sector of the Russian pharmaceutical market is still very uncertain.

Wholesale distribution of pharmaceuticals

Among the approximately 4,500 pharmaceutical distributors operating in Russia, most operate in their own regions. The largest national distributors are Protek Co., SIA International and Shreya Corporation. According to experts, their cumulative share of the market is estimated at about 50 per cent. In 2003, among the leading distributors a new national player, ROSTA, appeared (as a result of merger of Farm Tamda 77, Rossibfarmacia and Artromed). The share of these four leaders in total pharmaceutical imports in 2003 accounted for 17.4 per cent, 13.5 per cent, 6.1 per cent and 2.6 per cent respectively.

---

[2] Association of Russian Pharmaceutical Manufacturers, which includes such leading domestic companies as Veropharm, Pharmsintez, Nyzhpharm, Ufa-Vita, Otechestvennye Lekarstva, Akrikhin.

It should be noted, that today there is a tendency for the creation of vertically-integrated structures. As a part of this, the leading distributors also try to develop related sectors: pharmaceutical production and the retail sector. Thus, Protek has developed its own manufacturing company, Sotex, and the pharmacy chain in Moscow called Rigla, while another leader, SIA International, has announced its plans to manufacture drugs.

Retail sector

The pharmacy business in Russia includes about 65,000 retail outlets. The share of pharmacies accounts for about 30 per cent of total number of retail outlets, while the smaller drug outlets' share is 70 per cent. About 65 per cent of the pharmacies and 62 per cent of the smaller outlets are state or municipal owned.

According to experts, the main tendency in the pharmacy market is an aggressive growth of networks, especially in the private sector. This process of agglomeration of drugstores into pharmacy networks has been very noticeable during the last few years. In addition, since 2003 there has been an expansion of the large pharmacy networks (such as Rigla, 36'6) into regions. According to experts, the share of these networks today is estimated at 40 per cent of the pharmacy market.

Sales structure

The structure of retail sales by therapeutic groups for the last two years was quite stable: in 2003, changes of shares of ATC groups by first level codes in retail sales did not exceed 0.7 per cent compared to 2002 figures (the top selling therapeutic groups are shown in Figure 3.10.10). The most significant changes in sales structure were the growth of the drugs for treatment of the respiratory system (+0.7 p.p.) and the decrease in the group of medicines for the nervous system (by 0.6 p.p.). The analysis of the retail sales by second level ATC codes groups shows that in 2003 there were no significant changes compared to the corresponding period of previous year (see Table 3.10.1).

The structure of hospital purchases (see Figure 3.10.11) by therapeutic group in 2003 changed more significantly compared to the year 2002. The largest changes were a 2.5 per cent point decrease of the cytostatics & immune modulators and 1.7 per cent point increase of the anti-microbics' share.

188   Market Potential

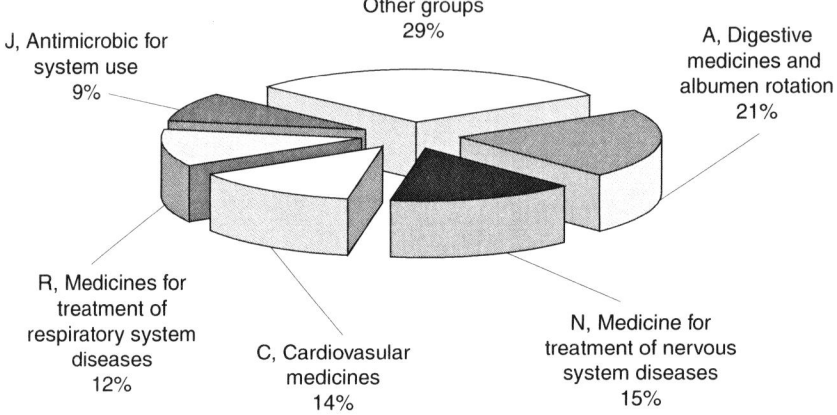

Source: RMBC

Figure 3.10.10 Top 5 ATC groups by retail sales in 2003, retail prices

Table 3.10.1 Top 10 therapeutic groups by retail sales in 2003

Rank 2003	Rank 2002	Code	ATC group	Sales value, in pharmacy purchasing prices, $Mln 2003	2002	Share in pharmacy sales, % 2003	2002
1	1	J01	Antibacterials for systemic use	186.7	170.8	6.9	7.4
2	2	N02	Analgesics	174.1	148.4	6.4	6.5
3	3	A11	Vitamins	141.1	116.8	5.2	5.1
4	4	C09	Agents acting on the renin-angiotensin system	108.5	87.4	4.0	3.8
5	5	N06	Psychoanaleptics	99.9	84.1	3.7	3.7
6	6	R05	Cough and cold preparations	95.3	66.8	3.5	2.9
7	9	G03	Sex hormones	78.4	58.4	2.9	2.5
8	11	M01	Anti-inflammatory and anti-rheumatic products	73.8	55.5	2.7	2.4
9	8	C01	Cardiac Therapy	72.7	63.5	2.7	2.8
10	7	N05	Psycholeptics	68.1	65.8	2.5	2.9
Total top 10				**1098.6**	**917.5**	**40.5**	**40.0**

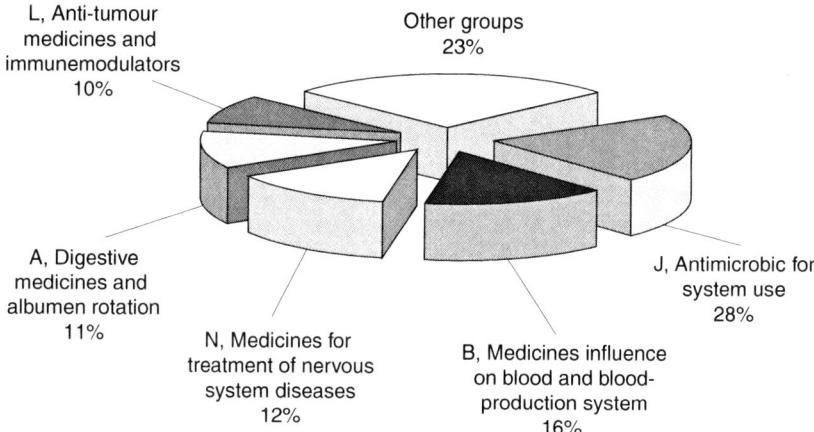

Source: RMBC

Figure 3.10.11 Top 5 ATC groups by hospital purchase value in 2003, wholesale prices

3.11

Investing in Russian Pharmaceuticals: Crisis or Renaissance?

Denis Matafonov, Analyst, Antanta Capital

The Russian pharmaceutical sector remains a 'minefield' for the investor. Purchasing shares in pharmaceutical companies today is considered high risk and we believe that the share's growth potential of the majority of trading companies does not make up for the risk of investments into the sector.

The overall industry and development trends

We believe that industry growth in 2003 may reach 12–15 per cent if the situation in the pharmaceutical sector does not worsen. In 2003, Russian producers will be placed into two categories: those investing in restructuring their production and in the production of new medicines, and those disregarding the problems in the industry. The latter category of producers are most likely to start dumping their products onto the market and might complicate the situation for leading generic companies. Only the best companies will be able to compete successfully with importers.

Currently there are at least 150 large, and a significant number of smaller, producers of finished medicaments in the pharmaceutical market. Their overall annual production has been fluctuating in the range of $850–$900 million over recent years.

How the Russian pharmaceutical sector lost its plants

To better understand the current situation in the sector it is necessary to mention a few very important assumptions upon which its development is based. In Soviet times, Russia produced only the raw ingredients ('substances') for medicines. The drugs themselves were prepared on the basis of these substances in production plants in Poland, Hungary, GDR and Czechoslovakia. This division of labour seemed appropriate, as the development of new substances (and the production of already existing ones) is, in fact, the most complex and highly-technological stage of the production process. The growth of the pharmaceutical sector was very dynamic: average production growth was over 7 per cent during the period of 1980–1991, which was significantly higher than GDP growth. However, the pharmaceutical boom was inevitable considering the level of highly-qualified manpower in the USSR, close integration with other sectors, a high technological level of production and significant investments into science and technology. The medicines produced were in compliance with all the international standards. The volume of substances produced was enough to supply both Russian plants and those in the member countries of the Council for Economic Mutual Assistance.

Unfortunately, the discrepancy in the structure of the production capacity, having been the main advantage of the existing specialization, turned out to have a negative impact on the sector during the mid-1990s, when the pattern of economic development in Russia changed. A significant number of facilities of substances production went out of operation due to lack of timely investment. As a result, Russia transformed from the largest producer into a consumer of substances within the period of a decade. Therefore, pharmaceutical companies in Russia have only one choice today – to build their own plants producing finished medicines on the basis of imported substances and participate in a highly-competitive market with importers, whose current share of producers of finished medicines in Russian is over 82 per cent.

Importers are winning the battle for the market share

Since the beginning of the 1990s, the number of imported goods in Russia has increased dramatically – these goods range from substances to finished medicines. These imported goods are better than the Russian products in quality and often in price.

The structure of imports has also undergone change. In 1999 almost half of Russia's imported medicines came from India, but in 2000 the share of medicines imported from developed countries increased dramatically, and currently stands at about 60 per cent. The flow of imported medicines that flooded the Russian market almost put Russian producers on the verge of extinction. Russian companies have lost the battle for the pharmaceutical market. In 1999, their share of the market was 60 per cent, while in 2002 their share fell to only 20 per cent.

The reduction in sales volumes of Russian medicines is connected first with the reduction in production volumes. While the volumes in

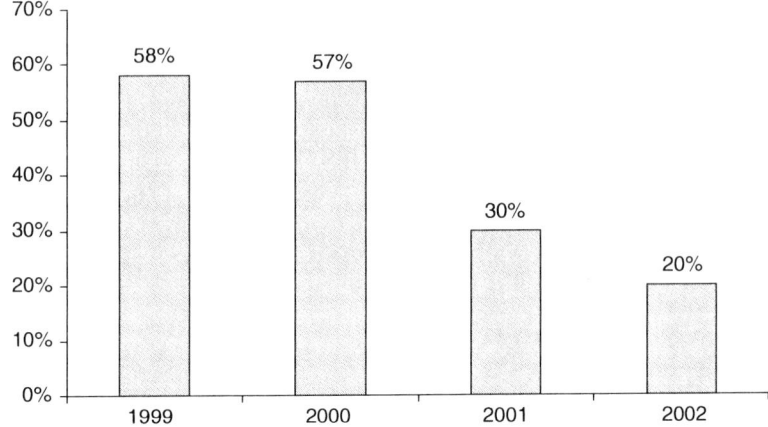

Source: CMI 'Farmexpert'

Figure 3.11.1 The share of the Russian pharmaceutical sector controlled by Russian companies

the pharmaceutical market are growing, the market share of the Russian producers is steadily declining. We believe that the main reason for this is the Russian producers' lack of funds to upgrade their basic assets and increase production – they simply fail to keep pace with market growth. A constant factor of the Russian producers' weakening market position is their failure to ensure they have the required range of medicines, which is mainly due to lack of funds for their own development or for the purchase of licences for production of foreign medications. As a result, the Russian pharmaceutical industry is based on the production of old medicaments and generics – replications of popular drugs that no longer have valid patent protection.

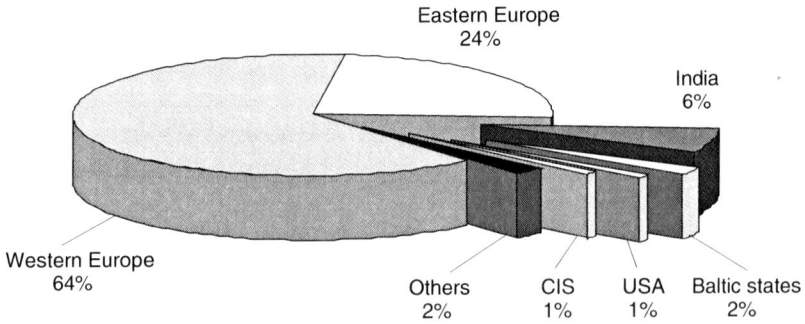

Source: CMI 'Farmexpert'

Figure 3.11.2 Countries supplying pharmaceutical products into Russia

Furthermore, the production of generics is becoming quite complicated due to the strengthening of patent control. Russian producers are becoming absolutely defenseless against importers, especially as at the moment no Russian enterprise fully complies with the international Good Manufacturing Practice (GMP) standards. The best that Russian producers tend to achieve is compliance with GMP using different technological methods.

A special feature of the Russian pharmaceutical sector is also connected to the fact that the enterprises sell their products only in Russia and some CIS countries. Such 'tightness' of the retail market is the result of a poor range and quality of product that does not allow the companies to capture a decent share of the overseas market. In fact, in the domestic market the medications made in Russia are being steadily directed into the low-income consumer sector. In this environment, changes in the Russian pharmaceutical sector are defined, first of all, by the increase in living standards and, as a result, changes in customer preference.

The market is to grow quantitatively, but not qualitatively

Data from Goskomstat suggests that the pharmaceutical sector in Russia is growing quite rapidly – the overall production in the sector increased in real terms by 5.6 per cent in the first quarter of 2004 compared to same period of 2003. But despite that, the market itself is growing much slower. According to the experts' estimates, the incremental growth of consumption in real terms was over 12 per cent, without taking into account 'shadow' (black market) turnover and fake medicines, which play an important role in the Russian market. Currently the volume of the legitimate share of the pharmaceutical market is around $2.8 billion, while another $700–$800 million represents the volume comprising the 'shadow' economy. However, according to expert estimates, there was a significant increase of actual consumption only in the lowest price group of goods; all other groups experienced a shift of demand towards expensive and effective medicines of better quality.

The potential of the pharmaceutical market remains very large. According to expert estimates, an average Russian consumes fewer drugs today than in the Soviet times. Nevertheless, we doubt that the growth dynamics of the sector will be very positive, as the volume of drugs consumption is highly dependent on the level of personal income, which is still quite low.

In terms of consumption of products in the industry in 2002, according to data from Komkon-Farma, only a small proportion of consumers who spend a minimum of $5 p.a. on drugs increased their spending by 12 per cent. The number of Russians spending over $15 p.a. on drugs increased by as much as 5 per cent compared to the previous year. The largest group with consumption in the range of $5–$15 p.a. fell by 7.4 per cent compared to 2001. Thus, we may sum up that the total consumption of drugs in 2002 experienced almost no growth, and in fact the demand shifted towards the more expensive and efficient medicines.

Production and producers

The year 2002 was rich with innovations in the pharmaceutical sector, which were mainly a result of government policies but also the result of large corporate events. A 10 per cent VAT on drugs introduced at the beginning of 2002 has changed the market landscape significantly. It caused a reduction in production volumes and imported deliveries in 2002 compared to 2001. Profit tax relief for the pharmaceutical companies was likewise removed.

The overall financial results demonstrate that the market is experiencing a period of stagnation. Despite the fact that in cash terms the pharmaceutical sector grew by 12 per cent and reached the amount of $2.8 billion, in real terms it fell by 10 per cent. This contradiction is easy to explain, however. At the end of 2001 importers bought a huge amount of medicines before VAT was introduced. Later these products were sold from their warehouses. Also, the increase in turnover was underpinned by appreciation of the euro, as the bulk of imported drugs are delivered through Europe.

According to the overall results from 2002, the output of drugs manufactured in Russia fell by 3 per cent in cash terms and totalled $865 million compared with $896 million in 2001. It is difficult for Russian producers to compete favourably with Western companies in this unstable economic environment. But certain successes are worth mentioning. Brand promotion complies with Western standards and importers treat the issue of competition with Russian pharmaceutical companies quite seriously.

Is the 'black' market the leader of growth?

The black market for medicines in Russia is estimated to be at least $250–$300 million, according to Gostorginspection of MEDT of Russia. This implies that around 10 per cent of the overall sales of drugs are 'fabricated' products, and 67 per cent of the overall amount of these fabricants are produced in Russia.

According to non-official data, illegal sales are $1 billion p.a. and the black market is growing much faster than the legitimate market. In 2002, the share of fabricants increased by 140 per cent compared to 2001, but the actual volume of fabricated products might be larger. The most popular violations in the trading of medicines relate to breach of storage and sales regulations, and the sale of products passed their expiry date.

From a customer's point of view, a 'fabricated' medicine is a fraudulent product that might damage health. From a professional's point of view it is:

- a medicine accompanied by false information about its composition and/or producer, in other words, produced with breach of patent law or without a license; or

- medicine packaged without comprehensive information, medicines with expired expiration date, and medicine with an incorrect composition of active ingredients.

The products in the second group (the majority of fabricants) are often harmless but undermine positions of the State and producers.

A new Pharmaceutical Inspection has been created in the Ministry of Healthcare of Russia, in addition to the system of licensing introduced by the Ministry, and its function of control over the pharmaceutical sector is confirmed by the Law. The Inspection is authorized to check all medical products supplied to the regions, issue certificates of compliance and so on. New rules of certification for all medicines, without exception, were introduced on 15 December 2002. No regulation can be identified either in the Criminal Code or the Administrative Code for production and sale of fabricated or substandard medicines. Inspectors will be actively suspending licences and refusing to certify medicines. These remain the only mechanisms that the State can employ against unscrupulous players.

However, the certification of medicines has not changed the situation in the pharmaceutical sector thus far. In 2002 the Pharmaceutical Inspection captured only an insignificant volume of fabricated products, with a total value of 7 million roubles (approx. $200,000). Fraud is mostly uncovered during public procurement of medicines.

A black list, of companies will soon be created. The regional healthcare authorities and medical networks operators will be able to identify from the list those companies with whom they should avoid dealing. The Ministry of Healthcare believes that such measures, accompanied by changing the regulatory regime for certification of medicines, will result in the establishment of order in the pharmaceutical industry. Furthermore, the high volumes of the certification of imported medicines will also give a competitive advantage to the Russian producers.

Investment barriers in sector

Three main factors underpin the low investment attractiveness of pharmaceutical companies:

- low profitability of the business and strong competition from importers;
- lack of transparency of the companies, combined with very low concentration of production;
- extremely low liquidity of shares of pharmaceuticals. The narrowest spread of a bid and an offer is over 100 per cent.

Low profitability

There are over 150 companies operating in the Russian pharmaceutical sector. However, only 70 companies have any significant turnover (over $1 million) and just a few companies operate with an income margin over 3 per cent. The overall financial situation in the sector is deteriorating. The pharmaceutical sector is not particularly attractive for investors mainly due to tough pressure from importers and the dumping of fake products onto the market by Russian producers. For example, in 2001 the overall revenue of the 50 largest Russian producers was some $914 million, and the overall profit was $87 million. During 2002 the overall sales increased by 9 per cent (up to $970 million), but profit decreased by 35 per cent (down to $57 million). This means that the production of medicines is becoming a less profitable business despite the overall growth of the market.

In theory, the potential of the pharmaceutical sector is quite large. If the welfare of the Russian people increases, their spending on drugs will grow exponentially. At present, the average amount spent by a Russian on drugs is less than $10 p.a., but in about 3–5 years the amount spent might reach $15–20 p.a. However, only the largest companies will benefit from this growth in the market, as they are the ones actively investing in their own production and capable of upgrading their equipment to fit GMG standards, which will become obligatory for Russian producers after 2005. Naturally low profitability and strong pressure from importers leave Russian producers only one possible way forward – to enlarge their businesses. Only if they achieve this, will it become possible to turn the pharmaceutical business into a genuine business, with reduced expenses on marketing and research. Only large companies will be able to access the capital markets and attract investments. The consolidation process has already started. There are three operating holdings in Russia at present. Their overall annual sales exceed $320 million. However, even the largest companies remain non-transparent for investors.

Lack of transparency

The majority of pharmaceutical companies operate in almost full isolation from the 'external' world. Even the largest holdings often do not have PR services or an Internet site. The only information that leaks out from the sector is obligatory financial reports prepared by companies and submitted to the FCSM and Goskomstat. Shareholders and investors gain access to these reports only after significant delay and sometimes they may not be published at all.

Under these conditions, investing in the pharmaceutical industry is a bit of a lottery, as it is risky to rely on the company reports, especially those prepared on the basis of Russian accounting standards. To forecast future results is even more difficult as the internal processes in the sector make it difficult to estimate the development trends of individual companies within it. This problem will be solved only with enlargement of companies and their subsequent access to the capital markets, when the transparency of their information will ensure the attraction of investment.

Low liquidity

Probably, one of the biggest problems facing an investor taking the risk of making portfolio investments into the industry is the liquidity of shares, or more precisely the lack of it. The majority of companies are either state-owned companies (GUP, FGUP) or closed companies (OOO, ZAO) as identified by their type of ownership. Those companies that are officially called joint stock companies in practice are in essence not different from ZAO (closed companies), as they also have a limited number of shareholders and they are likewise isolated from the rest of the world. In theory, an investor can buy shares in only eight companies in the market, and only three of these have a listing on the stock exchange (shares of other companies are available only via the 'phone', off-board market). Nevertheless, the presence of a company on the RTS or MICEX boards does not make its shares more liquid. For example, there is no quotation for the shares of the holding Drugstores 36.6, which completed the IPO on MICEX not long ago. Shares of Biokhimik, Farmakon and Krasfarma are in the same situation. At best, spread between a bid and an offer is over 100 per cent, at worst there is no quotation at all. Thus, the low liquidity of shares in pharmaceuticals automatically implies fixed limited periods of investments. We believe that the minimal period of purchase of shares in Russian pharmaceutical producers is one year.

3.12

The Development of Retail

Alexander Raifeld and Andrei Kouzmin, Deloitte & Touche

Introduction

Retail is arguably the fastest developing industry in Russia. Starting in 1999, the country has made a fast recovery from the economic crisis. Its GDP has grown at an average of 6.3 per cent per year resulting in remarkable growth over the five-year period. This, against a backdrop of a declining population, has meant that per capita GDP has grown even faster. In addition to this, inflation has slowed down and is nearing its critical single-digit level. President Putin, who came to power in 2000, has continued and further strengthened the liberalization process that was already taking place within the Russian economy. Over the past few years Russian legislative bodies have approved many laws aimed at increasing the efficiency of the domestic economy and decreasing the country's dependence on oil monopolies. The political and social stabilization has inspired confidence in foreign investors and the amount of direct and indirect investment in Russia has increased greatly.

Retail has probably benefited the most from these changes. Russian retail chains have grown extraordinarily in size, fully satisfying consumer demand in Moscow and aggressively expanding into other regions. Major Russian retailers have acquired world-class expertise and developed their retail formats based on best Western benchmark operations. Some of the global retailers have also entered into the Russian market by opening their first stores in Moscow over the past three years. Western companies such as Metro, IKEA, Auchan, Obi and others are enjoying great demand within the Russian market. The performance of these companies has exceeded all expectations.

Domestic consumers have benefited from lower prices and better service as a result of the competition between domestic and Western retailers. However, all of the above only really applies to Moscow. There is still an enormous unrealized growth potential in the industry for both domestic and international retailers to expand into the country's regions.

Macroeconomic trends

Russia has experienced a surprisingly robust economic turnaround since the 1998 crisis. The country's GDP has risen dramatically, reaching approximately $380 billion in 2003. Economic growth has been based mainly on high oil prices, which have provided solid profits for domestic oil companies and strong tax revenues for the federal government. This favourable macroeconomic factor was used to strengthen domestic industries and to reorganize some of Russia's key industries. Vladimir Putin has also worked hard to reduce corruption within the State. Although corruption persists, it has diminished greatly since the 1990s. Another major achievement of the past few years is the stabilized social environment within the country.

All these steps have had a major influence on Russia's political and economic situation. Western companies have become more willing to invest in Russia. BMW, Ford, Mars, Gillette and others have opened factories here. British Petroleum has made a $3 billion direct investment in Russian TNK Oil Company. The economy has clearly benefited from accelerated foreign investment, a reflection of the increasing regard with which foreign investors hold Russia. They believe that Russia has turned the corner, having tackled corruption and accelerated the reform process. Indeed Russia's government debt has now achieved investment grade status, something that cannot be said for many leading Western corporations, reflecting confidence in the integrity of the country's financial management.

A significant growth in the disposable incomes of the Russian population coupled with increased future confidence has brought about an explosion in consumer spending. In 2003 real incomes grew by 14.5 per cent while real wages increased by 10.4 per cent and the retail industry was the greatest beneficiary of these trends. The turnover of Russian retail grew by 10.6 per cent in 2002 and by 8.0 per cent in 2003 to amount to $154 billion. The industry has become more structured and sophisticated. The number of self-service stores has risen dramatically, as consumers have been introduced to new store formats. Hypermarkets, discount outlets, DIY and cash-and-carry formats have quickly found their market niches. We believe that retail will continue to develop quickly in Russia due to the country's positive macroeconomic outlook and the fact that the national GDP is projected to grow 5–7 per cent annually until the year 2010. Moreover as the country begins to invest in non-oil related industries, more regions will be able to afford modern self-service retail outlets. Thus we believe that the recent macroeconomic trends provide a solid foundation for future development of retail.

Major trends in Russian retail

Russian retail in 2003 has been characterized by three major trends: the arrival of foreign players, the expansion into the regions by both domestic and international operators, and the rapid construction of modern shopping malls. These trends have had a major shaping influence on the Russian retail sector. We also consider them to be key determining factors in the industry's development.

Positive changes in the economic, political and social situation in Russia have made Western companies more willing to invest in the country. They have also been impressed by the positive experience of early investors in the Russian retail sector. The principal success stories were Ramenka, a Turkish hypermarket operator (Ramstore brand), and IKEA, the Swedish furniture retailer. In the latter case, IKEA's first store has been so successful that its primary challenge has been to supply enough merchandise to the store so it could to satisfy consumer demand. Now IKEA is expanding its operations in Russia. Not only is it opening new stores, it is developing sourcing relations within Russia, to supply its Russian stores and to supply stores throughout Europe. Moreover, IKEA is involved in developing shopping centres, an important new type of shopping venue for Russia. Ramenka was similarly successful with its Ramstore hypermarkets and supermarkets. Currently the company operates 26 stores in Moscow and in two other major Russian cities. It is these positive examples that have increased Western companies' willingness to invest in Russia.

Recently a few major European companies have opened their stores in Moscow. The most prominent ones are Germany's Metro, a cash-and-carry operation, Auchan, the French hypermarket chain, and Obi, a German DIY retailer. Metro expects to have 20 stores in Russia by the end of 2005. Six cash-and-carry stores were operating in 2003. The next 14 stores will include several Real hypermarkets, as well as Media Markt electronic stores. Auchan has three hugely successful hypermarkets already and the company plans to have 10 hypermarkets in operation within the next two or three years. Meanwhile, Obi opened its two stores in Moscow at the end of 2003. Other major global retailers known to be closely considering Russia are Carrefour, Tesco and Wal-Mart.

The other major trend is expansion into the regions by major domestic retailers. As the Moscow market becomes more and more crowded and the level of disposable income increases throughout the country, regional expansion becomes increasingly attractive. Almost all major retailers have opened their stores in major cities throughout Russia. Electronic retailers, some grocery stores, and a DIY chain, Starik Hottabych, are especially notable for establishing their regional presence. Eldorado, the largest Russian retailer, operates 439 stores in 295 cities. Pyaterochka, the leading grocery discount chain, has developed a very popular franchise programme and therefore has been successful in developing its national network. Metro has opened its first stores in St.Petersburg. IKEA is rapidly developing its regional network as well. We believe this trend will continue over the next few years as retailers try to occupy new local markets for themselves. Retailers understand the importance of establishing a presence in the regions ahead of competitors. We expect the market share of self-service chain stores will increase quickly in the regions.

Finally, the third trend that characterizes the development of Russian retail is the construction of modern shopping malls. Two major historical Moscow shopping centres, GUM and TSUM, are currently undergoing major renovation and market repositioning. The operators of these buildings plan to turn them into modern shopping centres with a full array of goods and services for consumers. In addition to that a large number of malls have been constructed in Moscow and other major Russian cities. Among the new largest Moscow malls are the Mega Mall, Atrium, Crocus City Mall, Rublevsky, Ramstore-City and others. Mega Mall occupies approximately two million square feet hosting three anchor stores – IKEA, Auchan and Obi, as well as an array of smaller retailers. Within the past couple of years shopping centres have become attractive to many Muscovites. People appreciate the extensive range of stores and entertainment facilities. We are confident that many new malls will be constructed not only in Moscow, but in all major Russian cities over the next few years.

Russia's largest retailers

Supermarkets

Perekriostok, Ramstore and Sedmoy Kontinent (The Seventh Continent) are the three major supermarket operators in Russia. These companies are based in Moscow, they each operate a chain of 20 to 50 stores and generate an annual revenue of $300–400 million. These companies possess a very strong world-class expertise in food retail; we expect them to continue expansion both within and outside the Moscow city region. Food retail is arguably the best-developed sector of the industry and consequently, is one of the most competitive ones. As competition increases in Moscow, these companies will move to other regions to open new markets for themselves.

Discount outlets

Discount chains arrived in Russia relatively recently, yet they have been able to find a large market niche by providing customers with high-quality low-cost products. Pyaterochka and Kopeyka are the two largest retailers in this format. Pyaterochka's sales exceeded $700 million in 2003, making the company Russia's second largest retailer. The company itself operates a total of 172 stores in Moscow and St. Petersburg. It also has 47 stores working in five other Russian cities under franchise and the company is currently completing its state-of-the-art distribution centre. Discount outlets have a very high chance of success in the regions, as the average income level there is significantly lower than it is in Moscow.

Electronics

Electronics stores are perhaps the best-developed in Russia. There are a few sector leaders, such as Eldorado, M-Video, MIR, Technosila, and Partya. Eldorado is the largest retail company in Russia with its annual sales exceeding $1 billion. The company has been able to establish its presence in all major Russian and CIS cities. The company established its first Russian nation-wide store network by opening branches in all the nation's regions. Eldorado has pursued a low-price strategy, undercutting its high-margin rivals. Its aggressive marketing strategy allows the company to attract consumers away from its competitors. M-Video is the third largest Russian retailer with its sales approaching $573 million. Electronics retailers have been the most active in building their stores in the regions. They have accumulated the necessary skills and experience as well as the finances to edge out the local retailers.

DIY

Starik Hottabych, Russia's first DIY operator, has been very successful. The Moscow-based company has moved into the regions, opening its stores in key Russian cities. Currently the company operates 19 stores in Moscow and 11 stores in different cities throughout the country. The company's success is based on its strong focus in certain categories, such as ceramic tiles, carpeting, bathroom accessories and flawless execution of merchandise planning and selection. The company has been preparing for the mass arrival of Western DIY leaders, such as Obi and Marktkauf, who opened their first store in Russia last year. We believe that the DIY retail segment will develop rapidly throughout Russia, primarily due to the presently unsaturated market and high consumer demand. Local players, such as Starik Hottabych, will be under severe pressure in Moscow, as the foreign retailers move in. It will force Moscow-based local retailers to intensify their regional development.

Cash-and-Carry

Metro was the first Western company to enter the Russian market with its cash-and-carry format. The company presently operates six outlets and announced plans to invest an additional $1 billion into its retail network over the next four to five years. It plans to develop its wholesale business and open up to 20 Real hypermarkets. Lenta is the most successful Russian cash-and-carry operator, although its format is more like US-style warehouse clubs. The company is based in St. Petersburg and is planning to start expansion into the regions next year. We believe that the cash-and-carry format can be successfully replicated in all major cities throughout Russia.

Hypermarkets

The Turkish retail chain Ramenka was the first one to build hypermarkets in Russia in 1997. Since then, several other players have pursued this format. The most successful entry into the Russian market has been made by Auchan, a French retailer. According to unofficial sources, the turnover of an average Moscow Auchan is close to $400,000, which greatly exceeds comparable Western operations. Another promising Moscow player is Mosmart, which is currently operating one hypermarket and is in the process of building several more. The company was able to attract Western specialists, who developed a similar format in Poland.

Perfumes

Arbat Prestige is a leading Moscow-based cosmetics and fragrances retailer. The company achieved sales of $200 million in 2003. Arbat Prestige has become a widely recognized brand due to its aggressive marketing policy and a strong merchandising programme. One of its rivals, L'Etoile, recently purchased a franchise from Sephora, a world leader in cosmetics retail. We believe that the fragrances market will become more competitive as more foreign companies continue to establish their presence in Russia.

Luxury clothes and accessories

One could say that in terms of the luxury goods market, Moscow is on par with Europe's and America's largest cities. The three largest luxury retailers are Bosco Di Chiliegi, DjamilCo and Mercury, with the latter being the sector's largest company with estimated sales of $250 million in 2003. Mercury occupies a large market niche selling various luxury goods from watches and jewelry, to top-brand clothes and luxury cars. Both Bosco and Mercury purchased historical shopping malls in the centre of Moscow, planning to develop them into upscale modern retail complexes. There are many smaller niche players in this retail market segment, serving a variety of tastes of local elite clientele. Moscow-based luxury goods retailers started to establish their presence in other Russian cities by opening their stores in other high-income regions and major cities.

Future outlook

We believe that the Russian retail industry will continue to develop according to present trends. The local retail market will become more sophisticated as the number of open-air markets and kiosks continues to diminish. Russians are slowly become more discriminating as consumers and local retailers are trying to improve their services to retain customer loyalty. We predict the future development and specialization of retail formats, with domestic retailers becoming even more professional and efficient as they compete with established Western companies. Regional expansion will continue to take place as both Russian and Western retailers open branches throughout Russia.

Shopping malls will become a hot topic for the next few years. This is especially true given the fact that most Russian cities have available space for shopping centre development. Modern shopping malls will not only provide convenient shopping for local residents but will also serve as entertainment complexes.

We also expect more successful foreign retailers to enter the Russian market in the medium term. Wal-Mart, Carrefour and other possible entrants will bring their own expertise, thus making retail in Russia even more efficient and competitive.

Conclusion

We believe that there is enormous unrealized growth potential within the Russian retail sector. So far only selected Moscow retail chains operate to Western standards. The development of modern retail formats in the regions, coupled with a fast-growing level in disposable income, creates a unique opportunity for both local and foreign retailers. We expect the retail industry to grow at a rate, exceeding those of most other sectors of the economy. We see unique opportunities in Russian retail as the country quickly accumulates wealth and moves towards a consumer society and market economy.

3.13

The Brewing Industry

Deloitte & Touche

Market potential

Over the past six years, the Russian beer industry has experienced a real boom. Since 1998 the Russian beer market has grown an average of 16 per cent per annum. This is in stark contrast to developed countries, where the beer industry is mature and has limited growth opportunities. The transition to a market economy in Russia has also changed lifestyles among part of the population, encouraging a shift away from 'hard' alcohol. Beer has become increasingly seen as a social drink on par with traditional vodka. According to industry experts, beer sales rose to approximately 40 per cent of the drinks market in 2003. The Russian Brewery estimates that in 2004 vodka and beer spending will be 36.6 per cent and 39.7 per cent correspondingly. Beer demand rose from 47 litres per person per year in 2002 to 49 litres per person last year.[1] This consumption is still low in comparison with other European countries (eg in the Czech Republic it is 160–180, and the world average is 60 litres per year) and thus could still have some growth potential.

In 2000–2001, most analysts were overly optimistic about beer market growth prospects, forecasting long-term growth of over 20 per cent per annum. However, the market situation proved different in 2002, when growth stopped. Between January and May 2003, production fell by 1.2 per cent and in June 2003 (the hottest time for brewers) it was 8 per cent lower compared to the same period in 2002. According to the results of the first quarter of 2003, production in value terms shrank by five per cent reaching $140.1 million as opposed to $147.3 million in the same period last year. At the same time volume grew by some 4.2 per cent (732 million decilitres), also falling short of analysts' expectations. Thus, beer production is still growing in volume terms, however at a significantly lower rate. This is no wonder, as beer market development prospects largely depend on the growth in beer price compared to other

---

[1] According to EIU.

alcohol. In the past the development of the beer market has clearly been affected by variations of excise taxes and changes in barriers to the distribution of cheap illegally produced alcohol. Consumption in terms of pure alcohol volume per capita has been impressively stable over the past two to three decades. This is due not only to changing drinking habits but also to the change in relative price. Thus, growth deceleration can, to a large extent, be attributed to the introduction of a higher 25 per cent excise on beer from 1 January 2003. The other factor could be changes and restrictions in advertising campaigns that came in due to the anticipated banning of beer commercials by the Duma. Nevertheless, the general growth in production continues. According to various estimates, in 2004 it will amount to 5–8 per cent.

The brewing industry has attracted about $1 billion in investment during the past five years, and domestic brewers are expanding production to meet the increasing demand. The size of the Russian beer market is now estimated at about $5 billion. By 2008 it will be worth even more. Investments in the industry are guaranteed for the coming 4–5 years, due to the anticipated long-term market growth. At the same time it is critical for investors to evaluate market potential, existing brewing capacity and distribution constraints, before investing.

Demographics and market characteristics

Young Russian consumers aged 18–35 have shown a clear preference for beer over vodka and other spirits, and this preference continues to strengthen and gain momentum. Brand awareness, once considered a capitalist manifestation and a scourge to be avoided, is likely to take hold as these educated consumers become increasingly dependent on brands to ensure consistent and world-class quality. However, industry analysts have noticed that consumers are still eager to explore new brands and, in general, brand loyalty remains low.

The major market participants invest heavily in advertising in the hope of developing the brand equity seen by their counterparts in established European, Asian and US markets. The competition is so high that advertising continues all the year round. Russian beer marketers spend about $90 million a year on advertising. Advertising is centred on television, radio and, to a lesser extent, print media. However, breweries have recently come under fire for allegedly targeting underage consumers. This criticism culminated in potential restrictions being imposed on beer advertising. On 16 September 2002 the State Duma passed the second reading of changes to the law on advertising, which would ban beer advertisements between 5pm and 10pm and the use of people or animals in beer ads. Although the restrictions have yet to become law it is a clear indicator that there will be some regulation of beer advertising in the future.

A few beer festivals have also sprung up, mainly in St. Petersburg and Moscow, attracting thousands each year. Point-of-sale advertising has begun in bars and restaurants. However, kiosks, which still account for the majority of sales, present their own unique problems.

Geographical trends are also clear. Moscow and St. Petersburg have a per capita consumption twice the average of other regions; however, less than one-tenth of the population lives in these two cities. Brewers must not only have a presence in Moscow and St. Petersburg, but also Siberia and the Urals to be considered an industry leader. The difference in these two markets further complicates this issue.

The capital cities: Moscow and St. Petersburg

Market saturation in Moscow and St. Petersburg (beer consumption more than 60 litres per capita a year) approaches the lower average European level (80 litres per capita a year). Analysts identify greater customer sophistication and an increase in price competition.

The Moscow and St. Petersburg markets are dominated by consumers with higher disposable incomes, who are more concerned with quality and brand, although price still remains a factor. If the economy is able to maintain its healthy growth rate, industry leaders may be able to reap some rewards for the massive investments they have made. However, it is clear that within the capital cities price is less important among the young and affluent, but shows significantly increased sensitivity among the less well off and consumers over 35. This differs dramatically from the regions – here price is the leading, and some would argue the only, factor.

The regions

For those unfamiliar with the Russian market, the difference between the capital cities and the regions can be mind-boggling to say the least. Realistic estimates place the country's wealth in its two historical capitals anywhere from 30 to 35 per cent. While Moscow and St. Petersburg have large populations with disposable incomes, vast portions of the population in the regions have little, if any, disposable income. Disposable income tends to be more concentrated in the hands of a very few in the regions when compared to the capital cities.

These regional markets were traditionally served by low quality/low cost manufacturers, not only in the case of beer, but also in that of all consumer goods. Historically, only one brand was available. Manufacturing decisions were based entirely on cost reduction implications. Advertising in the regions is difficult due to the lower population density. In addition, brand awareness and loyalty can seem foolish to some people. At present, beer consumption per capita does not exceed 20 litres a year per capita in some regions; for instance, in Khabarovsk or Tumen, beer consumption amounts to 15 litres a year per capita.

The regions have proved to be one of the most difficult issues facing market leaders. While branding, advertising and quality control (areas in which international brewers excel) work in the capital cities, price is the leading factor in the regions. Another issue is the sheer size of the regions. Operations in Vladivostok are geographically closer to the capitals of Canada, the United States, Japan and China, than they are to Moscow. Communications and travel logistics present another difficulty when managing these remote regions. Nevertheless, regional expansion is vital for market players who wish to gain a leading position in the Russian beer market.

The largest players have started considering establishing their own production facilities to the east of the Ural Mountains. Krasny Vostok opened a brewery in Novosibirsk in 2003 (its capacity is 30 million decilitres) and Baltika built its brewery in Khabarovsk (10 million decilitres). A branch of the Moscow-based Ochakovo will become operational in Tumen in 2004 (up to 15 million decilitres a year). Local brewers have also started increasing production, such as the Omsk-based Rosar (belonging to Sun Interbrew) and Pikra (belonging to Baltic Beverages Holding). In the summer of 2003, three large brewing companies – SUN Interbrew, Efes and TSEPKO – announced that they planned to buy new breweries. All three companies demonstrate the biggest interest in the markets of the Ural region, Siberia and the Far East, where beer consumption is growing much faster than in the European part of Russia. According to UFG, the capacity of the Siberian beer market is 80 million decilitres a year and production capacity in the region, taking into account the fact that breweries that are not operational yet, amounts to 72 million decilitres.

Analysts view large-scale overproduction in Moscow and St. Petersburg as the main reason for large brewing companies' interest in regional expansion. It is logical to presume that if growth slowed down slightly in Moscow and St. Petersburg, the overall positive trend would account for growth acceleration in the regional markets. Moreover the relocation of production lets them save a lot of money. According to the CEO of Business-Analytika, Andrei Sterlin, if companies start brewing the beer in Siberia that they sell in Siberia, they will be able to save up to 10 per cent on logistics and transportation.

Apart from the bottled beer market, the microbrewery/brewpub market is beginning to develop in Russian regions. Siberia provides an example of these developments in the Russian provinces. In Tomsk, Tomsk Beer has opened a bar and restaurant complex adjacent to its brewery, while the Omsk-based Sibirskaya Korona brewery (controlled by Sun Interbrew) has established its own bar/restaurant in Tomsk.

Competitive situation

The Russian beer market underwent a fundamental change at the end of 2002 – switching from extensive growth to consolidation. The beer market is already dominated by just three companies: Baltika, SUN Interbrew and Ochakovo, which together claim more than 54 per cent of the market. It is difficult to state the market share accurately, but reasonable projections are shown in Tables 3.13.1 and 3.13.2.

Table 3.13.1 Market share

Producer	Share (%) 1H2003	Share (%) 2002
Baltic Beverages Holdings (BBH)	33.4	32.8
SUN Interbrew	13.5	12.5
Ochakovo	7.5	8.3
Krasniy Vostok	7.0	7.1
Heineken	4.6	4.1
Ivan Taranov Brewery (owned by Detroit Brewing)	4.1	5.0
Efes Brewery	3.3	2.7
Stepan Razin	2.1	2.6
SUBMiller	2.0	1.9
Others	21.5	22.0
Imports	1.0	1.0

Source: Reuters, UFG, Goskomstat, Annual reports, companies presentations

Table 3.13.2 Beer output by the major players, 2002

Producer	Output 2002, HL mln.
Baltic Beverages Holdings (BBH)	16.1
SUN Interbrew	8.1
Ochakovo	5.7
Krasniy Vostok	5.2
Ivan Taranov Brewery (owned by Detroit Brewing)	3.2
Heineken	2.8
Efes Brewery	2.6
SUBMiller	1.8
Stepan Razin	1.7

Source: Renaissance Capital estimates

Three major trends that are expected to continue in the industry are further consolidations, mainly through foreign direct investment, struggling imports and regional expansion. The import segment, which accounted for nearly 15 per cent of the market in 1996, was dramatically affected by the economic crisis of 1998 as consumers shifted their loyalties to locally produced brands. The economic crisis, coupled with improved branding and the quality of local products, drove imports down to about 1 per cent in 2002. Many of the world's largest brewers have invested in the Russian market to capture the market share, not only with locally-produced international brands, but also by investing in the creation of Russian brands (see Table 3.13.3). Other international brewers, without local operations, have licensed the local production of their international brands.

Table 3.13.3 Brewers and their brands

International brewer	International and local brands
Baltic Beverages Holdings	Yarpivo, Cheliabinskoe, Zolotoy Ural, Kupecheskoe, Ubileynoe, Siberian Legend, Baltika, Don, Arsenalnoe, Carlsberg, Parnas, etc.
SUN Interbrew	Tolstyak, Klinskoe, Siberian Crownz, Stella Artois, Volzhanin, Bavaria
SUBMiller	Zolotaya Bochka, Staropramen (Licensed), Holsten (Licensed), Miller (Licensed), Tri Bogatirya
Efes Beverages Group	Stary Melnik, Efes (Licensed)
Bravo (now Heineken)	Bochkarov, Lowenbrau (Licensed), Bear Beer (Licensed), Ohota, Exportnoye, nonalcoholic Buckler
Ivan Taranov Brewery	Pit, Tri Medvedya, Doctor Diesel, Gosser (licensed, super premium brand)

Source: Renaissance Capital, Business Communication Agency

The brewing industry is one of the leaders in terms of attracting foreign direct investment, with several major companies active in Russia – South African Brewers is in Kaluga, SUN Interbrew (Belgian-Indian joint venture) in the Moscow region and Omsk, Efes (Turkey) in the Moscow region, and Heineken in St. Petersburg. This influx of foreign investment has engendered serious competition from Russian brewers (St. Petersburg's Baltika dominates the market, while Kazan's Krasniy Vostok and Moscow's Ochakovo are major players as well). Foreign capital dominance in the beer industry continues to grow, pushing out small domestic Russian brewers.

Branding: The national brand

As with all consumer goods, branding, once irrelevant in the Russian market, has become critical. The value of branding can differ between regions and between consumer groups. The race is on among the leading brewers to develop and promote a strong national brand and achieve national coverage.

Competition for consumers is becoming fierce against the background of slowing beer market growth. Brewing companies are attempting to protect their positions with the assistance of new brands, primarily in the premium segment, as price competition results in margin erosion. For companies, profits lie in the perceived extra value of brand names. And as the dominant brands establish their positions, the focus of competition shifts.

Table 3.13.4 Key brands share of total market, 2002

Key Brands	Owner	Volume (%)	Share (%)
Baltika	BBH	12.4	12.0
Ochakovskoe	Ochakovo	7.7	7.6
Arsenalnoye	BBH	5.3	4.5
Yarpivo	BBH	4.0	3.2
Klinskoye	SUN Interbrew	3.8	3.9
Tolstyak	SUN Interbrew	2.7	3.0
Volga	BBH	2.6	2.4
St. Razin	St. Razin	2.6	2.6
Bochkarev	Heineken	2.2	2.5
Medovoye	BBH	2.1	3.2
Don	BBH	2.1	1.6
Okhota	Heineken	1.6	0.8
Sib. Korona	SUN Interbrew	1.5	1.5
Nevskoye	BBH	1.5	1.3

Source: Goskomstat, companies presentations

While some international brewers have introduced domestically produced international brands, others have sought to further increase the brand awareness of a number of their selected local brands. Baltika launched four new brands with low-cost labels, packaging and advertising in March 2003. The new brands are called Krasnoyarskoye, Krasnodarskoye, Tyumenskoye and Sverdlovskoye after the cities where they will be marketed. Patra has added a new beer brand to its product range – the 'Knyazhe Gold'. Vinap has closed beer production in the Novosibirsk brewery, with production starting in the new Sobol brewery with new brands Kaltenberg and Sobol being produced alongside Zhigulyevskoe, the only one of seven previous brands to be continued. For the Vena Brewery 2003 was a turning point: the company rebranded their leader, Nevskoye, and also launched several new brands, including Triumph and Kronverk. The Stepan Razin Plant (St. Petersburg) invested $0.5 million into the production of Ordinar Premium, a new beer brand, in 2003. The successful introduction of new brands is partially explained by the fact that Russian consumers tend to be more loyal to new brands than to old brands that have been changed.

Table 3.13.5 Beer market segmentation, 2001 and 2002 (%)

	Segment share of total beer market	2002 (%)	2001 (%)
Import	KupecheskoyeBavaria, Staropramen, Heineken, Corona Extra, Foster's	1	1
Licensed	Miller, Lowenbrau, Holsten, Staropramen, Efes, Stella Artois, {Tuborg, Carlsberg}- BBH	2	1
Premium	Zolotaya Bochka, Stary Melnik, Solodov, Bochkarev, {Baltika0, Baltika2, Baltika5, Baltika7, Baltika 8 Parnas, Nevskoe}- BBH	16	11
Mainstream	Sibirskaya Korona, Klinskoye, Tolstyak, Stepan Razin,Volzhanin, Pit, Okhota, {Baltika3, 4, 9, Sibirskaya Legenda, Don, Yarpivo, Arsenalnoye, Medovoye, ZolotoyUral, Kupecheskoye}	60	59
Economy	Ohakova, Krasny Vostok, {Voronezhskoye, Chelyabinskoye, Uralskiy Master}	21	28

Source: UFG, companies' presentations

Overall, in the same year, mass-market brands lost their positions, and premium brands gained them. The premium segment grew rapidly, not only due to the appearance of new brands, but also as a result of changing several old mass brands.

Quality matters

Overall beer consumption may continue to grow in the future, as analysts predict, but it is already clear that the high-quality beers will dominate the market.

Since the 1998 crisis, there have been great profits to be made by investing heavily in domestic production facilities to meet new demands for quality. Additionally, as competition heats up, larger breweries have begun buying up smaller facilities. They have been working hard to increase the quality of locally-supplied ingredients and packaging materials, which is helping to cut operational costs and keep standards high. The marketing of beer on tap, an area that was almost entirely neglected during the Soviet era, has also been on the increase, with consumers appreciating the quality improvement over canned or bottled beers.

This high quality is supported by the fact that foreign brands are seeking to produce their beers locally under licensing agreements. Major international players have been quick to establish themselves in this growing market. For instance, the Baltika Brewery has entered an agreement with the Danish brewing company, Carlsberg, to produce approximately 10,000 hectolitres per year in Baltika's plant in Rostov-on-Don.

Active promotion of new kinds of beer packaging is another opportunity to increase sales. The effect of canned beer advertising is evident. According to AC Nielsen, the share of canned beer sales grew from 9 per cent between January and May 2002 to 12 per cent between January and May 2003.

Distribution channels

While traditional bars, pubs, restaurants and food outlets have their own slight deviations in the Russian market, no challenge is greater than that of the Russian kiosk. The equivalent to Western convenience stores, these independent outlets sell the vast majority of the hectolitres consumed in the Russian Federation. Often stocked through middlemen, they offer unique quality control issues to brewers intent on maintaining brand loyalty. While the brewing techniques are the primary focus for quality improvements, the brewers can lose all control at the point of sale. Often, sales are of the lower quality brands, which sell based on price. However, these issues create obstacles for premium brands to overcome.

Table 3.13.6 Store classifications selling beer, March 2002 (%)

Store type	Beer sales
Mixed and food stores	53%
Impulse kiosks and pavilions	38%
Open markets	9%

Source: ACNielsen

Geographical and structural problems are specific to the beverages industry in Russia. Russia's size, the relatively low concentration of population and weak retail network limit the opportunities for a greater degree of market dominance. It is difficult and costly to get products onto shelves – the result is a dominance of locally-produced local brands that holds back national consolidation. And it takes time for national players to emerge and establish dominance in the local marketplace.

Focus

Acquiring local breweries, as opposed to greenfield projects, has driven growth among the largest market players. In most instances, the local authorities and the local management see these local entities as part of the beverage market rather than the beer market. Many local Russian beer companies also bottle local-branded soft drinks, mineral water, juice or hard liquor. Larger brewers must constantly fight to maintain their focus on beer. Some have maintained these side businesses; others have spun them off or have simply stopped producing. As with any acquisition in the former Soviet Union, the 'other assets' accompanying the productive assets can present unique challenges to those who do not have a clear mission.

Conclusion

Although market growth is slowing down, making industry watchers nervous, the simple fact is that the Russian beer market remains extremely attractive. The main reason for beer companies to invest in Russia has not changed: Russia can still offer growth. There is additional growth in the regions, in shifting customers up to higher-margin beer products, in diversifying packaging, and finally there is growth as beer continues to replace other beverages among consumers in their consumption patterns. The main difference now for companies is to identify properly where the best opportunities are, whereas in the past growth was so rapid it was not very important which space one occupied in the market. Unlike some other consumer goods industries, there will always be room for small niche players, but this space will continually decrease and the niche must be better defined than simply by geography.

With the challenges of branding, market segmentation and distribution high on CEO agendas, winners and losers will begin to emerge over the next three to five years. It is estimated that the top three companies will produce 75 per cent of beer sold by 2010. While local antimonopoly committees will continue to scrutinize each acquisition by local breweries, market forces will prove as efficient as ever and drive the largest forward and the rest out or into niche roles.

Part Four

Getting Established: The Taxation and Legal Environment

4.1

Business Structures

CMS Cameron McKenna

Introduction

In the last few years Russia has introduced extensive corporate legislation governing the creation, management and liquidation of a range of legal entities and other structures through which business may be carried on. These include public and private companies, branches and representative offices and limited and unlimited partnerships. A basic description of each of these forms is set out in the Civil Code of 1994 and, in respect of some of the structures, further, more detailed regulations are set out in the laws governing particular types of structure, for example, the Law on Joint Stock Companies of 1995 and the Law on Limited Liability Companies of 1998.

The structures most commonly used or encountered by foreign investors are the representative office, the limited liability company and the joint stock company (of which there are two forms – 'open' or public and 'closed' or private). This chapter will focus on these principal forms.

Representative office

Status

A representative office with accredited status has been traditionally viewed as the simplest form of business presence that a foreign company could establish in Russia. In the USSR it was the only vehicle available to foreign companies and although foreigners can now set up a wholly-owned subsidiary company and may participate on an equal basis in the various forms of partnership prescribed under Russian law, a representative office remains an effective first entry vehicle either alone or in conjunction with a company of some form. Some of the reasons for this are explained below.

A representative office is not a separate legal entity but an office of the parent entity that is set up in Russia to represent the interests of that parent. Although a representative office may in practice conduct business in Russia and may be treated by the tax authorities as a separate profit centre from its parent company, the fact that, as a matter of civil law, a representative office does not have its own separate legal identity limits the types of business for which a representative office may be useful. For example, a representative office may not import goods for purposes other than its own needs, nor may it register title to immovable property in its own name. A representative office may also experience difficulties in obtaining licences and permits to conduct certain types of business.

A representative office may, however, carry out representative functions on behalf of its parent, including arranging marketing and advertising in Russia, negotiating the terms and conditions of agreements on behalf of the parent entity and facilitating the execution of those agreements by the parent company. It may also help in other commercial and legal transactions between the parent and Russian organizations, including the rental of property.

At one time an accredited representative office enjoyed a range of benefits that were not available to branches or companies. These benefits have been gradually withdrawn – for example customs exemptions on equipment imported for the use of the representative office were withdrawn in February 1999. Foreign employees of a representative office may still obtain personal accreditation, which confers certain practical benefits such as the right to import and export personal effects free of customs duty and VAT, and which assists with obtaining multi-entry visas. There has been considerable debate about whether accredited employees of a representative office require work permits but in practice having a work permit should avoid difficulties with Russian state and local migration authorities.

A significant advantage of a representative office is that it is not deemed to be resident for Russian currency purposes and, therefore, its foreign currency receipts are exempt from the mandatory requirement to convert those receipts into roubles. A representative office may have a number of different types of bank account: a foreign currency account; a rouble 'conversion' account (referred to as a type 'K' account) and a rouble 'non-conversion' account (known as a type 'N' account). These accounts enable the representative office to make payments in Russia to both residents and non-residents subject to certain currency control restrictions established by the Central Bank regulations and other applicable legislation. Proceeds from business operations may be accumulated either in a type 'K' or type 'N' account (depending on the type of proceeds) and, after conversion into foreign currency, may be transferred abroad.

Liability

As a representative office is merely an extension of its parent, the parent remains responsible for the debts and liabilities of the representative office.

Management

A representative office is managed by the 'Head of the Representative Office', who is empowered to conduct the business of the office, and so to represent the foreign parent company by way of a power of attorney. A representative office should also have a 'Chief Accountant'. There is no requirement for either the Head of the Representative Office or the Chief Accountant to be a Russian national, although an accountant who understands the intricacies of Russian tax and accounting law is a practical necessity. Since the foreign parent company is fully liable for the debts and obligations of the representative office, some consideration should be given to the management of the office and any internal controls that may be appropriate to mitigate the exposure of the parent company.

Setting up a representative office is often the first step that foreign companies take when entering the Russian market and may be used for certain service industries on an ongoing basis. For companies in many other business sectors, however, a representative office is not on its own sufficient, although one may form part of a larger structure including one or more companies or other entities.

Limited liability company ('*obshestvo s ogranichennoi otvetstvennostyu*')

Status

A limited liability company is designated by the letters 'OOO' before or after its name. It is the simplest form of Russian company and for that reason is often used for wholly-owned subsidiary companies of foreign investors. It is similar in concept to a German GmbH or limited liability company.

The establishment of a limited liability company is governed by Part 1 of the Civil Code and by the Law on Limited Liability Companies of 8 February 1998. It shares many similarities with another form of Russian company, the closed joint stock company, which is described below. The most significant difference between a limited liability company and a closed joint stock company is that a limited liability company does not issue shares. The charter capital is instead divided into 'participations' or 'interest' units ('*doli*'). Unlike shares issued by a joint stock company, these interest units are not considered to be securities and, therefore, do not need to be registered with the Federal Commission for the Securities Market, which goes some way to reducing the expenses of registration and also the level of bureaucracy to be dealt with by the company. Each holder of an interest unit is referred to as a 'participant'. The liability of participants in the company for the debts and obligations of the company is, as a general principle, limited to the amount of their respective contributions.

A limited liability company may be wholly owned by another business entity provided, however, that entity is not itself wholly owned by a legal entity or individual. At the other extreme, if the number of participants in the company exceeds 50 then, unless the number of participants is reduced, the company is obliged to re-register as an open joint stock company within a year.

Management

The management structure of a limited liability company is relatively straightforward and may consist of a general director and the meeting of participants. A board of directors is not required but can be provided for by the terms of the charter.

Although a participant of a limited liability company is generally entitled to the number of votes at the general meeting of participants that represents the value of his contribution to the company's capital, this principle can be changed in the company's charter either when establishing the company or by subsequent amendment to the charter, which requires the approval of two-thirds of the company's participants.

Transfer of interest units

Interest units or participations in a limited liability company are freely transferable, subject to a statutory right of pre-emption in favour of the other participants. This right cannot be excluded from a company's charter. Thus, a transfer to a third party can only take place once the other participants have had the opportunity to purchase the interest. The procedure for offering the interest units to the other participants and for determining the price at which the units are offered is usually set out in the company's charter.

The charter may even prohibit the transfer of an interest to a third party in which case, if the other participants decline to purchase units offered to them, the company itself is obliged by the Law on Limited Liability Companies to purchase this interest. Payment may be in cash or, with the agreement of the transferring participant, in kind. The participant has the right to receive payment for its interest within six months (unless a shorter period is provided for in the charter) of the end of the accounting year in which the participant offered its interest for sale.

Right to withdraw

Every participant of a limited liability company has the right to withdraw from the company, at any time without the consent of any of the other participants or of the company. If a participant exercises this right then, the interest unit is transferred to the company with effect from the time the withdrawal notice is served on the company. The company is then obliged to pay the exiting participant the 'actual value' of his portion of the capital in cash. The 'actual value' of the participant's interest will be calculated as a proportion of the net value of the company's assets equal to the proportion of the company's participation interests that he holds. Payment, however, is required to be made within six months after the end of the company's financial year in which the withdrawal notice was served. The company may pay the exiting participant its entitlement in kind provided the participant agrees to this.

This right to withdraw from a limited liability company cannot be excluded by the charter. Any provisions eliminating or limiting the right to withdraw are null and void. Although difficulties in valuing a participant's interest units and the procedure for repayment provides some practical disincentive to withdrawal, the existence of the right may undermine the usefulness of this type of corporate vehicle for anything other than a wholly-owned subsidiary.

Open and closed joint stock companies

Status

The legislation governing a Russian joint stock company is to be found in the Civil Code and the Joint Stock Company Law of 26 December 1995. The latest Law on Amendments to the Joint Stock Company Law was published on 27 February 2003.

A joint stock company can either be 'open' or 'closed'. An open joint stock company, (*'otkrytoye aktionernoye obshestvo'*) is designated by the letters 'OAO' and a closed joint stock company (*'zakrytoye aktionernoye obshestvo'*), by the letters 'ZAO' which appear either before or after the company's name. The distinction between the two corporate vehicles can be likened to that between a private company and a public company in jurisdictions such as England and Wales. The open joint stock company is the form used for public companies, as it can issue shares to the public and such shares are freely transferable without any pre-emption rights in favour of other shareholders or the company. A closed joint stock company, on the other hand, is designed for private or closely held companies and so, for example, cannot issue shares to the public.

Like a limited liability company, a joint stock company may not be wholly owned by another business entity, which in turn is wholly owned by an individual or a single legal entity.

The maximum number of shareholders for a closed company is 50. If this number is exceeded the company is obliged to re-register as an open joint stock company. There is no limit to the number of shareholders in an open joint stock company.

Management

The management structure of a joint stock company consists of three bodies: (i) the general meeting of shareholders; (ii) the board of directors; and (iii) the executive body, which can be either collective (eg a management board or board of directors), or a single individual, the general director.

The general meeting of shareholders is the supreme corporate body of a joint stock company and must be held annually. Extraordinary meetings may be called by the board of directors on its own initiative or on the initiative of the auditing commission, the independent auditor or a holder(s) of more than 10 per cent of voting shares. The Law on Joint Stock Companies defines certain decisions that are within the exclusive authority of the general meeting of the shareholders and that may not be delegated to any other management body within the company.

The board of directors is responsible for the general management of the company and has authority to decide on almost any issue except those within the exclusive competence of the general meeting of the shareholders. In a joint stock company with less than 50 shareholders, the functions of the board of directors may be performed by the general meeting of shareholders and authority to run the day-to-day business of the company can be delegated to the General Director. Directors are elected by the general meeting of shareholders usually for the period of one year but they may be re-elected any number of times.

The executive body of a joint stock company may consist of one person, the General Director, or of a General Director and a group of persons acting as a collective executive body. The executive body is responsible for the day-to-day management of the company. The executive body of the joint stock company is elected by the general meeting of shareholders unless the charter of the company transfers this authority to the competence of the board of directors.

Issue and transfer of shares

An open joint stock company may make public offerings of its shares, which are freely tradable on the market. There are no pre-emption rights or restrictions on the transferability of shares in an open joint stock company as there are for closed joint stock companies.

The shares of a joint stock company, whether open or closed, are treated as securities and, as such, are subject to the registration requirements of the Law on Securities Market of 22 April, 1996. When issuing new shares therefore, all joint stock companies must prepare and file with the Federal Commission for the Securities Market, a copy of any decision to issue shares, a report on the results of the share issue and, in certain cases, a prospectus for the share issue.

Title to shares in a joint stock company is determined by reference to the register of shareholders, which all joint stock companies are required to maintain. Share transfers take effect on their entry into the register and the shareholders' entitlement to participate in shareholders meetings is determined by the register. The register may be kept by the company itself or by an independent registry company duly licensed by the Federal Commission for the Securities Market. If the company has 50 shareholders or more then the register must be kept by an independent registrar.

Shares of a closed joint stock company may be distributed only to a limited group of persons. A closed joint stock company may not publicly offer its shares or otherwise offer them to an unlimited number of investors.

The transfer of shares in a closed joint stock company, is subject to pre-emption rights in favour of other shareholders. The procedure and terms for the exercise of pre-emption rights should be specified in the company's charter subject to the overriding requirements of the Joint Stock Company Law, which provide that these rights must be exercised within not less than 10 and not more than 60 days from the time the shares are offered for sale and at the same price as offered to any third person.

The strengthening of shareholders' rights is seen as a priority issue and there are a number of legislative and quasi-legislative initiatives underway to address the many concerns that investors have expressed about the corporate regulatory environment in Russia. The amendments made in August 2001 to the Joint Stock Company Law tidy up and clarify the procedures for approving what are known as 'major' and 'interested party' transactions by establishing more precise rules for conducting such transactions. Another major development in Russia has been the publication of a draft 'Code of Corporate Conduct', which the Federal Commission for the Securities Market introduced in 2003.

The Code is based around the general principles set out in the OECD Principles of Corporate Governance and is presently recommended for use by large joint stock companies. Like Corporate Governance Codes in a number of other countries, the Russian Code will not be legally binding, although it is expected that major joint stock companies will incorporate most of the provisions of the Code into their internal documents.

Recently, the Federal Commission for the Securities Market issued a number of documents governing particular issues related to the conduct of general meetings and other issues relevant to corporate governance. By expanding in greater detail some of the basic rights that shareholders are entitled to, such regulations should play a significant role in strengthening the protection provided to minority shareholder interests.

Other entities

The Civil Code provides for a range of other entities including branches and simple partnerships which are not legal entities, as well as full and limited partnerships and additional liability companies which are legal entities. There are also non-commercial organizational forms that may be used for charities, trade associations or other not-for-profit organizations.

4.2

Establishing A Presence

CMS Cameron McKenna

Introduction

Having decided the type of legal presence to establish in Russia, the next step is to register the presence with the relevant authorities. The registration procedure and the documents required for registration are very similar for a limited liability company or a joint stock company whether open or closed, while registration procedures for a representative office are different. As shares in a joint stock company, both open and closed, are treated as securities, there are certain additional requirements to register the securities with the Federal Commission for the Securities Market (FSCM).

Although it may be possible to purchase a company 'off the shelf', the registration requirements for transferring ownership of the shelf company, changing the charter so that it reflects the business to be carried on by the investor and changing the name is no less bureaucratic, burdensome and time-consuming than setting up a new entity from scratch. In addition, it may even be necessary to obtain the prior consent of the Anti-Monopoly Ministry for the acquisition of a shelf company. This is the case if the aggregate worldwide assets of the founders (and related companies) are greater than $680,000 (being 200,000 times the statutory minimum monthly wage, which on 1 January 2004 was 100 roubles or $3.4).

The registration procedure is quite simple, as in December 2000 the government announced a plan to streamline the laws for registering new companies by introducing a 'one-stop' registration process to reduce the time and cost it takes to establish a corporate vehicle, and which procedure has been recently successfully implemented.

Registration authorities

Representative offices

The accreditation of a representative office involves obtaining a permit from one of several federal accreditation agencies. Foreign companies wishing to open a representative office in Russia usually choose between the Chamber of Commerce and Industry of the Russian Federation, the State Registration Chamber (SRC) of the Russian Federation, or the Ministry of Foreign Economic Affairs of the Russian Federation. Accreditation with any of these agencies enables a representative office to operate at federal level irrespective of where the representative office is physically located.

In addition to federal accreditation, a representative office must be registered at the local level. This requires registration with the local tax inspectorate, the Russian Federation State Committee on Statistics and three employment-related funds, which collect mandatory contributions from the payrolls of all entities operating in Russia. Certain legal requirements that apply to the registration of a company (see below), such as procuring a guarantee of a legal address and the execution of a lease, also apply to a representative office and a branch.

If the federal accreditation was granted by an agency other than the SRC, the documents must also be filed with this agency, as the SRC maintains the register of representative offices of all foreign companies accredited in the Russian Federation.

Representative offices should also open one or more bank accounts, and for practical purposes, arrange to have a seal.

Companies

Pursuant to the Law on Registration of Legal Entities (the 'Law on Registration') as of 1 July 2002 the State Tax Ministry of the Russian Federation is responsible for the registration of legal entities. The Law on Registration made substantial changes to the procedure for the registration and re-registration of legal entities (which was similar to the registration procedure for representative offices, described above) in that it transfers the function of registration to a single federal executive body – the State Tax Ministry.

The Law on Registration establishes a uniform procedure for the registration of legal entities regardless of their organizational and legal form and the kinds of economic activities pursued by them. Regional branches of the State Tax Ministry are required to carry out registration in accordance with centrally prescribed rules. In accordance with Article 1 of the Law on Registration, the registration process is governed by federal legislative acts. This provision is intended to restrict the legislative powers of the regions.

Further, on 23 December 2003 the Russian President signed into law amendments to the Law on Registration, which successfully completed the implementation of the 'one-stop shop'.

Registration procedure

The Law on Registration provides for a 'one-stop' registration, avoiding the need for registration or notification with numerous other authorities as was required before.

State registration of legal entities should be made within five working days of the submission of the corresponding documents to the local branch of the Tax Ministry. A legal entity shall be deemed to be registered as soon as it is entered into the state register.

The application for registration and the requisite supporting documentation should be submitted to the local branch of the Tax Ministry in the administrative district stated in the application for state registration as the seat of its permanent executive body. The Law on Registration provides that the relevant documents can be submitted personally by the applicant, by its authorized representative, or can be sent by post. Upon receipt, the registration body is obliged to issue a receipt to the applicant. If the documents are sent by post the registration body is required to send the receipt to the address of the applicant by registered letter not later than the next day after the receipt of the documents and to obtain a confirmation of delivery.

All other authorities will be informed of the registration of a legal entity by the registration body and not by the applicant. The Tax Ministry shall, within five working days of state registration of a particular entity, provide registration data to employment-related funds of the Russian Federation, so that such Funds can effect their own registration of the entity (such as the Pension Fund, Social Security Fund and Medical Fund). The Tax Ministry shall be required to inform the employment-related funds not only of the fact of registration of a legal entity but also of all changes made to the data on such legal entity contained in the register.

Registration documents for representative offices

A list of the documents required by the authorities for a foreign company to register a representative office can be found in the Appendix to this chapter. Many of the documents required are straightforward, such as copies of incorporation certificates and copies of articles of association or charters. Reference letters are, however, required from third parties, including one from a bank in the home jurisdiction of the foreign company.

The registration authorities apply strict rules both as to the form and content of these documents and also as to the manner of their execution. Incorporation certificates and articles of association must be filed as notarized copies with an apostille affixed if originating from a country that is a member of the Hague Convention, or, if from any other country, the documents must be legalized. The procedure for obtaining an apostille varies from country to country and an investor should check with a locally-qualified notary or the requisite government office to determine how and where to obtain an apostille.

Reference letters from the bank as well as the letter from the tax authorities must also be notarized or have an apostille affixed, and thus it is necessary for an investor to liaise with the bank/local tax authorities to ensure that they understand the procedure to be followed. If documents have not been submitted in the prescribed manner the registration authorities may reject them and require them to be re-submitted. Documents that are dated any more than six months prior to the date they are filed with the Registration Chamber will not be accepted.

All documents must be in Russian or have a certified translation into Russian attached to them before the documents are submitted to the registration authorities.

The exact procedure for registering representative offices and companies may vary slightly from region to region within the Russian Federation; for example, in certain regions tax authorities may require a copy of an executed lease for office premises before it will register a representative office or a company.

Legistration documents for legal entities

The Law reduces the number of documents for registration of a new company to just four (five for entities with foreign participation) and these are as follows (from 1 July 2003):

1. an application;
2. a resolution on the establishment of the legal entity;
3. constitutional documents (charter and foundation agreement or decision on foundation); and
4. a document confirming the payment of the registration fee.

If one of the founders of the new company is a foreign legal entity, it will also be required to submit an extract from its trade register confirming its legal status. Other requirements with respect to the form of the documents have been determined by various pieces of Russian legislation. The documents prepared in foreign jurisdiction must be notarized and apostilled (or legalized, as applicable) and accompanied by a certified Russian translation.

The Law on Registration prohibits the registration authorities from requiring any other documents.

Contributions to capital

The minimum share or charter capital of a Russian closed joint stock company or a limited liability company is 100 times the statuary minimum monthly wage. On 1 January 2004 this was approximately $3.40 and the minimum US dollar capital therefore was $340.

Contributions to the charter capital of the Russian company may be made in cash or in kind. Contributions in kind may include securities, property, property rights or other tangible or intangible rights having monetary value. Certain rights that are granted exclusively to a shareholder or founder by Russian authorities – for example, licences – cannot be contributed to the company's capital if they are not fully transferable.

Exemptions from import duties and import VAT may be available for certain types of equipment that are contributed to the charter capital of a company by a foreign shareholder or participant. The equipment must be categorized as a fixed industrial asset and must not be subject to any Russian excise tax.

Generally any asset that is contributed to charter capital must be valued by an independent valuer.

Formation of charter capital

No less than 50 per cent of the charter capital of a limited liability company or a joint stock company must be contributed before the company is registered. The outstanding balance must be paid within one year from the date of the permanent registration certificate.

In order for a foreign investor to make cash contributions, an escrow account must be opened with a Russian bank in the name of the company being established.

Anti-Monopoly Ministry and FSCM

If the value of the assets contributed by the founders of a company is greater than $680,000 (being 200,000 times the statutory monthly minimum wage of 100 roubles as of 1 January 2004), the Anti-Monopoly Ministry should be notified of the registration of the company within 45 days of its registration. The information to be supplied to the Anti-Monopoly Ministry is prescribed by statute and the Anti-Monopoly Ministry may cancel the registration if the establishment of an entity may lead to a restraint of competition in the market. If an investor has any concern that the Anti-Monopoly Ministry may challenge the registration, there is a pre-notification procedure that can be used.

Shares in any joint stock company, whether closed or open, are considered securities and must be registered with the local subdivision of the FSCM before the registration of the company is completed.

Appendix: Registration documents

The following is a list of basic documents for the accreditation of a representative office of a foreign company in Russia:

1. Charter or Articles of Association of the parent company;
2. Certificate of Incorporation or Extract from the Trade Register for the parent company;
3. reference letter from the parent company's bank;
4. Power of Attorney for the head of the representative office;
5. Power of Attorney to complete the accreditation and registration;
6. letter from the tax authorities confirming the registration of the parent company with the tax authorities in the country of its residence;
7. resolution of the parent company or founder to set up a representative office;

   (Note: The above documents should be legalized or apostilled and a certified Russian translation of the documents should be attached to them.)

8. regulations of the representative office;
9. two letters of recommendation from Russian business partners; and
10. a letter of consent from the local authorities approving the location of the representative office (if it is to be established outside Moscow).

4.3

Russian Business Entities

*Gennady Odarich, Lawyer,
PricewaterhouseCoopers CIS Law Offices BV*

Introduction

Part One of the 1994 Civil Code contains the basic principles of the creation, management and liquidation of legal entities. These aspects of legal entities are regulated in greater detail by a number of subject-specific laws such as the Joint Stock Companies Law of 1995 and the Limited Liability Companies Law of 1998.

The following specific for-profit business forms are available:

- full partnerships;
- limited partnerships (*kommandit* partnerships);
- limited liability companies;
- additional liability companies;
- production co-operatives;
- joint stock companies (public and closed);
- unitary enterprises (these are state-owned legal entities not available to foreign investors).

Of the foregoing, only the joint stock company resembles a 'corporation', but the limited partnership and the limited and additional liability companies also limit the liability of investors to the extent described elsewhere in this chapter. This chapter concentrates on the legal entities and its subdivisions that are most commonly selected by foreign investors for setting up operations in the Russian Federation. These are: joint stock companies (with two forms – 'open' (ie public) and 'closed' (ie private)), and limited liability companies as well as representative offices and branches of foreign legal entities.

Joint stock companies

The main laws governing joint stock companies (JSCs) are Part One of the Civil Code and the Law On Joint Stock Companies of 1995, the latter having been amended numerous times.

The Joint Stock Company Law defines a JSC as a company with authorized capital that is divided into a specific number of shares; the participants of a joint stock company (ie the shareholders) are not liable for its obligations or any losses related to its activity only to the extent of the value of their participatory interests.

The Russian Civil Code provides that only joint stock companies may issue stock, which is considered a type of security under the law. A share issuance must be registered with the Russian Federal Securities Commission by filing a copy of the decision to issue the shares with the share issuance prospectus and, thereafter, the report on the results of share issue. All transactions involving the shares must be registered in the JSC register, which can be maintained either by a licensed independent company or by the JSC itself. If the company has more than 499 shareholders, it must have a licensed independent company to perform this function.

Management

The managing bodies of a joint stock company are:

- *The general meeting of the shareholders.* This is the supreme body of the joint stock company. The general meeting of shareholders is the only body that may take major decisions on behalf of the JSC. It is the only body of the JSC to decide about liquidation or reorganization of the company, expansion or reduction of the stock, amendments to and new editions of the charter, new shares issue and dividend amounts, etc. The general meeting may not delegate such decisions to other bodies or individuals. There are two types of general meetings: the annual meeting, to be announced one month in advance; and the extraordinary shareholders' meeting, which can be held in addition to the annual shareholders' meeting and can be called by the board of directors or at the initiative of an independent auditor or by the holders of more then 10 per cent of the voting shares.

- *The board of directors.* This is the general management body of the joint stock company. It has the authority to take any decisions except those that are subject to the general shareholders' meeting. The body can be either collective (required for JSCs with more than 50 shareholders) or single (ie an elected General Director).

- *The executive body.* This is either a single general director or a collective body that is responsible for implementing the decisions of the general shareholders' meeting and the board of directors.

'Open' and 'closed' joint stock companies

Russian legislation establishes two types of joint stock companies, specifically, 'open' (or 'public') and 'closed' (or 'private'). The main distinctions between an OAO (the Russian acronym for open joint stock companies) and a ZAO (the Russian acronym for a closed joint stock company) are as follows:

- *Transferability of stock.* While the stock of an OAO, as a rule, is freely transferable, stock of a ZAO is subject to the pre-emptive rights of other shareholders.

- *Limit on number of shareholders; open subscription.* Only an OAO has the right to offer its stock to an unlimited number of persons (in what might be loosely referred to as a 'public' offering). Thus, an OAO is a vehicle for raising funds from investors in the stock market. The number of shareholders of a ZAO is limited to 50.

A company may not have as a sole founder (or shareholder) another company consisting of one shareholder. This means that a joint stock company may not have as its sole founder or sole shareholder a company that in turn is owned by a single person. This rule also applies to limited liability companies.

- *Minimum capitalization requirements.* The amount of the charter capital of an OAO may not be less than 1,000 times the minimum monthly wage (approximately $3,000 at the current exchange rate), and the amount of charter capital of a ZAO may not be less than 100 times the minimum monthly wage (approximately $300 at the current exchange rate).

- *Public disclosure.* Public companies must make certain financial and related information public each year.

Limited liability company

Overview

In accordance with the Russian Civil Code and the Law On Limited Liability Companies (hereinafter 'OOO'), an OOO is company founded by one or several persons, its charter capital divided into participatory shares in the amounts determined by the foundation documents; the participants of an OOO are not liable for its obligations and bear the risk of losses connected with the activity of OOO only to the extent of the value of their contributions to it.

An OOO bears liability for its obligations with all of its property. The maximum number of participants of an OOO is 50.

Management

The management bodies of an OOO are:

- *Meeting of participants.* This is the main governing body of an OOO. The meeting of participants is the only body that may take major decisions on behalf of an OOO, such as liquidation or reorganization of the company, expansion or reduction of stock, amendments to the foundation agreement and charter, adoption of annual accounting reports and issue of debenture bonds and other issuing securities. Each participant's votes at the meeting are proportional to the value of their contribution to the company's capital. This can be changed by amendments to the charter.

- *General director.* This is the managing body of the OOO, responsible for implementing the company's policy.

The minimum amount of charter capital of an OOO is the same as that for a ZAO (100 times the minimum monthly wage: approximately $300 at the current exchange rate).

Differences between ZAO and OOO

Both a ZAO and an OOO are deemed legal entities under Russian law and are subject to the same corporate profits tax regime.

A ZAO and an OOO have very much in common. However, their primary differences are:

1. Shares in a ZAO are deemed securities and, therefore, are subject to registration with the Federal Securities Commission and payment of a 0.8 per cent securities tax on additional share issuances. Shares in a ZAO can be ordinary or preferred. A ZAO's shares of one and the same category have the same rights. Shares in OOO are not deemed securities and are exempt from the above requirements. All shares (or participatory interests) in an OOO are equal, ie there are no preferred shares. However, participants in an OOO can agree that voting and/or dividend rights under their shares can be different, eg a participant holding shares worth 20 per cent of the share capital of an OOO can have 80 per cent of the votes at the general meeting and dividends distribution and vice versa.

2. Shareholders' decisions in a ZAO can be taken by a simple majority vote or qualified majority vote (ie 75 per cent) of the shareholders present at the meeting provided that there is a quorum (ie shareholders holding 50 per cent +1 share are present at the meeting). In certain cases, the number of votes required for the adoption of a resolution can be changed by the charter of the ZAO. A unanimous

vote in a ZAO is required only for a decision to convert the OOO into a non-commercial partnership. In an OOO, shareholders' decisions can be taken by a majority, qualified majority or a unanimous vote of the participants of the company regardless of whether a quorum is present. The charter of an OOO can also provide that certain decisions require a higher number of votes than specified in the law.

3. Shareholders in a ZAO can only dispose of their investment in the company by selling their shares to other shareholders or a third party. In addition to sale, participants in an OOO have the right to withdraw from the OOO at any time. In this case, their shares are transferred to the company itself, which is obliged to pay the departing shareholder the actual value of its participatory interest, which is determined on the basis of the company's net assets.

4. The title to the shares in a ZAO is confirmed by an extract from the stock register, which each ZAO must hold. An OOO does not hold a share register; however, all the shareholders must be indicated in the charter and foundation agreement of the OOO, which are subject to state registration. Thus, each transfer of shares in an OOO requires registering the changes in its charter and foundation agreement.

5. The procedures for making charter capital contributions in a ZAO and an OOO are different. In short, the charter capital increase in an OOO is cheaper, shorter and easier since there is no necessity to register the shares with the Federal Securities Commission.

6. Unlike a ZAO, an OOO can accept from its shareholders so-called 'contributions' to its property that do not change the number of shares among the shareholders.

7. The charter of an OOO may provide for the prohibition of sale or any other disposal of shares to third parties. In such cases, only the company itself may buy the shares.

Antimonopoly (competition) filing

The Russian Antimonopoly Law establishes requirements of notification or even preliminary approval by the Russian Ministry of Antimonopoly Policy in certain cases. Thus, for instance, the Russian Ministry for Antimonopoly Policy must be notified not later than 45 days following the date of state registration of a Russian legal entity, provided the combined book value of assets of all its founders exceeds 200,000 statutory monthly wages (approximately $600,000 at the current exchange rate). The notification involves disclosure of certain documents and information on the founding company and its direct and indirect owners.

Foreign investors doing business in the Russian market usually choose to create a ZAO in all instances where disagreements between shareholders may occur or where the number of shareholders is significant. In addition, a ZAO is more attractive for structures designed for raising capital, while in all other cases (especially where a sole founder creates a company), an OOO is generally more convenient.

The Law On Foreign Investments in the Russian Federation nonetheless entitles foreign investors to trade without establishing a Russian legal entity – using representative offices or branches.

Representative offices and branches of a foreign legal entity

A representative office (abbreviated as RO) is a foreign legal entity's subdivision in Russia. A representative office represents and protects the legal entity's interests. Foreign legal entities are entitled to establish ROs in the Russian Federation only for international operations on behalf of the represented legal entity.

A branch, on the other hand, is a foreign legal entity's separate subdivision that performs all or some of the functions of the legal entity, as well as the functions of an RO. The authority of the subsidiary is broader than that of a representative office.

In accordance with the Law on Foreign Investments, a branch of a foreign legal entity is created to pursue all the activities in the Russian Federation that the head organization pursues outside the Russian Federation.

Neither representative offices nor subsidiaries are considered legal entities. While representative offices and branches are deemed to be integral parts of the legal entity that creates them, the parent legal entity remains responsible for their debts and liabilities. A representative office or a branch is directed by the Head (in other words, Director) of the representative office/branch who acts on behalf of the parent company within the authority of the respective power of attorney.

Formal registration requirements

Effective from 1 January 2004, the registration procedure for Russian legal entities was simplified by the introduction of a 'one window' approach and will normally be undertaken within two to two and a half weeks through local tax authorities, which are responsible for the registration process. 'Shelf' companies are generally not available and the incorporation process can take from two to three months.

Registration is also required for a branch or representative office of a foreign legal entity. However, unlike for Russian legal entities, the registration of a branch or representative office of a foreign legal entity must be undertaken through several federal and local authorities. Registration of a branch or representative office of a foreign legal entity is, in practice, always accompanied by 'accreditation' of a foreign legal entity through a variety of federal and local bodies. Accreditation confers certain benefits, including exemption from value added tax (VAT) on the rental of office space and accommodation for foreign staff. Although it is not, in theory, a legal requirement, in some parts of Russia accreditation is effectively compulsory, since the local banks and administrative authorities may not recognize the office without this form of registration.

The accreditation fee ranges from $1,000 to $3,500 depending on the period of accreditation (from one year up to three years for representative offices and from one year up to five years for branches). The registration and accreditation procedures are fairly complex, but can normally be completed within two months. If time is of essence, a fast-track accreditation can be effected for an additional fee of $1,500. This reduces time for accreditation and registration can be reduced from 60 to 30 working days.

Tax and social fund registration requirements

In addition to the state registration as mentioned above, a Russian legal entity must register with the tax authorities in the place of its location as well as in each tax district in which it has a branch, a representative office or real property and transportation vehicles that are taxable. A foreign legal entity is required to register with the tax authorities in each tax district in which it carries out business activities. A simplified registration procedure is available for foreign legal entities that do not carry out activities in Russia, but have property in Russia or wish to open a rouble investment account with a Russian bank. A foreign legal entity must notify the tax authorities in each tax district in which it has a source of income. Notification should also be sent to the tax office with jurisdiction over the location in which property belonging to the foreign legal entity is situated.

Separate registration procedures are required for each of the three Social Funds to meet the liability with respect to the remuneration of personnel. Entities are also required to register with the State Statistics Committee. As mentioned above, Russian legal entities may enjoy a 'one window' registration procedure through the tax authorities, while a branch or representative office of a foreign legal entity must visit Social Funds offices to get registered there.

Legal entities are required to collect receipts in a bank account in Russia, unless permission to do otherwise has been granted by the Central Bank of Russia. There are special rules for petty cash operations, which should be observed by Russian legal entities, representative offices and branches of foreign legal entities.

Opening bank accounts to Russian residents

In accordance with new currency legislation, most aspects of which came into force on 18 June 2004, a foreign legal entity (non-resident) shall open special bank accounts in the currency of the Russian Federation (roubles) for itself or its representative office or branch (if any) (CBR Instruction No. 116-I) for the following types of operations:

1. S-account – for purchase from and sale to a resident of bonds on the domestic market issued on behalf of the Russian Federation, including settlements and remittance related to transfer of such bonds;

2. A-account – for purchase from and sale to a resident of shares and investment units of unit investment funds on the domestic market, including settlements and remittance of such shares and investment units;

3. O-account – for purchase from and sale to a resident of bonds issued by residents and non-residents on the domestic market, including settlements and remittance of such bonds, save for bonds issued on behalf of the Russian Federation;

4. B1-account – for settlements and remittance in roubles under loans from a resident; for receipt from a resident of roubles obtained from the initial issue of shares and bonds on the domestic market and from issue of promissory notes on the domestic market to a resident;

5. B2-account – for providing a loan to a resident in roubles; for purchase from and sale to a resident of internal non-issued securities, including settlements and remittance related to transfer of such securities.

Operations with Russian roubles, which are not listed above, may be carried out by a non-resident on ordinary rouble accounts. Foreign currency accounts are opened to non-residents without any limitations.

Russian legal entities (residents) shall open the following types of special banking accounts in a foreign currency for operations listed below.

1. R1-account – for settlements and remittance under a loan in a foreign currency from a non-resident; for raising foreign currency

from a non-resident received from primary issue of external securities and from issue of external promissory notes to a non-resident;

2. R2-account – for settlements and remittance under a loan in a foreign currency to a non-resident; for purchase of external securities from a non-resident; for sale of external securities to the benefit of a non-resident.

Operations not listed above may be carried out by a resident on ordinary rouble accounts. Rouble accounts are open to residents without any limitations.

Foreign employees

Visa requirements

Foreign personnel must obtain a visa to enter the Russian Federation (except citizens of most of the former Soviet republics and citizens of some other countries). Upon registering their visas within three days of arrival, they may stay freely in the country, provided their visa is valid. Visa applications must be supported by an invitation from a Russian individual or legal entity.

Work permits

On the basis of the Law On the Status of Foreigners in the Russian Federation, effective from 1 November 2002, employers must obtain a special employment permit if they wish to hire or attract foreigners. Employees in turn must receive a work permit from the Migration Authorities before being allowed to work in the Russian Federation. In this regard, the Russian government adopted a procedure for obtaining work permits for foreign employees, according to which work permits must be obtained for *all* foreign national employees, including highly-skilled specialists and senior managerial staff (CEOs, deputy CEOs, heads of divisions, including heads of representative offices and branches). The above requirement applies to foreign nationals who work for either a representative office/branch or a Russian legal entity. A procedure for obtaining special employment permits by the employers is still regulated by the 1993 Presidential Decree to the extent it does not contradict the Federal Law 'On the Status of Foreigners in the Russian Federation'. Since the Law took effect, practice has shown that both employment and work permits are required not only for foreigners working under employment agreements but also for those providing services under civil law (services) contracts, engaging in entrepreneurial activity (except in some cases expressly provided for in the Law).

The Law On the Status of Foreigners in the Russian Federation envisages severe sanctions for breaches of its rules, including expulsion (deportation) of foreign employees, which may create difficulties or even the impossibility for such foreign nationals of obtaining another entry visa, while employers are also likely to encounter complications in the processing of their requests for issuance of further permits and invitation letters for Russian visas.

Conclusion

While it is usually possible to obtain a work permit and register a Russian legal entity or a representative office/branch with the various relevant bodies without professional assistance, it is highly recommended that foreign investors seek out tax and legal advisors to assist in the process, especially when attempting to determine the type of Russian legal entity to be registered or to provide foreign personnel to either a representative office of a foreign legal entity or a Russian legal entity under the provision of the personnel agreement.

4.4

Business Taxation

Paul Quigley, Deloitte & Touche

Introduction

With growing demand for consumer goods and an abundance of natural resources, Russia offers some of the best business opportunities in Europe. In the current environment of improving political and economic stability, it is widely expected that foreign investment will increase considerably in the next few years.

After the government debt crisis in August 1998 and the subsequent devaluation of the rouble, many Russian-based businesses benefited from a reduction in their costs, and the economy as a whole saw a reduced reliance on imported goods. Furthermore, the country was blessed by an increase in the price of oil, and since 2000, Russia has been enjoying a period of significant economic growth. Many foreign investors, having been badly burned once before, have begun to show renewed, albeit cautious, interest.

In the past, one of the areas of greatest concern to foreign investors was the uncertain legal framework in which they had to operate. Much work has been done in this area over the last 10 years, notably with the introduction of the Civil Codes of 1994 and 1995 followed by comprehensive laws on joint stock companies, limited liability companies and bankruptcy. Further legislation is being enacted at a remarkable pace.

Similarly, the tax system has undergone significant developments since 1991. It is now focused around the development of Russia's Tax Code. As components of the Tax Code are implemented, the problems of earlier years are being addressed and the system is becoming increasingly compatible with modern business. Part I of the Code, which sets out the administrative framework of the tax system, came into force on 1 January 1999. This was followed, in Part II, by a revamp of the laws on personal income tax, VAT, excise and social fund contributions; these came into force on 1 January 2001. Most recently, the laws on profits tax and property tax were also codified.

Russia is now able to claim one of the most generous tax regimes in the industrialized world, with a flat personal income tax rate for residents at 13 per cent and a combined total corporate profits tax burden at a maximum rate of 24 per cent.

There are, of course, a number of continuing problems. For example, frequent changes and a lack of clarity of interpretations by the tax authorities, and certain grey areas in VAT and currency control continue to present significant challenges. However, we also see that in many areas of business taxation, the problems today are less often about the failure of the law to understand concepts, fairness or the substance of transactions, but are more often about the inappropriate application of the law and inconsistencies of treatment across the cities and regions of Russia.

The following overview of taxes and related legislation is based on the laws in effect as of 1 March 2004.

Profits tax

As of 1 January 2002, a new chapter of the Tax Code, Chapter 25, introduced many substantial changes to Russia's previous profit tax regime. The main changes include:

- a reduction in the corporate profits tax rate to a maximum of 24 per cent;
- an 'open' list of deductible expenses (an expense that is not expressly listed as a non-deductible expense is therefore considered to be deductible);
- most tax concessions are abolished (although the loss carry forward concession will still be applicable with the term extended for 10 years);
- taxpayers need to establish an accounting policy for tax purposes and also implement a system of tax accounting;
- the accrual basis of taxation for taxpayers whose average revenue was in excess of one million roubles per quarter for the previous four quarters. Those whose average revenue per quarter during the preceding four quarters was less than this amount, however, may choose between the accrual or the cash basis of taxation;
- dates of income/expense recognition are established for various types of income and expenses;
- the introduction of thin capitalization rules, which affect the deductibility of interest expenses.

Tax incentives

Although the new Profit Tax Chapter abolishes all tax incentives, including the Capital Investment Concession, legislation was included that states that all privileges received by companies as part of their approved investment agreements with the regional authorities will continue for the full life of the original agreement. If the life of the investment agreement was not explicitly defined, the privileges will continue until the end of the term of recouping the investment project, but for no more than three years as from the moment of their granting.

Tax rates and timing of payments

Russia's standard corporate tax rate has been reduced to 24 per cent. Additionally, the regional governments have been given the authority to reduce their portion of the profits tax by up to four per cent. In other words, the overall profit tax rate may vary from 20 per cent to 24 per cent depending on the region in which the taxpayer is located.

Profits tax is subject to quarterly filing of returns and monthly advance payments.

Russian source income for foreign companies

Depending on the type of income, the following withholding tax rates apply:

- 10 per cent on income from international freight and the renting of property involved in international shipping;
- 15 per cent on dividends received by foreign companies from Russian legal entities, interest on state and municipal bonds;
- 20 per cent on royalties, interest (other than that received from state and municipal bonds), leasing activities (income is determined as the difference between the gross lease income less the cost of the asset);
- 20 per cent on all other income subject to withholding tax (with the exception of income received from the sale of shares in a Russian entity, which may be subject to withholding tax at the rate of 24 per cent as explained below).

The sale of shares in Russian entities is only subject to withholding tax if more than 50 per cent of the assets owned by the entity is comprised of immovable property. In this case, the shareholder may elect to be taxed either at the rate of 20 per cent on the gross sales price, or at the rate of 24 per cent on the difference between the sales price and original purchase price plus expenses related to the sale. The same rule applies to the income from the sale of immovable property located in Russia.

Transfer pricing

In general, the tax authorities should accept the price of goods as stated by the parties to the transaction. However, Russia's Tax Code provides for four instances in which the tax authorities are entitled to verify the prices used:

- if the agreement was concluded between related parties;
- in the case of barter transactions;
- in foreign trade transactions;
- if the contract price varies by more than 20 per cent of the market price for identical (similar) merchandise within a short period of time.

In these instances, the Code empowers the authorities to apply the market price for tax purposes where the latter varies from the transaction price by more than 20 per cent.

Value added tax

Value added tax (VAT) is charged on the majority of sales of goods and services 'realized' in Russia and on most imports into Russia. The tax is payable by all corporate businesses, including offices and branches of foreign companies and also individual entrepreneurs. However, companies and individual entrepreneurs can apply for VAT exemption if their taxable revenues (VAT and sales tax exclusive) remain below one million roubles for three consecutive months.

Tax rates

The standard VAT rate is 18 per cent. A reduced rate of 10 per cent applies to certain medicines and medical products, printed periodicals and books, foodstuffs and children's goods. A zero per cent rate applies (amongst other things) to the export of goods and related shipping and forwarding services as well as passenger transportation when the destination is outside of Russia.

Place of supply rules

There are specific rules to determine the place of supply for cross-border works and services. For example, consulting, advertising, information processing, legal, accounting, engineering, educational, scientific research and development, and also services related to patents, licences and the like are subject to VAT if rendered to an entity with a place of activity in Russia. Payments to a non-registered foreign entity for such services are subject to withholding at source by a Russian payer.

Exemptions

Major VAT-exempt activities include the lease of office space and accommodation to accredited foreign representative offices and individuals; medical services; banking and insurance services; operations with securities and derivative financial instruments; interest on loans; and gambling. The import of technological equipment and spare parts as a contribution to the charter capital is also exempt.

Individual income tax

Personal income tax applies to tax residents on their worldwide income and to non-residents on their Russian source income. Russian source income includes any remuneration for duties performed in Russia, regardless of where or when it is paid. A tax resident is an individual who has spent no less than 183 days in Russia during a calendar year.

Tax rates

Resident's income is subject to a flat rate of 13 per cent except for specific types of income, which attract different rates. Unless otherwise protected by a double tax treaty, non-residents are subject to a flat rate of 30 per cent.

Incomes subject to the different rates include:

- dividends: 6 per cent;
- winnings, prizes etc: 35 per cent;
- interest on loans in excess of established norms: 35 per cent;
- insurance payments in excess of established limits: 35 per cent.

Non-residents

The 30 per cent tax rate is applicable to non-residents irrespective of the nature of their income.

Date of receipt

Income is taxed when 'received' in cash, in kind or by way of 'material benefit'. Receipt includes power of disposition.

For salaries, the date of income receipt is the last day of the month for which the salary is accrued.

Deductions

In accordance with the current legislation, taxpayers may deduct 400 roubles from their monthly income if their accumulated annual income does not exceed 20,000 roubles. An additional deduction in the amount of 300 roubles can be taken for each dependant within the same limits.

Social deductions include:

- charitable donations to Russian-financed entities are deductible within the limits of 25 per cent of the income.
- payments for the education of taxpayers and their children (up to the age of 24) at licensed Russian institutions are deductible up to a limit of 38,000 roubles per person per year.
- payments for medical services made by the taxpayer for him/her and his/her family are deductible up to a limit of 38,000 roubles per year.

Property deductions

Proceeds from the sale of residential property owned for a period of at least five years should not be taxable. If the residential property is owned for less than five years, however, the taxpayer may elect to either pay tax on the difference between the sale price and one million roubles or pay tax on the difference between the sale price and the documented expenses.

Proceeds from the sale of other property owned for a period of at least three years should not be taxable. If the other property is owned for less than three years, however, the taxpayer may elect to either pay tax on the difference between the sale price and 125,000 roubles or pay tax on the difference between the sale price and the documented expenses.

The limit on the deduction of expenses on the purchase/construction of a house or apartment is one million roubles. If this deduction is not used in full during a particular tax period, its balance may be used in subsequent tax periods (this deduction is not available in respect of property purchased from related parties). Interest on a loan to construct or acquire such property is also deductible.

Non-taxable income

Non-taxable income includes:

- state pensions;
- most statutory allowances and redundancy payments;
- work injury compensation within certain limits;
- statutory insurance benefits and certain limited voluntary insurance benefits;
- interest on bank deposits within certain limits.

Taxation of foreign nationals

The only specific provision in the Tax Code relating to the income of foreign nationals is concerned exclusively with staff of diplomatic or international bodies. In general, foreigners' taxation is governed by common procedures and depends on residency. Specific exemptions for certain benefits provided to foreign citizens (including residential accommodation and company cars) were abolished from 1 January 2001.

Foreigners may only claim benefits under a double tax treaty upon presentation of proof of residence in the country with which Russia has concluded the relevant double tax treaty. Such proof must be presented by the end of the year following the year for which exemption is being claimed.

Tax agent

For purposes of withholding personal income tax, Russian organizations, entrepreneurs and permanent establishments of foreign companies are considered as tax agents and are required to calculate, withhold and remit income tax from payment to individuals. Those who have received income where the correct amount of tax was deducted at source and remitted to the budget do not need to file a Russian tax return within a given calendar year unless they wish to apply for social or property deductions.

Unified Social Tax (UST)

Russian employers, including Russian representative offices or branches of foreign legal entities, are obliged to make UST payments for their employees. The law gives no indication as to where the employing entity should be located, or where the duties, for which remuneration is received, should be performed. As such, foreign entities effecting payments to individuals are considered to be payers of UST.

Taxable base

The taxable base for UST is calculated for each employee individually, based on remuneration in cash or in kind. As employees are not payers of UST, it is only payable by the employer and calculated on a regressive basis ranging from 35.6 per cent on the first 100,000 roubles of salary to 2 per cent on salary payments in excess of 600,000 roubles.

Exemptions

Exemptions include most statutory allowances, healthcare services paid by the employer and obligatory insurance payments. There are also certain exemptions for companies employing disabled staff.

Excise tax

Excise tax is imposed on both the import and the manufacture of a list of goods, the primary categories of which are: alcohol, tobacco, oil, gas, petrol, jewellery and automobiles. The payers of excise tax are Russian residing manufacturers and sellers (including those with foreign investments) of excisable goods, both companies and individual entrepreneurs, or importers of excisable goods.

Exemptions

Exports of excisable Russian goods outside the CIS countries are free from excise tax. To receive the exemption, however, a set of documents proving the export must be presented to the tax authorities.

Property tax

Property tax is a regional tax and is levied at a maximum rate of 2.2 per cent per annum on the property of commercial enterprises and organizations in Russia, including the property of foreign enterprises that is located in Russian territory.

Taxable base

The tax is levied on the property of enterprises and organizations. Exemption is available under a number of double tax treaties, which provide that movable property should only be taxable in the country of residency of the owner of the property, provided the property is not connected with a Russian permanent establishment.

Generally, the taxable base includes most fixed and intangible assets, inventory, stocks of goods, work-in-progress and unfinished construction. Land and certain non-productive property are specifically excluded.

In general, the taxable base is the average net book value (cost less depreciation) of the property of the enterprise.

Exemptions

A limited number of exemptions are available depending on the type of organization and the type of property concerned.

Several types of property are exempt from property tax, including land and property used in nature protection.

Customs duties

A new Customs Code was introduced with effect from 1 January 2004. Import duties are levied according to the type of goods imported and their origin. Duties are normally expressed as a percentage of the value of the goods imported (*ad valorem* duties). However, they may also be expressed as a set amount of euros per unit or kilogram ('specified' duties) or as a combination (the greater of the two).

A new system of tariffs was introduced with effect from 1 January 2001. Prior to 1 January 2001, there were seven *ad valorem* rates of duty ranging from zero per cent to 30 per cent. There are now five rates: 5 per cent, 10 per cent, 15 per cent, 20 per cent and 25 per cent. Certain goods may also continue to be imported duty free.

Other taxes

Additional taxes, payments and fees may exist from region to region. Some of these include: the use of subsoil resources; the charge for the use of the words 'Russia' and 'Russian Federation' in the name of a legal entity; payments for generating pollution; various licence fees; water tax; timber duty; hard currency cash purchase tax; and the charge for street cleaning in populated areas.

4.5

Russian Taxation

Natalia Milchakova, Tax Partner, PricewaterhouseCoopers, Moscow

The modern Russian tax system has continued to evolve since 1999 when Part I of the Tax Code took effect, with laws and administrative resolutions dedicated to specific types of tax introducing numerous procedural and substantive changes to the tax regime. As of January 2004, Russian law establishes the following major business-related taxes:

Federal taxes

- profits tax;
- value added tax (VAT);
- excise tax;
- Unified Social Tax;
- customs duties;
- Mineral Resources Extraction Tax;
- payment for the use of natural resources.

Regional taxes

- property tax;
- transport tax;
- gambling tax.

Local taxes

- advertising tax;
- land tax.

Individuals are subject to Personal Income Tax.

Profits tax

Corporations and shareholders are taxed separately. Partnerships are taxed at the partner level, ie have the benefit of 'pass-through taxation'. A Russian legal entity is taxed on its worldwide income, whereas a foreign legal entity is taxed on Russian-source income only. No tax consolidation within a group of companies is allowed.

All entities are required to maintain, in addition to statutory accounting records, tax accounting registers.

Companies are generally taxed on income generated from the sale of goods, work, services or property, or on any other type of non-exempt income. Sales income and most expenses are generally recognized on an accrual basis. Most expenses are deductible for tax purposes if they meet general deductibility rules, ie if they are incurred for the purpose of deriving income, can be economically justified and are supported by appropriate documents. There are still some expenses that are wholly non-deductible or deductible only to a limited extent as established by government regulations (eg voluntary insurance premiums, entertainment expenses, certain types of advertising expenses etc).

Depreciable assets are classified into 10 groups depending on the useful life of the asset. For most assets, the company may choose to apply either the straight-line or the reducing balance method of depreciation. Intangible assets are amortized over the life of the asset.

Tax losses can be carried forward for 10 years; however, the amount of losses claimed each year cannot reduce the reporting year taxable profit by more than 30 per cent.

While there are no special tax avoidance provisions in the tax law, the Tax Code contains transfer pricing provisions. According to these rules, the tax authorities have the right to adjust the prices of transactions between related parties, barter transactions, foreign trade transactions and on goods (works, services) sold where the prices fluctuated by more than 20 per cent within a short period of time. If a transaction is one of the above types, the tax authorities may adjust the price if it differs from the market price by more than 20 per cent.

In addition, thin capitalization rules apply to transactions between group companies. According to the thin capitalization rules, a portion of the interest payable by a Russian organization to a foreign legal entity owning (directly or indirectly) more than 20 per cent of its charter capital, may be disallowed as a deduction and reclassified as a dividend. The thin capitalization rules are only applicable if the taxpayer's outstanding debt owned to the foreign legal entity exceeds the foreign company's proportionate ownership in the taxpayer's capital by more than three times.

The current profits tax rate is 24 per cent. Regional administrations have the right to reduce the portion of the profits tax payable to the regional budget by a maximum of 4 per cent. Small enterprises meeting certain criteria may apply a simplified system of taxation and accounting, and pay a unified tax on income and a reduced number of other taxes.

Enterprises, farms and individual entrepreneurs producing agricultural products may be exempt from most taxes by paying a single agricultural tax, subject to certain conditions. Regional authorities have the right to tax imputed income in their jurisdictions of legal entities and individual entrepreneurs engaged in certain industries, for example, retail sales to the general public and transport services, provided that certain criteria (eg floor space of a trading hall) are met. The tax rate has been established at 15 per cent. The imputed income is determined in accordance with a special formula. Payers of the tax on imputed income are relieved from payment of most other taxes.

Taxation of shareholders

Dividends paid to a resident corporation or a Russian resident individual from Russian subsidiaries are subject to a 6 per cent withholding tax (9 per cent from 1 January 2005). This tax is withheld at source by the payer. Russian source dividends are exempt on receipt. No credit for underlying profits tax is available.

Capital gains of a resident business entity are included in worldwide income, which is subject to corporate income tax. Losses from the sale of securities are deductible only to the extent of gains earned on the same class of securities (although certain exceptions apply for banks, brokers and other financial institutions).

Losses from the sale of fixed assets may be deducted for profits tax purposes in equal installments during the remaining economic life of the asset sold.

A 15 per cent tax is levied on dividends paid to non-resident corporations, unless a double tax treaty provides otherwise. The tax rate applicable to individuals who are treated as non-residents for purposes of Russian taxation is 30 per cent. However, such amounts may be exempt from the Russian tax or taxed at a reduced rate pursuant to the provisions of the respective double tax treaties, provided that certain conditions are met.

Reorganizations

The tax law does not contain detailed provisions with respect to corporate reorganizations. The Profits Tax Chapter of the Tax Code establishes a limited number of rules related to profits tax implications of reorganizations (eg loss carry forward).

Any transfer of assets in the course of any form of corporate reorganization (including merger, absorption, division, and split-off) is not considered a sale for tax purposes. In particular, there is no taxable gain that arises in the process of re-organization. Such taxable gain may arise at a later stage, at the moment of a future disposal of assets.

Taxation of foreign legal entities (FLEs)

Foreign corporations are subject to corporate income tax on income generated from sources in Russia. In general, taxation of business profits is limited to those attributable to a permanent establishment (PE). A PE is defined in the Profits Tax Chapter of the Tax Code as 'a branch, division, office, bureau, agency, or any other place through which a foreign legal entity regularly carries out its business activities in Russia' (double taxation treaties may contain different definitions of a PE). A foreign legal entity also creates a PE if it conducts business activity in Russia through a dependent agent as provided in the Profits Tax Chapter of the Tax Code.

Representative offices and branches are subject to tax on substantially the same basis as Russian legal entities. However, in cases when a foreign legal entity conducts free-of-charge preparatory and/or auxiliary services for third parties and cannot calculate profit directly, a deemed profit at 20 per cent of the PE's expenses on such activities may be used as the tax base.

Income earned by FLEs from sources in the Russian Federation, which are not related to business activities, is taxed at the source of payment at the following rates:

- 15 per cent in relation to dividends;
- 10 per cent in relation to freight income;
- 20 per cent in relation to other income from Russian sources, including royalty and interest.

These rates may be reduced under the terms of the respective double tax treaties. To enjoy double tax treaties' exemptions, the foreign legal entity must present a confirmation of tax residence in the country of the double tax treaty to the Russian tax agent.

VAT

Sales of goods (works and services) on the territory of Russia, and import of goods into Russia, are subject to VAT. Goods are considered to be sold in Russia if, at the beginning of their transportation or dispatch, they were located in Russia. The VAT Chapter of the Tax Code establishes special place of supply rules for different categories of services. Under these rules, services of a consultancy nature, or services related to patents, licenses or similar rights or a lease of movable property and some other types of services are regarded as supplied at the place of activity of the customer. The Tax Code defines Russia as a place of a company's activity if the company has received state registration in Russia, or if the company's management or a permanent executive body or a permanent establishment (if services are provided through this permanent establishment) is located in Russia. As for other types of services, the place of supply for VAT purposes is determined based on the place of activity of the supplier. Works and services related to movable or immovable property located in Russia are subject to Russian VAT.

Starting from 1 January 2004, VAT is charged at the rate of 18 per cent on most goods and services (until 31 December 2003, a 20 per cent rate was applied). A 10 per cent reduced rate applies to a limited range of basic food items, children's goods, medicines and some mass media products. Export of goods and certain services is zero-rated.

VAT is charged to customers at the applicable rate and paid to the budget net of input VAT paid on purchases and expenses (including import VAT paid at customs) provided these purchases and expenses are incurred in connection with carrying out VAT-able activities (otherwise, input VAT must be included in the cost of goods (work, services)). Input VAT is only recoverable if the goods and services are actually received and the relevant VAT, including import VAT, is paid. In addition, adherence to VAT-invoicing procedures is critical for input VAT recovery. Recovery of input VAT with respect to certain business trip, entertainment and advertising expenses is limited in accordance with the same limits that apply to the Profits Tax deduction. If sales are exempt from VAT, as a general rule, the relevant input VAT is not recoverable but added to the cost of goods (work, services).

Import VAT is applied to the customs value of goods (including freight, insurance and other costs incurred prior to the customs border), and increased by any applicable import and excise duties. Certain medical equipment and contributions of technological equipment, related components and spare parts to the charter capital of a Russian legal entity are exempt from import VAT.

If services (goods) subject to Russian VAT are supplied by foreign entities not registered with the Russian tax authorities, VAT is collectible via a 'reverse charge' withholding mechanism applied by a resident agent. Withheld VAT is recoverable by the tax agent as input tax, provided recovery requirements are met.

VAT exemptions apply to loans in cash, insurance and banking operations (with some exceptions applying to banking operations), circulation of securities, medical equipment (in accordance with the list approved by the Russian Federation Government) and medical services, etc.

Payroll taxes

Currently, the following taxes and contributions are paid by companies on the employee's compensation:

1. Unified Social Tax (UST);
2. Obligatory Pension Insurance Contributions;
3. Social Insurance Contributions for mandatory social insurance against work-related accidents (Social Insurance Contributions).

Unified Social Tax

Unified Social Tax (UST) is generally levied on total income payable to Russian and foreign employees and contractors at regressive rates from 35.6 per cent (for low-income employees) to 2 per cent (applies to annual incomes in excess of R600,000). UST includes Federal budget, Medical Funds and Social Fund contributions.

Some changes to the UST Chapter of the Tax Code will be introduced, effective from 1 January 2005, including reduction of the maximum UST rate of 35.6 per cent to 26 per cent and changes in the structure of groups taxed at regressive rates and applicable tax rates for these groups.

The Federal budget portion of the UST is reduced by the amount of Obligatory Pension Insurance due to the Pension Fund. The portion of UST attributable to the Social Fund is not applied to contractors.

Obligatory Pension Insurance

Similar to the Unified Social Tax, Obligatory Pension Insurance contributions are accrued on total income payable to employees and contractors at regressive rates depending on the cumulative remuneration. Remuneration of foreign nationals temporarily residing in Russia is exempt from such contributions.

Social Insurance Contributions

Social Insurance Contributions rates vary from 0.2 per cent to 8.5 per cent (depending on the employer's activity) of each employee's compensation. Income payable to contractors working under civil contracts is exempt from Social Insurance Contributions provided that accident insurance is not stipulated in the relevant contracts.

Property tax

Starting from 1 January 2004, the property tax base has significantly decreased and currently includes only net book value of fixed assets reflected on the taxpayer's balance sheet. Intangible assets, inventories and WIP now are excluded from the property tax base of a legal entity. Foreign legal entities may enjoy tax relief under the relevant double tax treaties. Foreign legal entities that do not create a PE in Russia pay property tax only on the net book value of immovable property located in Russia.

The maximum property tax rate was increased from 2 per cent to 2.2 per cent. The legislative bodies of the regions of the Russian Federation retain the right to introduce lower property tax rates, as well as grant the property tax exemptions.

Transport tax

Starting from 1 January 2003, the regional authorities received the right to introduce a transport tax. The tax is, in most cases, based on the capacity of a vehicle. The exact tax rate is established by the regional authorities within the allowed limit.

Advertising tax (will be abolished starting from 1 January 2005)

Advertising tax is established by the local legislative bodies. The tax rate cannot exceed 5 per cent. In general, advertising expenses incurred by the company are subject to advertising tax.

Taxation of individuals: Personal income tax

For both Russians and foreigners, tax residence in Russia is determined by the number of days of physical presence in Russia in a calendar year. For Personal Income Tax (PIT) purposes, an individual is considered resident if physically present in Russia for 183 days or more in a calendar year, counting the day of departure but not counting the day of arrival.

Russian residents are liable to PIT on their total worldwide income received in a calendar year. Non-residents are taxed on income received from sources in Russia, which includes income attributable to work in Russia, rental income from property located in Russia, dividends from Russian organizations etc. Benefits in kind are treated as taxable income valued at market prices. A number of allowances, deductions and exemptions are provided by the Tax Code. It is possible to apply a relevant double tax treaty to exempt certain types of income from Russian taxation.

A flat rate of 13 per cent applies to most types of incomes. Different rates are established for dividends (6 per cent [9 per cent from 1 January 2005]), all types of income received by non-residents in Russia (30 per cent) and certain income gained from receipt of prizes, insurance benefits, excessive interest on bank deposits and loans (35 per cent).

PIT should be withheld at source by an employer – a tax agent, with respect to all remuneration paid to individuals (employees and individual contractors, except for those who are duly registered individual entrepreneurs). Under current rules, the responsibility to be a tax agent lies with Russian entities, individual entrepreneurs and permanent establishments of foreign legal entities in Russia. In addition to withholding obligations, employers are required to provide information to the tax authorities on income paid and tax withheld, and to notify the tax authorities about the amounts of income received by individuals from whom tax could not be withheld.

An individual is required to file his/her annual tax return with the Russian tax authorities and pay PIT himself/herself in the following cases:

- he/she is self-employed;

- he/she received income from which Russian tax was not withheld by a tax agent;

- he/she is a Russian tax resident and received income from sources outside Russia;

- he/she is entitled to, and intends to take, an income tax deduction provided for under Russian law.

Personal income tax withheld by a tax agent is credited against total tax liability for the year as stated in the tax declaration.

Appendix A: Taxes and other Obligatory Payments (Except for Customs Payments) Payable by Russian and Foreign Legal Entities in 2004

TAX	TAX BASE	TAX RATE	DEADLINE FOR FILING REPORTS	DEADLINE FOR TAX PAYMENT
Profits tax	For a Russian legal entity (RLE) – profit calculated according to the Tax Code provisions based on tax accounting records. For a Foreign legal entity (FLE) – profit earned from business activities in the Russian Federation (RF) through a permanent establishment is calculated according to the Profits Tax Chapter of the Tax Code provisions based on tax accounting records using direct method. The use of 'indirect' method is allowed only for preparatory and auxiliary activity in favour of third parties for free of charge.	Maximum aggregate rate of 24% Rate may be decreased by the legislative bodies of the RF constituents to 20% for certain types of taxpayers.	*Quarterly filings* – within 28 days after the end of the reporting quarter (for the first 3 quarters); *Annual filings* – no later than 28 March following the reporting year.	**RLE** *If quarterly payments of the tax with monthly advance payments are made:* Advance payment – not later than the 28th day of the reporting month; final quarterly/annual payment is made not later than the deadline for quarterly/annual filings. *If the tax is paid monthly on actual profit earned:* the payments are made not later than the 28th day following the reporting month. The final annual payment is made by 28 March following the reporting year. **FLE** The payments are made within the deadlines stated for filing of the report.
Tax on dividend income, interest income on state bonds	Dividend income, interest income on state and municipal bonds (some of municipal bonds are tax-exempt).	6% on dividends received by RLEs or individuals – Russian tax residents from RLE. Tax agents could deduct the amount of dividends received from RLEs from the sum of dividends to be paid to RLEs when the tax base is calculated. 15% on dividends received by FLE from RLE and by RLE from FLE, interest income on state and municipal bonds (except for those that are tax-exempt).	*Quarterly filings* – within 28 days after the end of the reporting quarter (for the first 3 quarters); *Annual filings* – no later than 28 March following the reporting year.	*Withheld* when income is paid *by the entity that pays income*, and remitted to the budget within 10 days from the payment date.[1]

[1] For some state and municipal bonds – 10 days from the end of a month of income payment.

Russian Taxation 259

TAX	TAX BASE	TAX RATE	DEADLINE FOR FILING REPORTS	DEADLINE FOR TAX PAYMENT
Withholding tax on Russian sourced income	Income earned by FLEs from sources in the RF, which are not related to business activities performed in the RF through a permanent establishment.	Unless otherwise provided in the applicable double tax treaty: 10% on freight income; 15% on dividends; 20% on all other kinds of income subject to withholding.	Submitted by the person or entity that pays the income (tax agent) on a quarterly basis 28 days after the end of the reporting quarter, for the reporting year – not later than 28 March.	Tax is withheld by the tax agent from each payment of income to FLE. The tax must be paid by a tax agent to the budget simultaneously with the income payment to FLE (possibly within 3 days).
Value added tax (VAT)	• Value of realized goods (work, services), including excises (for goods and mineral raw materials subject to excise duties); • Market value of goods/services transferred without charge; • Value of imported goods; • Expenses on self-construction; • Value of goods (works, services), used for company's own needs, in cases the related expenses are not profits tax deductible.	• 0% – exported goods, works and services connected with export of goods; realization of goods to diplomatic representative offices; realization of precious metals etc.; • 10% – some types of foodstuff, goods for children, books, printed production and medical supplies, according to the list prescribed by article 164 of Part II of the Tax Code of Russia; • 18% – all other goods (works, services).	*Filings:* no later than the 20th day of the month following the reporting month[2] (for companies paying VAT on monthly basis) or no later than the 20th day of the month following the reporting quarter (for companies paying VAT on a quarterly basis).	Payments on a monthly basis are made not later than the 20th day of the month following the reporting period; Payments on a quarterly basis are made not later than the 20th day of the month following the reporting quarter.

[2] Entities with a monthly turnover less than R1,000,000 (approx. $30,000) file returns and pay tax on a quarterly basis.

TAX	TAX BASE	TAX RATE	DEADLINE FOR FILING REPORTS	DEADLINE FOR TAX PAYMENT
Property tax	Average annual net book value of the fixed assets and immovable property. Land plots, aquatic facilities, and natural resources shall not be taxed. FLEs may enjoy tax relief under the relevant DTT provisions. ROs of FLEs must account for taxable objects according to the Russian accounting rules. There are several exemptions available (eg for housing and infrastructure objects until 1 January 2005, for religious organizations and organizations for disabled persons, etc.).	No more than 2.2% (the actual rate in regions are established by the legislative bodies of RF).	On a quarterly basis within 30 days after the end of reporting quarter (during the first three quarters); and by the 30th March following the reporting year for the annual filing.	On a quarterly basis within 30 days after the end of reporting quarter (for the first 3 quarters) and by the 30th March following the reporting year end for annual tax payment.
Advertising tax[3]	Advertising expenses (VAT exclusive).	No more than 5% (established by local legislative bodies).	By the deadline established by the local legislative bodies.	Within the deadline established by local legislative bodies.

[3] Advertising tax will be abolished starting from 1 January 2005.

TAX	TAX BASE	TAX RATE	DEADLINE FOR FILING REPORTS	DEADLINE FOR TAX PAYMENT
Transport tax	• Engine capacity (based on horsepower) of vehicles, depending on the type of transport vehicles. • Gross tonnage (in gross tons) of non-wind-propelled waterborne craft. • Each unit of air transport and waterborne craft (other than non-wind-propelled waterborne craft).	Fixed rates (per unit of horsepower, gross ton or unit of transport), which are differentiated, based on the engine capacity, gross tonnage and type of transport. The actual rates in regions may be subject to the maximum 5-fold increase/decrease by legislative bodies of RF constituents.	Reporting rules are established by the legislative bodies of RF constituents.	Established by the legislative bodies of RF constituents.
Unified Social Tax and pension fund contributions[4]	Remuneration, bonuses and other income paid in cash and in kind, accrued by an employer in favour of employees on any basis, including remuneration paid under civil law contracts for provision of works/services, and copyright agreements. The tax is calculated for each employee.	The rate depends on the volume of the annual wage/salary of the employee: • Not more than R100,000 (approx. $3,000) – 35.6%; • From R100,001 to R300,000 (approx. $3,000–$9,000) – R35,600 + 20% of the amount, exceeding R100,000; • From R300,001 to R600,000 (approx. $9,000–18,000) – R75,600 + 10% of the amount, exceeding R300,000; • More than R600,000 (approx. $18,000) – R105,600 + 2% of the amount, exceeding R600,000.	*Quarterly returns* – not later than the 20th day after the reporting quarter. *Annual return* – not later than 30 March following the reporting year. In addition, a special return must be submitted to the Social Insurance Fund by the 15th day after the end of the reporting quarter.	Advance monthly payments are made not later than the 15th day of the next month; pension funds payments – within the deadline, established for the receipt of funds for salary payments, but not later than the 15th day of the next month. The final payment is due within 15 days after the quarter (annual) filing deadline.

[4] Some changes to the UST Chapter of the Tax Code will be introduced effective from 1 January 2005, including reduction of the maximum UST rate of 35.6% to 26% and changes in the structure of groups taxed at regressive rates and applicable tax rates for these groups.

TAX	TAX BASE	TAX RATE	DEADLINE FOR FILING REPORTS	DEADLINE FOR TAX PAYMENT
Pension tax	Remuneration, bonuses and other income paid in cash and in kind, accrued by an employer in favour of employees on any basis, including remuneration paid under civil law contracts for provision of works/services, as well as on license and copyright agreements, payments in the form of material assistance and other gratuitous payments. Individual entrepreneurs: income related to the entrepreneurial activity, excluding related expenses.	Tax rates depend on age and gender of employees and also on the amount of tax base. Pension tax amounts decrease Unified Social Tax that is paid on contributions to the pension fund.	*Quarterly returns (advance payments)* – not later than the 20th day after the reporting month. *Annual return* – not later than 30 March following the reporting year.	*Employers*: advance monthly payments within the deadline, established for the receipt of funds for salary payments, but not later than 15th day of the next month.
Statutory accident insurance	Similar to the base for the Unified Social Tax.	The rate varies depending on the industry in which the taxpayer is engaged. For the majority of industries the rate is 0.2%.	The return must be submitted to the Social Insurance Fund by the 15th day after the end of the reporting quarter.	Monthly payments within the deadline, established for the receipt of funds for salary payments (pay day).

Appendix B: Double Tax Treaties Concluded with the Russian Federation

Country	Treaty benefits available from	Dividends (%)	Interest (%)	Royalties (%)	Construction site durations (months)
1. Albania/RF	1 January 1998	10	10	10	12
2. Armenia/RF	1 January 1999	5 [vii] or 10	0	0	18
3. Austria/RF	1 January 2003	5 [vii] or 15	0	0	12 [vii]
4. Azerbaijan/RF	1 January 1999	10	0 [vii] or 10	10	12
5. Belarus/RF	1 January 1998	15	0 [vii] or 10	10	0
6. Belgium/RF	1 January 2001	10	0 [vii] or 10	0	12
7. Bulgaria/RF	1 January 1996	15	0 [vii] or 15	15	12
8. Canada/RF	1 January 1998	10 [vii] or 15	0 [vii] or 10	0 [vii] or 10	12
9. China/RF	1 January 1998	10	0 [vii] or 10	10	18
10. Croatia/RF	1 January 1998	5 [vii] or 10	10	10	12
11. Cyprus/RF	1 January 2000	5 [vii] or 10	0	0	12
12. Czech/RF	1 January 1998	10	0	10	12
13. Denmark/RF	1 January 1998	10	0	0	12
14. DPRK/RF	1 January 2001	10	0	0	12
15. Egypt	1 January 2001	10	0 [vii] or 15	15	6
16. Finland/RF	1 January 2003	5 [vii] or 12	0	0	12 or 18 [vii]
17. France/RF	1 January 2000	5 [vii] or 10 or 15	0	0	12
18. Germany/RF	1 January 1997	5 [vii] or 15	0	0	12
19. Hungary/RF	1 January 1998	10	0	0	12
20. Iceland/RF	1 January 2004	5 [vii] or 15	0	0	12
21. India/RF	1 January 1999	10	0 [vii] or 10	10	12
22. Indonesia/RF	1 January 2003	15	0 [vii] or 15	15	3
23. Iran/RF	1 January 2003	5 [vii] or 10	0 [vii] or 7,5	5	12
24. Ireland/RF	1 January 1996[i]	10	0	0	12
25. Israel/RF	1 January 2001	10	0 [vii] or 10	10	12
26. Italy/RF	1 January 1999	5 [vii] or 10	10	0	12
27. Japan/USSR	1 January 1987	15	0 [vii] or 10	0 [vii] or 10	12
28. Kazakhstan/RF	1 January 1998	10	0 [vii] or 10	10	12
29. Korea/RF	1 January 1996	5 [vii] or 10	0	5	12 or 24 [vii]
30. Kuwait/RF	1 January 2004	0 [vii] or 5	0	10	6
31. Kyrgyzstan/RF	1 January 2001	10	0 [vii] or 10	10	12
32. Lebanon/RF	1 January 2001	10	0 [vii] or 5	5	12
33. Luxembourg/RF	1 January 1998	10 [vii] or 15	0	0	12
34. Macedonia/RF	1 January 2001	10	10	10	12
35. Malaysia/USSR	1 January 1989	0 or 15 [vii]	0 [vii] or 15	10 [vii] or 15	6 [vii] or 12
36. Mali/RF	1 January 2000	10 [vii] or 15	0 [vii] or 15	0	0
37. Moldova/RF	1 January 1998	10	0	10	12
38. Mongolia/RF	1 January 1998	10	0 [vii] or 10	rates in accordance with domestic law	24
39. Morocco/RF	1 January 2000	5 [vii] or 10	0 [vii] or 10	10	8
40. Namibia/RF	1 January 2001	5 [vii] or 10	0 [vii] or 10	5	9
41. Netherlands/RF	1 January 1999	5 [vii] or 15	0	0	12
42. New Zealand/RF	1 January 2004	15	10	10	12
43. Norway/RF	1 January 2003	10	0 [vii] or 10	0	12

Appendix B continued overleaf

264 Getting Established: The Taxation and Legal Environment

Appendix B continued

Country	Treaty benefits available from	Dividends (%)	Interest (%)	Royalties (%)	Construction site durations (months)
44. Philippines/RF	1 January 1998	15	0 [vii] or 15	15	183 days
45. Poland/RF	1 January 1994	10	0 [vii] or 10	10	12 or 24 [vii]
46. Portugal/RF	1 January 2003	10 [vii] or 15	0 [vii] or 10	10	12
47. Qatar/RF	1 January 2001	5	0 [vii] or 5	0	6
48. Romania/RF	1 January 1996	15	0 [vii] or 15	10	12
49. Slovakia/RF	1 January 1998	10	0	10	12
50. Slovenia/RF	1 January 1998	10	10	10	12
51. South Africa/RF	1 September 2000 1 January 2001	10 [vii] or 15	0 [vii] or 10	0	12
52. Spain/RF	1 January 2001	5 [vii] or 10 or 15	0 [vii] or 5	5	12
53. Sri Lanka/RF	1 January 2003	10 [vii] or 15	0 [vii] or 10	10	6
54. Sweden/RF	1 January 1996	5 [vii] or 15	0	0	12
55. Switzerland/RF	1 January 1998	5 [vii] or 15	0 or 5 or 10 [vii]	0	12
56. Syria/RF	1 January 2004	15	0 [vii] or 10	4.5 [vii] or 13.5 or 18	6
57. Tajikistan/RF	1 January 2004	5 [vii] or 10	0 [vii] or 10	0	24
58. Turkey/RF	1 January 2000	10	0 [vii] or 10	10	18
59. Turkmenistan/RF	1 January 2000	10	5	5	12
60. UK/RF	1 January 1998 [ii]	10	0	0	12
61. Ukraine/RF	1 January 2000	5 [vii] or 15	0 [vii] or 10	10	12
62. USA/RF	1 January 1994 [iii]	5 [vii] or 10	0	0	18
63. Uzbekistan/RF	1 January 1996	10	0 [vii] or 10	0	12
64. Vietnam/RF	1 January 1997	10 [vii] or 15	10	15	6
65. Yugoslavia/RF	1 January 1998	5 [vii] or 15	10	10	18
Signed but non-effective treaties					
Australia/RF	Status unclear [iv]	5 [vii] or 15	10	10	12
Cuba/RF	Not effective	5 [vii] or 15	0 [vii] or 10	5	12
Ethiopia/RF	Status unclear [v]	5	0 [vii] or 5	15	9
Hellenic Republic/RF	Not effective	5 [vii] or 10	7	7	9
Lithuania/RF	Not effective	5 [vii] or 10	0 [vii] or 10	5 [vii] or 10	9
Malta/RF	Not effective	5 [vii] or 10	0	0	6
Mauritius/RF	Status unclear [v]	5 [vii] or 10	0	0	12
Oman/RF	Not effective	5 [vii] or 10	0	5	9
Argentine/RF	Not effective	N/A [vi]	N/A [vi]	N/A [vi]	
Estonia/RF	Not effective	5 [vii] or 10	0 [vii] or 10	10	9
Georgia/RF	Not effective	10	0 [vii] or 10	5	9
Singapore/RF	Not effective	N/A [vi]	N/A [vi]	N/A [vi]	
Thailand/RF	Not effective	15	0 [vii] or 10	15	6

i In Ireland tax relief is available from 1/01/96 or 6/04/96 (depending on the tax).
ii In the UK tax relief is available from 1/04/98 or 6/04/98 (depending on the tax).
iii In the USA and RF tax relief is available from 1/01/94 or 1/02/94 (depending on the tax).
iv The Double Tax Treaty with Australia was ratified by the Russian Federation on 9 December 2003, however, the Treaty has not been officially published yet.
v There is no information whether the treaty is concluded (awaited from the RF Ministry of Foreign Affairs).
vi Details of the treaty are not available (awaited from the RF Ministry of Foreign Affairs).
vii Certain requirements/conditions are provided in the DTT for application of the rate/definition of construction site duration.

4.6

Auditing and Accounting

Andrei Elinson, Deloitte & Touche

Current state of the auditing profession in Russia

History

The auditing profession has a relatively short history in the Russian Federation. As with other professions that are part of the economic infrastructure of a market-oriented society, it simply did not exist as such prior to the start of the political and economic market reforms in the mid-1980s. In a state-planned and managed economy, where the only owner and user of resources was the State itself, the only relatively similar profession that existed was that of the state controllers who worked for various governmental ministries, as well as the higher-level controllers working for the Ministry of Finance and specifically, in the area of foreign trade, the Ministry of Foreign Trade.

With the introduction of market reforms prior to the dissolution of the Soviet Union, for the first time the concept of auditing was introduced. Its inception followed the first Governmental Decrees of 1987 and 1988 on Joint Venture Activities in the USSR. The first audit firm ever to commence work in the country was AO Inaudit – a state-owned and controlled company, which was the sole empowered auditor working in the market.

The actual creation of the profession started later, during the 1980s to early 1990s, when the largest international accounting and auditing firms (the Big Six) began to enter the market, and the newly-obtained economic freedom enjoyed by entities created the need and demand for consulting and accounting services.

In the early 1990s the auditing profession was not governed by any specific legislation, although many attempts were made to create and introduce such laws. Various professional unions and associations were created. The first attempts were made to adopt auditing standards at least at firm or association levels. The first certification procedures were put in place by the most prominent professional associations and the local authorities. The process was chaotic until at last, in 1993, a

Presidential Decree was issued enforcing 'The Temporary Regulations on Auditing Activities in the Russian Federation' (the Decree). This decree was subsequently superseded by the Law on 'Auditing Activity' in 2001.

Legislation

The Decree attempted to fill the legislative vacuum that existed at the time, and served its purpose in pulling together the various practices that existed, both international and domestic. It established the basic principles of independence and created a structure for the certification and licensing process. The basic feature of the Decree was that it empowered the Government to regulate the profession through its bodies (such as the Ministry of Finance). The regulation of bank audits was then under the separate responsibility of the Central Bank of the Russian Federation.

The 1993 Decree also established the Presidential Audit Commission (PAC). The PAC has so far set 34 Russian Standards on Auditing (RSA).

In 1994, the Government issued Regulation #482, 'On the Approval of the Supervision of Auditing Activities', to initially form three audit industry licensing bodies, known as the Central Certification Licensing Auditing Commissions (*Tsalak*), covering general, banking and insurance, as well as budget funded and exchange organizations. In the summer of 1996, following a government reorganization, the two non-banking Tsalak bodies merged to form a single Tsalak (MinFin Tsalak), which was comprised of 25 representatives, including representatives from the Ministry of Finance, the PAC, the Central Bank, and other governmental and professional bodies.

The Tsalaks of both the Ministry of Finance and the Central Bank had the responsibility for audit examinations, attestation and licensing issues. The PAC was responsible for professional standards insofar as that it issued recommendations on exams and, more importantly, introduced auditing standards.

In May 1997, the PAC, the Ministry of Finance and the Financial Scientific Research Institute published a collection of 11 rules (standards) for auditing activity and a list of terms and definitions thereto. However, in the absence of any auditing law, some auditing firms disputed the compulsory nature of these rules. Some clarification on the matter was provided by Resolution #472 of the Russian Government, dated 27 April 1999, 'On the Licensing of Some Types of Auditing Activity in the Russian Federation', which established that the quality of audits should correspond to the standards approved by the PAC. By the end of 2000, work on Russian auditing standards within the framework of the 'Action Programme for the Audit of

Financial Statements of Economic Entities Using Internationally-based Auditing Standards in the Period 1998 to 1999', adopted in accordance with an assignment of the Russian Government dated 4 January 1998, was essentially complete.

In October 2000, with the participation of the ICAR, the 'Big Five' and several major Russian auditing firms, the official Russian translation of the International Auditing Standards and Ethics Code of the IFAC was first published, and the second official edition of the Code, including some new documents, was published in August 2001. The two publications were of a referential nature, and were to be used in the process of developing new auditing standards.

Government Regulation #1355, dated 7 December 1994 (amended by Government Regulation #408, dated 15 April 1995), originally established the criteria for economic entities subject to a compulsory annual audit as follows:

- open joint stock companies; banks and other credit organizations; insurance companies and mutual insurers; commodities and stock exchanges; investment institutions;

- extra-budgetary funds that collect mandatory contributions; charity and (non-investment) funds that collect voluntary contributions;

- companies with foreign-owned capital;

- other economic entities if total annual revenues and assets exceed specified amounts.

The aforementioned decrees and pronouncements of the Central Bank and Presidential Commission have served as the legislative basis for the profession to date.

Provisions elaborating on the auditor's functions during the audit of certain types of entities were included in the laws on joint stock companies and limited liability companies. The Federal Law 'On Joint Stock Companies', dated 26 December 1995, established that an auditor may have access to statutory documents of a joint stock company, assess property contributed in payment for shares and other securities, check the correspondence of the company's net asset value to the size of its share capital, issue an opinion based on the results of the annual audit of the company and require that an extraordinary meeting of shareholders or the board of directors be convened. Similar functions and authorities were granted to auditors by the Federal Law 'On Limited Liability Companies', dated 8 February 1998. An audit opinion, confirming the financial statements of an entity subject to an obligatory audit in accordance with the Federal Law 'On Accounting', dated 21 November 1996, became an integral part of the financial statements.

Current developments in the regulatory environment

As time passed, business communities, as well as the auditing profession, realized that the existing legislative infrastructure was not sufficient to protect the public and State's interests, nor to protect the auditing profession. The process of instituting a comprehensive audit law was embarked upon. In the summer of 2001, following a long discussion, with the participation of the Russian auditing community, the Federal Law 'On Auditing Activity' was finally adopted and took effect on 9 September of the same year.

The law stipulates that the following entities should be subject to obligatory audit:

- open joint stock companies;
- credit institutions, insurance and mutual insurance companies, commodities and stock exchanges, investment funds, state extra-budgetary funds that collect mandatory contributions;
- entities or individual entrepreneurs whose annual revenue exceeds 500,000 times the minimum statutory monthly wage, or whose balance sheet assets at the end of the reporting year exceed 200,000 times the minimum statutory monthly wage;
- state unitary enterprises if their performance falls within the above limits.

Where before the adoption of the Law audit certificates were issued for a limited period, now a certificate of qualification is issued to auditors who have successfully passed the qualification exam without any time limitation. However, auditors are still obliged to undergo professional training each calendar year.

The Law established that an authorized federal body should regulate auditing activity, and the Russian Government assigned this function to the Department of Organization of Auditing Activity of the Ministry of Finance. In order to achieve a balance between state regulation of auditing activity and the ability of the auditing community to influence the auditing market, an Auditing Activity Board was established under the above body. The Board, as well as representatives of the federal executive bodies, other state authorities and the Bank of Russia, also includes representatives from seven professional auditing associations accredited with the Board, including: the Institute of Professional Auditors of Russia (member of IFAC), the Russian Auditors' Collegium, the National Federation of Consultants and Auditors, and the Auditing Chamber of Russia, etc.

In accordance with the Law, the Government was also obliged to develop and approve national auditing standards. With the participation of the above Board, the following federal auditing rules (standards) were developed and approved by Resolution #696, dated 23 September 2002:

- *Rule #1*: Objective and Main Principles of an Audit of Financial Statements established that the objective of an audit is to express an opinion on the financial statements of the audited entity and the compliance of its accounting procedures with the legislation of the Russian Federation. The auditor should express an opinion on the reliability of the financial (accounting) statements in all material respects.

- *Rule #2*: Audit Documentation Maintenance stated that the auditing firm or individual auditor should document all the information that is important in terms of providing evidence supporting the auditor's opinion, as well as evidence that the audit has been performed in accordance with the federal rules (standards) of auditing activities. Working documents can be in the form of data recorded on paper, on film, in an electronic file, or in other formats.

- *Rule #3*: Audit Planning, based on International Auditing Standards, established unified requirements for the planning of an audit of the financial (accounting) statements, which should be applied primarily to repeat audits of the audited entity (ie not the first year that the auditor has audited the entity). According to this rule, audit planning involves, in particular, the development of a high-level strategy and a detailed approach to the expected nature, timing and scope of audit procedures.

- *Rule #4*: Audit Materiality, also based on International Auditing Standards, established unified requirements in respect of the materiality concept and its connection to audit risk. It requires that the auditor use professional judgment in determining materiality. In developing an audit plan, the auditor should set an acceptable materiality level to ensure the detection of material misstatements (on quantitative grounds). However, account should be taken of both the value (quantity) and the nature (quality) of misstatements.

- *Rule #5*: Audit Evidence established, in particular, that audit evidence should be obtained through a series of tests of internal controls and substantive procedures. In certain situations, evidence can be obtained exclusively by performing substantive procedures. According to this Standard, audit evidence includes the information received by the auditor during the audit and the results of their analysis of this information, and forms the basis of the auditor's opinion. Audit evidence includes, in particular, the source documents and accounting records that underlie the financial (accounting) statements, as well as written representations of the audited entity's authorized employees and information received from various sources (third parties).

- *Rule #6*: Auditors' Report on Financial (Accounting) Statements. According to this rule, an auditors' report is an official document intended for the users of the financial (accounting) statements of the audited entity, prepared in accordance with this rule and containing the opinion of the audit company or individual auditor. This report should be expressed in a prescribed format, and should comment on the reliability of the financial (accounting) statements of the audited entity, as well as the entity's compliance with the accounting laws of the Russian Federation. The reliability of the financial statements refers to the accuracy of the data contained within the financial (accounting) statements, which enables the users of the statements to draw correct conclusions as to the performance, financial position and property status of the audited entities and make reasonable decisions based on these conclusions. In order to assess the degree of compliance of the financial (accounting) statements with the legislation of the Russian Federation, the auditor should establish the tolerable limits of deviation by determining the materiality of the accounting records and financial statements data for the purposes of the audit, in accordance with federal Rule #4 'Audit Materiality'. At present, the Board continues to develop other rules (standards) on auditing activity, and professional auditing organizations have begun to develop rules to guarantee the quality of audits performed by their members.

- *Rule #7*: Internal Control of the Quality of the Audit, based on International Accounting Standards, established unified requirements for audit internal control of quality. It requires that measures be taken both at the overall level of the audit firm itself and on individual projects. These measures include professional requirements, professional competence, challenging tasks, recommendations, and monitoring the efficiency of internal control procedures.

- *Rule #8*: Auditor's Risk Estimation and Internal Control of the Audited Entity, based on International Accounting Standards, required that the auditor achieve understanding of the accounting and internal control systems, and of audit risk and its components: inherent risk, control risk and detection risk. According to this rule the auditor should obtain sufficient understanding of the accounting and internal control systems to plan the audit. The auditor should use professional judgment to assess audit risk and to design audit procedures to ensure that it is reduced to an acceptably low level.

- *Rule #9*: Related Parties, based on International Accounting Standards, stipulated that the auditor should perform audit procedures designed to obtain sufficient appropriate audit evidence regarding the identification and disclosure of related parties by management, and the effect of related-party transactions that are material to the financial statements. In this rule the term 'related parties' means natural and legal persons who have the ability to impact upon the activity of legal and/or natural persons engaged in business activity. However, an audit cannot be expected to detect all related-party transactions.

- *Rule #10*: Subsequent Events, based on International Accounting Standards, established standards and provided guidance on the auditor's responsibility regarding subsequent events. In this rule, the term 'subsequent events' is used to refer to both events occurring between period end and the date of the auditor's report, and facts discovered after the date of the auditor's report.

- *Rule #11*: Going Concern, based on International Accounting Standards, set standards on the auditor's responsibilities, including consideration of management's assessment of the entity's ability to continue as a going concern. Under the going concern assumption, an entity is ordinarily viewed as continuing in business for the foreseeable future with neither the intention nor the necessity of liquidation, cessation of trading or seeking protection from creditors pursuant to laws or regulations.

Additionally the *Code of Audit Ethics,* which is based on International Accounting Standards, was established in August 2003. It endorses the concepts of objectivity, integrity and professional competence, and is applicable to all professional auditors.

Conclusion

In conditions where most Russian auditors focus their attention on tax-related issues, one must also take steps to ensure audit quality, auditor independence and financial liability in case of negligence, recklessness or fraud.

In the present Russian audit environment, an audit infrastructure is required to ensure a high quality statutory audit function, and the issuance of correct and credible financial statements by all that practice in the profession is in the process of active development. While some firms that practice in the profession do perform high-quality audits, others do not. Such an infrastructure could be broadly broken down into the following categories:

- control over the quality of audit services using the principles established by the respective International Auditing Standard;
- rules on audit firms and mutual recognition;

- unification of the currently disconnected professional auditing and accounting associations;
- completion of the development of professional standards on auditing, based on International Auditing Standards;
- ethical rules and independence, based on the IFAC's ethics code;
- disciplinary procedures and sanctions infrastructure;
- liability regime.

Accounting standards in the Russian Federation

The Russian Federation's move to a market economy has also necessitated a change in the standards of accounting for the financial position and results of operations of Russian enterprises.

While the Russian Accounting Standards (RAS) have gone through reform over the years, the major reform needed for the standards to be in full compliance with International Accounting Standards (IFRS) has fallen short.

The Ministry of Finance of the Russian Federation has been given the responsibility of instituting reform of the RAS. This holds true for all organizations, except those that are required to report to the Central Bank of the Russian Federation, which have their own rules for reporting.

Since 1998 the Ministry of Finance has increasingly instituted revisions in an effort to account for transactions under more internationally accepted methods. For example, accounting for revenue under the accrual method has been introduced and accruing expenses incurred but not paid is now required in certain situations. In particular, provisions on accounting (termed PBU) have been issued.

These PBUs include the following topics: Financial Statement of Organization; Financial Investment Accounting; Income Tax Accounting; Expenditure on Research and Development and Technological Works Accounting; Activity Terminated Accounting; Conditional Facts of Economic Activity; Inventory Accounting; Fixed Assets Accounting; Affiliated Parties; Organization's Income; Organization's Expense; Organization's Accounting Policy; Subsequent Events; Loans and Credits Accounting; Intangible Assets Accounting; State Financing Accounting; Segment Information; Accounting of Assets and Liabilities valued in foreign currency; Accounting for Construction in Progress.

Nevertheless, even with the issuance of these accounting policies, fundamental differences still remain. While the PBUs may be similar to IFRS, they are not IFRS, and therefore important differences remain.

Despite the stated intention of the Chairman of the Russian Government to transfer to IFRS by 2004, there are still many differences between IFRS and RAS. GAAP 2000 and 2001 surveys of National Accounting Rules in 53 countries showed the existence of multiple variances between national accounting rules and IFRS in a number of European countries, including in more than 42 accounting areas in Russia.

Russian accounting may differ from IFRS because of the absence of specific Russian rules on recognition and measurement. Some of the more significant areas include:

- the distinction between acquisition and unification of interests in business combination situations;
- provisions in the context of business combinations accounted for as acquisitions;
- consolidation of special-purpose entities;
- accounting for associate companies;
- the restatement of financial statements of companies reporting in the currency of a hyperinflationary economy in terms of the measuring unit currency at the balance sheet date;
- the translation of the financial statements of hyperinflationary subsidiaries;
- impairment of assets;
- the recognition of operating lease incentives;
- restatement of financial statements;
- accounting for changes in enacted tax rates for deferred tax;
- accounting for an issuer's financial instruments.

It is unfortunate that RAS have not moved closer to IFRS. As a result, many companies, particularly those that are interested in obtaining Western investment, have the double burden of preparing their accounts under both methods, one to fulfill legal requirements and one to attract the interest of Western investors. Moreover, with the adoption of Chapter 25 of the new Tax Code, Russian companies also need to keep tax accounts.

Conclusion

Whilst many would say that reform has already occurred, one only needs to compare company accounts prepared under RAS to those prepared under IFRS to see that more reforms are needed. Many international organizations are anxious for these reforms to be carried out. At present, it is difficult to estimate when these reforms will take place. In the meantime, in order for external investors to be able to properly evaluate the financial position and results of operations of enterprises, credible financial statements prepared under IFRS (or another internationally-accepted method, ie US GAAP) must be requested and obtained.

4.7

New Russian Customs Legislation

Alexander Dragunov, Director, Customs Practice, PricewaterhouseCoopers

The enactment of the new Russian Federation Customs Code, which took effect on 1 January 2004, resulted from the objective need to bring customs legislation into line with the Constitution of the Russian Federation and with a number of important federal laws that were passed after the old version of the Customs Code had come into force, as well as the need to account for international practice, Russia's growing foreign trade turnover, and the creation of an attractive investment climate in the country. On the whole, as statute law, the old Customs Code did not necessarily create any particular difficulties for entities engaged in foreign trade.

The customs value is determined in line with GATT/WTO principles and is generally equivalent to the DAF/Russian border transaction price of the goods concerned. Classification of customs codes follows the international Harmonized Commodity Description and Coding System.

From a real business perspective, the greatest achievement of the new Customs Code is that, effective 1 January 2004, *it has substantially simplified the procedure for appealing the unlawful actions (or inaction) of the customs authorities through the arbitration courts.* Under the old customs rules, before filing with an arbitration court, the appeal first had to be submitted to the superior customs body, and only if the claimant remains unsatisfied with the decision of the superior customs body could a secondary appeal be filed directly with the arbitration court. This procedure was excessively harsh on business, since it was virtually impossible to resolve disputes with customs quickly and with minimal financial losses. However, it is now possible to file suit in court immediately, thus bypassing the lengthy process of having a problem reviewed in the depths of customs bureaucracy. Moreover, the new procedural options available for defending one's rights in court open up a wider range of possibilities for identifying the most efficient means of responding to a given scenario. Previously, in cases where the customs authorities took unlawful actions with respect to a business, the company was forced to exclude the affected goods or exacted funds from its turnover for a whole six months. However, it now seems likely that this will cease. In addition to allowing the direct filing of lawsuits in arbitration courts, the new Customs Code also permits the claimant to simultaneously petition the court to bar the customs authorities from exacting funds.

The RF Federal Customs Service (former State Customs Committee) has been divested of its powers to issue legal acts. From now on, *all major legal acts regulating customs affairs will be issued directly by the Ministry of Economic Developments and Trade and the government.* The Ministry of Finance will dictate policy on customs payments, and customs valuation of goods and means of transport.

As of 1 January 2004, *an importer will be able to clear its goods at any customs office without requesting additional authorization to do so.*

The new Customs Code provides many opportunities for applying *simplified customs clearance procedures.* If an entity engaged in foreign trade is not in continued breach of customs rules and has engaged in foreign trade for at least three years, it may declare goods by submitting documents and then submitting a customs cargo declaration within 45 days. It may also apply the periodic declaration procedure by submitting one declaration for goods imported in several shipments over a certain period of time. Other options are now also available for reducing logistics costs.

Particular attention should be paid to new provisions on the *temporary storage of goods.* The old Customs Code mandated that goods could be stored and customs clearance performed only at temporary storage warehouses. Many importers had to pay expensive fees for temporary warehouse storage. The new Code now permits the storage of such goods at the recipient's own warehouse. Moreover, the given warehouse does not have to be a customs temporary storage warehouse, equipped according to strict customs rules. In addition, it will now be sufficient to merely submit a substantiated application to the customs office to have the storage period extended by two to four months.

At the same time, however, one should not get the impression that importers now have unlimited freedom of choice as regards *the place of customs clearance.* For example, depending on the means of transport used to perform the international carriage of goods, or for goods frequently found in breach of customs rules, the customs authorities may establish a list of specific customs offices at which such goods must be cleared. Thus, the current system of specialized customs offices will continue to exist.

In addition, as regards *declaring goods*, another aspect worthy of mention are so-called 'technical errors' that frequently 'turn up' unintentionally in customs declarations. From now on, all errors detected during customs control that have no effect on customs payments made shall not be deemed an obstacle to the release of goods. Moreover, no charges may be brought for customs offences if such errors are detected.

Under the simplified procedure for confirming *the country of origin of goods*, a certificate of origin must be submitted only in those cases when the goods in question qualify for customs benefits in applying import customs duty rates. But, even the lack of such a certificate does not entitle the customs authorities to apply the base duty rate, increased by two.

There have been positive changes concerning *release of goods* as well. The customs authorities will have only three days to carry out an inspection, after which the goods must be released. Moreover, regarding acceptance of customs declarations, the new Customs Code does away with the requirement to prove that customs payments have been made. For the purposes of releasing goods, it will be necessary either to have funds available on the appropriate accounts or to have submitted a guarantee that customs payments will be made. Given all the specific features of customs procedures, one should bear in mind that, aside from the general grounds for releasing goods, there are those that are merely 'implied' for different regimes. For example, special authorization must be obtained to place goods under the customs processing regime.

Regulation of customs regimes has also undergone a number of changes. The most positive changes concern customs regimes with an economic impact. Customs processing regimes make it significantly easier to repair goods, while the customs warehouse regime permits the sale of goods directly from the warehouse. Special regimes for means of transport are also provided.

The *temporary import customs regime* deserves particular attention. For fixed production assets, it is now permitted to use temporary import for 34 months and make partial customs payments in the amount of 3 per cent per month. This is a unique procedure for making payments; the taxpayer not only makes its customs payments in installments, but such installment payments will be interest-free. At the end of the temporary import period, the goods are automatically recognized as released for home use.

Effective 1 January 2004, *the procedure for making customs payments* has come under the purview of the new Customs Code. However, taxes and duties are set in accordance with the rules of the Tax Code. Interestingly, the new Code has established a number of innovations not envisioned under tax legislation. For example, it sets a minimum value for imported goods (R5,000) that will not be subject to customs duties and taxes provided that such deliveries occur no more than once per week. In contrast to the Tax Code, the new Customs Code establishes new rules for determining the taxable base for goods being transferred when calculating value added tax, which is equal to the customs value only. Also, businesses do not need to make customs payments where a loss of goods occurred as a result of natural operational wear and tear. The new Customs Code also sets its own rules for calculating interest for installment payments or deferments of customs payments, but does not establish any fixed fee for customs clearance. These innovations in customs legislation probably represent the legal manifestation of the government's efforts to reduce the tax burden. One more important innovation introduced by the new Customs Code is a statute of limitations for effecting customs payments, namely one year from the date the taxpayer's liability for customs payments first arose.

However, the new Customs Code has expanded the list of customs operations that may require providing *security for customs payments*. All goods not subject to customs payments (due to tax exemptions or preferential customs regimes, or goods released under simplified procedures) will be considered foreign goods. It is precisely in these cases that provision of security for customs payments could be required. Given a choice of the type of security provided, importers should bear in mind that all forms of security are regulated by the norms of civil law, where relations between parties are based on equality, autonomy, and independence. This means that the customs authorities may not accept any type of security, and, in particular, this concerns guarantees and pledges of property. Therefore, analyzing which form of security to use will take time, and the final choice must be agreed upon with the relevant customs post. However, security is not now mandatory. A security is required only if the customs office has serious and valid grounds to believe that the importer's obligations will not be met. Such grounds may include the existence of unpaid debts for customs payments or frequent breach of customs rules, as well as bankruptcy proceedings with respect to the importer, etc.

The new Customs Code limits the *period during which goods may be under customs supervision after their release*. According to the general rule, all goods that lose their status while under customs supervision may be subject to subsequent customs control only within the course of one year. This rule does not apply to those goods that will be placed under customs regimes that are under the continuous supervision of the customs authorities; for example, the placement of goods in a customs warehouse, where the goods are monitored throughout the entire storage period. The new Customs Code does not limit the timeframe for performing customs supervision after the release of goods with customs payment exemptions. An example of such goods would be the importation of equipment as a contribution to a company's charter (joint) capital, or goods imported as humanitarian aid.

The real potential stumbling block concerns how the new Customs Code will actually be applied in practice by various customs authorities. Certainly, as enacted, the new Customs Code is aimed at making customs procedures as transparent and simple as possible, while painless and fast. However, all the progressive innovations of the new Customs Code notwithstanding, only actual practice can answer the major questions now being raised by all parties involved in customs relations. That said, the time has finally come when all parties involved in customs relations have a real opportunity to form a new, civilized customs practice.

Here we list the most significant changes in Russian customs legislation:

- The RF Federal Customs Service was divested of its powers to issue legal acts.

- It is now possible to directly file claims with a court of law against actions (or inaction) of customs authorities and officials.

- Customs legislation provides for a comprehensive list of documents to be submitted when applying for customs clearance.

- In cases of conditional release, it may be required to put up security for the period of conditional release (such as goods as collateral, a bank guarantee, cash deposit or surety).

- The maximum time period for customs inspection was reduced from 10 to 3 days.

- The customs authorities are prohibited from refusing to accept a declaration that contains inaccurate information, but which has no impact on the defrayal of customs payments or on the application of foreign trade restrictions.

- The customs clearance of goods may now be carried out through any customs office. The old Customs Code had stipulated that the place of customs clearance should be the customs office in the region where the specific entity, or its structural subdivision, was registered.

- The new Customs Code provides urgent customs clearance for perishable goods, express cargoes, media materials, and other categories of goods.

- Following the release of goods, the customs authorities are entitled to verify the reliability of information declared at customs clearance within one year from the date when the goods in question are released from customs control.

- Goods that qualify as fixed assets may be temporarily imported for 34 months with periodic customs payments. Such goods are recognized as released for free circulation when the amount of periodic customs payments reaches the total amount of customs duties payable when the goods are imported for free circulation. No interest is charged in this case.

- Foreign individuals may temporarily import goods that are neither for production nor for other commercial activity, but for personal use, and are intended to be re-exported, without payment of duties.

- Individuals may import goods for their personal use in accordance with the regulations set forth in the Customs Code. Currently, individuals may bring in goods up to a value of $2,000 (subject to certain conditions).

- Cultural valuables are imported by individuals duty free.

Part Five

Business Development: Operating an Enterprise

5.1

The Property Regime in Russia

CMS Cameron McKenna

Introduction

The Russian Constitution of 1993 proclaims a right to hold land in private ownership. This is supported by the Civil Code of 1996, but Chapter 17 of the Civil Code, which was intended to establish a framework for transactions in land, was not brought into effect until 29 October 2001 when the new Land Code of the Russian Federation came into force. On 30 October 2001, almost 84 years to the day after the October Revolution of 1917, Russia passed a federal law overturning one of the remaining legacies of the USSR: state ownership of land. The new Land Code at long last permits private ownership of commercial land and, together with Chapter 17 of the Civil Code that now comes into effect, governs transactions in land. In general, foreign individuals and companies are allowed to buy and sell commercial land except in certain border and other designated areas. Agricultural land, however, has been excluded from the provisions of the Land Code and is dealt with in a law on agricultural land dated 24 July 2002. Perhaps the greatest practical significance of the Land Code is that it applies to the whole of the Russian Federation and the existing patchwork of regional land legislation is to be amended to bring it into line with this federal law. The Land Code has therefore removed the many discrepancies and inconsistencies that have appeared between regional and federal land law in the last few years, as certain regions had forged ahead with their own land law reform programmes.

Land

Article 9 of the Constitution provides that land and other natural resources may be held in private, state, municipal or certain other forms of ownership.

The Land Code divides land into several categories on the basis of a designated prescribed use. These are as follows:

- agricultural land;
- land for housing;
- commercial land for use by industrial enterprises, power companies, communications companies etc;
- land that is situated beneath an object which is itself specially protected (eg nature parks);
- forestry land;
- water-front land; and
- reserve land (land which is owned by the State, is not used for commercial purposes, and which can be transferred to any of the other categories – in effect, a miscellaneous grouping).

It is important, therefore, for a potential purchaser to check the prescribed use of any land before buying it. The prescribed use should be stated in all title documents, any agreement for use of the land and all registration documents. Each category has different conditions for usage and the Land Code requires that each plot of land is used and exploited only in accordance with the category in which it is designated. So, for example, it will not be permissible to build a factory on agricultural land. It should be noted, however, that in such a situation an application can be made to the relevant State authority to have the prescribed use of a particular plot of land changed.

Many of the 'subjects' of the Federation, (namely the 89 regions and cities), had their own local laws governing land and some of these had permitted commercial land ownership for some time. The Land Code requires all regional land legislation to be brought into line with the provisions of the Land Code itself.

As a general rule, the Land Code only applies to transactions occurring after its enactment. Pre-existing ownership rights, which are now inconsistent with the provisions of the Land Code, however, have to be re-registered. In particular, a permanent right to use of land should be re-registered as a lease or the right of ownership to the land should be purchased prior to 1 January 2006. Only state and municipal institutions, federal state-owned enterprises, governmental and local government bodies do not need to re-register their permanent rights to use of the land plots. Individuals or legal entities whose permanent right to use of the land plot has not been re-registered are not entitled to dispose of their land plots. Similarly, where a building (or other item of immovable property such as a rig or a bridge) has been acquired, the land underneath that structure, or the land which is necessary for its use, and which had previously been granted as a permanent right of use should be re-registered as a lease or the land acquired outright.

Unless and until land plots to which an earlier registered right of permanent use is attached are re-registered, further dealings with that land will not be permitted. In particular, it should be noted that it is no longer permissible for a permanent right to use land to be contributed to the charter capital of a company.

It is a general principle of the Land Code that foreign individuals and legal entities are to have the same rights to land as local residents. Despite this, there are certain restrictions applicable to foreigners. A foreign national, for example, may not own land located in border and other special territories. A list of such land plots is still to be approved by the President of the Russian Federation. The Land Code also provides that further restrictions may be imposed on foreigners leasing land but no additional restrictions have yet been enacted.

In some instances described in the Land Code, and in the regional land legislation, residents may be entitled to receive land free from the State. Foreigners, on the other hand, may only acquire land for a valuable consideration.

Lease of land

There is no limit to the term of a lease of land. A lessee has a priority over any subsequent lease of the same plot and, on the sale of the land, a priority right to its purchase. Leasehold rights may themselves be sub-let, assigned, sold or contributed to the charter capital of another entity. Unless otherwise provided for by the lease agreement, the aforementioned transactions can be entered into without the consent of (but after notification to) the lessor.

Land may be leased by companies and individuals whether Russian or foreign. In practice, leases are generally granted for a maximum term of 49 years and a lessee usually has a preferential right to renew the lease on expiry. The exact terms and conditions of a lease agreement will depend on negotiations between the lessor and lessee, but every lease should conform with the detailed requirements set out in the Civil Code and the Land Code.

Any change to the terms of the lease agreement requires the consent of both parties. Early termination by the lessor of a lease agreement with a term of five or more years will require a court order. An application for such an order can only be made where there has been a material breach of the terms of the lease agreement by the lessee.

Agricultural land

Agricultural land has been excluded from the provisions of the Land Code and a specific law on agricultural land was adopted on 24 July 2002.

The Law on Agricultural Land provides that foreign legal entities, foreign individuals and Russian legal entities in which foreigners control more than 50 per cent of the charter capital may not own agricultural land. They are instead only permitted to lease agricultural land and for up to a maximum period of 49 years.

The further amendments made to the Law on Agricultural Land adopted in June 2003 provide for preferential rights of the State and, if provided by the law, municipal authorities to acquire agricultural land in all cases except by acquisition at a public auction.

Buildings

One of the principles of the Land Code is to keep buildings and the land on which they are situated in the same ownership. The Land Code only allows buildings to be disposed of separately from the land on which they are situated if: (a) it is not possible to separate out the land (for example, a condominium); or (b) the sale and purchase of the land is restricted (army land, border areas etc).

Where land is to be sold by a private entity, the owner of any building situated on that land will have priority in acquiring the land. If the owner of the building chooses not to buy the land then the landowner can sell it to a third party. Where the land is to be sold by the State, however, the owner of any building on that land will have an exclusive right to purchase it: if the building-owner chooses not to so purchase, the State cannot sell the land to anyone else. Thus, buildings may be owned by individuals and companies including foreign investors, but the land beneath those structures, if not owned with the building, will remain state (or private) property.

Mineral resources

Ownership of a plot of land will not include ownership rights of the resources situated beneath that land. Such resources remain state property and may be exploited only in accordance with the provisions of the relevant sub-soil legislation.

Building leases

Buildings and parts of a building may also be leased. The terms and conditions of the lease agreement are regulated by the provisions of the Civil Code. These include, for example, general duties imposed on the lessee to pay the rent agreed, to maintain the property in good repair, to pay compensation on alterations for any improvements made, and gives a preferential right to renew the lease. Leases for more than one year must be in writing and must be registered with the relevant authority, which in Moscow is the Committee for the State Registration of Real Property Rights and Transactions Therewith within the territory of the City of Moscow.

Rent payable on real estate leases is subject to VAT at a rate of 18 per cent. An exemption from VAT is provided on lease payments made by the representative offices of companies incorporated in most Western European countries and the United States.

Mortgage

There are no restrictions in the Land Code on the grant of security over land. Article 3 of the Land Code expressly states that this issue is to be regulated by the general civil legislation unless there are specific provisions to the contrary (thus, for example, a pledge cannot be taken over land that cannot itself be owned by foreigners). The Civil Code provides that a land plot can be mortgaged, while Article 22 of the Land Code authorizes lease rights to be pledged.

It should be noted that the Land Code does not prescribe any particular requirements as to the form or content of agreements for the mortgage of land, which are regulated by the Civil Code and the Law On Mortgages of 22 July 1998. Mortgages must be certified by a Russian notary and registered with the appropriate registration authority. Buildings and other real estate may be mortgaged but only together with whatever rights the building owner has to the land beneath the building. Residential houses and apartments can also be subject to mortgage as can leasehold interests in real property.

In the event of default, a mortgagee may enforce its right to possession of real estate only through court proceedings unless the parties agree otherwise. In either case, the property that is subject to the mortgage will be sold at a public auction organized either by the court or by specially registered auction companies.

The Law on Mortgage Securities came into force in Autumn 2003. The Law sets out the requirements and conditions for the issue, certification and allocation of mortgage securities and their execution. The Law on Mortgage Securities provides for the further development of the real estate market in Russia.

Dispute resolution

The Land Code stipulates that disputes involving land are to be settled in court proceedings although, prior to such proceedings commencing, any dispute can be referred to arbitration.

In accordance with the Civil Procedure Code and the Arbitration Procedure Code, disputes concerning immovable property (including land) are within the exclusive competence of the courts of the Russian Federation. In connection with this, Article 64 of the Land Code, which allows a dispute to be referred to arbitration, would appear to be in conflict with the legislation on jurisdiction. Pending an official explanation of this provision, we would recommend incorporating into contracts for transactions involving immovable property a clause providing for the submission of disputes to the non-exclusive jurisdiction of a pre-determined arbitration body.

Registration

The ownership and other property rights in immovable property, encumbrances over these rights, their acquisition, transfer and termination should be registered by the relevant local registration authority under the Ministry of Justice in accordance with the Law on State Registration of Rights to Immovable Property and Transactions Therewith. Such registration is effective as confirmation of title. Rights that are created or transactions that are completed without registration (other than lease agreements for less than one year) are not valid unless and until they are properly registered. The appropriate authority in Moscow is the Committee for the State Registration of Real Property Rights and Transactions Therewith within the territory of the City of Moscow. The information contained in the State Register is available for inspection after payment of a fee.

Payments for real estate

Payments for real estate in Russia made to Russian individuals or Russian entities, whether lease payments or payments of a purchase price, are subject to Russian currency control and should be made in roubles.

It is not uncommon for the price of many commodities, including land, to be quoted in a foreign currency, usually US dollars. Payment is then made in roubles by reference to the Central Bank rate of exchange applicable for the day of payment.

Use

The specific use of land and buildings is usually defined by the State Register of Real Property Rights and Real Property Transactions. The most significant distinction is between residential and non-residential use.

5.2

Land Relations in the Russian Federation

Andrey Goltsblat, Managing Partner, Pepeliaev, Goltsblat & Partners

The coming into force of the Land Code in 2001 and the adoption of the Law 'On Farm Land Turnover' caused an increased investor interest in land. The Land Code made more favourable the terms and conditions for the turnover of land plots and their acquisition, including through privatization.

Current Russian legislation sets forth the principle of plurality of ownership rights to land: the law treats as legally equal the right of land ownership of the Russian Federation (federal property), the constituent entities of the Russian Federation, municipalities, legal entities and individuals. All land owners enjoy equal protection. Unless otherwise provided by law, the right of ownership in a plot of land extends to the surface (soil) layer and closed reservoirs within the boundaries of this land plot and to the forest and plants that grow on it.

Rights to land plots are primarily acquired in Russia through:

- a transaction with a land plot itself (purchase and sale, lease, exchange, gift, contribution to authorized capital, etc);

- acquisition of ownership interests in land (interests in common ownership of farm land) with a possibility of subsequent land apportionment;

- acquisition of shares (ownership interests) in a legal entity owning a land plot.

Owners of a land plot have the right to sell it, give it as a gift, erect buildings and structure thereon, pledge, lease out or otherwise dispose of it with regard to particularities, as set out in land laws.

The types of objects of land parcels that are barred from circulation should be expressly specified by law. For example, withdrawn from circulation are the lands of wildlife sanctuaries and national parks, lands under defence, security and atomic energy facilities, lands used for military and civil burials, etc. Restrictions have been imposed on the circulation of plots of forested land, farm land contaminated by hazardous waste and radioactive substances, other lands that have been subjected to degradation, etc.

Purchased, sold, leased out or otherwise disposed of can be only those land plots that are recorded in the State Land Cadaster and the rights to which are registered, as required by Russian laws. Marketable land plots are identified by means of cadastre registration – the description and individualization of a land plot that results in assigning attributes to the land plot that unambiguously distinguish it from other real estate assets. The coming into force of the amendments to the Law 'On Farm Land Turnover' made it possible in a number of constituent entities of the Russian Federation to privatize farm land after 1 January 2004.

One of the specific features of the new Russian legislation is a special legal framework for land possession applicable to foreign individuals, foreign legal entities and stateless persons. For these categories of landholders certain restrictions have been imposed by the current laws:

- their rights to land plots require payment in all cases and in no event may such rights be transferred gratuitously (unlike Russian condominiums and individuals who are allowed, in a number of specified cases, to acquire such rights gratuitously);

- foreign legal entities, foreign individuals and stateless persons are not allowed to own land in frontier areas (the list of which should be set up by Presidential decree) and in other specially designated territories, as provided by federal law.

In addition, there are certain statutory restrictions in relation to the acquisition of title to plots of farm land:

- foreign individuals, stateless persons and foreign legal entities may only possess and use plots of farm land based on a lease agreement;

- Russian legal entities with more than a 50 per cent ownership interest held by foreign individuals, stateless persons and foreign legal entities may only hold plots of farm land on lease;

- the constituent entities of the Russian Federation should set the lower limits for plots of farm land and overall upper limits for farm lands that may be concurrently owned by an individual, his/her relatives and legal entities where this individual and his/her relatives have more than 50 per cent of the votes; such limit of the total area of farm land in the territory of one constituent entity of the Russian Federation may not be less than 10 per cent of the total area of farm land within the boundaries of one administrative and territorial unit.

However, the vagueness and ambiguity of certain statutory provisions are raising apprehension among investors conducting land transactions. This apprehension is indeed well-grounded for there are no clearly identified market benchmarks and no objective methods to assess the market value of land; the land registration system is in its infancy stage and there has been no delimitation of state-owned lands. Quite often investors face difficulties in identifying the actual owner of a particular land plot or interests in land.

For instance, in the event of shared land ownership, if an investor (not one of the land co-owners but a third party) wishes to acquire a land plot that is in shared ownership, under the Civil Code (unlike that required under the Law 'On Farm Land Turnover') the investor is required to obtain all co-owners' consent. This may prove difficult in reality, since more often than not the number of land owners runs into hundreds. We have developed and are successfully using our own methods to cope with potential difficulties.

Investors frequently have apprehension related to the land plot forming procedure: it is difficult not only to find a suitable land plot but also to obtain this particular land plot for a project (be it construction of a plant, crop growing, etc).

Given that the Russian Constitution refers privatization laws and land legislation to the joint competence of the Russian Federation and its constituent entities, the specifics of legislation in each particular constituent entity of the Russian Federation need to be taken into account when conducting transactions. In addition, the regional and local authorities use different approaches to offering incentives for buying out or leasing land in their regions. When choosing a land plot it is important to take into consideration the specific features of regional legislation, which affect the terms on which the land plot may be granted, and deal with the local authorities individually.

The Russian land legislation distinguishes between seven basic land categories depending on the intended use of land, including farm land, lands under settlements, industrial land, etc.

The lands pertaining to a certain category must be used only as intended. Legal framework for lands depends on the category they fall under and permitted use in accordance with territorial zoning. Any type of permitted use is chosen by the land user independently and does not require any additional permits or approvals.

For objective reasons and for reasons of expediency, economics, social issues and the like, it is possible to convert land from one land use category to another. Such conversion requires that special rules and conditions be observed. The decision on land conversion falls within the competence of different authorities, depending on how the land plot is categorized and who its owner is.

The land legislation highlights as a priority the need to preserve especially valuable lands and lands of especially guarded territories.

The law provides that withdrawal of valuable farm lands, forested lands, lands under first-class forests, lands occupied by especially guarded natural territories and facilities, lands occupied by cultural heritage assets, other especially valuable lands and lands of especially guarded territories for other purposes is limited or prohibited, as provided by federal laws. For the construction of industrial facilities on farm land and for other non-agricultural needs, lands unfit for farming or farm lands of inferior quality in terms of cadastre value are granted.

Withdrawal for non-agricultural purposes, including by means of a buy-out, of farm land with a cadastre value exceeding the average figure across the district is allowed as an exception, if required for the performance of the international obligations of the Russian Federation, for defence or security reasons, development of mineral deposits (except for common minerals), maintenance of cultural heritage assets of the Russian Federation, construction and maintenance of cultural, social and educational facilities, motorways, trunk pipelines, power supply lines, communication lines and other similar facilities.

Particularly valuable productive farm lands, including farm lands of experimental production units of research institutions and training and experimental units of higher educational establishments, and farm lands with a cadastre value exceeding the average figure for the district may be included in the list of lands that are not allowed to be used for other purposes, as provided by the laws of the constituent entities of the Russian Federation.

The conversion of forested land to non-forested land for purposes other than forestry operation or forest use, and/or withdrawal of forested land in first-class forests fall within the competence of the Russian Government, while in second and third-class forests such conversion and/or withdrawal are the responsibility of the authorities of a particular constituent entity of the Russian Federation.

In any event, when construction or mining operations are performed damaging the soil layer, the fertile layer of soil is removed and used to improve low-productive lands. Provided the removed fertile layer of soil is put on low-productive or non-productive farm lands, the rate at which farm industry losses are required to be reimbursed may be halved.

To avoid unpleasant surprises in land transactions attention should be paid to certain inconsistencies and discrepancies in regulatory acts such as:

- the inconsistency between the provisions of civil laws and land laws in relation to the legal destiny of land plots and real estate assets located thereon, when the owner of the land and the assets separates out only the land or only an asset;

- the discrepancy between the provisions of land legislation and privatization laws governing price calculations for land plots that are subject to privatization;
- the discrepancy between the provisions of land legislation and privatization laws as to the gratuitous or not gratuitous basis of land privatization under certain circumstances;
- insufficient legal regulation for situations where there is a combination of rights *in personam* and rights *in rem* in relation to one and the same land plot. What we mean by this is a fairly common situation where a party holding a land plot based on the right of perpetual (indefinite) use, leases out this land plot with the owner's consent to a third party for real estate development, etc.

When conducting transactions with land plots, in each particular case it is necessary to consider all surrounding circumstances and the specific features of the legal status of the objects of and parties to each single transaction.

Copyright © 2004 Pepeliaev, Goltsblat & Partners LLC. All Rights Reserved.

5.3

Intellectual Property and E-commerce

CMS Cameron McKenna

Introduction

The main types of intellectual property that are recognized and protected by Russian law include:

- trade marks;
- copyright (including computer programs) and neighbouring rights;
- patents.

Trade marks

Principal legislation: Laws and normative acts

Trade marks are subject to the following principal legal acts:

- the Civil Code;
- the Law On Trade marks; and
- regulations of the Patent Office.

Concept of a trade mark

According to the Law On Trade Marks, a trade mark is a designation that distinguishes the goods and services of one economic entity from those of another. A trade mark may take the form of a design, a symbol or a three-dimensional object, or a combination of these, and may be any colour or combination of colours.

The Law On Trade Marks provides a list of designations that may not be registered as trade marks. These include state flags and emblems, the names of state and international organizations, official marks such as hallmarks or stamps of approval, generally used designations of particular kinds of goods, and generally accepted symbols and terms.

The owner of a trade mark has an exclusive right to use and dispose of the trade mark and to prohibit its use by others. Any manufacture, use, import, offer for sale, sale or other putting into commercial turnover or storage with a purpose to put into commercial turnover of a trade mark, goods marked with the trade mark or a designation confusingly similar to the trade mark in respect of similar goods without the owner's consent is a violation of the exclusive right of the trade mark owner. Goods bearing trade marks that violate the exclusive right of a trade mark owner, will be considered counterfeit and may be seized and destroyed pursuant to a court decision.

Trade mark criteria

To be registered as a trade mark, a designation should not lead to confusion on the part of the public or be contrary to the public interest or principles of humanism or morality.

Designations that are identical to or confusingly similar to registered trade marks, well-known trade marks, names of characters or quotations from literature, science or art, names, pseudonyms or portraits of famous people may not be registered as trade marks.

Protection of trade marks

Registration of trade marks
According to the Law On Trade marks, protection is granted on the basis of registration. A trade mark may be registered only by a legal entity or an individual entrepreneur registered as such with the tax authorities.

Trade marks are registered with the Patent Office, which issues a trade mark certificate. The legislation sets out the procedure, fees and requisite documents for registration. Applications by foreign entities/foreign individuals must be submitted only through trade mark attorneys registered with the Patent Office.

Priority is given from the date an application for registration is made, or an earlier date if the application was first made under the Paris Convention in another member state or the goods were first exhibited in a member state. The priority date may also be established according to the date of international registration under an international treaty of the Russian Federation.

Registration is a time-consuming process, which may take from 18 to 24 months to complete. The Patent Office will make an entry in the State Register of Trade Marks and issue a certificate of registration.

Information concerning the trade mark is also published in the official bulletin of the Patent Office.

Time period and conditions of protection
A trade mark certificate is valid for ten years from the date of application. This term may be extended for another ten years upon application by the trade mark owner in the last year of the ten-year period. Extension is subject to a fee and is reflected in the State Register and the certificate.

The registered trade mark must be used. The use of the trade mark is its application on goods or packaging either by the owner or a licensee. Protection may be revoked if the trade mark was registered in the name of a person who is not an individual entrepreneur or in breach of trade mark criteria or was not used in the Russian Federation during the previous three years.

Troubleshooting

If the rights of a trade mark owner are infringed, he may apply to the Chamber for Patent Disputes of the Patent Office or to an arbitrazhniy (commercial) court.

The registration of a trade mark may be challenged by application to the Chamber for Patent Disputes of the Patent Office. If the trade mark was registered, for example, in the name of an individual who is not an entrepreneur or the trade mark is not used, the Chamber for Patent Disputes may consider the registration void.

Disputes regarding violation of rights of a trade mark owner or relating to licensing or assignment agreements fall within the jurisdiction of state arbitrazhniy (commercial) courts.

Remedies available to the owner of a trade mark include suing for damages and/or obtaining injunctions against the infringer requiring the infringer to delete the trade mark from goods or to destroy a designation, or goods bearing a designation that is confusingly similar to the trade mark. Alternatively, instead of claiming for damages the owner of a trade mark may claim for a fixed amount of compensation ranging from $3,400 to $170,000 (being correspondingly 1,000 times and 50,000 times the statutory minimum monthly wage, which on 1 January 2004 was 100 roubles or $3.4).

The owner of the trade mark may also apply to the Ministry of Anti-Monopoly Policy with a request to delete a particular designation that is so confusingly similar to a registered trade mark that competition would be affected and consumers confused.

Trade mark owners may also apply to the police with a request to open a criminal case against an infringer. According to the Criminal Code of the Russian Federation, an individual who intentionally repeatedly and illegally uses a registered trade mark may be fined up to $6,800, fined an amount equal to his income for a period of up to 18 months, or subjected to mandatory works for a period from 180 to 240 hours, or be sentenced to up to two years of hard labour.

Foreign companies may also request to the customs authorities to prevent the import of goods having a designation infringing the rights of a trade mark owner.

Assignment, licences, need to register

Trade marks may be assigned and the right to use the trade mark may be licensed to a third party. Both an assignment agreement and a licence agreement must be made in writing and must be registered with the Patent Office. Failure to register renders these agreements void.

Copyright and neighbouring rights

Principal legislation: laws and normative acts

The principal laws governing copyright and neighbouring rights are:

- the Civil Code;
- the Fundamentals of the Civil Legislation (Part IV of the Civil Code of the RF governing the IP rights is expected to be submitted to the Russian Parliament for consideration during 2004, replacing the Fundamentals of the Civil Legislation);
- the Law On Copyright and Neighbouring Rights;
- the Law On the Legal Protection of Computer Programs and Databases.

Concept of copyright

Copyright protection is granted to a work that is the product of creative activity and that is expressed in any material form. Such works include literary, dramatic, musical, choreographic and audio-visual works, sculptures, designs, photography and computer programs. Copyright protection does not apply to ideas, methods, concepts, principles, discoveries, facts, official documents, state symbols and information on events.

Rights of the author that may and may not be assigned

The author is entitled to:

- be recognized as the author of the work;
- protect his name as the author;
- preserve the integrity of the work;

- publish and use the work;
- access the work.

These rights are not transferable and rest with the author even if other exclusive rights, such as, for example, the right to reproduce, distribute, import, demonstrate, communicate, translate and redraft the work, are assigned to other people.

The author is entitled to receive remuneration from the use of his work by other people. There are very limited circumstances where the protected work may be used without permission of the copyright owner and without remuneration.

Concept of neighbouring rights

Neighbouring rights belong to performers. According to the Law On Copyright, a performer is an actor, singer, musician, dancer or other person who performs the work in any way, including a director of a film and a conductor.

No registration, by act of creation

Copyright protection is granted by virtue of creation. No registration or other special procedure is required.

Time period for protection

As a general rule, copyright is valid during the lifetime of the author and for 50 years after his death. Some rights of the author, such as a right to be recognized as the author, are protected with no time limit.

Troubleshooting

According to reservations made by Russia on joining international conventions, protection under international treaties is granted for works first published after Russia joined those conventions.

With regard to copyright, the earliest date for granting protection is 27 May 1973, when the Universal Convention on Copyright became effective for the Soviet Union. Any work first published before this date in any other member state of the convention was not protected in the Soviet Union and is not protected in Russia. In addition, works first published later but in a country that is not a member of the Universal Convention are not protected either.

In order to protect their rights, copyright owners may apply to the courts, to arbitration and to the police. Remedies available to the owners include the recognition of their rights and compensation for damage. Counterfeit goods and equipment for the manufacture of counterfeit goods may be seized and destroyed in accordance with a court decision.

Upon filing an application to the court, copyright owners are also entitled to obtain an injunction to prevent counterfeiting activities of an infringer and to seize counterfeit goods and equipment for their manufacture.

An infringement of copyright also constitutes a criminal offence, which may be investigated by the police. Under the Russian Criminal Code (Criminal Code) an individual who intentionally infringes an author's intellectual property rights and purchases, stores and/or transports counterfeit works may be fined up to $6,800, fined an amount equal to his income for a period of 18 months, be subjected to mandatory works for a period from 180 to 240 hours, or be imprisoned for a period of up to two years. Plagiarism is also considered a criminal offence under the Criminal Code, which stipulates that an individual who intentionally uses someone else's works may be fined up to $6,800, fined an amount equal to his income for a period of 18 months, be subjected to mandatory works for a period from 180 to 240 hours, or be sentenced to hard labour for a period from three to six months.

Infringers of an author's intellectual property rights, the intentional and illegal purchase, storage and transportation of counterfeit products with a value exceeding $8,500 or infringement by a group of people or by an official are punishable by imprisonment of up to five years and a fine of up to $17,000 or an amount equal to the infringer's income for a period of up to three years.

Patents

Principal legislation: laws and normative acts

The principal laws regulating patents are:

- the Civil Code;
- the Patent Law;
- the Regulations of the Patent Office.

Concept of a patent

A patent may be granted for:

- an invention;
- a utility model;
- an industrial design.

A patent holder has exclusive rights to use an invention, utility model or industrial design, and to prohibit its use by others.

A patent holder may assign their rights or license the patent by way of a licence agreement to third parties. Such assignment and licence agreements must be registered with the Patent Office and failure to register will render a licence agreement and assignment agreement invalid.

Patent criteria

In order to qualify for protection by patent, an invention must be new, have an element of invention and be capable of industrial application. A utility model to qualify for the same must be new and be ready for an industrial use. For an industrial design to be registered, it must be new and original.

Registration

Patents must be registered with the Patent Office. The registration and issuing of patents involves application, expert examination and publication of information about the patent. The Patent Office sets out the rules for application.

The priority date is the date of application for registration or an earlier date if the application was first made under the Paris Convention.

Time period of protection

Protection is granted for a period of 20 years for an invention, five years for a utility model and ten years for an industrial design. The protection period can be extended by the Patent Office upon application of a patent holder for up to five years for an invention industrial design and up to three years for a utility model.

Troubleshooting

If the rights of the patent holder are infringed he may apply to the Chamber for Patent Disputes of the Patent Office, to courts, or to arbitration. The registration of a patent may be challenged by application to the Chamber for Patent Disputes of the Patent Office.

Disputes regarding violation of exclusive rights of the patent holder or relating to licensing and assignment agreements, as well as the illegal use of the patent, fall within the jurisdiction of courts of common jurisdiction if one of the parties is an individual, or the state arbitrazhniy courts if all parties are legal entities, or individual entrepreneurs.

The patent holder is entitled to injunctive relief, compensation for damages caused by illegal use of the patent. Infringement of a patent also constitutes a criminal offence within the jurisdiction of the police. Under the Russian Criminal Code an individual who intentionally and illegally uses or discloses (prior to official publication) a patented invention, a utility model or an industrial design may either have to pay a fine of up to $6,800, a fine of an amount equal to his income for a period of up to 18 months, or be subjected to mandatory works for a period from 180 to 240 hours, or be imprisoned for a period of up to two years.

Infringement by a group of people is punishable either by a fine of between $3,400 and $10,200, a fine of an amount equal to the infringer's income for a period of between one and two years, or be arrested for a period from four to six months, or by imprisonment for up to five years.

International treaties: Russia as legal successor to the Soviet Union

Russia is a member of the World Organization of Intellectual Property. As legal successor to the Soviet Union, Russia is also party to a number of international treaties including the Paris Convention for the Protection of Intellectual Property (1883), the Geneva Convention for the Protection of Phonograms (1971), the Madrid Agreement for the International Registration of Marks (1891), the Universal Copyright Convention (1952), and the Treaty on Patent Co-operation (1970). On 3 March 1995 Russia became a full member of the Berne Convention.

Russia is also party to a number of bilateral agreements on the protection of intellectual property – for example, with Austria, Bulgaria, Sweden and Slovakia. Bilateral agreements extend protection to works published both before and after the signature date. Finally, in 1993 Russia and other CIS countries signed the Agreement on Measures for Protection of Intellectual Property and the Agreement on Co-operation in the Sphere of Copyright Protection.

E-commerce

Lack of regulation

The legal regulation and enforcement of the Internet in Russia is an area that is only now starting to be developed and thus court practice remains undeveloped and somewhat contradictory. For example, registration of domain names is not regulated by any legal act of government or parliament, nor has the legal status of domain names been clearly defined by the courts.

The registration of domain names is carried out by the Russian Institute for Public Networks, a non-commercial partnership established by the Ministry of Science, the Ministry of University Education and the Scientific Research Institute named after academic, Kurchatov. It is responsible for the development of the Russian zone on the Internet. This authority was delegated to the Russian Institute for Public Networks by the International Network Information Centre (InterNIC).

Squatting, piracy, domain names and IP rights

Prior to 1 June 2000 the registration of domain names was a low cost procedure. Any person willing to register a domain name simply applied to the Russian Institute for Public Networks and had to pay a registration fee within three months of registration. Maintenance of the registration was also subject to a nominal annual fee. Failure to pay the fee did not prevent the person from applying for registration of the same domain name again. This led to a rush of cyber-squatting activity.

Of growing concern is copyright protection on the Internet. Russian law does not provide clear guidance as to what remedies may be available to a copyright owner when his rights are infringed by a site operator. The owner of the copyright might find limited comfort in the Copyright Law, which prohibits unauthorized communication of copyright-protected works by means of cable or wire transfer and other analogous means, or unauthorized distribution by means of copying and distribution of copies of the work by any means.

To register a domain name, an applicant must pay a registration fee of $20 (VAT excluded) and an annual registration maintenance fee of $15.

Domain names are divided into the categories of geographical and generic (for example, ac.ru, org.ru, net.ru), public (those that are not geographical or generic) and corporate (all other domain names).

The Rules for Resolving Disputes Over Domain Names were developed on the basis of the Uniform Domain Name Dispute Resolution Policy recommended by WIPO and accepted by ICANN. The Rules provide protection for trade mark owners against owners of domain names that infringe the intellectual property rights of trade mark owners.

According to the Rules, the registration of a domain name should be cancelled if it is proved that the domain name (i) is identical or confusingly similar to a trade mark, and (ii) was registered or used in bad faith.

A domain name is deemed to be registered or used in bad faith if it was registered or used:

- mainly with the purpose of a later assignment to the trade mark owner for a remuneration considerably exceeding the cost of registration;
- to prevent the trade mark owner from registering the domain name;

- to obstruct the activities of the trade mark owner as a competitor of the domain name owner; or

- in commercial interest and with an intention to attract third parties to the Internet resources of the domain name owner thus creating a possibility that the trade mark will be considered by third parties as having a connection with the domain name holder.

Although the Rules that apply to disputes considered by an arbitration forum at the Russian Institute for Public Networks do not provide for compensation for damages, they do leave open the possibility to apply to state courts for an award of damages.

Contracts via the Internet: Legislation on electronic signatures

The regulatory framework for e-commerce is only now emerging in Russia and only the Law on Electronic Signatures has been adopted so far. A number of other drafts exist and some of them are presently at committee stage in the Russian parliament.

There are drafts of the Law On Electronic Commerce, the Law On Electronic Documents and the Law on Electronic Financial Services. There is even a proposed draft of a federal programme on e-commerce.

The first step in developing e-commerce was the adoption of the Law on Electronic Signatures, which came into force on 12 January 2002.

The Law On Electronic Signatures defines an electronic digital signature as a cryptographic symbol that depends on public key cryptography technology to decode it. The cryptography is the exclusive public domain of the Federal Agency of Governmental Communication and Information (FAPSI), which allows additional state control over the electronic transactions.

A draft of the Law on Electronic Commerce was passed by the Russian State Duma (the lower chamber of the Russian Parliament) in its first hearing on 6 June 2001. The draft law is designed to establish procedures for electronic transactions. It has yet to be passed in a further two hearings, adopted by the Federation Council and signed into law by the President.

At present there is no sub-regulation applicable to electronic contracts that would recognize electronic transactions.

Taxation of purchases made through the Internet

Purchases of goods transferable through the Internet are not taxed, as a means for tracking such purchases and assessing taxes does not presently exist. If goods are bought through the Internet and then delivered to customer in a material form, they would be subject to all existing Russian taxes and customs duties.

5.4

Arbitration and Dispute Resolution

CMS Cameron McKenna

The courts

The financial crisis of 1998 led to a significant increase in the number and complexity of disputes being referred to the commercial courts in Russia, particularly the Moscow Arbitrazhniy (commercial) Court. This was something of a baptism of fire for many of the judges who found themselves being asked to consider complex issues of fact and law, often under close scrutiny both from at home and abroad. Although many Russian lawyers will claim that Russia is a civil law system and, therefore, individual court decisions do not create precedents that are binding on other judges and courts, in practice the significance of case law has increased greatly in the last few years. As in other civil law jurisdictions, Russian judges and lawyers are realizing the value of case reports that can give guidance on how previous cases were decided. A judge may not be required to follow precedents but he may be persuaded by them.

This chapter describes the court structure and the basic elements of litigation in Russia. Calls for the reform of the Russian legal system can often be heard but perhaps the most pressing need is to improve the quality and number of judges and the court facilities in which they are required to work. An average judge in the Moscow Arbitrazhniy Court is reportedly required to handle around 450 cases each year – an intolerable workload.

Structure

The jurisdiction of the Russian courts is principally divided between the courts of common jurisdiction and the state arbitrazhniy courts (see Figures 5.4.1 and 5.4.2), which between them deal with civil, criminal and commercial matters. There is also a separate constitutional court. It should be noted here that the arbitrazhniy courts are often referred to as arbitration courts. This can be confusing since the arbitrazhniy courts are state-run like their counterparts in the West. They should not be confused with commercial arbitration bodies that administer private arbitrations by agreement between the parties. These arbitration bodies operate independently from the State.

The Russian court system also includes federal military courts and so-called 'specialized' courts. In addition, a system of 'single judges' (*mirovye sudyi*) has recently been created to hear minor disputes.

The structure, jurisdiction and procedure of the courts of common jurisdiction are set out in the Federal Law On the Court System of the Russian Federation. The courts of common jurisdiction are organized on the basis of first instance district or municipal trial courts; second instance regional appellate courts with geographically discrete jurisdictions; and a single national Supreme Court (based in Moscow), which hears appeals from the regional appellate courts.

Under the Federal Law On Arbitrazhniy Courts in the Russian Federation a system of arbitrazhniy courts was set up to deal with commercial disputes. These separate state arbitrazhniy courts have their own structure, jurisdiction and procedure as defined by the Arbitrazhniy Procedural Code.

Arbitrazhniy Courts of the Constituent Subjects of the Russian Federation are courts of both first instance and of appeals. Next there are the Federal District Arbitrazhniy Courts, of which there are roughly 10 throughout Russia. These district courts hear cassation applications (which are described below) from the regional courts. The Russian Supreme Arbitrazhniy Court occupies the highest level and exercises a supervisory role over the regional and district arbitrazhniy courts.

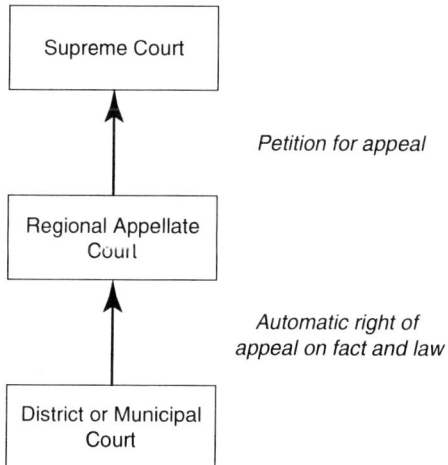

Figure 5.4.1 Courts of common jurisdiction

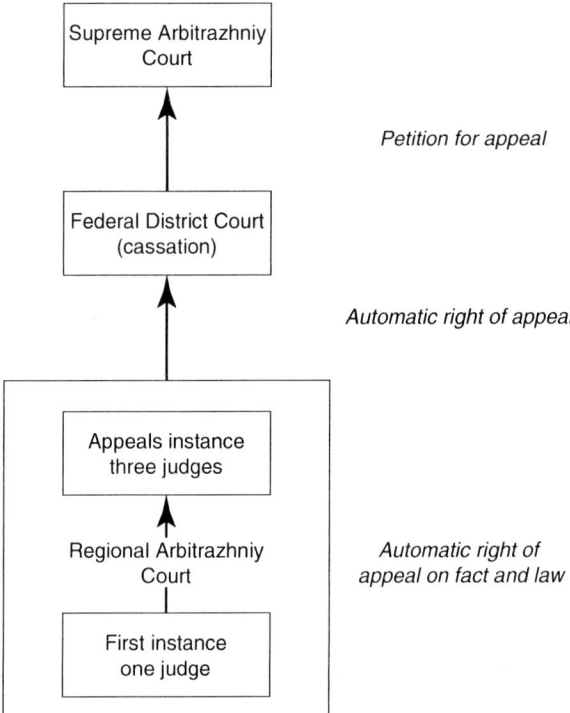

Figure 5.4.2 Arbitrazhniy or commercial courts

Although jurisdictionally separate, the Supreme Court and the Supreme Arbitrazhniy Court occasionally publish joint resolutions summarizing their practice in relation to particular issues and giving an authoritative interpretation of current law.

Courts of common jurisdiction: First instance jurisdiction

In effect, any matter not assigned to be dealt with elsewhere is dealt with by the courts of common jurisdiction.

Cases are normally commenced in the first instance district or municipal courts. In very limited circumstances, for example, in cases involving state secrets, a second instance regional appellate court may act as a tribunal of first instance. The Supreme Court acts as the first instance court for disputes arising in connection with the presidential and parliamentary elections and some other administrative matters.

A defendant should usually be sued in the first instance court for the area in which he resides, or, if the defendant is a firm, in the first instance court for the area in which it has its registered office. If the defendant's whereabouts are unknown or if the defendant is resident abroad, then the claimant may be able to issue proceedings in the court of the region in which the defendant's property is located.

The quorum of a first instance district or municipal court is usually one professional judge, but in some circumstances the quorum will be three such judges.

Courts of common jurisdiction: Appellate jurisdiction

The final judgement of a first instance court becomes enforceable after ten days. During this period each party has a right of appeal on fact and/or law to a regional appellate court. The appeal must be filed with the court whose judgement is being appealed.

No new evidence may be adduced on appeal unless it was not possible to present that evidence to the lower court. Respondents may reply to the points raised in the appeal by submitting a written response.

The quorum of an appellate court is three professional judges.

Decisions taken by a regional appellate court can be further appealed to the supervisory appeal instance, the Presidium of the regional appellate courts, and then to the Supreme Court. The Supreme Court acts as the final court of appeal. It has the authority to reverse decisions of all first instance courts and rulings by appellate courts.

State arbitrazhniy courts: First instance jurisdiction

The jurisdiction of the state arbitrazhniy courts is confined to cases of a commercial or business nature. Any other type of dispute requiring a hearing in a public forum must be tried by the court of common jurisdiction.

Arbitration procedure rules set out that organizations may be represented in arbitrazhniy courts only by their respective heads within the scope of their authority, by employees of the said organizations, or by advocates. Thus, lawyers without the status of an advocate and those not employed by an organizsation are not entitled to represent the interests of their clients in arbitrazhniy courts.

As a general rule, an action should be started in the regional court for the area in which the defendant resides. If the defendant is a firm, then the action should be begun in the first instance court for the area in which it has its registered office.

If there are two or more defendants and they are located in different constituent subject territories of the Russian Federation, the claimant can start the action in the relevant court for any of the relevant constituent subject territories.

If the defendant's whereabouts are unknown or if the defendant is resident abroad, then the claimant may be able to issue proceedings in the court for the region in which the defendant's property is located. In addition, if it is a contractual claim, legal action can be started in the first instance court for the region in which the agreement is meant to be performed. Whatever the location of the first instance court, it is sometimes possible to transfer a case to an alternative arbitrazhniy court of the same level of competence.

The quorum in a first instance state arbitrazhniy court is usually one professional judge.

State arbitrazhniy courts: Appellate jurisdiction

Decisions of first instance arbitrazhniy courts become enforceable after one month and during this time a party has the right of appeal on fact and/or law to the appeals instance of the regional court that first heard the case. The appellant cannot put forward new claims or adduce new evidence, unless it was not possible to present that new evidence at the first instance trial.

The appellant must serve a copy of the appeal documents filed with the court on all the other parties at the first instance trial. They then have a chance to enter a written response to the points raised in the appeal. The response must be filed with the appellate court before the date of the appeal hearing and served on any other parties.

Under the Arbitrazhniy Procedural Code of 2002 there is a distinct appeal procedure called causation, under which a Federal District Arbitrazhniy Court has the power to cancel a decision or ruling of a regional arbitrazhniy court or find against appeal rulings by such courts.

The final court of appeal is the Russian Supreme Arbitrazhniy Court, which has a supervisory appellate function empowering it to revise the decision of any state arbitrazhniy court that is illegal or lacking in legal substance.

The quorum of an appellate arbitrazhniy court is always an uneven number of judges. A minimum of three is required, irrespective of the level at which the appeal is heard.

Procedure

Generally speaking, the courts of common jurisdiction are open to all members of the public over the age of 16. In principle, state arbitrazhniy court proceedings are also open to the public. However, in practice, special permission must be obtained to gain access to any hearing. In addition, state arbitrazhniy courts will sit in closed hearing in order to protect industrial secrets or commercially sensitive information.

Pleadings

Actions are begun in the court of common jurisdiction when a claimant files a statement of claim with the appropriate first instance court. The statement of claim will contain a mixture of alleged fact and law, coupled with details of the evidence that the claimant proposes to adduce at trial. However, the claimant can modify or add to his claim at any stage up until the moment when the court retires to consider its verdict. The service of the pleadings will be effected by the court.

Under state arbitrazhniy court procedure, the claimant files a written and signed statement of claim, just as he would do in a court of common jurisdiction case. The statement of claim should also be sent to the defendant, along with all supporting documents, prior to filing the case with the court, and all post receipts should be attached to the filings. While the defendant in a state arbitrazhniy court is expressly entitled to service a written defence as well as a counter-claim, the claimant in the court of common procedure has no such express right, although he will equally be permitted to serve a written reply.

Evidence

Under both the Civil Procedural Code of 2002 and the Arbitrazhniy Procedural Code of 2002, the judge handling the case is responsible for preparing a case for trial. He will question the parties in an attempt to clarify the issues in dispute between them. The judge may also instruct the parties to deliver further documentary or other evidence to the court and has the power to examine the parties' experts before commencement of the main hearing.

There is no mechanism for the pre-trial exchange of expert evidence. In state arbitrazhniy court cases such evidence will be in written form. In courts of common jurisdiction cases – where experts are usually court appointees in any event – expert evidence will be required in oral and written form.

Judgements

Usually the judgement will be given orally at the end of the proceedings and a full verdict will be issued in writing within five days after the proceedings have ended. If the court has consisted of more than one judge, this will (if necessary) be a majority judgement.

Enforcement

The enforcement of all court judgements and orders by both courts of common jurisdiction and state arbitrazhniy courts is dealt with by the enforcement officer for the district in which the enforcement is to be executed. Should it prove necessary, the officer can be assisted in his duties by both the police and the militia.

Litigation costs

In the courts of common jurisdiction, the costs consist of the court fee plus the costs related to the trial of the case. In general, the claimant has to pay the necessary state court fee when starting an action, although there are certain exceptions.

The level of the state court fee will vary according to the value of the claim. It is calculated using the fixed table set out in the Law Of the Russian Federation Of the State Duty. The maximum fee for state arbitrazhniy courts is approximately $3,470. The maximum fee for the courts of common jurisdiction is 1.5 per cent of the value of the claim. Losing parties are usually ordered to pay the winner's costs (including, among other things, reasonable attorney's fees). If a claim or a defence is only partially successful, then the cost award will reflect this.

Costs are dealt with in the same way in the state arbitrazhniy courts.

Alternative dispute resolution mechanisms

Under the Arbitrazhniy Procedural Code of 2002, the judge has a duty at the pre-trial preparation to encourage the parties to settle their differences rather than engage in full-scale litigation. However, judges in the courts of common jurisdiction do not have a similar statutory duty and thus the public policy support for non-litigious civil dispute resolution remains patchy.

In addition to these limited alternatives to dispute resolution provided by the public court system, many arbitral bodies offer conciliation as well as arbitration services. However, formal alternative dispute resolution procedures are rarely used in Russia at the present time. Indeed, people are reluctant to use the new facility of private arbitration even for their domestic disputes.

No concept of 'without prejudice' negotiations or settlement

Neither the Civil Procedure Code of 2002 nor the Arbitrazhniy Procedural Code of 2002 restrict the ability of any party to plead in evidence any negotiations or offers made by any other party before or after proceedings are commenced. The practical effect of this is to severely hamper any opportunity for the parties to resolve and settle disputes without admitting liability. If an offer to settle is made then it may be introduced into court proceedings as evidence of admission of liability, and hence great care must be taken when dealing with customer complaints and disputes of any kind.

5.5

Employment Law and Work Permits for Expatriates

CMS Cameron McKenna

As of 1 February 2002 a new Labour Code of the Russian Federation came into force. The new Labour Code replaced the previous Labour Code, which was adopted 30 years ago when the Soviet state was the only employer and concepts such as entrepreneurship and private property were largely unknown in Russia.

The new Labour Code deals with the following principal issues: the rights and obligations of employees and employers; trade unions and their regulation; the procedure for making, amending and terminating employment contracts; salary payments; the State as employer; and the procedure for dealing with employment disputes.

Employment contracts

Russian law distinguishes between an employment contract, which is subject to the Labour Code, and a civil law contract between an organization and an individual for the provision of services. For the purposes of this chapter, we will be dealing with the former unless otherwise stated.

Employment agreements should be made in writing although the Labour Code provides that an employee who starts working without a written agreement is nevertheless to be treated as an employee to whom all the provisions of the Labour Code will apply.

Employment agreements may be concluded:

- for an indefinite period of time; or
- for a fixed period of time (but not exceeding five years).

The application of fixed term contracts is generally limited to work requiring fixed term employment (ie to replace a sick employee, for fixed term projects, etc), but the new Labour Code specifically extended the possibility of fixed term employment contracts for directors and deputy directors of legal entities, chief accountants, retired persons and employees working outside Russia.

A probation period of up to three months may be specified, although this maximum limit can be extended to six months for certain executive staff including directors, managers and chief accountants. Three days prior to the expiration of the probation period both the employer and the employee have to notify each other in writing of the termination of the contract. Moreover, the employer should indicate reasons for the termination.

The new Labour Code provides a list of mandatory provisions, which should be included in the Employment Agreement and sets out a list of documents that an employer may request from an employee at the time of hiring.

Working hours and holidays

The statutory working week may not exceed 40 hours. Despite this, the Labour Code does envisage extra hours being worked and the procedure for this is strictly regulated. Thus, employees are required to agree in writing to work overtime and cannot work more than four extra hours on any two consecutive working days and the total number of hours overtime cannot exceed 120 hours per year. Overtime pay is set at time and a half for the first two hours and double time for each subsequent hour.

The minimum statutory paid holiday entitlement is 28 calendar days, although longer periods are possible by agreement. Compensation for unused holidays will only apply to those holiday days in excess of 28. Finally, note that an employee is generally only entitled to holiday after serving a minimum of six months in the firm, though a shorter period may be agreed upon by the parties. Vacations may be divided into several periods but one part per year may not be less than 14 consecutive days. The Code provides for mandatory extra vacations for employees working in certain industries and for those with no fixed working hours.

Minimum statutory wage and currency control issues

The minimum salary must be no less than the minimum subsistence level established by the federal legislation (currently the minimum subsistence level is approximately $80 per quarter, although legislation sets out a minimum salary level of $20 per month). The Labour

Code provides that a salary must be paid at least twice a month, although it does not specify whether these payments should be of equal amounts. Salaries should be paid in Russian roubles by bank transfer to the employee's account or in cash. Payment in foreign currency is not permitted, although salary levels may be fixed in foreign currency or by reference to a foreign currency amount. Some banks offer payment schemes that allow employees to convert rouble salary payments into dollar deposits or even, in the case of representative office employees, to receive dollar salary payments on employees' credit cards. Salaries may be a fixed amount per month or may be linked to performance. Any changes to salary should be notified to the employee at least two months in advance of the change coming into effect and the change should be agreed in writing. Employers who pay late may face fines on the due but unpaid amount for each day the payment of wages is delayed. If wages are delayed for more than 15 days, employees may stop working until the wages are paid in full.

Termination of employment agreement

An employment agreement may be terminated with the mutual consent of the employer and the employee; at the initiative of one or other party; or upon the effluxion of time.

If it was entered into for an indefinite period of time, an employee may terminate his employment agreement by giving two weeks' notice to the employer. Any longer period of notice required by the employer and specified in the agreement will not be capable of enforcement. Post-termination restrictive covenants are also largely unenforceable.

An employer's ability to terminate an employee's contract of employment is severely limited by the Labour Code. The grounds for termination include:

- liquidation of the employer;
- redundancy (for specific economic or technical reasons);
- lack of qualification (this does not extend to poor performance) or poor health of the employee;
- repeated and systematic breach of duty after disciplinary action has already been taken;
- absence from work for more than four hours without a valid reason;
- intoxication (alcohol or drug): this must be medically verified;
- committing theft at the workplace and the theft having been confirmed by the court or an appropriate state authority;
- unauthorized disclosure of confidential information.

Employment contracts with members of the executive body of a legal entity may also be terminated in accordance with the grounds provided in those contracts.

The change of ownership of a legal entity may not result in the termination of its employees' labour contracts. The new owner may, however, terminate the employment contracts of the head of the company, his deputies and the chief accountant within three months of the change of ownership.

In each case care must be taken to comply with the strict procedural requirements of the Labour Code and due regard given to the priority rights granted to certain groups of employees. For example, the employment of pregnant women and women with young children may only be terminated if the employer is to be liquidated. Working students, war veterans and employees with more than two dependants have priority to remain employed in cases of redundancy. Decisions must be carefully documented and, in certain cases, an employee should be offered alternative employment within the organization. Compensation for dismissal will be payable in an amount equal to between two weeks' and five months' salary. Compensation for any untaken holiday is also to be paid.

If the provisions of the Labour Code are not followed when dismissing an employee or employees then the employee may bring legal proceedings. Among the various rulings that the court can give is that of reinstatement, a ruling that is not uncommon.

Data protection

An employer is obliged to protect the personal data of employees that is in his possession and may disclose such data to third persons only with the prior written consent of the employee. The employer must also develop internal procedures for safeguarding employees' personal data and notify each employee of such internal procedures.

Work permits for expatriates

Russian companies that wish to employ foreign labour in Russia must apply for a general permit to do so. General permits are issued by the regional divisions of the Federal Migration Service and are valid for one year; they may be extended on request. For each individual foreign national, a Russian company requires a 'Confirmation' of the right to work which is, in effect, a personal work permit. Certain categories of employees are not covered by these requirements, including employees of foreign embassies, scientists and artists working in institutions established in accordance with international agreements, journalists accredited in Russia, ships' crew and students on study internships.

Employment Law and Work Permits for Expatriates   315

As work permits are not issued centrally by the Ministry of Ethnic and Migration Policy, the exact terms and conditions thereof tend to vary from region to region. In Moscow, for example, the processing of a work permit usually takes between 2–4 months.

The procedure of obtaining a work permit in Moscow for a foreign employee can be split into three stages:

1. Initially the authorization of the local employment authorities must be obtained. In Moscow this authority is a local branch of the Employment Board, which is responsible for issuing opinions on whether it is reasonable for a Russian employer to hire foreign nationals. It performs a formal check to confirm whether there are any Russian citizens with the same educational background and work experience as the foreign national who has been proposed for a specific position.
2. The second stage is for an employer to obtain a permit to employ foreign nationals. This permit is issued by the Federal Migration Service. The applicant must attach its constitutional documents to the application.
3. The last stage is to obtain a work permit for the employee. The work permit is issued by the Migration Department of the Ministry for the Internal Affairs of the Russian Federation.

Personal accreditation of foreign employees of representative offices

Individuals employed by the representative offices of foreign companies may apply to the registration body where the representative office is accredited for their own personal accreditation. For example, the State Registration Chamber will accredit a representative office and usually will allow that representative office to accredit up to five individuals. On application this number may be increased.

Personal accreditation confirms the official status of a representative office's employee and allows an accredited person to obtain a visa with less difficulty than a non-accredited person. Family members of employees may also be granted personal accreditation. The validity of the personal accreditation is linked to the term of accreditation of the representative office, so the personal accreditation may be extended only after the accreditation of the representative office of a foreign company has been extended.

Visas

As well as a personal work permit or personal accreditation, a foreign employee may require a visa to enter, remain in and leave Russia.

Registrations with the Ministry of Interior

Foreign employees of Russian companies and their representative offices in Russia must register with the Department for Visas and Registrations of the Ministry of Interior (UVIR). Foreign nationals visiting Russia must register their passports and visa with the UVIR within three days of arriving in Russia. If the foreigner is staying at a hotel, the hotel will usually organize registration with UVIR, but if not, then registration is still required. UVIR will place a stamp in the visa to confirm registration. A foreign national without this stamp is likely to encounter difficulty with the militia and other authorities.

5.6

An Investment Project in Russia: Applicable Laws

Andrey Goltsblat, Managing Partner, Pepeliaev, Goltsblat & Partners

The following chapter is designed to take the reader through the basic stages that an investor may want to consider when formulating their business strategy for the Russian market. In summary, these stages, and the elements of a structured investment strategy that potential businessmen may want to consider for Russia, include the following:

- basic stages of an investment project (direct investment);
- land legislation;
- corporate law;
- investments tax allowances;
- Russia's international treaties;
- customs allowances for investments;
- foreign investment law.

We will take the reader through each of these components of an investment strategy point by point.

Stages of an investment project in Russia

Below is an approximate outline of an investment project/construction/reconstruction of manufacturing facilities in Russia.

Stage 1: Establishment of a Russian legal entity

One month. This stage includes:

- producing a charter and other necessary corporate documents;

- building up charter capital;
- registration of the legal entity with tax authorities, state funds, state statistic committee, and other authorities;
- opening of bank accounts.

Stage 2: Work permits for foreign personnel

Three to six months; may be implemented simultaneously with stages 3–10. If required, permits are issued by the Interior Ministry.

Stage 3: Selection of a land plot

One to four months; may be implemented simultaneously with stages 1–2 or even before stage 1. This stage includes conclusion of a contract with a professional realtor company.

Stage 4: Acquisition of a land plot

Three to seven months. Possible options are *lease* or *purchase* of the selected site (generally 'green-field' or 'brown-field' sites).

This stage includes various actions depending on the category and/or location of a particular site, for example:

- due diligence;
- boundary marking and cadastre registration of a land plot,
- change of category of the site (for all non-industrial lands), this may be accompanied by statutory crop losses compensation and negotiable compensation for losses incurred by land users;
- negotiating the transaction terms;
- conclusion of a purchase or lease contract;
- state registration of title to the site or the right to lease it (purchase or lease).

Land plots may be acquired both from the state/municipalities and from private persons.

From the state/municipalities land plots are normally acquired in two ways:

1. *Upon prior approval for the location of the facility* [to be constructed] which includes:

- filing an application for land plot selection with the state or municipal authorities;
- selection of a land plot by the municipal authorities and issuance of a relevant act and a decision on prior approval for the location of the facility;

- demarcation of the boundaries of the land plot and its cadastral registration;
- adoption of a decision by the state or municipal authorities to lease out the land plot;
- reimbursement of losses incurred by the holders of rights to land plots (if it is necessary to withdraw the land plots);
- signing and state registration of a land lease.

2. *Without prior approval for the location of the facility*, which includes:
- completion of formalities for the land plot by and at the expense of the governmental authorities;
- decision of the state or municipal authorities to hold bidding (tenders, auctions) and publication of a relevant announcement;
- filing an application to participate in the bidding;
- holding the bidding for the sale of the land plot or the right to enter into a lease thereof;
- signing and state registration of the sale and purchase agreement or the lease of the land plot.

The acquisition of land plots from *private persons* (individuals or legal entities who own land plots) normally includes:
- due diligence review of documents evidencing the rights to a particular land plot and corporate documents of the right holder;
- obtaining various certificates and opinions from the state and municipal authorities concerning the legal status of the land plot and the options to use it;
- acquisition of the land plot through the execution of a sale and purchase agreement (or a lease), purchase of shares or ownership interests in the legal entity or otherwise depending on the circumstances;
- state registration of the right to the land plot.

The acquisition of land plots both from the State and from private persons may require a change of land category and compensation for crop losses (eg conversion of agricultural lands into industrial ones) or forest losses (eg conversion of forest fund lands).

Stage 5: Development of necessary pre-project documentation

Five to eleven months. This stage includes:
- development of town-planning documentation and getting it approved by state and municipal authorities;

- obtaining Technical Conditions for using municipal electricity, gas, water, waste water treatment plant and other resources;
- obtaining a construction permit (crucial state permission is necessary for nearly all types of construction operations); etc.

Stage 6: Development of design documentation

A design project includes various types of documents (eg Feasibility Study {abbreviated in Russian to 'TEO'}, 'working project', etc) depending on the purpose, function and technical characteristics of the facility to be erected.

This stage includes:

- choosing a designing company and conclusion of a contract for development of design documentation;
- obtaining official approvals for design documentation (for instance, ecology experts, Fire Inspectorate, architecture authorities etc);
- obtaining a favourable governmental expert opinion on project documentation and environmental impact of the project, etc.

Stage 7: Construction

Six to ten months. This stage includes:

- obtaining a municipal construction permit;
- choosing a General Contractor and conclusion of a general construction contract;
- supervision over construction operations;
- preliminary acceptance of the facility erected and elimination of discovered construction drawbacks.

Stage 8: Import or purchase and installation of production machinery

Two to five months; as a rule this is implemented simultaneously with stage 7. This stage may include:

- conclusion of import and installation contracts;
- customs clearance of imported machinery (imported technological machinery is, under certain circumstances, exempt from VAT and customs duties);
- installation of machinery; etc.

Stage 9: Final official acceptance of erected facility by state accepting commission

One month. This is a crucial act, which is necessary for commissioning the facility erected and future registration of title. An official acceptance report is followed by an appropriate Mayor's Resolution.

Stage 10: Registration of title to facilities, buildings, constructions

One to three months. As a result, title is confirmed by an entry in the State Realty Registry and an Ownership Certificate.

Total: 20–30 months

Land relations under investment projects

Choice of a land plot, title examination

Circulation of non-agricultural privately-owned lands:

- purchase and sale;
- lease (term is not limited, except for agricultural lands whose lease term is 49 years);
- mortgage;
- contribution to the charter capital.

Circulation of non-agricultural state- and municipally owned lands:

- lease (term – 49 years);
- privatization;
- perpetual (indefinite) use.

Provision of land plots for construction purposes

- Restrictions on foreign ownership of land plots:
  - purchase and sale of a land plot out of agricultural lands;
  - lease of land plots out of agricultural lands;
  - privatization or lease of agricultural state- or municipally-owned lands;
- circulation of ownership interests in the common property;
- special considerations relating to the use of farm lands for constructing industrial facilities;
- land categorization, change of category;
- compensation for crop losses and forestry losses.

Investment projects in terms of corporate law

An investment project normally presupposes one or another corporate structure and registration of a Russian legal entity.

Such legal entities are most commonly set up as a limited liability company (abbreviated in Russian to OOO) and a closed joint-stock company (abbreviated in Russian to ZAO).

When choosing a legal status for the company, the main consideration to be taken into account is the number of investors/participants, whether they are associated entities or not, and whether a joint venture is planned to be set up. If a foreign legal entity sets up, directly or through a group of entities, a company in Russia that is fully owned by such legal entity, the most suitable legal status for the company will be OOO. An OOO gives an opportunity to promptly increase its charter capital, while with a ZAO registration of the issue of shares will be required and the issuing company, in case of any additional issue of shares (ie with the exception of the initial issue of shares at the time when the company is established), will incur a securities trading tax liability. An OOO is easier to manage than a ZAO. In relation to the establishment and operation of an OOO (except where the OOO decides to issue bonds), unlike for a joint stock company, there is no Federal Commission on the Securities Market as an additional 'supervisory' body over OOOs.

When a joint venture is planned to be set up, the choice of legal status may depend on the prospective ownership interest of a particular investor and the availability of a sufficient number of discretionary rules in the laws concerning those provisions of foundation documents which relate to decision-making. Another argument in favour of an OOO is the possibility for any of its members to secede from the company. During six months of the year following the year in which an application for secession was filed, the seceding member should be paid the actual value of his ownership interest as of the end of the fiscal year in which the application was filed.

Apart from choosing a legal status, of great importance is the establishment of branches and representative offices. More often than not regional authorities insist that a new legal entity be set up in the region where a particular investment project is being carried out, even if in another region there is already a legal entity (involved in this project). They believe that by doing this, more taxes will be paid to the budget of the appropriate constituent entity of the Russian Federation, but this is not true.

In tax terms, due to the impossibility for a holding company to make consolidated tax payments, it is beyond any doubt more advantageous to set up a branch. It is also possible to open a representative office or a detached subdivision. However, the presence of a branch makes it easier to handle customs formalities in the region and does not affect payment of taxes into the budget of that region.

Investment tax allowances

Russian laws currently offer practically no essential investment tax allowances and those that were previously available are now suspended. For example, in Moscow Oblast in 2003 investment allowances were suspended.

The only investment allowances that are available now are those that can be obtained from local governments. Local authorities are empowered to offer a property tax allowance and an allowance in relation to advertising tax, which is a tax on costs.

Russia's international treaties

Some of the international treaties to which Russia is a party contain provisions allowing a reduction of the tax burden for a Russian company where an ownership interest is held by an investor originating from a country that is a party to a relevant treaty.

A good example is the Double Taxation Agreement between Russia and Germany. According to the Additional Protocol to this Agreement, advertising costs incurred by a company with German participation are fully deductible for profit tax purposes. Although the new version of chapter 25 of the Russian Tax Code allows the deduction of basic advertising expenses from the profit tax base, large FMCG companies still end up with huge advertising expenses associated, for instance, with promotional campaigns that are treated by the law as a promotional sweepstake, the costs of which continue to be treated as non-deductible for profit tax purposes.

Investment allowances for customs payments

Customs allowances for the importation of goods

Goods that are imported as a foreign investor's contribution to the charter capital of a company with foreign participation are exempt from import duty if these goods:

1. are not excisable;
2. can be categorized as fixed assets;
3. are imported within the time limits set by the foundation documents for charter capital build-up.

1. The goods should not be excisable.
The list of excisable goods is set out in part two of the Russian Tax Code.

2. The goods should fall under the category of fixed assets.
For categorizing instruments of labour as non-current (fixed) assets, the criterion of their circulation (service life) is applied, while the value criterion is not used. Thus, it makes no difference how the goods imported as a contribution to the charter capital are assessed by the investor in terms of their value.

3. The goods should be imported within the time limits set by the foundation documents for building up the company's charter capital.
Tariff benefits are offered only if the goods were imported into the customs territory of Russia and declared as goods imported as a contribution from a foreign founding member into the charter capital of a company with foreign participation before the expiration of the deadline for charter capital build-up set by the company's foundation documents or Russian laws.

A customs allowance may be provided either in the form of exemption from customs duty or refund (off-set) of customs duties paid earlier. Everything depends on the availability of the list of imported property. If such a list is known, the customs allowance will be granted in the form of an exemption. However, under certain circumstances this procedure is more complicated, because it requires a classification decision from the State Customs Committee of Russia.

VAT allowance

Art. 150 of the Russian Tax Code 'Non-Taxable (Tax-Exempt) Importation of Goods into the Territory of the Russian Federation' treats as non-taxable (tax-exempt) manufacturing equipment, and components and spare parts for such equipment imported as contributions to the charter capital of companies.

Foreign investment law

The Foreign Investment Law does not contain any fundamental provisions that would, one way or another, regulate foreign investments. This Law declares the principle of equal treatment for foreign investors and Russian investors. The Law stipulates guarantees for foreign investors, which are of rather a declarative nature. The Law provides that a foreign investor or its company in Russia will be protected against unfavourable consequences of newly adopted tax or customs legislation (for not more than seven years). At the same time this protection is only afforded to priority projects, the list of which is to be approved by the Russian Government. We are not aware of any such projects. Neither are we aware of how this legal provision is applied. Thus, the Law offers no practical help either for the implementation of investment projects or for the protection of investor's interests, although it does confirm that both investors and companies with foreign capital are being treated in a civilized manner.

Copyright © 2004 Pepeliaev, Goltsblat & Partners LLC. All Rights Reserved.

5.7

Entrepreneurial Start-ups

Jamison Firestone, Firestone Duncan

Most entrepreneurial start-ups in Russia will be what Western countries define as small businesses – businesses with anywhere from thousands to several millions of dollars of investment. These businesses are typically owned by small groups of people with limited resources to invest in the start-up, although at times they can also be the local operations of large multinational corporations. While this chapter should prove useful to the latter, it is directed at the former as a guide to the 'nuts and bolts' of starting an entrepreneurial venture in Russia.

Setting up a venture

Planning the structure

Russian law is neither intuitive nor forgiving. What seems like a straightforward contract in the US or the UK most likely will not be enforceable in Russia. What seems like a simple way to operate might have very unfavourable tax or legal consequences for a company operating in Russia. In short, proper planning with legal and tax advisors who specialize in Russian law is essential before registering a company or even concluding a seemingly simple contract.

The first issue that needs to be determined is the structure of operations. This not only includes choosing the correct form of legal entity to register in Russia but also determining how that entity will be owned and how it will contract with suppliers and with clients.

Many issues will be taken into consideration at this time, including the ability of the various types of legal entities to carry out the business as envisioned, Russian hard currency control legislation, Russian taxation, and how best to protect the rights of the various shareholders if there are going to be several shareholders in the venture.

Application of the simplified taxation system for small businesses
One of the first issues that should be considered at this time is the possible application of the simplified taxation system for the company.

The present simplified taxation system was introduced by the Federal Law No. 104-FZ of 24 July 2002, and is a special system that can only be used by small businesses and individual entrepreneurs. The system allows legal entities and individual entrepreneurs to replace the obligation to pay a number of significant taxes (corporate profit tax, VAT, assets tax, unified social tax and tax on income from the entrepreneurial activities) with a single unified tax.

The unified tax under the simplified taxation system is chosen by the taxpayer as either 6 per cent of turnover or 15 per cent of the difference between revenues and certain allowable expenses.

The simplified taxation system is intended for small business and therefore there are certain restrictions that prevent larger companies from using the system. The system cannot be used by:

- companies and entrepreneurs earning more than 15 million roubles (about $525,000 at the time of writing) of income during a calendar year;
- companies having branch offices and/or more than 25 per cent corporate ownership;
- companies and entrepreneurs engaged in certain activities (banking, insurance, gambling, and some other businesses);
- companies and entrepreneurs employing more than 100 employees;
- companies having amortized assets worth more than 100 million roubles (about $3,500,000);
- other companies and entrepreneurs meeting some specific criteria.

It should be noted that Russian accounting requirements are very demanding and time consuming. They often require a large number of forms to be completed and filed even if the company is not conducting any business. Often these forms must be filed in person by a company employee and this can mean waiting in line outside the tax office for hours. For this reason, simplified accounting and reduced tax filing requirements are often a bigger bonus to small businesses than reduced taxation!

Although the limits placed upon turnover and the limits placed upon corporate ownership effectively limit the application of small business tax preferences to the very smallest of small businesses, the benefits of the system are significant enough that any business that could be structured to use these benefits should seriously consider doing so.

It is important to note that at the time of writing this chapter, the Russian Government is seriously considering expanding the definition of companies and entrepreneurs that will qualify to use the simplified taxation system. It is anticipated that a new definition would vastly raise the turnover limits and might remove the corporate ownership limitation.

Therefore, when planning a start-up in Russia it will be important to see if the current simplified taxation regime could be applied to the venture in question. If it could be applied based on turnover but not based on corporate ownership, it may be appropriate to consider whether the very real advantages offered by the legislation are worth the individual owners holding a Russian company directly.

One very important point to keep in mind: a company wishing to use the simplified system of taxation for small businesses must notify the tax authorities of this simultaneously with the registration of the company or between 1 October and 30 November of the year preceding a new calendar year where the company wishes to switch to the simplified system. It is not possible to start using the system in any other fashion.

Implementing business registration

The legal address of the business

Chapter 18, Article 288 point 3 of the Russian Civil Code requires that the business has a non-residential address. Furthermore, this address must be given to the tax authorities before the company can be registered. Legally the address must be the actual non-residential address of the executive body of the business. This means that compliance with the law demands that a business find premises first before being registered. While it is possible to buy a fake business address and while this is often done for start-ups that do not yet have a place of operation, the management of the company is risking criminal liability by doing this.

Buying a ready-made company vs registering one from scratch

Registering a company in Russia to a foreigner or a foreign corporation takes about three weeks from the time the process is started until the company is fully operational. However the process cannot be started for foreign citizens or foreign companies that will participate in Russian companies until they produce certain documents. In the case of foreign citizens who will not come to Russia to appear before a Russian notary or in the case of foreign corporations, those documents will have to be apostilled in the home country, a process that can take a bit of time. Due to the length of the entire procedure many foreigners often consider buying ready-made companies. Although buying a ready-made company can at times be a way to get into business quickly, the time savings are more often than not illusory. Furthermore, there are several things that buyers should be aware of.

Part of the reason it takes so long to register ownership of Russian companies to foreign citizens and foreign companies is because they often must provide apostilled documents from abroad. If these documents are not on hand there is no way to put a ready-made company under the control of the foreign citizens or foreign corporations that wish to buy it. While some people will choose to put the business under the temporary control of a local person, this is generally not a prudent thing to do. Even if the proper documents are on hand the amount of time it will take to transfer a ready-made company to the buyer and to open bank accounts in a decent bank is roughly equivalent to the time it will take to set up a new company. For this reason there is often little reason to buy a ready-made company.

Furthermore there are significant risks in buying ready-made companies. In the overwhelming number of cases the companies have never been used and have no liabilities but they often have technical defects that make them dangerous to use.

The two most common defects are:

- *Company transferred to new owner before capital has been paid in*
  Almost all ready-made companies are capitalized upon their formation with equipment that in fact does not exist (which means that the charter capital has never paid in). If the company is transferred without first paying in the capital, the company is subject to liquidation. This is a principal defect that can never be remedied. While the Russian authorities are not out to find such companies, it would be risky in the extreme to entrust significant assets to such a business because this defect could always be used as a reason for the authorities to liquidate the business. Often it is possible to prepare a ready-made company for a clean sale by having the buyer of the ready-made company buy the fictitious equipment from the ready-made company and pay the purchase price to the company. After this has been done the company can then be transferred to the buyer's ownership.

- *Company charters are poorly written*
  The charters of most ready-made companies are very crude and tend to have a lot of passages that say things like 'to be resolved in accordance with the law'. In other words, if there is to be more than one shareholder, the charter will need substantial revision to protect the interests of the shareholders.

Operational issues

Once the overall structure is clear and once company registrations are underway, there are many legal and tax issues that need to be resolved that relate to overall operations. Some of the most important ones are listed below.

Hiring a full-time or part-time Chief Accountant and the qualifications necessary

Most operative Russian companies will require a full-time Chief Accountant. This is not a legal requirement, it is a practical requirement. The volume of accounting work and the intricacies of Russian tax law usually require a full-time in-house person if the company is to operate effectively. Once again, Russian accounting is not intuitive. It is designed to help tax inspectors collect as much tax as possible, it is not designed to be a financial tool that allows managers to gauge the health of a business. For this reason it is often possible to owe tax even when a business is losing money.

Three things to consider are:

1. How many people are issuing or collecting 'source documents'? Source documents are the documents that form the basis for accounting such as invoices, dispatch notes, expense reports, bank and petty cash payment orders, receipts for expenses etc. When more than one person in the company generates all these documents, the company has generally grown to the point where a part-time or outsourced accountant will not be a good solution.

2. Almost any company will save money if its accountant is very knowledgeable regarding tax law and is proactive. This is the difference between hiring a 'bookkeeper' and a specialist as Chief Accountant. A bookkeeper will file all accounting statements correctly and inform company management after the fact that they have a large tax bill to pay, often when the company has not made any profits. A knowledgeable proactive Chief Accountant will understand the tax and accounting issues that arise from the way a company is operating and will often be able to find a legal way of structuring transactions and accounting for them that will not result in punitive taxation. This type of proactivity can only be carried out by a knowledgeable accountant who is familiar with the day-to-day operations of the company and who is on site often enough to take corrective action before a problem arises.

3. Management must be able to speak directly to the Chief Accountant. Although it is possible to use a translator to speak with your accountant, it is not advisable. If you can't speak Russian, it is almost always worth paying more for a skilled chief accountant who can speak your language.

Hiring Russian staff: Employees vs independent contractors

Russian employment law is not very favourable to the employer. The old labour legislation was designed for Soviet times when everyone was guaranteed a job with the State and if the State fired you it was often impossible to find another job. Although the new Labour Code, which was made effective as of 1 February 2002, is a progressive change, it is still targeted at protecting primarily the interests of the employee, not of the employer.

For the most part an employer can have a three-month trial period, during which it is relatively easy to dismiss the employee; after this it is very difficult (but often not impossible) to dismiss an employee who refuses to accept being fired. Even if there is no contract but the employee can prove that he worked for the company, Russian employment law will apply. Furthermore, there are also significant payroll taxes associated with paying employees.

One way that small businesses can get around unfavourable labour regulations and high payroll taxes is to contract staff as contractors and not as employees, and for those contractors to use the simplified system of taxation. In this case there are no payroll taxes, the staff's personal taxes are reduced by half, the relationship does not fall under Russian labour law, and therefore it can be terminated at any time.

Working with independent contractors presents some difficulties. In Russia it is still a criminal offense for a person to work as an independent contractor without first officially registering as an independent entrepreneur. Although this registration is not difficult, it must be done in the city where the worker is registered to live (which may be a different city to where he actually lives and works) and the worker must then file and pay taxes quarterly instead of having everything done for him by the company. Often the company will assume the responsibility for preparing and filing the tax returns but the worker must still pay his own tax. One further difficulty is that only Russian citizens or foreigners with residency permits can register as individual entrepreneurs.

Visas and work permits for foreigners working in Russia

Foreign citizens who work in Russia for a company registered in Russia require either a work permit or a work visa from the company they will work for, or a residency permit. The process of arranging a work permit and work visa or a residency permit will take four to six months. Working in Russia for a company registered or accredited in Russia without such documentation is a violation of the law and can result in deportation. Furthermore, two administrative violations are now grounds for refusal to issue a Russian visa.

In the past foreigners setting up a new Russian venture would often order a one-year commercial multi-entry/exit visa from a travel service provider and then they would begin working for their new venture. Today it is clear that this practice is illegal and could result in the foreigner being deported or denied visa renewals. While ordering such a visa may be a good way to initially enter and leave Russia during the start-up phase of the business, it is completely inappropriate if the foreigner wishes to work for that company.

Thus, it is important that foreign citizens assume no official positions in their Russian businesses until such time as they have obtained a Russian work permit and work visa or a residency permit. It should be noted that while in the past work visas and residency permits did not grant the right of exit (a foreigner had to apply for an exit visa a week to two weeks ahead of any planned exits!), this problem seems to have been recently resolved for work visas. Since January 2004 work visas have been issued as multi-entry/exit. The situation with residency permits is still unclear at the time of writing.

Conclusion

Although Russian regulations do not make it quick, cheap or easy to establish and maintain entrepreneurial ventures, a little advance knowledge of the issues facing entrepreneurial start-ups can go a long way to avoiding problems later on. Knowledge combined with prudence, a rapidly growing economy and an abundance of opportunities ensures that many entrepreneurial ventures will be well worth the effort.

5.8

Property Rights

Andrei Soukhomlinov, Partner, Baker & McKenzie – CIS, Limited

Introduction

Both the Constitution of the Russian Federation and the Civil Code of the Russian Federation uphold the right to own private property. The Land Code of October 2001 and other federal laws adopted as a follow-up to the Land Code are another important step ensuring that this policy becomes a reality.

President Vladimir Putin and the Government of the Russian Federation have always recognized the importance of statutory regulation of the status of land. As a result, the Land Code was adopted by the State Duma, approved by the Federation Council, and signed by the President on 25 October 2001. As provided in the Federal Law On Implementation of the Land Code No. 137 FZ of 25 October 2001 (the Implementing Law), the Land Code came into force on the date of its publication, 30 October 2001. The Land Code, together with the Federal Law No. 101-FZ On Circulation of Agricultural Lands of 24 July 2002 (the Circulation Law), which entered into force in January 2003, put an end to the political debate as to whether land ownership in Russia is possible.

At the present time, land is treated separately from buildings under Russian law, although there are plans to develop a concept of a single object of real estate on the basis of the rights to land. The Land Code sets out the principle of a single approach to land and buildings that are located on such land. The implementation of this principle will, however, require further extensive changes in the existing laws and regulations.

Under current Russian law, investors have choices in terms of using, leasing, and owning property. In addition, Russia's recent economic growth has introduced new opportunities to those investors that are interested in participating in the Russian real estate market. However, in looking at these details, it is important to understand that there are, for the moment, different regulations for land and for buildings.

Ownership of land

The general principles of land ownership are set forth in the Constitution of the Russian Federation, which was adopted in December 1993. Article 9 of the Constitution proclaims the principle of private ownership of land, but does not, however, stipulate the procedure for the transfer of land (which had historically been owned by the State) into private ownership. This legislative vacuum has prompted the rise of a number of regional laws and regulations, as well as the Presidential Decrees adopted in an attempt to regulate various land issues. Regional initiatives raised, however, a more serious concern with respect to the overall validity of all of the regional laws on land ownership. According to Article 72 of the Constitution, decisions on issues on the possession, use and disposal of land are the joint responsibility of the Federation and its 'subjects' (constituent members). Article 76 of the Constitution further provides that a federal law must govern such issues of joint responsibility. Such federal law may be supplemented by laws and other regulations that the 'subjects' of the Federation may issue in compliance with the federal law in question. In addition, Article 36 of the Constitution provides that a federal law must determine the 'terms and procedures of land use'.

The Land Code therefore represented a significant reform, particularly because of the federal sanctions and encouragement that it gives to the creation of private ownership rights in land. Although fundamental terms and procedures of land use are determined in the Land Code, it provides that other Federal laws will have to be adopted. The Land Code has limited applicability to agricultural land, as it is expressly provided that the circulation of such land is the subject of a separate Federal law.

Possession, use and disposal of land plots designated for agricultural use are regulated by the Circulation Law. Not all agricultural land, however, is subject to the Circulation Law. It does not extend, for example, to those land plots that were provided to individuals for the construction of individual homes or garages, or for carrying on a small-holding or dacha garden. Such land plots are covered by the provisions of the Land Code. Agricultural land plots may be held by right of ownership, perpetual (indefinite) use, lifelong inheritable possession, or free fixed-term use, and such plots may also be leased. Ownership of land plots in state or municipal ownership is to be awarded to individuals and legal entities, as a rule, through bidding by tender or auction. Such bidding is also to be held during such land plots' lease when they are claimed by two or more potential lessees. The way the corresponding tenders or auctions should be organized is described in Article 38 of the Land Code.

Although there is no express provision permitting land ownership by foreigners, the Land Code may clearly be interpreted as allowing such ownership, except in cases where it is specifically prohibited. The rights to acquire land ownership rights under existing buildings or for construction are equally applicable to foreigners subject to the following restrictions set out in the Land Code:

1. The relevant rights must always be paid for and can never be granted free of charge; and

2. Foreigners are specifically prohibited from owning land plots in border areas, a list of which is to be drawn up by the President, or in other special territories of the Russian Federation pursuant to other federal laws. Additionally, the President may establish a list of types of buildings and other structures to which pre-emptive buy-out or lease rights to land plots for foreigners may not apply. Under the Implementing Law and pending the preparation of the Presidential list, the border restrictions apply to all border areas. Foreigners are also prohibited from owning agricultural land. The Circulation Law further specifies the rights to agricultural land that may be granted to foreign nationals and foreign legal entities (and stateless persons). Those in this category may only lease agricultural land plots. This restriction on foreign legal entities also extends to Russian legal entities in which the equity participation of foreign nationals, foreign legal entities, and/or stateless persons exceeds 50 per cent. Pursuant to recent amendments to the Federal Law On Mortgages (Real Property Pledges), it may now be possible for foreigners to mortgage certain categories of agricultural land. Mortgage rights do not, however, automatically entail ownership rights.

Under the Land Code, the rights to land now consist of ownership (by the State, municipalities, private individuals, and legal entities), perpetual or indefinite use, free fixed-term use, lease, lifelong inheritable possession, and easements.

In the future, new rights of perpetual or indefinite use may only be granted to state and municipal institutions, Federal Treasury-owned enterprises, and state and local authorities. Legal entities (other than those listed in the previous sentence) with existing rights of perpetual use will no longer be able to transfer these rights. Under the terms of the Implementing Law, these entities had until 1 January 2004 to convert and re-register their rights as (at their option) either lease or ownership rights. Recently, the term for conversion of the rights as either lease or ownership was extended until 1 January 2006 in accordance with Federal Law No. 160-FZ of 3 December 2003. Presently, any legal entity looking to transfer its land rights to another legal entity, such as a joint venture, will first need to upgrade its rights accordingly before any contributions can be made.

The Land Code sets out detailed procedures for acquiring rights over land that is intended for new construction. In particular, the Land Code distinguishes two scenarios. Under the first, a land plot must first have been 'prepared' for sale or lease: its boundaries defined; a cadastral number (a special number assigned to land plots indicating their area, location, type category, etc) assigned; and technical conditions for the utilities connections determined. In such cases the Land Code provides either for acquisition of land directly into private ownership or for lease.

The second scenario for the allocation of land for construction purposes will be used when a new project will require a thorough investigation of ecological, sanitary, architectural, and other issues, and a specific request for land rights from an investor. This may involve the investigation of public opinion regarding construction in the area. In such cases no tender is required. The land will, however, be given on lease only.

Of particular interest to owners of existing buildings and structures is an option to privatize or to obtain land lease rights over the land plots on which their buildings are located, where such land plots are owned by the State or a municipality. Owners of existing buildings, facilities or structures located on land owned by a third party will now enjoy the pre-emptive right to purchase or lease the land plot beneath such buildings.

Ownership of buildings

The current Russian law permits both Russian and foreign nationals and legal entities to own buildings. In general, the rules relating to the use, disposal and sale of buildings are set forth in the Russian Civil Code, which guarantees the freedom to sell, rent, and carry out other transactions with buildings. The process of the acquisition of buildings through privatization is also less complicated. In general, provided that the building in question was recorded on the balance sheet of the state enterprise at the time it was privatized, the successor company has the right to own that building.

In the past, state-owned buildings were granted to state-owned enterprises for economic management or use. During privatization, however, such buildings and other structures were usually transferred into the ownership of those enterprises that operated and used them on the basis of various use rights. Thus, the newly privatized enterprise would 'inherit' such buildings and structures from the state-owned enterprise, provided that they were recorded on the company's balance sheet and were included in the privatization documentation.

The special authority that is in charge of the state registration of the rights to real estate must issue an ownership certificate certifying the right of ownership of buildings and structures (see section below). In accordance with the Civil Code, the rights to real estate arise after the state registration of such rights, except in the case where such rights have been obtained prior to the adoption of Federal Law No. 122-FZ of 21 July 1997, On State Registration of Real Property Rights and Real Property Transactions, as amended (the Registration Law). In this case, the owner is not obligated to register the rights unless it wants to enter into any transaction related to the real estate object. Obtaining the relevant certificate is a fairly straightforward, although sometimes lengthy, process, as long as the private company that is seeking to obtain such a certificate can clearly demonstrate that the buildings in question were purchased or privatized in accordance with the prescribed procedures. Before an ownership certificate is issued, the local office of the Bureau of Technical Inventory (BTI) needs to carry out a detailed assessment of the building and to produce an updated BTI 'technical passport' for the building. Quite often, this becomes a problem since no such updated BTI 'technical passport' exists and building owners are often reluctant to incur the costs involved in securing the required BTI assessment.

Leases

Foreign legal entities may be granted either land leases or building leases. Such leases on state- or municipally-owned property are usually based on a standard local form. Although the Civil Code does not stipulate a statutory maximum length of time, the current practice is that such lease terms rarely exceed 49 years.

However, in Moscow the recently adopted Moscow City Law No. 27 on Land Uses and Construction in the City of Moscow of 14 May 2003, which came into force on 26 June 2003, fixes those periods for which leases may be obtained for Moscow-owned land plots. Lease terms for sites free of any capital buildings, structures, or facilities may not exceed five years. Land plots on which such property is located are, however, available for leases of 25–49 years, confirming existing practice. In some cases, in extension of current practice, they may even be leased for as long as 99 years. This will require a Moscow Government decision in respect of projects of special significance to the city.

The level of rent payments for the majority of land leases granted by the State or municipalities is set either by a general local decree or by a specific decree for the lease in question. In Moscow, where the demand for land remains relatively high, a lessee must pay rent calculated on the basis of a formula. In addition, a Moscow lessee must pay for the right to lease any land in excess of the area of the existing building on that land. In St. Petersburg, the level of rent is determined by a decree of the Governor; the levels differ depending on the location of the site and the type of activity of the lessee, and in some instances, it is possible to negotiate the lease rent with the local St. Petersburg authorities.

The basis for granting a lease for a municipal- or state-owned building, as well as the rental payments, is normally established by a local decree. The parties themselves may negotiate leases for a part of or for the entire privately-owned building. To date, few office and retail sector leases have exceeded a 10-year term; with 5-year terms being the most common. Longer leases of 25 years or more have been executed in the industrial sector. All three markets, however, are changing rapidly. Subleases are also permitted, subject to any contractual restrictions in the primary lease.

Whether the lease concerns land or a building, the Land and Civil Codes provide a lessee with certain basic rights. When the property is transferred, it must be in the condition required by the lease. Thereafter, unless the lease specifies otherwise, the lessor is liable for the repair of defects on the premises. If the lessor fails to carry out the necessary repairs, the lessee's options include compensation and the right to terminate the lease. A lessee that properly fulfills its obligations under the lease has a priority right of renewal at the end of the term. The renewal rights of a lessee under a land lease are to be treated in conjunction with the pre-emptive rights to purchase or lease the land plot that are granted to the owners of the existing buildings and structures.

Significantly, the provisions of the Civil Code, insofar as they apply to land leases, are supplemented by the Land Code in a number of areas. In particular, the Land Code sets forth a series of modified rights for land lessees. Their applicability will, in part, depend upon the precise drafting of a lease. For example, the presumption under Article 615 of the Civil Code that a lessee needs a lessor's consent to sublease has been reversed for lessees of land. Of particular significance is the provision that lessees of state- or municipally-owned land under lease, with a term exceeding 5 years, now have a free right to assign their rights, subject only to the delivery of a notice to the lessor. In other land leases, this rule will also apply (in contrast to the provisions for prior consent under Article 615(2) of the Civil Code). A notable improvement is also made in conveyancing procedures, with the new provision that the assignee of a land lease does not need to enter into a new land lease.

Both the lessor and the lessee may terminate the lease contract, but only with a court order. The Civil Code also suggests that the lease contract may provide for other termination opportunities. Additional protection is given to the lessees of residential premises. The Land Code contains new provisions that deal with the termination of land leases in conjunction with a court order. Presently the following will also constitute grounds for termination:

1. misuse of the land plot (a more stringent test than that under Article 619 of the Civil Code, which requires either substantial or repeated violations);
2. use of the land plot that results in a decline in fertility of agricultural land or, important for industrial users, a material deterioration in the environmental situation;
3. failure to correct a range of other intentional environmental violations of applicable land use regulations; and
4. failure to use the land plot for its designated purpose for a period in excess of three years.

Most leases must be state-registered to be valid. The only exception is for leases of buildings for a period of less than one year, which do not need to be state-registered to be valid. The principles and procedures of state registration are discussed below.

State registration of rights to immovable property

As discussed above, the right to real estate arises only from its state registration. The current Russian legislation contains a specific procedure for the registration and identification of rights (title) to immovable property. In many cases, such registration is a prerequisite for the validity and enforceability of transactions involving immovable property.

According to the Registration Law, transactions involving immovable property (buildings, land, etc) are also subject to state registration, and they become effective and enforceable only upon such registration. The registration authorities in the place where the immovable property is located carry out the registration process. The registration authorities maintain the Unified State Register of Rights to and Transactions With Real Property, which indicates the history and the current status of the immovable property in question. This Register also records various encumbrances over immovable property, including leases. The registration authorities issue a certificate in a prescribed form that certifies the rights to immovable property. Information on state-registered transactions with immovable property is also included in the Register.

Land plots are also required to undergo the cadastral registration. The procedures and rules of the state cadastral registration of land are outlined in Federal Law No. 28-FZ On the State Land Cadastre, dated 2 January 2000 (the Land Cadastre Law), which came into force in July

2000. The State cadastral registration applies to all land plots located in the Russian Federation, regardless of the form of ownership, the designation, or the authorized use of the land plots. Under the Land Code, only land plots that have State cadastral registration can be the subject matter of a sale-purchase transaction. In practice, especially in Moscow, this applies to all transactions with land plots. The Unified State Register of Land (the Land Register) is established pursuant to the Land Cadastre Law and contains detailed information on land plots, including their cadastral number, location, land category and authorized use, the borders of the land plots, the registered proprietary rights and encumbrances over the land plots, and information about any immovable property on the land plots. The information from the Land Register is open to the public. The Land Cadastre Law states that such information will also be provided in the form of extracts and copied documents from cadastral files. Additional regulations and rules will define the procedures for filing the relevant applications to obtain such information.

Classifications of real estate

Russian real estate is classified on the basis of its intended use (ie either for residential or non-residential purposes). The specific use should be identified in the lease, the certificate of ownership, or the act of permanent use, as well as in the BTI. The use of buildings is also governed by the decree or other document that was originally issued in relation to that building. The property of a privatized enterprise may also be subject to additional use restrictions imposed by its specific privatization plan.

It should be noted that all real estate construction requires state permits and consent.

Payments for real estate

At present, when a foreign investor purchases or simply leases real estate from Russian residents, payments for the real estate purchased and, usually, lease payments effected in foreign currency, are classified as 'capital transfer transactions'. Previously, every such capital transfer transaction required a specific licence from the Central Bank of the Russian Federation (the CBR). However, the licensing requirement for foreign currency payments by foreign tenants to Russian landlords or sellers has been recently abolished. Furthermore, under the new Federal Law On Currency Regulation and Currency Control, the greater part of which will come into effect on 17 June 2004, foreign currency payments made by foreign investors to Russian residents in consideration for purchased or leased immovable property will no longer be deemed 'capital transfer transactions'. This development certainly testifies to further liberalization of Russian currency control legislation. Additionally, when both the seller and the buyer, or the lessor and the lessee, are foreign legal entities, a payment in foreign currency to an offshore bank account is also possible. Such transactions, however, may have tax consequences, particularly with regard to withholding tax.

Residential real estate

By now, many apartments have been privatized and are in private ownership. Federal Law No. 72-FZ of 15 June 1996, On Partnerships of Home Owners (the Condominium Law), provides the basis for the formation of condominiums, including those formed by a developer prior to their construction, although such ventures are limited to buildings that consist primarily of residential premises. Additional regulations are also required, some of which have already been passed in Moscow and St. Petersburg. Presently, simple condominiums are also being registered.

Mortgage of real estate

Federal Law No. 102-FZ On Hypothec (Mortgage of Real Property) of 16 July 1998 came into effect on 22 July 1998 and was subsequently amended on a number of occasions (the Mortgage Law). The Mortgage Law significantly improves the importance of a mortgage as a creditor's instrument for securing its investment. It is important to note that buildings and structures can be mortgaged only simultaneously with the land plots on which such buildings and structures are located.

The concept of a mortgage under Russian law differs from that in common law jurisdictions. In Russia, a mortgagee cannot automatically acquire rights to the mortgaged property if default occurs under the secured obligation. In most cases the mortgaged property must be sold at a public auction. The proceeds will then be used to repay the debt. There are two types of foreclosure on mortgaged property: judicial and extra-judicial. The parties may also enter into a contract for the transfer of the mortgaged property to the mortgagee to set off the secured obligation. However, such an agreement can be concluded only after the default has occurred under the secured obligations.

In order to be valid, a mortgage agreement must be certified by a Russian notary and registered with the relevant state real property registration authority. The local office of the state real property registration authority and all of the land committees can provide information on the absence or presence of a valid mortgage over immovable property.

According to the Mortgage Law, the following types of property can be subject to a mortgage:

1. land plots (with those exceptions stated in the Mortgage Law);
2. enterprises registered as real estate;
3. buildings, structures, and other immovable property that are used for business activities;
4. residential houses, apartments and parts thereof, consisting of one or several isolated rooms;
5. cottages, garages, and other structures for personal use;
6. aircraft, sea and river vessels; and
7. a lessee's interest in leased real estate, which may be the subject of a 'leasehold mortgage'.

The terms and conditions of a mortgage may restrict the owner's or user's capability to dispose of the property, including its contribution to charter capital and/or lease to third parties. Therefore, confirmation of the absence or existence of a valid mortgage over the property is important. If there is a valid mortgage, the purchase can be effected only with the consent of the mortgagee. Even then, notwithstanding such consent, the mortgage will follow the immovable property unless and until the primary obligation secured by the mortgage is performed and the property is released from it.

The Mortgage Law as amended includes some significant changes that are important specifically for securing financing through mortgages. Thus, revised Article 78 of the Mortgage Law provides that foreclosure by the mortgagee on a mortgaged residential house or apartment and disposal of such property constitutes grounds for termination of occupancy rights of a mortgagor and his family members residing together in this residential house or apartment, provided that this residential house or apartment was mortgaged under a mortgage agreement to secure the return of a loan granted for the purchase or construction of this residential house or apartment.

This means that now (unlike prior to the revision of the Mortgage Law) a mortgagee can demand that a mortgagor vacate the mortgaged property if the mortgagee intends to foreclose on it. However, this rule would apply only if the mortgaged property was mortgaged to secure the repayment of a loan taken by a mortgagor to purchase or construct the property. It is also important that those individuals who occupy the mortgaged property, pursuant to a lease or a 'naim' agreement (under Russian law, a specific type of residential lease where the lessee is a private individual), cannot be moved out upon foreclosure on the mortgaged property. Such a lease or a 'naim' agreement concluded prior to the mortgage agreement will remain in force and can be terminated only in the specific circumstances provided for by the Russian Civil Code or applicable housing legislation.

Some new changes were introduced in the Mortgage Law as amended in respect to the extension of an existing mortgage on a newly-constructed building. The previous version of Article 65 of the Mortgage Law provided that a mortgage did not extend to buildings and structures constructed on the mortgaged land plot unless otherwise stipulated by the mortgage agreement. Based on this provision of the Mortgage Law, real property registration authorities demanded that an addendum to the existing mortgage be signed each time the existing mortgage was to be extended to cover a newly-constructed building or structure. This slowed the process down and increased the cost, specifically a notary fee of 1.5 per cent of the mortgaged property value had to be paid each time such an addendum was executed. Currently, according to Article 65 as amended, the existing mortgage of a land plot automatically extends to cover a building or a structure erected on this land plot by the mortgagor, unless otherwise provided by the mortgage agreement. The revised Article 65 of the Mortgage Law allows a mortgagee to extend the mortgage over a land plot to all buildings and structures that may be constructed on the plot without need for a subsequent addendum.

The amendments to the Mortgage Law introduced by Federal Law No. 1-FZ of 5 February 2004 now permit the mortgage of any land plot, including agricultural land, unless it has been withdrawn from or is limited in circulation, or if it is held in state or municipal ownership.

5.9

Competition Law

Paul Melling, Partner and Sergei Voitishkin, Partner, Baker & McKenzie – CIS, Limited

The basic law regulating antimonopoly questions is the Russian Federation Law on Competition and the Restriction of Monopolistic Activity in the Commodity Markets (the Competition Law), enacted 22 March 1991, as amended. The Russian competition watchdog is the Federal Anti-Monopoly Service (the FAS).

The Competition Law regulates four areas of particular interest to a foreign investor:

1. abuse of a dominant position;
2. agreements limiting competition;
3. establishment of companies; and
4. mergers and acquisitions.

Abuse of a dominant position

Dominant entities are subject to certain restrictions on their activities. Determining whether a particular entity enjoys a dominant position involves a complex evaluation of various factors. The most important factor is the entity's market share.

For entities with a market share of 65 per cent or greater, there is a presumption of market dominance. If a market share is between 35 and 65 per cent, there is a rebuttable presumption of non-dominance. However, the FAS may deem that such a non-dominant entity still holds a dominant position based on the stability of the entity's market share, the market share of its competitors, the barriers to market entry and/or other factors. For entities with a market share of 35 per cent or less, there is a conclusive presumption of non-dominance.

For those in a dominant position, the Competition Law prohibits any of the following activities:

- withdrawal of goods from circulation with the intent to create or maintain a shortage of such goods;
- creation of conditions that place one or more legal entities in an unequal position as compared to other entities in their ability to access the market for particular goods;
- imposition on a contracting party of contractual terms that are disadvantageous or do not relate to the subject matter of the contract;
- creation of barriers to market entry for other legal entities;
- support of high or low prices (ie price fixing);
- discontinuance of production of goods for which there is a consumer demand if it is possible to produce them without a loss; or
- unjustified refusal to consummate a contract with particular customers if it is possible to produce or deliver the relevant goods to such customers.

Any of the above activities may be allowed if the dominant entity can prove that the positive effects of a particular activity outweigh its negative consequences.

Agreements limiting competition

The Competition Law prohibits agreements, transactions, or other business activities of business entities operating in the same or similar commodities markets that lead or may lead to the following:

- control or fixing of prices, discounts, bonus payments, or surcharges;
- increase or reduction of prices, or the manipulation of prices at auctions/tenders;
- division of the market by reference to territories, or according to the volume of sales/purchases, the range of marketable goods, or the range of sellers or buyers;
- restriction of access to the market or the removal from the market of other entities that sell or purchase particular products; and
- refusal to conclude agreements with particular sellers or buyers.

The Competition Law further prohibits other agreements between business entities operating in the same or similar commodities markets, including agreements between non-competing entities, which will or may result in exclusion, limitation, and elimination of competition or derogation of interests of other business entities.

Finally, the Competition Law prohibits agreements or other concerted actions between non-competing legal entities (such as potential sellers and potential buyers) acting in a particular market if such agreements or other actions result or may result in the exclusion, restriction, or elimination of competition. This rule, however, only applies to legal entities with a joint market share in a particular commodity market exceeding 35 per cent.

In certain cases, the above-mentioned activities may be permitted if the business entity can prove that the positive effects of the action, including effects in the socio-economic sphere, outweigh its negative consequences, or if the entity can prove that federal laws permit such agreements or business activities.

Establishment of companies

The founders of a new company must notify the FAS within 45 days following the company's registration if the aggregate asset value of the founders exceeds 200,000 times the monthly minimum wage (in May 2004 this corresponded to approximately $690,000).

Mergers and acquisitions

Mergers

Entities involved in a consolidation or a merger must receive prior approval from the FAS if the aggregate asset value of the entities exceeds 200,000 times the minimum monthly wage. The procedures for obtaining such approval are similar to the procedures used for acquisitions.

Acquisition of an interest in a Russian company

Acquisition of shares/participatory shares in a Russian company
Entities involved in an acquisition must receive prior approval from the FAS if:

1. the aggregate asset value of the acquiror, its group of persons, and/or the target company exceeds 200,000 times the minimum monthly wage; or
2. either the acquiror, any entity of the acquiror's group, or the target company is included in the FAS Register of Entities with a Market Share Exceeding 35 per cent in the relevant market.

In determining the threshold for asset values, the FAS takes into consideration not only the acquiror and the target company, but also all persons (individuals or legal entities) in the acquiror's 'group of persons'. The broad term 'group of persons' includes all individuals or legal entities related to the acquiror as a result of controlling share ownership or through certain management contracts, familial relations, and/or other *de facto* control mechanisms.

It is common practice for a foreign investor to buy Russian shares/participatory shares and to become such a shareholder/participant in a Russian company. However, there are some legal formalities associated with the acquisition of a stake, non-compliance with which may seriously damage the interests of an investor.

The two most popular forms of organization for Russian companies are joint stock companies (JSCs) and limited liability companies (LLC). JSCs issue shares, which, under Russian law, are classified as securities. Therefore, Russian securities legislation provides additional regulations on transactions involving securities:

1. Each share issue must be registered with the Federal Financial Markets Service. A failure to register will forfeit the share purchase transaction under Article 168 of the Civil Code;

2. Sold shares must be paid for in full by the shareholders. Otherwise, the transaction will be deemed invalid and may be challenged by any interested party; and

3. Most shares exist in non-documentary form as entries in a shareholders' register, which is maintained by the JSC or by third party registrars. The title to such non-documentary shares is transferred as a legal matter only at the moment of entry in the shareholders' register. Accordingly, it is very important to receive an excerpt from the shareholders' register, confirming the buyer's title to the acquired shares.

Participatory shares in an LLC are not classified as securities and do not need to be registered. However, an existing participatory share can be transferred only after it has been fully paid for. In addition, a buyer will obtain the participant's rights in the LLC only after the LLC is notified of the sale of the participatory share. Moreover, since all of the participants in an LLC must be included in its charter and foundation agreement, it is very important to make sure that the LLC participants approve the relevant amendments to the LLC charter and foundation agreement naming the investor as a new participant.

The advantages of a share (participatory share) purchase scheme are that:

- exposure of the purchaser to the liabilities of the target company is limited to the nominal value of the purchased share (participatory share); and

- in most cases, the procedure for the share (participatory share) purchase does not require any lengthy or onerous state registration (with the exception of the LLC itself, as to which the charter and the foundation agreement must be amended to reflect that the purchaser has become a participant in the LLC).

Unfortunately, there are also some disadvantages to such a scheme:

- due to LLC shareholders' right of first refusal, the purchaser must be approved by the existing shareholders in the company, which can be difficult if the company has shareholders other than the seller;
- potential problems may arise when returning to a foreign purchaser its investment upon the liquidation of a company (especially a JSC); and
- the purchaser must complete certain corporate formalities prior to the share sale.

The purchaser of shares should take the following steps:

1. perform due diligence on the target company;
2. obtain prior approval from the FAS as required by the Article 18 of the Competition Law;
3. ensure that the appropriate corporate procedures are followed (such as the waiver by other shareholders of their pre-emptive rights);
4. sign a share purchase agreement and any other required documents (such as a share transfer instruction in the case of JSCs, or a notification to the company in the case of LLCs); and
5. ensure that the purchaser of the shares is entered into the shareholders' register of the JSC or that a new version of the charter and foundation agreement, reflecting the purchaser of a participatory share as a participant in the LLC, is properly approved and registered.

Acquisition of the sssets of a Russian company
The main purpose in purchasing assets from a third company is to use the acquired assets in one's own business.

Under Russian law, two main methods of purchasing assets are available:

1. purchase of particular assets; and
2. purchase of an enterprise.

The advantages of purchasing particular assets are:

- the procedure is simple and does not require state registrations (except for specific objects, for example, in the case of the purchase of real estate objects and intellectual property objects, such as patents and trade marks); and

- the purchaser does not acquire any of the liabilities of the seller, unlike in the case of the purchase of an enterprise or shares.

An asset purchase also has some disadvantages:

- encumbrances over pledged assets will be transferred along with the assets;
- there is possibly an obligation to pay VAT; and
- acquisition of certain assets can require state registration (real estate objects, some intellectual property objects, etc).

Purchase of an enterprise
An acquisition of an enterprise is advantageous because the purchaser acquires a block of tangible and intangible assets, which allows it to launch or maintain a business. The purchase of an enterprise is, in reality, the acquisition of a business.

However, there are also disadvantages to enterprise acquisition:

- the purchaser acquires not only the assets but also the liabilities of the seller attributable to those assets;
- applicable Russian legislation provides for the joint liability of the purchaser and the seller of the enterprise to its creditors; and
- if an enterprise owns any tangible property (eg a house, a car, a lake, or a satellite dish), it is necessary to register the enterprise as a real estate object and to register the purchase agreement with the body of justice for State Registration of Real Property Rights and Real Property Transactions.

A purchaser of assets and/or enterprise(s) must take the following steps:

1. perform due diligence on the purchased assets (mainly, due diligence as to the title and the legal status of the seller and the powers of its officers);
2. obtain prior approval from the FAS as required by Article 18 of the Competition Law;
3. ensure that the appropriate corporate procedures are followed (such as the approval of a 'major transaction', the approval of an 'interested party transaction');
4. sign an asset/enterprise purchase agreement and the other required documents; and
5. complete required state registrations (registrations of the rights to and transactions with real estate objects, the registration of enter-

prise purchase agreements and/or the registration of assignments of patents and trade marks, etc).

Procedures and timing

If the FAS determines that the establishment, merger, or acquisition may restrict competition or strengthen a dominant position, it may request additional information and documentation. The FAS may also require the parties to take measures to ensure competition.

After all documents have been submitted, the FAS must issue a written decision within 50 days. In practice, the investor can expect a much longer time period to pass before the FAS decision is issued.

Appendices

Appendix 1

Learning from the Russian Experience: Regional Debt Defaults and Recovery 1998–2003

Eugene Korovin and Elena Okorotchenko, Standard and Poor's Ratings Direct

Russian local and regional governments (LRGs) are once again borrowing on the capital markets after a deep slump during 1998–2000 that followed numerous defaults. Over 2003, the Russian LRG bond market more than doubled in size and now totals $3.3 billion (as of mid-2004). Since 2001, there have been no publicly recorded defaults, except for that of Primorskiy Krai, which defaulted on a small bond issue in 2001.

As the bond market reaches new heights and new issuers enter the market, investors have become ever more concerned about potential defaults and adequate assessment of entities' creditworthiness. This appendix analyses common default triggers and recovery rates, and compares the circumstances of the 1998–2000 default wave with the present situation.

For the purposes of this study, a default is a non-payment of interest or principal or coercive exchange in which the creditor has no real alternative but to accept the offer, which is unfavourable.

Delay or non-payment to the federal government is not regarded as a default for the purposes of this study. Borrowing from the federal budget is a component of the Russian intergovernmental budgetary system. Budget loans are repeatedly prolonged, written off, or used to replace grants.

Publicly available data only represents the top of the 'default iceberg'. Poor disclosure of LRG defaults is common in Russia, as in many other European countries. Lack of data on municipal defaults makes it impossible to include them in this study.

Numerous defaults after the crisis of 1998

Russian RGs' direct debt started growing rapidly after the stabilization of the national capital market in 1996. By 1998, direct regional debt amounted to at least 25 per cent of consolidated regional budget revenues, up from 15 per cent in 1997. The simultaneous increase in debt service payments caused by a high proportion of short-term debt, with an average duration of less than one year, combined with yawning gaps in budget balances, increased exposure to debt refinancing risks.

An increase in interest rates significantly worsened borrowing terms in the first half of 1998. Coupled with urgent social expenditures, this increase prompted several RGs to default in May/June.

On 17 August 1998, the federal government announced the devaluation of the rouble, the halt of federal government bond trading, and a moratorium on corporate external debt payments. This prompted an avalanche of regional defaults, driven on by the growth of debt service payments on foreign currency debt, the collapse of the national capital market, and RGs' poorer liquidity.

During 1998–2001, at least 57 Russian RGs, out of a total of 89, defaulted. Information on 123 overdue obligations, with a total amount of 22 billion Russian roubles ($771 million in current prices), is publicly available. By 2001, the number of defaults had fallen sharply (see Figure A.1).

Foreign currency-denominated debt accounted for two-thirds of total defaulted obligations. The largest defaults, representing more than R2 billion each, were committed on foreign currency-denominated obligations. For example, Nizhniy Novgorod Oblast's obligation was eurobonds, and those of the republics of Tatarstan and Sakha, the

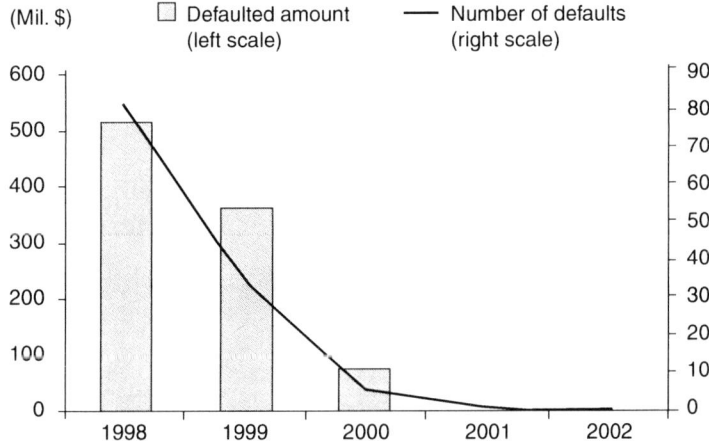

Figure A.1 Defaults by Russian regions

Leningrad Oblast, and the Yamal-Nenets Autonomous Okrug (YNAO) were syndicated loans.

Bonds and bank loans each account for about one-half of total defaulted obligations. In practice, however, the proportion of bank loans is inevitably higher because loan restructurings are often not made public (see Figure A.2).

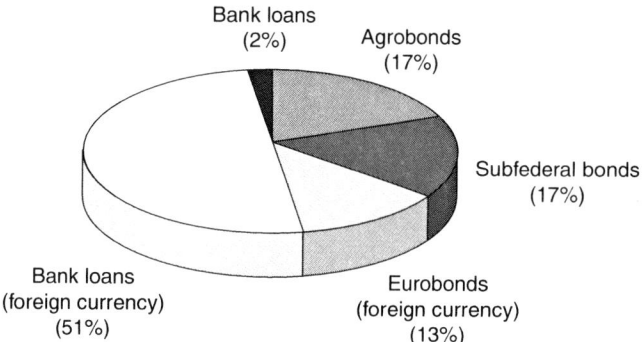

Figure A.2 Russian regions' default by debt instrument

Default triggers

In general, RGs defaulted due to a lack of debt service capacity or a general unwillingness to pay. In 1998–1999, several RGs including Tatarstan, Nizhniy Novgorod, and YNAO defaulted because impending debt service payments totalled 26–29 per cent of their budget revenues.

In contrast, in 2000, the cities of Moscow and St. Petersburg met their obligations in full and on time, even though their debt service was at the critical level of 27 per cent of revenue for both cities. This divergence in behaviour highlights the importance of willingness to pay as a factor for LRGs' creditworthiness. In difficult financial situations, and unlike corporates, which are subject to bankruptcy and liquidation laws, prioritization of payments plays a crucial role.

Moscow, St. Petersburg, and some other regional governments managed to meet their debt obligations owing to an efficient set of emergency measures. Their initiatives included active debt management, such as purchase on the secondary market, postponing and cutting current expenditures, and suspending capital projects.

Common default triggers included:

- poor liquidity – non-cash payments, high seasonality of revenues, and high arrears;
- lack of financial flexibility – inability to raise revenues or cut expenditures;

- economic and financial crises;
- high-risk debt profiles – short-term debt, bullet maturities, and high foreign exchange risk;
- poor debt management; and
- an unsupportive intergovernmental budgetary system.

The unwillingness of RGs to pay during this period was often caused by:

- refusal to pay debt contracted by previous governments – corruption or inefficiency was often blamed;
- the forced nature of debt obligations – the obligatory conversion of enterprises' debt into regional debt by the Ministry of Finance, for example;
- inefficient enforcement procedures – regions used loopholes in legislation that made it almost impossible for creditors to get their money back through the courts; and
- the default example set by the federal government.

Poor liquidity

RGs' liquidity was constrained by the widespread practice of collecting budget revenues in non-cash forms, such as mutual settlements, commercial paper, the delivery of goods and services, and tax exemptions. This practice was very specific to Russian RGs. In 1997, non-cash revenues accounted for half, on average, of regional budget revenues, and up to 90 per cent in some regions.

The actual financial position of RGs accustomed to non-cash budget execution was considerably poorer compared with that arising from official financial statements in 1998–1999. Below-par actual value of non-cash revenues and expenditures differed widely across RGs and prevents any reliable adjustment of RGs' financial figures for that period.

Cash reserves were consequently insufficient to support liquidity when LRGs faced significant debt payments. Reserves totalled only 2.5 per cent of revenues in 1997.

Revenues are often highly seasonal. In some cases, only 15 per cent of revenue is collected during the first quarter of the year and 40 per cent during the last. Mounting arrears aggravated the problem.

Lack of financial flexibility

Rigid spending structures did not leave RGs much opportunity to cut budget expenditure. Capital expenditure covered only pressing investment needs, was already low, and was usually urgent. The majority of current expenditure was obligatory – wages and social allowances – earmarked, or delegated by federal government. Deferrable expenditure had already been postponed by accumulating accounts payable, which reached 21 per cent of total expenditure on average in 1999, even on 'obligatory' expenditures. Due to tight control over tax rates, shares, and collection by the central government, LRGs also had little room for manoeuvre in terms of revenues.

Economic recession and financial crisis

The recession of 1998 – manifested in a 6.4 per cent drop in GDP – affected budget revenue collection. Several RGs barely managed to collect 70–80 per cent of their budgeted revenue. In addition, the collection of a large part of revenues in non-cash forms meant that they could not be used for salaries or debt repayment.

The collapse of the banking system, a typical event for countries in default, undermined liquidity and complicated tax collection and debt payments. Cash reserves deposited in insolvent banks were frozen. Tax arrears rose because insolvent banks, having no funds, could not execute taxpayers' payment orders.

Risky debt profiles

RGs' financial positions were further sapped by their exposure to high foreign exchange and refinancing risks. Debt was largely short term, only 200–250 days on average in 1998, with bullet maturities. This was the natural result of the shallow and speculative Russian capital market. In 1997, borrowing for refinancing purposes exceeded net borrowing and amounted to 9 per cent of consolidated regional budget revenues. Sharp increases in interest rates, up to 100–150 per cent in the summer of 1998, prevented new borrowing by most LRGs. High foreign-exchange risk manifested itself when the rouble value of foreign currency denominated obligations tripled in summer 1998.

RGs with onerous foreign currency debt could not cope with the increased debt burdens and had to default. The Republic of Sakha's debt burden, for example, increased to 60 per cent of budget revenues from 17 per cent.

Poor debt management

Excessive borrowing was the predictable result of RGs' aggressive and shortsighted financial policies and inefficient regulation by the federal government.

Speculative use of borrowed funds and the channelling of borrowed money to cover current expenditure deficits undermined debt service capacity. Some RGs invested borrowed funds in risky securities, such as federal government bonds, or deposited them in commercial banks.

These investments were lost as a result of the federal government's default and the collapse of the banking system.

Unsupportive intergovernmental budgetary system

General financial support from the federal government was irregular and could not be relied upon. Even grants were distributed unevenly within a financial year. Financial assistance in distress situations was not forthcoming because the government had problems of its own. Such a break of intergovernmental fiscal arrangements in a period of sovereign distress is typical for developing countries and represents a significant risk for RGs, especially those highly dependent on the intergovernmental budgetary system.

Unwillingness to repay debt contracted by preceding administrations

Some RGs defaulted after changes in administration owing to regional elections. Newly elected governors refused to repay debt contracted by their predecessors, claiming that these obligations were contracted illegally or used ineffectively and therefore should not be repaid.

The forced nature of debt obligations

RGs often refused to repay debt that they considered to be 'imposed' on them. This was the case with the 'agrobonds' issued in 1997–1998 by 70 RGs. They were 'forced' to convert the guarantees they issued to support agricultural enterprises into direct obligations in the form of bonds. Issued bonds were passed to the Ministry of Finance. The ministry then placed the bonds among private creditors through auctions. Many regions felt that this debt was not their true obligation.

Inefficient enforcement procedures

Inefficient and irregular enforcement procedures contributed to the corruption of RGs' credit culture. RGs missed debt payments, supposing that creditors would not succeed in enforcing payment. The Budget Code stipulates that the claims of creditors may only be satisfied after all other planned budget expenditures. Even if creditors obtained a court judgement in their favour, the authorities often failed to enforce the payments.

In 2000, the Budget Code introduced an alternative legal procedure for dealing with insolvent RGs. The federal government could now impose external control over regional budgets. To date, however, the federal government has not applied this regulation to any insolvent RGs. Attempts by creditors to oblige the government to do so have also failed.

Default by the federal government

Several RGs followed the example of the federal government and defaulted on certain debt obligations in 1998–1999. These RGs claimed to have a moral right to default because their debt service capacity was affected by the impact on the federal government of the growth of foreign currency debt service, the collapse of the banking system, and the tax base recession. The federal government's examples of 'selective default' and protracted negotiations regarding the terms of debt restructuring were often followed by RGs.

Restructuring and recovery

The restructuring of overdue debt was generally protracted and coercive. Restructuring terms were usually unfavourable for creditors. Enforcement procedures could not protect creditors' rights, and so they had no alternative but to accept the terms offered by the RGs. They consequently incurred significant losses.

Duration of default: one to two years

Restructuring was usually protracted. No more than one-third of overdue debt was restructured within the year of default (see Figure A.3). About one-quarter has not yet been restructured.

The length of the restructuring period depended on the willingness of the RG to pay, the creditor's efforts to recover debt, and the type of

Figure A.3 Russian regions period of defaulted debt restructuring

debt obligations. In general, external debt obligations, such as eurobonds and bank loans, were restructured more quickly. The restructuring of agrobonds, often overdue because of unwillingness to pay, dragged on for years.

Coercive restructuring terms

Overdue debt was often repaid in non-cash assets, such as new bond issues, stocks, property, and goods obtained through non-cash budget revenue collection, with only a few exceptions, including bonds held by individuals. Overdue debt could also be exchanged for tax exemptions or accepted as tax payments or budget loan repayments.

Creditors exchanged overdue debt obligations for assets offered by the RGs at auctions, usually for less than face value. Many creditors incurred losses by attempting to convert debt obligations into cash as soon as possible, because the market price of assets offered by RGs was obviously significantly below par. There were also several cases of forced debt swaps at below-par rates, including by Novosibirsk Oblast.

Low recovery rates on both domestic and external debt

Non-cash repayment schemes and the lack of data complicate the assessment of recovery values. Lack or unreliability of data on the prices of defaulted regional bonds is explained by the fact that the liquidity of overdue issues was extremely low. Moreover, RGs often suspended trading of overdue regional bonds on the stock exchange until restructuring was complete. Trading on Novosibirsk's three bond issues, which had a total value of R233 million, for example, was suspended for 54 months.

Generally, creditors incurred significant losses due to protracted restructuring even if the overdue debt was repaid in full nominal value.

Recovery rates on rouble-nominated bonds were quite low. Low recoveries originated from a protracted restructuring process, the low liquidity of defaulted bonds, unclear restructuring terms, and great uncertainty about repayment of debt instruments received by investors in exchange for defaulted bonds. Recovery on Omsk Oblast's bonds, which defaulted in 1998–1999, for example, averaged 47 per cent, varying from a mere 33 per cent up to a more significant 75 per cent, owing to the non-simultaneous redemption of different issues. This was completed by December 2003.

Recovery rates on bank loans were even more dispersed than for bonds. The lower dispersion for bonds was a result of the general uniformity of bond obligations and similarity of court procedures. Bank loans, regulated by uniquely structured contracts, experienced more differentiation and less predictable recovery.

Recovery rates on external obligations, such as eurobonds and syndicated loans held mainly by foreign creditors, were on a par with recovery rates on rouble-denominated obligations. Creditors recovered 38–48 per cent on the Nizhniy Novgorod Oblast defaulted Eurobonds, for example.

Similar recovery rates on external debt could be explained by the balance of RGs' stronger willingness to pay on the one hand, but poorer debt service capacity where RGs had substantial external debt on the other. RGs' concerns about their reputation among foreign investors and better documentation of external debt deals strengthened RGs' willingness to pay. It resulted in shorter periods and better terms of restructuring for creditors, including full repayment in cash and accrual of interest on capitalized amounts of debt. Heavy debt burdens, however, which had tripled after the drastic devaluation of the rouble, exhausted their debt service capacity and demanded extension of repayment schedules.

Continued default

Some RGs are still in default. Overdue debt obligations include agrobond issues, bank loans, foreign currency guarantees (Kaliningrad Oblast), and domestic bonds (Primorskiy Krai). In total, 17 RGs still have overdue debt obligations.

It is evident that less favourable borrowing conditions are offered to RGs with poor credit histories. Nizhniy Novgorod, therefore, did not issue bonds in 2003 because potential underwriters offered placement at yields of 30 per cent. Yields on bonds issued by the cities of Moscow and St. Petersburg, the most creditworthy RGs, were 9–12 per cent.

The future

Debt expected to grow in the medium term

Raising funds from capital markets is becoming an ever more important source of infrastructure investment for RGs because current resources – budget surpluses – cannot meet growing regional investment needs.

RGs' debt burdens are expected to grow in the medium term, although they remain low by international standards (see Figure A.4). During 2002–2003, regional direct debt as a percentage of operating revenues increased by 5.5 percentage points compared with 2001. The central government's initiatives to reduce regional borrowing from the federal budget and delegate additional expenditure responsibilities, such as raising the salaries of budget-sphere employees, will prompt RGs to borrow from capital markets. Debt limits set in the Budget Code are quite generous and should not limit debt growth in the medium term.

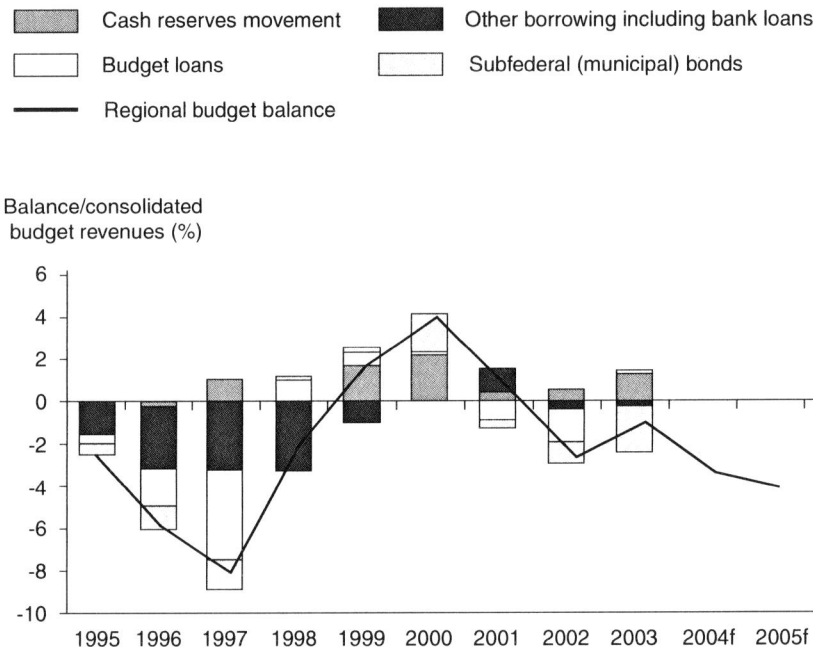

Figure A.4 Russian regional budgets deficit financing by instrument

Creditworthiness remains low despite some improvements

The current financial and debt situation of Russian RGs is very different from the pre-crisis, pre-default position of 1997–1998. In 2002, the stronger financial performance of rated RGs was indicated by higher operating budget balances (a median of 21.7 per cent compared with 13.5 per cent in 1998 and deficits of 1.3 per cent in 1997) and manageable debt service (a median of 5.2 per cent of revenues compared with 12.4 per cent in 1998). Budget revenues are collected wholly in cash because non-cash settlements were prohibited in 2000. Liquidity is supported by growing cash reserves (4 per cent in 2002 compared with 2.5 per cent in 1997) and better borrowing terms.

Although RGs' creditworthiness has improved, credit risks remain high, as the non-investment-grade credit ratings continue to indicate. Major constraints on creditworthiness include low-quality financial management, weak financial flexibility, and exposure to economic risks and a volatile intergovernmental system. The RGs' debt structure still involves significant refinancing and currency risks.

Legal restrictions remain ineffective

As a partial answer to the numerous LRG defaults in 1998–1999, the Russian federal government introduced the legal debt limits set in the 2000 Budget Code. These limits include requirements that:

- total debt is less than budget revenues minus transfers from the federal budget;
- total budget revenues are greater than current expenditures;
- budget deficits are less than 15 per cent of budget revenues minus transfers from the federal budget (this regulation indirectly limits net borrowing to 15 per cent of own revenues);
- interest payments are less than 15 per cent of budget expenditures; and
- guarantees issued within one year are less than 5 per cent of budget expenditures.

These limits are quite generous, however, and in Standard & Poor's opinion they fail to restrict borrowing to a level manageable by emerging countries. In addition, poor discipline undermines the effectiveness of these restrictions. At the beginning of 2003, 41 RGs were in breach of at least one of these restrictions.

Refinancing and currency risk exposure is lower but remains important

The structure of regional debt has improved considerably compared with its pre-1998 levels, but it still carries some currency and refinancing risks. Although the duration of debt liabilities has extended significantly, the debt obligations of even the most creditworthy RGs mature over two to three years – a lower average than international standards. Many RGs also remain exposed to foreign exchange risk because foreign currency denominated debt amounted to 25 per cent of total regional debt in 2002. Although the 2000 Budget Code prohibited foreign currency denominated borrowing by RGs, they can still refinance foreign currency debt or incur debt fixed to an exchange rate.

Poor debt management quality still a concern, but trends positive

Debt management remains inadequate in most Russian RGs. Only the most progressive administrations are moving forward in terms of management quality. The debt policies of the majority remain short-sighted and poorly institutionalized compared with their peers in developed countries. Borrowed funds are spent ineffectively because borrowing plans are not incorporated into investment programmes. Even though debt structures remain perilous, risks are not assessed and most risk management techniques are ignored. The transparency of debt operations remains low, due to poor disclosure and the weakness of accounting.

RGs may suffer significant shortfalls in budget revenues due to high exposure to large taxpayers or industries. Rainy day funds, conservative financial planning, and other hedging techniques are not applied widely among the regions.

Intergovernmental budgetary system and local self-government reforms lead to uncertainty

The ongoing intergovernmental budgetary system and local government reforms undermine the stability of regional finances in the short term. Irregular and sudden redistributions of tax revenues, financial aid, and expenditure responsibilities inherently lower the stability of regional finances and render any longer-term financial policies practically impossible. Recent federal government initiatives, including further equalization of per capita tax revenues and delegation of additional expenditure responsibilities, are expected to have a negative effect on the wealthier rated RGs.

The vulnerability of RGs to possible sovereign distress remains high. Their strong dependence on ever-changing intergovernmental fiscal arrangements represents a considerable risk factor despite the recent improvements in sovereign creditworthiness.

Weak enforcement mechanisms do not offer protection to creditors

The default by Primorskiy Krai in 2001 clearly indicates that Russian RGs cannot be compelled to pay. In the meantime, creditors continue their unsuccessful attempts to recover debts, some more than five years old, such as the agrobonds issued by Saratov Oblast. Expected recovery rates remain low, owing to poor enforcement, which results in higher borrowing costs for all RGs. Until creditor rights are protected, long-term loans will be beyond the reach of most RGs.

In 2007–2008, the federal government plans to introduce a mechanism to enforce insolvent RGs to pay their debts – Temporary Financial Administration (TFA). TFA will be established in RGs with overdue obligations exceeding 30 per cent of budget revenues. The TFA is expected to prepare a debt repayment plan and oversee its implementation. TFA does not, however, guarantee the protection of the creditor's rights because only the federal government can establish it. It cannot be introduced if overdue debt does not exceed 30 per cent of revenues. Furthermore, the mechanism seems quite opaque.

Bailouts remain ad hoc

Recent bailout practices are likely to cause debt discipline problems if repeated. The federal government helped Nizhniy Novgorod, for example, to repay its first tranche of the restructured eurobonds. Ad hoc bailouts do not contribute to the supportiveness and predictability of the intergovernmental budgetary system but rather worsen entities' unwillingness to pay. RGs may expect similar bailouts when in financial distress or when considering a default. This may encourage unsound financial policies and more reckless borrowing.

Will there be more mass defaults?

Low credit ratings in general suggest that single defaults are likely. Only one regional default occurred during 2001–2003, however. Regional borrowing on the capital markets is now concentrated among the most creditworthy regional governments (RGs). On the other hand, less creditworthy RGs are now entering the market, and defaults are more likely to occur because these new borrowers are more exposed to the risks that were common default triggers in 1998–2000.

Most credit risk factors, including an unstable intergovernmental budgetary system, tax base concentration, and dependence on a shallow national capital market, are ubiquitous among Russian RGs. On the other hand, improved liquidity, due to the elimination of non-cash payments and longer debt maturities, is a significant improvement on the late 1990s. Willingness to pay will continue to play a crucial role in the determination of RGs' probability of default.

Improvements in financial management quality give Standard & Poor's Ratings Services some hope that mass defaults will not be repeated and that more attention will be paid to the credit quality of individual entities in the sector. Improved enforcement mechanisms and credit discipline – such as clear mechanisms or the complete absence of *ad hoc* bailouts by the federal government – will be key to the provision of creditor protection and reduced borrowing costs for RGs.

Copyright © 1994–2004 Standard & Poor's, a division of The McGraw-Hill Companies. All Rights Reserved.

Appendix 2

Placing Investment Projects within the Context of National Significance

Vitaly Mozharowski, Partner and Maxim Popov, Senior Attorney, Pepeliaev, Goltsblat & Partners

For investment projects time is crucial. So each day spent trying to have the documents approved and re-approved by the authorities matters. An additional impetus can be given to an investment project if it is made nationally significant. This will also help to speed up and very often to facilitate the execution of the necessary documentation.

Practically any investment project for the construction of manufacturing facilities starts from searching for and purchasing a land plot where these facilities will be located. If a facility is made nationally significant, within the meaning given to this term by art. 49.1 (2) of the Russian Land Code, it will simplify the withdrawal of the land plot chosen for locating this facility. The literal interpretation of art. 49 of the Russian Land Code identifies two conditions which, if met simultaneously, make it possible to withdraw the land plot for national needs:

1. The facility proposed to be located on the land plot is nationally significant.
2. There are no other options for locating this facility.

National significance of the facility

The Russian Land Code does not have a clear list of nationally significant facilities. Neither does it contain any criteria that would set these facilities apart from facilities having any other significance (municipal, private, etc). 'Nationally significant facilities' should be understood to mean federally significant facilities and facilities significant at the level of a constituent entity of the Russian Federation. So the real meaning of art. 49 of the Russian Land Code can be revealed through a system analysis of other regulatory acts.

Quite illustrative in this context are the Rules for issuing permits for the construction of federally significant real estate items and real estate items in the territories of federally significant specially regulated town-planning entities (Resolution of the Russian Government No. 221 of 10 March 2000). One of the grounds for issuing special permits for the construction of real estate items in the territories of federally significant specially regulated town-planning entities is *the decision of the executive authority of a particular constituent entity of the Russian Federation with respect to the construction of a real estate item which is significant at the level of this constituent entity* and preparation of documents required for obtaining a special permit for its construction (clause 25).

The meaning and contents of the above-mentioned Rules definitely suggest that, in any case, the basis for recognizing a facility as being nationally significant is the decision of the competent governmental authority adopted as appropriate.

Indeed, under the Russian Constitution the people exercise their power directly and through the governmental authorities and local governments. In other words, the decision of the governmental authority to recognize a facility as being nationally significant actually constitutes unconditional acknowledgement of public interests and needs in respect of the land plot proposed for withdrawal. Public interests and needs can justify legal restrictions on the rights and freedoms of individuals (particular land owners, land users, land holders and tenants) but only if such restrictions are commensurate with the socially necessary result.

The provisions of federal legislation concerning the withdrawal of land plots for national and municipal needs can and must be made more specific in the laws of the constituent entities of the Russian Federation for two basic reasons:

1. Under the Russian Constitution land legislation falls within the joint competence of the Russian Federation and its constituent entities (issues falling with their joint competence are regulated by federal laws and the laws and other regulatory acts of the constituent entities of the Russian Federation passed in accordance with federal laws);

2. Withdrawal, including though buy-out, of lands for the needs of a constituent entity of the Russian Federation is handled by the

constituent entities of the Russian Federation (art. 10 of the Russian Land Code).

The legislation of the constituent entities of the Russian Federation in this area first of all defines:

- the governmental authorities empowered to pass decisions recognizing facilities as being nationally significant;

- criteria that make it possible to recognisze a facility as being nationally (regionally) significant.

For instance, in the Moscow Region issues related to the construction of real estate items that have regional or inter-district significance are dealt with by the Moscow Region Government. The drafts of Moscow Region regulatory acts concerning the location and development of industrial facilities of federal, regional or inter-district facilities are prepared and submitted to the Moscow Region Government for consideration by the Economy Ministry of the Moscow Region.

In some of Russia's regions, for example in the Voronezh Region, the standing co-ordinating executive authority responsible for governmental regulation of the development and location of manufacturing facilities is the relevant Inter-departmental Commission for locating manufacturing facilities in the territory of the region. It is the responsibility of this Commission to give prior consent for the location and construction of manufacturing facilities.

Very often Commission Regulations provide that with respect to regionally significant facilities, governmental regulation of the development and location of manufacturing facilities in the region is effected and prior consent for the location and construction of manufacturing facilities is given by the Regional Administration as agreed with the relevant district and municipal administrations.

With regard to regionally significant facilities, if the Commission's opinion is positive, the decision that serves for the project owner as a basis for starting work on a statement substantiating investments into the construction is made by the Regional Administration.

Quite often an additional lever of influence over the Inter-departmental Commission is a positive opinion from the Expert Council for the Strategy of Social and Economic Development of the Region under the Head of the Regional Administration. Almost each Russian region has bodies vested with similar functions.

In addition, there are formal criteria set out in regional legislative acts that make it possible to recognize a facility as being nationally (regionally) significant. One example is Voronezh Region Law No. 27-OZ of 15 May 2002 'On Governmental (Regional) Support for Investment Activities in the Territory of the Voronezh Region'. Under this law, if an investment project appears on the Register of investment projects of the Voronezh Region (the list includes projects selected through competition), it means that this project is in line with the priority avenues for the economic development of the Voronezh Region and has economic and/or social significance for the region.

An additional argument in favour of recognizing a facility as being nationally significant is inclusion of the investment project into the Programme for the Economic and Social Development of the Region, which exists in every constituent entity of the Russian Federation and is subject to the approval of the regional legislature.

Absence of other options for locating this facility

The second condition for the withdrawal of the land plot for national needs is the absence of other options for locating nationally significant facilities. It is primarily aimed at protecting individuals and legal entities from groundless termination of their rights to the land plots they hold.

In the course of selecting a land plot for construction purposes pursuant to art. 31 of the Russian Land Code, the local government is obliged to make sure that there is only one option for locating the facility that meets all requirements listed by the applicant (landscape, geological structure of the land plot, access to resources, accessibility and well-developed condition of the infrastructure, etc). This option should also envisage locating the facility not on reserve lands but within the boundaries of a land plot held by an individual or a legal entity on the basis of a particular right.

The absence of other options for locating this facility should be confirmed by a formal decision of the local government. It is quite obvious that the applicant will stand a better chance of success if the application for land plot selection and prior consent for the location of the facility, as provided in clause 1 art. 31 of the Russian Land Code, lists the strictest possible requirements in respect of the land plot, including:

- the area of the land plot (with due regard for the need to set up a buffer zone, as the case may be);
- landscape;
- geological parameters of the land plot;
- specifications for connecting to service lines (power supply, water supply, sewerage, purification works, communications);
- access to transport and social infrastructure facilities;
- availability of qualified labour resources, etc.

By ensuring that these conditions are met and by having the facility to be constructed under the investment project recognized as being nationally significant, the investor will essentially simplify the procedures of land withdrawal and facilitate further implementation of the project in general.

Copyright © 2004 Pepeliaev, Goltsblat & Partners LLC. All Rights Reserved.

Appendix 3

Useful Business-Related Websites

www.gksoft.com/govt/en/ru.html
A directory of all of the federal government institutions of the Russian Federation, including a list of all ministries.

www.embassyworld.com/embassy/russia1.htm
A directory of all of the Russian embassies and consulates around the world.

www.embassiesabroad.com/embassy.cfm?embassy=home&fkcountry=75
A directory of foreign embassies and their websites in Russia.

www.users.globalnet.co.uk/chegeo/ or *www.russiaexport.net*
Interesting English language site providing information about Russia's foreign trade since 1994, detailing different products imported and exported to and from the Russian Federation, main trading partners, and companies involved in foreign trade with Russia, etc.

www.rmg.ru
English language site containing information about breaking news from the Russian financial markets, including market analysis, daily quotes and indices, corporate finance, etc.

www.fipc.ru
The website of the Russian Government's foreign investment promotion centre under the Ministry of Economy.

www.mid.ru
The Russian Ministry of Foreign Affairs' English language site providing current political information and various documents.

www.rbcc.com/
Russo-British Chamber of Commerce in the United Kingdom.

www.amcham.ru/
American Chamber of Commerce in Russia (Moscow based).

www.russianbusinesssite.com
The website of the Russian government entity set up to promote the development of the small- to medium-size business sector in Russia.

www.britemb.msk.ru
Website of the British Embassy in Moscow, listing the services the embassy provides for British companies.

www.tradepartners.gov.uk
Advice and information from the UK government network that helps UK companies trade internationally, including basic information about Russia's business environment and economy.

www.tradeuk.com
Trade partners UK's Internet service for international buyers and UK exporters.

www.russianembassy.org
The website of the Russian embassy in Washington, DC – a useful resource providing excellent information on contemporary society as well as recent and ancient history, plus links to news sources, etc

www.bisnis.doc.gov / bisnis / country / rusfed.cfm
US Department of Commerce site, established to provide Business Information Service for the Newly Independent States (BISNIS) – a massive web-based resource pertaining to all aspects of business in Russia. This includes a commercial overview of Russia, comprising an economic profile, a foreign trade profile, a foreign investment summary (giving information on intellectual rights and existing US-Russia bilateral agreements), a banking and finance summary, a section on practical information for travellers, and a section on useful contacts/addresses.

www.eia.doe.gov / emeu / cabs / russia.html
US-DOE Energy Information Administration: Country Analysis Brief on Russia – a description of Russia's energy economy, including oil, natural gas and electricity. Elsewhere on this site are: a somewhat dated (2000), but still useful, 'Country Energy Balance' (*www.eia.doe.gov / emeu / world / country / cntry_RS.html*) for Russia with information on oil, coal, natural gas, and electricity; a 'Russian Oil and Gas Exports Fact Sheet' (*http:/ / www.eia.doe.gov / emeu / cabs / russexp.html*); and an 'Environmental Issues Briefing' (*www.eia.doe.gov / emeu / cabs / russenv.html*) with information on air pollution, energy intensities, carbon emissions, renewable energy, and an outlook for the 21st century.

www.odci.gov / cia / publications / factbook / geos / rs.html
CIA World Factbook 2003 – a very useful information summary about Russia, including sections on geography, people, government, economy, communications, transportation, military forces and transnational issues.

Appendix 3: Useful Business-Related Websites

www.russialink.org.uk/embassy
Online Russian international visa service. This is a non-government site affiliated to the Russian Embassy in London, offering a full range of visa support services for visitors to Russia (including arranging invitations for business and tourist visas).

www.visatorussia.com/
Russian visa support services available online.

www.russiangateway.co.uk
Another of the Internet-based visa and travel support service agencies serving the Russian Federation, providing information on visas, tours and hotels from the UK's leading Russia experts.

http://www.russia-travel.com
Official website of the Russian national tourist office.

www.city.ru
Russian cities on the Web – a complete Internet-based guide to numerous large (as well as not so large) Russian cities.

Appendix 4

Contributor Contact Details

Allan & Overy
One New Change
London EC4M 9QQ, UK
Contact: Eric Zuy
Tel: +7(095) 725 7900
Fax: +7(095) 725 7949
Email: Eric.Zuy@AllenOvery.com

American Chamber of Commerce in Russia
7–9 Dolgorukovskaya Street, 14th floor
Moscow 103006, Russia
Contact: Alexander Kravtsov
Communications Director
Tel: +7 (095) 961 2141
Fax: +7 (095) 961 2142
Email: AKravtsov@AmCham.RU
Website: www.amcham.ru

Antanta Capital
8a Strastnoi Boulevard,
Moscow 107031, Russia
Email: info@antcm.ru
Contact: Denis Matafonov
Research Department
Tel: +7 (095) 783 9626
Fax: +7 (095) 783 9627
Trading Department
Tel: +7 (095) 783 4444
Fax: +7 (095) 783 9627

Baker & McKenzie – CIS, Limited
Moscow Office
Sadovaya Plaza 11th Floor
7 Dolgorukovskaya Street
Moscow 127006, Russia
Tel: + 7 (095) 787 2700
Fax: +7 (095) 787 2801
Email: moscow.office@bakernet.com
Contact: Paul Melling
Email: paul.melling@bakernet.com

St. Petersburg Office
57 Bolshaya Morskaya Street
St. Petersburg 190000, Russia
Tel: + 7 (812) 303 9000
Fax: + 7 (812) 325 6013
Email: stp.office@bakernet.com
Contact: Maxim Kalinin
Email: maxim.kalinin@bakernet.com

Branan
10 Vostochnaya ul
Moscow 115280, Russia
Contact: John Marrow, Director
Email: jem@branan.ru
Additional contact:
Tatyana Baeva
Email: tab@branan.ru

CMS Cameron McKenna
Pavaletskaya Square 2/3
Moscow 115054, Russia
Contact: David Griston
Tel: +7 (501) 258 5000 (office)
Tel: + 7 095 108 7106 (mobile)
Email: David.Griston@cmck.com

Deloitte & Touche CIS
16/2 Tverskaya Street
Moscow 103009, Russia
Contact: Michael Bolan, Director of Marketing & Administration
Tel: +7 (095) 787 0600 x.2421 (direct)
Tel: +7 (095) 787 0600 (main)
Fax: +7 (095) 787 0601
Email: mbolan@deloitte.ru

William Flemming
Tel: +7 (095) 937 3399
Fax: +7 (095) 937 3393
Email: flemming@imedia.ru

Firestone Duncan
Staropimenovskiy Pereulok 13, Stroyeniye 2, 6th Floor
Moscow 127006, Russia
Tel: +7 (095) 258 3500
Fax: +7 (095) 258 3501
Website: www.firestone-duncan.com
Contact: Jamison R Firestone
Email: jamison@fda.ru

OTAC Limited
47 Falcon Drive
Hartford
Huntingdon
Cambridgeshire PE29 1LP, UK
Tel: +44 (0) 7971 588437
Email: otac@ntlworld.com
Contact: Sergey Maslichenko
Email: Maslichenko@yahoo.co.uk

Pepeliaev, Goltsblat & Partners
Krasnopresnenskaya nab. 12, Entrance 7
15th floor, World Trade Center-II
Moscow 123610, Russia
Tel: +7 (095) 967 00 07
Fax: +7 (095) 967 00 08
Email: info@pgplaw.ru

St. Petersburg Office
25 Nevskiy Prospect, Atrium
St. Petersburg 101000, Russia
Tel: +7 (812) 346 7708
Fax: +7 (812) 346 7709
Email: spb@pgplaw.ru

Website: www.pgplaw.ru

PricewaterhouseCoopers
Kosmodamianskaya Nab.52, Bld.5
Moscow 115054, Russia
Tel: +7 (095) 967 6000
Fax: +7 (095) 967 6001
Website: www.pwc.com/ru

Contacts:
Keith Rowden
Leader, Energy Industry Services
PricewaterhouseCoopers
Email: keith.rowden@us.pwc.com

Igor Lotakov
Senior Manager, PricewaterhouseCoopers
Email: igor.lotakov@ru.pwc.com

Alexander Chmel
Partner, PricewaterhouseCoopers
Email: alexander.chmel@ru.pwc.com

Vyacheslav Solomin
Senior Manager, PricewaterhouseCoopers
Email: vyacheslav.solomin@ru.pwc.com

Natalia Milchakova
Partner, PricewaterhouseCoopers
Email: natalia.milchakova@ru.pwc.com

Alexander Dragunov
Director, Customs Practice, PricewaterhouseCoopers
Email: alexander.dragunov@ru.pwc.com

Gennady Odarich
Lawyer, PricewaterhouseCoopers CIS Law Offices BV
Email: gennady.odarich@ru.pwc.com

Raiffeisen Bank Austria
17/1 Troitskaya Street
Moscow 129090, Russia
Contact: Elena Romanova
Head of Research
Tel: +7 (095) 721 9934
Fax: +7 (095) 721 9900
Email: eromanova@raiffeisen.ru

RosBusinessConsulting
78 Profsoyuznaya Street
Moscow 117393, Russia
Tel: +7 (095) 363 1111 (switchbox)
Fax: +7 (095) 363 1125
Email: http://research.rbc.ru/
Websites: www.rbc.ru and www.rbcnews.com
Contact: Vyatcheslav Masenkov
Email: masenkov@rbc.ru

RMBC ('Remedium' group of companies)
Bakuninskaya 71
Moscow 105082, Russia
Tel: +7 (095) 780 3425
Fax: +7 (095) 780 3426
Contacts: Sirma Gotovats, Anton Timergaliev
Emails: evargashkina@rmbc.ru, antony@rmbc.ru
Website: www.rmbc.ru

Standard & Poor's Ratings Direct
11 Gogolevsky Blvd, 9th floor
Moscow 121019, Russia
Contacts:
Ekaterina Novikova
Email: Ekaterina_Novikova@standardandpoors.com
Elena Anankina
Tel: +7 (095) 783 4130
Email: elena_anankina@standardandpoors.com
Robert E Richards
Tel: +7 (095) 783 4011
Email: rob_richards@standardandpoors.com

Index

References in *italic* indicate figures or tables.

accident insurance   *262*
accountants   330
'Accounting' Law   267
accounting standards   272–74, 330
accreditation of representative offices   225–26, 237
advertising, brewing industry   206
advertising tax   256, *260*
Agency for Restructuring of Credit Organizations (ARCO)   87
agricultural land   286, 289–92, 334
AKM-com index   154
Alfa Bank   47, 80
alternative telecom operators   150–51
AmCham   39, 40–41
American investment   38
Anglo-American corporate governance model   99
Anti-Monopoly Law   235–36
Anti-Monopoly Ministry   166, 229–30, 235
appellate jurisdiction   307, 308
arbitration   310
Arbitration Court   84–85
arbitration managers   85
arbitrazhniy (commercial) court system   32, 33, 304, 305–06, *306*, 307–08
   procedure   308–10
ARCO *see* Agency for Restructuring of Credit Organizations
Asian corporate governance model   100
assets acquisition   348–49
Auchan   200, 203
auditing   265–72
   current developments   268–71
   history   265–66

legislation   266–67
rules   269–71
Auditing Activity Board   268
'August 1998 Crisis'   70
automotive industry   174–79
   'big three'   176–77
   major FDI projects   177–78
Avtotor   178
AvtoVAZ (Volgski Automobile Plant)   175, 176, 177

Baltika   208, 209
bank accounts
   non-resident companies   96, 238
   representative offices   218
   resident companies   238–39
banking sector   23–28, 69–78, *78*
   credits, assets and investments   *24*
   current status   71–72
   deposits   *24, 25, 26*
   effect on risk ratings   65–66, *65*
   history   70
   legislation   72–73
   lending   *24, 27, 28*, 73–74, 80–81
   mortgage financing   76
   reform plans   76–77
   regulation   69–70
   retail   25–28, 74–76, 79–81
   structural reform   47–48
bankruptcy *see* insolvency regime
Banks Insolvency Law   87, 88
Bashkortostan, government economic involvement   62
bilateral investment treaties   37
'black market', pharmaceuticals sector   194–95
BMW   178
boards of directors   232

bonds 94
  yields on 20–23
Bosco di Chiliegi 203–04
branches of foreign legal entities
    236, 322–23
  taxation 253
branding, brewing industry 210–12,
    210, 211, 212
brewing industry 205–14
  cities 207
  competition 209–10, *209, 210*
  demographics and market
      characteristics 206–07
  distribution channels 213–14, *213*
  national brand 211–12, *211, 212*
  quality 212–13
  regions 207–08
bribery xxix, 51
BTI *see* Bureau of Technical
    Inventory
buildings
  ownership 336–37
  regulations 286–87
Bureau of Technical Inventory (BTI)
    337
bureaucracy, effects on credit quality
    58–59
business addresses, legal
    requirements 328
business culture xxviii–xxxi
Business Ethics Commission 40
business structures/entities 217–24,
    231–40, 317–18, 326
  bank accounts 96, 218, 238–39
  foreign employees 239–40
  limited liability companies
      219–21, 233–34
  open and closed joint stock
      companies 221–24, 232–33
    differences between ZAO and
        OOO 234–36
  registration 225–30, 236–38
  representative offices 217–19, 236

cadastral registration of land 339
capital currency control 35, 96–97
capital inflows, exchange rate effect
    17–20
capital outflows, trend towards 46
capital transfer transactions 340
cash-and-carry format 203
CBR *see* Central Bank of Russia
CDR-FOREM 129
CDU-System Operator 129
CED *see* Commercial Energy
    Dialogue
cellular communications 158, *158*
Central Bank of Russia (CBR) 47,
    69–70, 75, 77
  exchange rate options 13–15
Central Certification Licensing
    Auditing Commissions 266
centralized political system, problems
    with 61–63
Chief Accountants 330
Circulation Law 334, 335
Civil Code 34, 217, 219, 221, 231,
    232
  currency 95
  property 283, 287, 338
  securities 92, 94
civil law system 33–36
closed joint stock companies 221–24,
    233
clothes market, luxury 203–04
coal consumption and production
    140–41, 142–43, *144*
Code of Audit Ethics 271
Code of Corporate Conduct 223
commercial court system *see*
    arbitrazhniy court system
Commercial Energy Dialogue (CED)
    40
communications equipment
    manufacture 162–63
communications facilities market
    156–62, *157, 158, 160, 161*
companies *see* joint stock companies;
    limited liability companies
Competition Law 344
competition law 344–50
  abuse of a dominant position
      344–45
  agreements limiting competition
      345–46
  mergers and acquisitions 346–50

Concept for Automotive Industry Development   174
Conception for Developing the Russian Telecommunications Equipment Market   163
Condominium Law   341
Constitution   4, 30–31, 334
Constitutional Court   32, 33
constitutional structure   30–32
construction stage, investment projects   320
consumer-services sector growth   43–44, *44*
contractors, as alternative to employees   331
contracts of employment   311–12
  termination   313–14
contributor contact details   374–78
copyright   297–99
  Internet   302
  troubleshooting   298–99
corporate credit ratings   56–58, *57*
corporate governance   51–52, *53*, 99–106
  effect on country risk ratings   59–61
  oil and gas industries   121–22
Corporate Governance Code   104
corporate Intranet equipment   161
corporate law, investment projects   322–23
corporate securities   92
Corporate Wealth Maximization Model (CWM)   99–100
corporations, largest   xxv
corruption   xxix, 51
court systems   32–33, 304–10, *305, 306*
  procedures   308–10
courts of common jurisdiction   304–05, *305*, 306–07
  procedures   308–10
credit assessment difficulties   80
credit bureaux, plans for   47
credit ratings, corporate   xxvi, 55, 56–58, *53*
Criminal Code   299

currency legislation   35, 72–73, 95–98
  movement of capital   96–98
  penalties   98
  resident status   96
  salary payments   313
Currency Law   95, 97–98, 340–41
custom programming of IT market   169, *170, 171*
Customs Code   36, 249, 275–79
customs legislation   36, 249, 275–80, 323–24
CWM *see* Corporate Wealth Maximization Model
cyber-squatting   302

data protection, employee data   314
debt defaults and recovery, regional   353–65
  default triggers   355–59
  future   361–65, *362*
  1998 crisis   354–55, *354, 355*
  restructuring and recovery   359–61, *359*
Decree for the Support of Insolvent State Enterprises   82–83
Decree on the Temporary Regulations on Auditing Activities   266
Department for the Organization of Auditing Activity   268
Department for Visas and Registrations (UVIR)   316
deposit insurance system   75, 80
'Development of Telecommunications' programme   163
digital communications channels   157
directors, limited liability companies   234
disclosure, and transparency levels   63–64
discount outlets   202
disposable income growth   45
dispute resolution processes   32, 33, 40–41, 304–10
  alternative procedures   310
  courts   304–08, *305, 306*
  procedure   308–10
  property   287–88

dividend income, tax on *258*
DIY stores 202–03
documentation
  design development 320
  pre-investment project 319–20
domain names 302–03
double taxation treaties 37, *263–64*
Duma *see* State Duma

EBRD *see* European Bank of Reconstruction and Development
e-commerce 301–03
economic context xxiv–xxv, 11–29, *29*, 38
  concentration issues 63
  investment climate 42–46, *44, 45*
  retail industry 199–200
  see also monetary issues
Efes 208
Eldorado 202
electricity industry 128–35
  consumption 140, 141
  investment opportunities 134–35
  stakeholders 134
  structural reform 48, 131–34, *131, 133*
  supply 144
electronic signatures 303
electronics stores 202
employment contracts 311–12
employment law 239–40, 311–16, 330–31
  contracts 311–12
  hours and holidays 312
  minimum wage and currency control 312–13
  personal accreditation 315
  termination of employment agreements 313–14
  work permits 314–15
Energos 130, 132
energy industry 136–45, *144*
  balance forecast 139
  consumption 139–42, *142*
  efficiency constraints 137–39, *138*
  GDP growth 136–37, 138, *138*
  investment constraints 144–45, *144*

structural reform 48
supply 142–44, *142*
see also electricity industry; gas industry; oil industry
entrepreneurial start-ups 326–32
  operational issues 329–32
  setting up a venture 326–29
environmental regulation, oil and gas industries 121
Europe, convergence with 50
European Bank of Reconstruction and Development (EBRD) 46
European corporate governance model 99–10
exchange rates 11, 12–15, *12, 13*
  implications for economy 17–20, *18, 19*
excise tax 34, 248
executive body of companies 232
executive branch of government 31
exports 11
  energy infrastructure problems 111–12, *112*, 118
  implications of appreciating exchange rate 17
Exxon Mobil Corp 62

'fabricated' pharmaceutical products 194–95
farm land 286, 289–92
FAS *see* Federal Anti-Monopoly Service
FDI *see* foreign direct investment
Federal Agency for Government Communication 166
Federal Anti-Monopoly Service (FAS) 93, 344, 346, 350
Federal Assembly 31–32
Federal Commission for the Securities Market (FSC/FCSM) 91, 93, 94, 229–30
  Corporate Governance Code 104
Federal Financial Markets Service (FFMS) 69
Federal Grid Company (FGC) 129, 132
Federal Security Service 33
Federal Service for the Financial Markets (FSFM) 91, 93

federal structure   31
federal taxes   250
Federation Council   7, 8–9, 32
FFMS *see* Federal Financial Markets Service
FGC *see* Federal Grid Company
financial reserves   45–46
first instance jurisdiction   306–07, 307–08
First Law on insolvency   83
Fitch ratings   45
fixed communications facilities   158–59
fixed-term contracts   311–12
Ford Motor Company   178
foreign direct investment (FDI)   xxxi, *19*, 43
  automobile industry   177–78
foreign employees   239–40
  taxation   246–47
foreign investment   *19*
  latest developments   38–41
  legislation   36–37
  restrictions   37
  retail sector   200
  see also foreign direct investment
Foreign Investment Law   236, 324–25
foreign legal entities, taxation   253
FOREM   129, 132
forest land   292
Fradkov, Mikhail   6
free trade arrangements   49–50
FSC/FCSM *see* Federal Commission for the Securities Market
FSFM *see* Federal Service for the Financial Markets

gas industry   114, 116
  consumption   139–40, 141–42
  dependence on   63
  key investment issues   117–22
  regulatory and legal environment   123–27
  structural reform   48, 49
  supply   144
GAZ *see* Gorky Automobile Plant
Gazcom   161

Gazprom   114, 116, 119, 126
  credit rating   62–63
GDP growth   38, 43, *44*
  energy industry   136–37, 138, *138*
  implications of exchange rate appreciation   18
general jurisdiction, courts of   33
General Motors   177–78
geography   *xx, xxi, xxii*
German corporate governance model   99–100
Globalstar   161
Golden Telecom   151
goods sector growth   43, *44*
Gorky Automobile Plant (GAZ)   175, 176
government   5–7, 38–39
growth of the economy, exchange rate effect   17
Guta Bank   47, 75

High Arbitrazhniy Court   32, 33
holidays   312
hospital pharmaceutical purchases   187, *189*
hours of work   312
'household department'   5
hypermarkets   203

ICLG *see* Institute of Corporate Law and Corporate Governance
IFC *see* International Finance Corporation
IFRS *see* International Accounting Standards
IKEA   200
Illarionov, Andrei   5
immovable property rights registration   339–40
import and installation contracts   320
imports
  brewing industry   210
  implications of appreciating exchange rate   17
  pharmaceuticals   183–84, *184*, 191, *192*
income tax, personal   34, 245–47, 256–57

inflation   15–17, *16*, 44
Insolvency Law   88–90
insolvency regime   82–90, *86*
  current status   88–90
  history   82–88
Institute of Corporate Law and Corporate Governance (ICLG)   52
institutional telecom operators   150
intellectual property   294–301
  copyright and neighbouring rights   297–99
  e-commerce   301–03
  patents   299–301
  trade marks   294–97
interest rates   11, 20–23, *20, 21, 22*
  arbitrage   17
interest units, limited liability companies   220
International Accounting Standards (IFRS)   272, 273
International Finance Corporation (IFC)   46
international law   36
Internet   159
  e-commerce   301–03
  trading on   170–71
Intranet equipment   161
investment
  current climate   42–54
    corporate governance   51–52, *53*
    economy   42–46, *44, 45*
    law   51
    politics   49–50
    structural reforms   47–49
  energy industry   144–45, *145*
  pharmaceutical industry   196–97
  see also foreign direct investment
investment banking   74
investment projects   317–25
  corporate law   322–23
  customs payments   323
  foreign investment law   324–25
  land relations   321
  nationally significant   366–70
  stages   317–21
  tax   323
IT market   168–73, *168, 169, 170, 171*
  largest participants   *172*

Japanese corporate governance model   100
joint stock companies (OAO and ZAO)   221–24, 232–33
  contributions to capital   229
  formation of charter capital   229
  investment projects   322–23
  limited liability companies compared   234–36
  registration   228, 346
  share acquisition   347–48
Joint Stock Companies (JSC) Law   91, 94, 221, 223, 231, 232
  auditing   267
judicial system   32–33

Kasyanov, Mikhail   6
Khlebnikov, Paul   51
Khodorskovsky, Mikhail   xxvii, xxviii, 10, 111
Kosmicheskaya Svyaz   159
Kozak, Dmitry   6–7
Krasny Vostok   208

Labour Code   311
labour productivity index   *18*
land acquisition stages   318–19
Land Cadastre Law   339–40
Land Code   35, 286, 287, 289, 333
  land ownership   334, 335, 336, 283–85
  leasing   338–39
  nationally significant projects   366–67
land legislation   283–86
land ownership   334–36
Land Register   340
land relations   289–92, 321
land taxes   34
Law on Agricultural Land   286
Law on Arbitrazhniy Courts   305
Law on Auditing Activity   266, 268
Law on Banks and Banking   91
Law on the Court System   305
Law on Electronic Signatures   303
Law on Farm Land Turnover   289, 290, 291

Law on Foreign Investments 236, 324–25
Law on Gas Supply 124
Law on Mortgage Securities 287
Law on Registration 226, 227, 228
Law on Restructuring of Credit Organizations 87, 88
Law on the Status of Foreigners 239, 240
Law on Trade Marks 294, 295
LDPR party 8
leases 337–39
  of buildings 286–87
  of land 285
legal entities *see* business structures/entities
legal framework 30–37
  civil law system 33–36
  constitutional structure 30–32
  foreign investment legislation 36–37
  judicial system 32–33
  property 35–36
legal system 304–10
  courts 304–08, *305, 306*
  procedure 308–10
legislative branch of government 31–32
lending by banks *24, 27, 28*, 73–74, 80–81
liability, representative offices 219
licensing
  oil and gas industry 120–21, 124
  telecommunications industry 166–67
limited liability companies (OOO) 219–21, 233–34
  contribution to capital 229
  formation of charter capital 229
  investment projects 322
  joint stock companies compared 234–36
  registration 226, 228, 346
  share acquisition 347–48
Limited Liability Companies (LLC) Law 91, 94, 219, 231
  auditing 267

liquidity issues, pharmaceutical industry 197
litigation costs 310
LLC *see* Limited Liability Companies Law
'loans for shares' programme 102
local taxes 250
luxury clothes market 203–04

management
  joint stock companies 222, 232
  limited liability companies 220, 234
  representative offices 219
maps *xx, xxi, xxii*
'market economy' proclamation xxvi
Mass Privatization Programme (MPP) 52, 101
MBS *see* Mortgage-Backed Securities Law
McCarthy, Tim 47–48
Medvedev, Dmitry 4
Mercury 203–04
mergers and acquisitions 346–50
  assets acquisition 348–49
  banking sector 71
  mergers 346
  procedures and timing 350
  purchase 349–50
  shares acquisition 346–48
Metro 200, 203
microbrewery/brewpub market 208
mineral resources, ownership 286
MinFin Tsalak 266
minimum wage 312–13
ministers 6–7
Ministry of Anti-Monopoly Policy 166, 229–30, 235, 296
Ministry of Communications and Information Science 165–66
Ministry of Economic Developments and Trade 276
Ministry of Finance 268, 276
Ministry of Health Communication 166
Ministry of the Interior 316
Ministry of Internal Affairs 33
Ministry of Justice 33

Mironov, Sergei 9
monetary issues 11–29
　banking sector 23–28, *24, 25, 26, 27, 28*
　exchange rate 12–15, *12, 13,* 17–20, *18, 19*
　inflation 15–17, *16*
　interest rates 20–23, *20, 21, 22*
Moody's xxvi, 45
Mortgage-Backed Securities (MBS) Law 91
Mortgage Law 341–43
mortgage financing 76
mortgage regulation 287, 341–43
Moscow
　brewing industry 207
　property leasing law 337
Mosmart 203
MPP *see* Mass Privatization Programme
M-Video 202

National Banking Council 70
National Council for Corporate Governance (NSKU) 104
nationally significant investment projects 366–70
natural gas sector, structural reform 48, 49
Natural Monopolies Law 87
natural resource sector, diversification away from 43
neighbouring rights 297–99
　troubleshooting 298–99
New Currency Law 95, 97–98
nominal wages averages *19*
non-residents
　bank accounts 96, 238
　status 96
　tax rates 245
non-taxable income 246
notarization requirement, mortgage financing 76, 341–42
NSKU *see* National Council for Corporate Governance

OAO *see* joint stock companies
Obi 200

Obligatory Pension Insurance 255, *261*
Ochakovo 208, 209
oil industry 109–14, 115–22
　consumption 139–40
　dependence on 63
　key investment issues 117–22
　pipeline system 111–12, *112,* 118–19
　production levels 109–10, *110,* 116, *117*
　regulatory and legal environment 123–27
　supply 143
oil prices 13
oligarchs, limiting power of xxix–xxx, 9–10, 50
OOO *see* limited liability companies
open joint stock companies 221–24, 233
ownership
　buildings 336–37
　concentration xxix–xxx
　land 334–36

PAC (Presidential Audit Commission) 266
parliament 7–9, 31–32
participants' meetings, limited liability companies 234
Patent Office 295, 296
patents 299–301
　registration 300
　troubleshooting 300–01
payroll taxes 255
　Unified Social Tax 247
PBU (provisions on accounting) 272
PE ('permanent establishment') 253
pension fund contributions *261*
pension system reform 49
pension tax 255, *262*
perfume retailers 203
'permanent establishment' (PE) 253
personal accreditation of foreign employees 315

Index   387

personal income tax   34, 245–47, 256–57
personalities, importance in business culture   xxviii–xxix, 61–63
Pharmaceutical Inspection   195
pharmaceuticals market   180–89, 190–97
  development trends   190–95, *192*
  investment barriers   196–97
  retail sector   187, *187, 188, 189*
  size and structure   180–82, *180, 181, 182*
  supply   182–86, *183, 184, 185, 186*
  wholesale distribution   186–87
'physical line' modem market segment   156–57
pipeline system, energy industry   111–12, *112*, 118–19, 127
piracy   302–03
political environment   xxiii–xxviii, 3–10
  investment climate   49–50
  problems with centralized system   61–63
presidential administration   4–5, 31
  problems with centralized system   61–63
Presidential Audit Commission (PAC)   266
prime minister, role of   6
privatization   52, 101–02
  telecommunications industry   164–65
probation periods   312
Production Sharing Agreements (PSAs)   113–14, 125–26
Production Sharing Agreements (PSA) Law   124, 125–26
Procurator General   33
profitability levels, pharmaceutical industry   196
profits, exchange rate effect   17
profits tax   34, 242–44, 251–53, *258*
property deductions, income tax   246
property legislation   35–36, 283–88
  buildings   286–87
  dispute resolution   287–88
  land   283–86

  mineral resources   286
  mortgages   287
  registration   288
property rights   333–43
  immovable property rights registration   339–40
  leases   337–39
  mortgage of real estate   341–43
  ownership of buildings   336–37
  ownership of land   334–36
  real estate classifications   340
  real estate payments   340–41
  residential real estate   341
property taxes   34, 248, 255–56, *260*
provisions on accounting (PBU)   272
PSAs *see* Production Sharing Agreements
purchase of enterprises   349–50
Putin, Vladimir   xxiii, xxv, 3, 9–10
  influence on business culture   xxix
  influence on investment climate   49–50
Pyaterochka   202

RABD *see* Russian American Business Dialogue
Raiffeisen Bank   80
railway system, and oil transport   118
Ramenka   200, 203
RAO UES Rossii *see* Unified Energy Systems
RAS *see* Russian Accounting Standards
ready-made companies   328–29
real estate classifications   340
real estate payments   288, 340–41
regional taxes   250
regions
  brewing industry   207–09
  debt defaults and recovery   353–65
  future   361–65, *362*
  1998 crisis   354–55, *354, 355*
  default triggers   355–59
  restructuring and recovery   359–61, *359*
  retail sector   201
registration authorities   225–26

Registration Law   337
registration requirements
  business entities   225–30, 236–37, 328–29
  foreign employees   316
  property   288, 321
'rent-seeking' behaviour   xxix
reorganizations, taxation   252–53
reporting requirements   64
representative offices   217–19, 236, 322
  accreditation of foreign employees   315
  registration authorities   225–26, 237
  registration documents   227–28, 230
  taxation   253
residency permits   331–32
resident status   96
residential real estate   341
retail banking   25–28, 74–76, 79–81
  statistics   *25, 26, 27, 28*
retail industry   198–204
  largest retailers   201–04
  macroeconomic trends   199–200
  major trends   200–01
retail pharmacy sector   187, *187, 188, 189*
RF Federal Customs Service   276
risks ratings, country   55–66
  banking system   65–66, *65*
  bureaucracy   58–59
  centralized system   61–63
  corporate credit ratings   56–58, *57*
  corporate governance   59–61
  economic concentration   63
  transparency incentives   63–64
Rodina party   8
Rosenergoatom   129
Rostelecom   155, 165
Rotek   157
rouble *see* currency legislation; exchange rates
RSPP *see* Russian Union of Industrialists and Entrepreneurs
Rules for Resolving Disputes Over Domain Names   302

Russian Accounting Standards (RAS)   272, 273
Russian American Business Dialogue (RABD)   39
Russian Institute for Public Networks   301–02
Russian Standard Bank   80
Russian Union of Industrialists and Entrepreneurs (RSPP)   39, 40–41

Sakhalin projects   113–14, 126
  Sakhalin-3   40, 62
satellite communications   159–61
Sberbank   47, 75, 77
Sechin, Igor   4, 5
Second Law on insolvency   84–86, 88
Securities Law   91, 92, 94
securities markets and transactions   91–94
  regulation   93–94
  stock exchange   91–92
security, global   50
self-regulating organizations (SROs)   93
service sector growth   43–44, *44*
Services Purchasing Managers' Index (SPM)   44
services sector of IT market   169, *170*
Severstal   178
Shareholder Wealth Maximization Model (SWM)   99
shareholders
  electricity industry   134
  meetings   232
  taxation   252
shareholding structures   64
shares
  acquisition   346–48
  issues and transfers   222–24
shopping mall development   201, 204
Siberian Aluminium (SibAl)   178
small and medium-sized enterprises (SMEs)
  bank credit problems   80
  see also entrepreneurial start-ups
social deductions   245–46

social fund registration requirements   237
Social Insurance Contributions   255
software sector of IT market   169, *170, 171*
SPM *see* Services Purchasing Managers' Index
squatting   302–03
SROs (self-regulating organizations)   93
St. Petersburg, brewing industry   207
stakeholders, electricity industry   134
Standard & Poor's   xxvi, 55–56
Starik Hottabych   202–03
start-ups, entrepreneurial   326–32
   operational issues   329–32
   setting up a venture   326–29
state arbitrazhniy (commercial) courts   32, 33, 304, 305–06, *306*, 307–08
State Commission on Electronic Communication   166
State Committee for Radio Frequencies   166
State Duma   4, 7–8, 32
State Registration Chamber (SRC)   226
stock exchange   91–92
stock market, telecom operators in   151–54, *153*
storage of goods (temporary), customs regulations   276
Strategy, Energy   136
Strategy for the Development of the Banking Sector   76
structural reforms   47–49
Sub-soil Law   123, 124–25
SUN Interbrew   208, 209
supermarkets   301–02
Supreme Courts   32, 33, 307, 308
Surkov, Vladislav   4–5
Svyazinvest   154–56, *155*, 159, 165
switching equipment manufacture   161–62, *161*
SWM *see* Shareholder Wealth Maximization Model

tax agents   247
Tax Code   34, 241
tax incentives, abolition of   242–43
tax rates
   income tax   245
   profit tax   243
   VAT   244
tax system   34, 241–49, 250–57
   advertising tax   256
   customs duties   249
   double tax treaties   *263–64*
   effect on bank lending   73–74
   excise tax   248
   individual income tax   245–47, 256–57
   Internet purchase   303
   investment projects   323
   oil and gas industry   112–13, 119–20, 125–26
   payroll   255
   Unified Social Tax   247, 255
   profits tax   242–44, 251–53
   property tax   248, 255–56
   registration of business entities   237
   small businesses   327–28
   summary   *258–62*
   transport tax   256
   value added tax   244–45, 253–54
telecommunications market   146–63, *149*, 164–67
   communications equipment manufacture   162–63, 167
   communications facilities market   156–62, *157, 158, 160, 161*
   governing agencies   165–66
   key players   150–56, *152, 153, 155*
   licensing   166–67
   privatization   164–65
   volume   147–48, *147, 148*
territorial generation companies   132
thermal power stations   141
thin capitalization rules   251
Thuraya   161
trade marks   294–97
   registration   295–96, 297
   troubleshooting   296–97

traditional telecom operators   150
transfer pricing   243–44, 251
Transneft   118, 119, 126
Transnefteprodukt   126–27
transparency and disclosure levels   63–64
  pharmaceutical industry   197
transport infrastructure, energy industry   118–19, 126–27
transport tax   256, *261*
treaties
  bilateral investment   37, 323
  double taxation   37, *263–64*, 323
  intellectual property   301
Tsalak   266
TSEPKO   208

UAZ *see* Ural Automobile Plant
UGS *see* Unified Gas Transmission
Unified Energy Systems (UES) of Russia (RAO UES Rossii)   128–29
  restructuring   48
Unified Gas Transmission (UGS)   119
Unified Social Tax (UST)   247, 255, *261*
United Russia party   8, 61
Ural Automobile Plant (UAZ)   175, 176–77
Uralsvyazinform   154–55
US-Russian bilateral processes   39–40
US-Russian Commercial Energy Dialogue (CED)   40
UST *see* Unified Social Tax

utilities sector, structural reform   48
UVIR *see* Department for Visas and Registrations

value added tax (VAT)   34, 244–45, 253–54, *259*, 324
VEB bank   76–77
Vimpelcom   61
visas   239, 316, 331–32
Vneshtorgbank (VTB)   47, 76–77
Voentelecom   161
VolgaTelecom   155
Volgski Automobile Plant (AvtoVAZ)   175, 176, 177
VTB (Vneshtorgbank)   47, 76–77

wage, minimum statutory   312–13
websites, business-related   371–73
wholesale generation companies   132
withdrawal rights, limited liability companies   221
withholding tax   243, *259*
'without prejudice' negotiations   310
work permits   239–40, 314–15, 318, 331–32
World Trade Organization (WTO) accession   39, 50

Yeltsin, Boris   xxiii–xiv, 7
Yukos case   xxvi–xxviii, 9–10, 50, 60, 61, 111
  Kenneth Dart   103–04

ZAO *see* joint stock companies
Zhukov, Alexander   6

Index of Advertisers

Adam Smith Conferences	ii
Argus Media	v, 108
ITE Group plc	vi
SGS	xiii–xiv